Judaism for Universalists

Everett Gendler

Blue Thread Communications

Judaism for Universalists. Copyright © 2015 by Everett Gendler. All rights reserved. Printed in the United States of America. No part of this book may be used or reproduced in any manner whatsoever without written permission from the publisher except in the case of brief quotations embodied in critical articles or reviews.

For information, write to: JEWISH CURRENTS, PO Box 111, Accord, NY 12404.

Photographs by Mary Gendler.

ISBN 978-0-9903524-2-6

Judaism
for Universalists

Table of Contents

INTRODUCTION
    A Universalist with a Rabbinical Degree   1
        How an Insult Became a Badge of Honor

PART ONE

Judaism and the Natural World

    On a Judaism of Nature   11
        God as the Life of the Universe

    A Time to Sow and a Time to Reap   19
        Jewish Agricultural Time

    The Life of His Beast   34
        Our Kinship with Other Creatures

    The Universal Chorus   40
        Joy and Vegetarianism

    A Sentient Universe   44
        The Underlying Mystery of Nature

    A Matter of Spirit   50
        The Gift of Genesis

    Perek Shirah: Marginal or Mainstream?   69
        Time to Reassess

    Through the Zen Garden of the Hebrews   75
        A Scriptural Stroll

    The Solar-Powered Eternal Light   84
        "See My Works!"

    Our Environment: Study and Action   86
        Judaism's Festival Rituals

    Sustaining the Soil, Sustaining the Spirit   89
        Gardening as a Jewish Spiritual Practice

Haystacks and Haybales, Pumpkins and Seeds   94
On the Transmission of Legacies

Part 2
War, Peace, and Community

War and the Jewish Tradition   109
"Just Wars" and the Issue of Conscience

Can a Jew Be a Conscientious Objector?   130
Jewish Teachings and Military Violence

" . . . Therefore Choose Life"   135
In the Face of Nuclear Annihilation

Teaching Shalom in the Shadow of Tibet   142
Nonviolent Resistance for National Survival

Universal Nonviolence Training   149
A Moral Alternative to Universal Military Training

The Loving Rebuke   160
Personal Confrontation and Human Harmony

Rabbi Nachman's "OD"   175
An Ode of Human Redemption

Community/Kehillah   183
A Keystone of the Jewish Tradition

Reflections on Cuba   188
Three Eyewitness Accounts

The U.S. Bicentennial and the Jubilee Year   204
A Right We Must Reclaim

Part 3
Israel and Diaspora

To Be a Jew in the Diaspora   225
An Affirmation

Ancient Visions, Future Hopes   236
Rabbi Aaron Samuel Tamaret's Objection to Zionism

A Year to Remember Gedaliah   249
Peacemaking in Ancient Times

Israel and America   254
A History of the "Special Relationship"

Immigration as Approval of Israeli Policy   263
Why Jews Stay Away

Martin Luther King, Jr. in the Holy Land   275
The Tragedy of His Absence

PART 4:
Between Ourselves and Judaism

The Return of the Goddess   290
A Revised Confessional

Identity, Invisible Religion, and Intermarriage
An Evolving New Social Form of Religion

Ever Since Eden   317
Trees, Tradition, and Tu B'Shevat

The Tree That Sustains All Life   327
Reviving the Tu B'Shvat Seder

Three Contributions to Prayer   328
In loving tribute to the memory of Abraham Joshua Heschel

The Process of Becoming   341
A Verse of Scripture Framed by Memories

Turn, Turn, Turn   346
Prayer Wheels and Judaism

From Chore to Ceremony   349
Reconnecting Work with Worship

The Parsley Versus the Potato   355
A Passover Remembrance

Lag B'Omer and May Day   357
Counting the Omer with Actual Plantings

Post-Biblical Paganism   359
The Case for Tammuz

Illumination and Renewal   361
The Markers of Rosh Hashanah

On Illuminating the Sukkah   364
The Yaakov (Jacob) Lantern to the Rescue

Cupid Comes to Shul   366
For Valentine's Day

Part 5
Political and Personal Reflections

Darkness and Light   373
Rabbi Gendler's Senior Sermon, 1957

Not Tired, Merely Retired   380
Loosening the Daily Ties

Fifty Years in the Rabbinate   385
Delighted Amazement

Woodchucks in the Garden, Beavers in the Stream   387
And Messiah Nowhere in Sight

A Conversation with Everett Gendler   395
May Day, 2015

Introduction

A Universalist with a Rabbinical Degree

How an Insult Became a Badge of Honor

The exact words were these: "Everett Gendler, a radical universalist with a rabbinical degree . . ." They introduce a paragraph in the *American Jewish Year Book* of 1972, part of a long essay by a prominent Jewish sociologist entitled, "Confrontation and Reconstitution: Selections from the Literature of Jewish Public Affairs, 1969-1971."

One could interpret these words as simply an attempt to characterize, briefly, my religious outlook. In context, however, it was clear that they were an attempt to diminish my standing within the Jewish community and to dismiss my position paper about intermarriage. The remark seemed designed to say: "Careful, folks, Gendler is not a rabbi, he is only a universalist with a rabbinical degree. The rabbinic aspect is an add-on, an appendage, not a core part of his being. And his argument? Since it comes from one of such dubious dedication to the continuity of the Jewish community, it can be dismissed out of hand."

The barb was aimed at me during a particularly vulnerable period of my life. At the end of six turbulent yet satisfying years serving the Jewish Center of Princeton, New Jersey, my wife Mary and I had spent 1968-1969 in Cuernavaca, Mexico, at the Center for Intercultural Documentation (CIDOC), directed by Monsignor Ivan Illich, a maverick (some would say notorious) priest who challenged many of the accepted religious and societal truisms of that period. At the beginning of our stay, we had entertained fantasies about living among the poor and dispossessed rural inhabitants of Latin America, helping them organize more effective communities for advocacy while also introducing more productive methods of small scale organic food growing.

Fortunately, a number of stark realities did manage to penetrate our romantic bubble that year. Apart from our own lack of adequate personal preparation for the realization of our fantasy, we had two very young children whose healthy development would surely be compromised were we to live in such primitive rural circumstances.

Of course, there were urban opportunities as well. During my two extended visits to Cuba in 1968 and 1969, I learned of possibilities for Mary to teach French to Cuban diplomats who were cultivating closer relations with Vietnam. At CIDOC, we learned of interesting possibilities for teaching at the Catholic University in Santiago, Chile, while also doing work with Jewish youth in the city. We found this quite appealing, especially under the Allende government – but we finally decided to return to the U.S. at the end of the year. (We still sometimes speculate about our fate had we been living in Chile during the overthrow of the Allende government.)

Back in the U. S., we found our way to Packard Manse, a social-action-oriented interreligious and interracial center with houses in Stoughton and Roxbury, Massachusetts. We also were involved with Havurat Shalom, the community seminary in Somerville founded by Rabbis Arthur Green and Zalman Schachter-Shalomi. Classically "Sixties" in spirit and structure, Havurat Shalom made me realize how much I missed serving a congregation.

Mary, meanwhile, was discovering the feminist movement and reclaiming her own personality and sense of purpose beyond the traditional wife-mother roles. This meant significant changes in our family dynamics and structure, compounding an already dizzying fluidity in our lives. To boot, I endured a bit of brain surgery at this time, which kept me in the hospital for thirty days.

It was during this period of disorientation and self-doubt that I found myself characterized as "a radical universalist with a rabbinic degree." Had this taunt come my way when I was buoyed by a sense of who and how I was, I'd surely have replied internally: Of course I'm a universalist! How could I dare to be a rabbi without being concerned for all human beings? Abram's original command from God, as he was sent on his journey and assured that "I shall make of thee a great nation," was "Be thou a blessing… in thee shall all the families of the earth be blessed" (Genesis 12:2, 3). Not to be a universalist, not to be concerned that through the quality of Jewish life all human families should be blessed, would represent a betrayal of the original purpose of God's call to Abram become Abraham, the father of all three monotheistic traditions, Judaism, Christianity, and Islam!

Sadly, at that dispirited time in my life, I felt invalidated by the accusation. Looking back now, I can hardly believe my internal reaction. Why didn't I welcome those words as an unsought testimonial to the truth of my calling, even if they were dismissively intended? Why didn't I summon Amos and Isaiah to strengthen the case?

Amos (9:7) said it briefly and bluntly:

> Are you not like the Ethiopians to me,
> O people of Israel? says the Lord.

> Did I not bring Israel up from the land of Egypt,
> and the Philistines from Caphtor,
> and the Arameans from Kir?"

How clear the message: God, the Liberating Redeemer, is concerned for all lands and all peoples, not only for Jews.

Do I claim too much? Isaiah would not concede so. Foreseeing a time when the Egyptians themselves will discover and turn to the Liberating Deity, he declared (19:24-25): "On that day Israel will be the third with Egypt and Assyria, a blessing in the midst of the earth, whom the Lord of hosts has blessed, saying, 'Blessed be Egypt my people, and Assyria the work of my hands, and Israel my heritage.'"

Amos and Isaiah thus unite in the assertion that God works toward and welcomes the awakening to liberation of all peoples.

Indeed, the holder of a rabbinical degree had better be a universalist! How else could he or she serve adequately and with integrity such a universalist God, whose liberating concern extends to all peoples and all persons? Sadly, I had forgotten the penetrating words of our dear friend from Princeton, Erich Kahler, who characterized the Jews (in *The Jews among the Nations,* 1967) as "a tribe directed toward the achievement of an all-embracing, super-ethnic humanity . . . The substance of its particularity is universality . . . a tribe directed toward humanity at large." Nor did I remember Heschel's trenchant remark about idolatry: "What is an idol? Any God who is mine but not yours, any God concerned with me but not with you, is an idol."

Eventually, of course, with such texts to support me, I did find healing, and a positive reengagement with life and with Judaism as I understood it. This reengagement found especially inviting institutional settings at Temple Emanuel of the Merrimac Valley and Phillips Academy of Andover, both in Massachusetts. My gratitude to those institutions, from which I retired nearly twenty years ago, remains fresh and strong. Both technically "part-time" positions, they added up to far more than full-time, but the stimulation and satisfaction I derived from each far exceeded whatever energies I gave.

And today, well into my eighties and well finished with crises of confidence, I have chosen to entitle my collected writings *Judaism for Universalists.* I embrace the supposed insult with pride.

The oldest piece in this collection, my Senior Sermon, dates from Spring, 1957, just prior to my ordination. Reading it again today, I am startled by how it anticipated and articulated a basic, persistent element in my understanding of the world: *y'tziat mitzrayim,* the release from *mitzrayim,* the Narrow Place (as Egypt is identified in the Hebrew Bible), as the basic trajectory of human history. To say this is not to identify uncritically every change and upheaval as a manifestation of this Divine urge towards human liberation; destructive hostility and nihilism are not, as I understand it, Divine manifestations of God's liberating power at work in history. Still, how prescient I find that pre-ordination utterance to be, with many of its examples referring to what we now call nonviolent means for social change. Many of the articles in this collection are elaborations upon that theme, which is one of the two central motifs of what I think of as "our Friday evening catechism," the blessing of wine known as the *kiddush: zekher litziat mitzrayim,* "a reminder of the departure from Egypt."

A second doctrine articulated in the *kiddush* – and likewise introduced by a Hebrew term from the root *zakhar,* the act of calling to mind or remembering – is *zikaron l'maasei v'reshit,* the recollection of Creation. Here, too, is a theme that undergirds many of the essays in this book. There are numerous articles about Nature – some more theoretical, some detailed and practical, exploring details from Jewish tradition that I have found helpful in connecting my personal actions to rhythms of the cosmos. Such rituals are invaluable for increasing our awareness of the living connections with our immediate natural environment, for translating what we have in our heads to how we move with our bodies, for connecting to the kind of joy and aesthetic wonder that Nature evokes – and for plumbing the depths of Judaism for our contemporary exploration.

Other essays seek to affirm God's presence in social movements dedicated to greater social justice and human dignity. Implicit throughout these "political" essays, and explicit in some of them, is my conviction that abiding results from good intentions require proper means for their realization, that is, nonviolent methods that respect the inherent Divinity within each human participant in the conflicts, personal and political, that are an inescapable part of our daily experience. This belief is especially evident in the article on Universal Nonviolence Training, jointly authored with Mary, who has for nineteen years shared my involvement with the Tibetan exile community in India. Another example, necessarily speculative and tentative, is my attempt to imagine how Dr. Martin Luther King, Jr. might address the Israeli-Palestinian impasse guided by nonviolent principles.

Many of the articles in this book might benefit from an introductory update beyond the sentence or two inserted at the start of each essay, but I'm afraid that would swell the already formidable bulk of the volume beyond acceptable size. Let me limit this indulgence, then, to the essay that provoked the epithet, "universalist with a rabbinic degree."

The essay is "Identity, Invisible Religion, and Intermarriage," originally published in *Response* magazine in the Winter of 1969-70. Were I writing it today, there is one element I would modify: While affirming that there is, indeed, a new, broader, more inclusive religious identity in the making, I would also explicitly emphasize the value of preserving, developing, and strengthening our treasured Jewish religious ideas and practices. Overarching commonality with distinctive individual expressions seems to me a worthy goal. Many of the essays in this volume do, in fact, seek to preserve and renew precious, traditional Jewish practices, and show my life's work to have been as much about the enhancement of Jewish religious expression as about the cultivation of a universalist, Divinity-anchored, religious humanism. My belief is that the former is an invaluable resource for the latter.

As for the remainder of the *Response* essay, I am struck by how many of its ideas and theories can help our comprehension of such recent findings as the Pew Report on Religious Affiliation and Participation. I also remain convinced that the current movement guidelines for rabbinical practice with respect to intermarriage are woefully inadequate. The official discouraging of officiation when one member of the couple is not Jewish, even when there is a commitment to rearing anticipated offspring as Jews, is both pastorally problematic and strategically inept. What are the personal consequences of denying young people our presence and blessing at the very moment when they make the relational commitment that enables the next generation to come upon the scene? Usually these are not strangers; they are the young people we've educated and come to cherish. This is both personally painful and, I think, destructive of the future of Judaism.

I dare to hope that my essays will offer readers some guidance for the future, not simply a nostalgic view of "once upon a time." At first glance, they may seem out of touch with some current political atmospheric readings – the strong conservative winds, the tightening boundaries, the turning toward the past, the enchantment with fundamentalist doctrines, that are ascendant in Jewish life in the 21st century. Yet my reading of the long-range spiritual forecast, Biblically anchored, predicts that the overall direction of future Jewish and human development will find accurate markers in the spirit of these collected essays. They represent, I hope, both the appreciation and celebration of the particulars of Jewish tradition along with their reappropriation and expansion in light of current challenges and opportunities. They also, I hope, are largely faithful to Erich Kahler's description of the quintessential Jewish character of tribal universality, and to Abraham Joshua Heschel's depiction of idolatry as the exclusion of any person or people from the caring concern of the true God Who Unites All.

A few specific words of appreciation for help and support in enabling this volume to see the dark of print:

My first and most profound appreciation is to the Great Giver of Life, Who has been unbelievably gracious in granting me so many rich years, time sufficient for this, my very first book, to appear. I do hope, in all humility, that along with remarkable patience on the part of the Granter during some of these now 86 years (please God, may they continue yet a while longer), I have been fulfilling the purpose to which I was summoned.

Through the decades, the refreshingly critical yet lovingly appreciative support of Mary, my wife, has been invaluable. The inadequacies of the outlook underlying this collection surely would be much greater had I not enjoyed, and at times been sobered by, Mary's special spirit of affirming skepticism. (And how naturally our very accomplished daughters, Tamar and Naomi, joined her in this family pastime!) What a joy to have had, until now, a full half century of such companionship! I pray that we be granted still a few more years of the richness, the adventure, the pleasure, and the challenges of this treasured relationship.

Crisse MacFadyen came into our lives a few years ago, after we had been living several years in the Berkshires and the accumulation of papers and books in my study had become more and more forbidding. Our late beloved friend, Rabbi Jack Stern, assured me that Crisse would help me straighten out the mess in firm but not officious fashion. How right he was! Her exceptional organizing abilities quickly earned her the accolade of "our very own Mary Poppins," and she has re-earned the title, time and again, during what, without her, might have been the helter-skelter, chaotic process of locating, gathering, and organizing this scattered material from more than half a century.

Finally, to Lawrence Bush, the editor of *Jewish Currents* and its publishing imprint, Blue Thread Books (what a name for an avowedly secular

Jewish press!), my inexpressible appreciation for the attention and care he has accorded these essays. Larry's artistry, creativity, and energy are notable, and I am humbled by his willingness to give time to producing this collection. His editorial sensibility has helped these various writings assume a coherent sequence, and his brief introductions to the essays provide a bit of background, all of which, I hope, will help the reader make overall sense of the outlook here conveyed.

Everett Gendler
Great Barrington, Massachusetts
May 2015

Part One

Judaism and the Natural World

Where is the God Whom in joy we may worship? . . .
Wherever the feeling of life flows — in animals, plants,
In stones — there you will find God embodied. . . .
  God-in-Creation
                —Saul Tchernichovsky (c. 1900)

On the Judaism of Nature

God as the Life of the Universe

More and more Jews today, particularly young Jews and their communities, have become involved in efforts to live 'green' lives and curb pollution, especially the carbon emissions that are fueling global climate change. In this essay, published in 1971 – which Rabbi Gendler actually wrote just before the inauguration of Earth Day in 1970 – he explores the nature-oriented and ecologically aware elements embedded within the Jewish tradition.

Each of us, I think, approaches the 'official' tradition of Judaism with a particular set of inherited tendencies and experiences: archetypes, somatotypes, infantile impressions and childhood visions, adolescent agonies, and all the rest. For each of us, therefore, the living tradition of Judaism must be somehow distinct and individual. If not, what is the meaning of our religious being?

I was born in Chariton, Iowa, and lived there eleven years, in a small town surrounded by open country where nature was omnipresent. Des Moines, the "city" of my adolescence, also enjoyed nature's presence – as did I.

Not that I was conscious of it at the time. It seems to me, in retrospect, that not until after ordination from seminary and a period of time spent in Mexico did I become more fully aware of nature.

Its relation to my religious outlook took more time still. The entire process, I now know, was furthered by graduate academic studies and by poetry. J.J. Bachofen, Johannes Pedersen, Erich Neumann, Erwin Goodenough, Mircea Eliade, D.H. Lawrence, e.e. cummings, William Blake, Saul Tshernikhovsky, Lao Tzu, Kenneth Rexroth, the Besht, Reb Nachman: these, finally, were among my latter-day teachers, and I mention them for others more than for myself. It is true, their names do constitute for me a doxology of sorts, and their effect on me is mildly magical. They helped make me known to myself.

From this came my reevaluation of 'official' or traditional American Judaism, and my pained perception of its present plight: sea-sited synagogues with sea-views bricked over! tree-filled lots with windowless sanctuaries! hill-placed chapels opaque to sunsets! the astonishing indifference to natural surroundings!

Was Judaism always this way? I very much doubt it.

However powerful the Biblical assault on ancient nature cults, elements of those cults persisted, purified and sublimated, among loyal Jews for centuries after that Biblical assault. This much, I think, is convincingly established by the evidence in Raphael Patai's *The Hebrew Goddess*. This underground stream, flowing from the most ancient of times down to the present, reemerges strikingly at times – in kabbalah, Hasidism, and in the writings of recent Hebrew poets such as Saul Tchernikhovsky – as the reassertion of both the natural and the feminine components of religion.

Further, whatever merit there may be to the claim that post-Biblical Judaism is very much an urban development, it must be remembered that cities until quite recently were rarely so totally cut off from natural surroundings as are our present megalopolitan sprawls. However removed from landholding by legal disabilities, the Jews of Eastern Europe were nevertheless constantly aware of the land and often envious of those privileged to have direct proprietary contact with it. Many are the reminiscences of Hebrew and Yiddish writers that focus on *kheder* memories of their natural surroundings. And a perusal of the very moving photos in the Polish volume *Wooden Synagogues* (by Maria and Kasimierz Piechotka) makes quite vivid the rural locations (at least by our standards) of so many of these incomparably expressive structures.

Important, also, is the evidence from the persistence of various folk customs into recent decades. An especially telling instance concerns Shavuot, the least nature-oriented of the three pilgrimage festivals (in J.D. Eisenstein's *A Digest of Jewish Laws and Customs*):

> It is a custom to put trees in synagogues and homes on Shavuot . . . and to spread grass about in the synagogue . . . to recall that at the giving of the Torah the Jews stood upon a mountain surrounded by foliage. The Maharal used to spread fragrant grass and flowers on the floor of the synagogue in celebration of the holiday, and if Shavuot fell on Sunday, the Maharal would bring them in before Shabbat . . . On Shavuot the *shamash* used to distribute fragrant grass and herbs to every worshipper . . .

And what of the seder traditionally celebrated by the Sephardim on Tu Bishevat, when some thirty varieties of fruits, nuts, grains, and wines are consumed with special *kavanot* (intentions) and accompanied by readings from the Bible and the Zohar?

Most significant of all, however, has been the faithfulness of the folk to the rhythms of the moon throughout the ages.

In the biblical period, Hodesh or Rosh Hodesh (New Moon) was a holiday at least comparable to the Sabbath. Commerce was prohibited (Amos 8:5), visits to "men of God" were customary as on Sabbaths (II Kings 4:23), and New Moon is grouped with Sabbaths and festivals as a major holiday in the Jewish religious calendar (Hosea 2:13, II Chronicles 2:3, 8:12-13, and others). It is interesting to note that, quantitatively speaking, the New Moon offerings prescribed in Numbers (28:9015) and Ezekiel (46:3-7) exceeded those prescribed for Sabbaths.

The moon was, of course, the most visible heavenly marker of the passage of time. As such, it was essential to the determination of festivals and sacred celebrations. At the same time, however, its numinous quality constantly tempted people to worship the moon (Deuteronomy 17:2-7, Jeremiah 7:18, 44:15-19). It seems likely, then, that Hayyim Schauss is correct in suggesting (in *The Jewish Festivals*, 1938) that the prevailing rabbinic attitude toward the moon was also hostile, and that insofar as Rosh Hodesh survived at all, it was due to the loyalty of the folk, not the representatives of the severely anti-pagan official tradition.

This folk feeling for the moon should not be hard to comprehend, even in our own terms. As Mircea Eliade has pointed out (in *Patterns in Comparative Religion*, 1996):

> The sun is always the same, always itself, never in any sense "becoming." The moon, on the other hand, is a body which waxes, wanes and disappears, a body whose existence is subject to the universal law of becoming, of birth and death. The moon, like man, has a career involving tragedy, for its failing, like man's, ends in death. For three nights the starry sky is without a moon. But this "death" is followed by a rebirth: the "new moon." . . . This perpetual return to its beginning, and this ever-recurring cycle make the moon the heavenly body above all others concerned with the rhythms of life . . . they reveal life repeating itself rhythmically . . . it might be said that the moon shows man his true human condition; that in a sense man looks at himself, and finds himself anew in the life of the moon.

Small wonder, then, that a folk desirous of maintaining some significant connection both with cosmic rhythms and with the self should preserve its lunar festivities despite official frowns. Nor is it surprising that women, whose bodily functioning includes built-in, periodic natural rhythms, were most closely related to the lunar rhythms. As J.D. Eisenstein writes:

> Work on Rosh Hodesh is permitted . . . but women are accustomed not to work on Rosh Hodesh . . . weaving and sewing were especially avoided on Rosh Hodesh.

Other observances on Rosh Hodesh include these:

> It is a mitzvah (recommended practice) to have an especially ample meal on Rosh Hodesh. . . .

> In some countries, Yemen, for example, it is a custom to light candles on the eve of Rosh Hodesh, both in the synagogues and on the tables at home, just as on Sabbaths and Festivals. Some people prepare at least one additional special dish in honor of Rosh Hodesh and wear special festive garments.

Of all this and more, how much is practiced today? Except for the announcement of the new month in the synagogue on the Sabbath preceding – and I do mean new month, not new moon; it is all very calculated, calendrical, and non-lunar – very little, from what I have noticed. As for the ceremony of *kiddush hal'vanah* (the sanctification of the waxing moon), an out-of-door ceremony dating from Talmudic times that requires visual contact with the moon between the third and fifteenth days of the lunar month, and which also includes dancing before the moon – except for a few Hasidim, how widely is this practiced or even known today? Yet it is prescribed even in the Shulkhan Arukh, the classical 16th-century code of Jewish law.

These few examples do, I trust, establish that the present Jewish insti-tutional alienation from nature was not always the case, and that it is, in fact, a comparatively recent development.

An attempt to analyze why this has happened would take us far afield and lengthen this essay beyond its appointed limits. More important are some of the psycho-religious consequences of this estrangement from nature — an estrangement that is by no means unique to Judaism or Jews.

Two or three poetic formulations are among the best brief statements on this subject that I know.

> Great things are done when Men & Mountains meet;
> This is not done by Jostling in the Street.
>
> *William Blake*

> They know not why they love nor wherefore they sicken & die,
> calling that Holy Love which is Envy, Revenge & Cruelty,
> Which separated the stars from the mountains, the mountains from Man
> And left Man, a little grovelling Root outside of Himself.
>
> *William Blake*

> Oh, what a catastrophe for man when he cut himself off from the rhythm of the year, from his union with the sun and the earth.
>
> Oh, what a catastrophe, what a maiming of love when it was a personal, merely personal feeling, taken away from the rising and setting of the sun, and cut off from the magic connection of the solstice and the equinox!
>
> That is what is the matter with us.
>
> We are bleeding at the roots, because we are cut off from the earth and sun and stars, and love is a grinning mockery, because poor blossom, we plucked it from its stem on the tree of Life, and expected it to keep on blooming in our civilized vase on the table.
>
> *D.H. Lawrence*

Nor should one overlook the important lament by Tchernikhovsky over

> the distress of a world whose spirit is darkened,
> for Tammuz, the beautiful Tammuz is dead.

It seems increasingly clear that whatever the penalties that humans may have suffered when subjugated to nature, our 'liberation' from nature has become, in fact, truly a dreadful freedom. No longer attuned to the cosmic rhythms about us, increasingly entombed by the contrived, human-made elements of our environment, we neither knows ourselves as microcosm nor have any felt, enlivening connection with *khey ha-olamim*, the Life of the Universe (a term for the Divine that twice occurs in the traditional morning service).

Where, today, does one find that confirmation of being expressed in this rabbinic statement?

> Whatever the Holy One, blessed be He, created in the world, He created in man . . .
> He created forests in the world and He created forests in man . . .
> He created a wind in the world and He created a wind in man . . .
> A sun in the world and a sun in man . . .
> Flowing waters in the world and flowing waters in man . . .
> Trees in the world and trees in man . . .
> Hills in the world and hills in man . . .

> Whatever the Holy One, blessed be He, created in His world, He created in man . . .
>
> *Avot de Rabbi Natan, Version A, Chapter 31*

The self shivers in solitary confinement, and each detached attempt to discern one's true being seems to catapult the self into an abyss, or finds the self facing sets of mirrors that merely cast further and further back, in dizzying regress, that very image of the self that was seeking its substance.

Without grounding in felt being, what of relating, of love? The ever-shifting, estranged-from-the-universe subjectivity often means simply a mutual sense of being lost together – hardly a solid basis for lifelong relationship, which should help children also gain some orientation in this world.

Also, what does it mean to grow up, as increasing numbers of children do today, with so little contact with other growing things? How does it affect personal growth when almost all easily-observed, rapid developmental paradigms are of other-determined end products, not self-determined growth? What does it mean to have numerous examples of making and processing all around one, but few if any examples of that slow, deliberate, self-determined unfolding of inner potential that is so amazing to watch in the transformation of seed into plant? The separation from the vegetation cycle may have consequences for the spirit that we have hardly begun to comprehend.

And what may be the effects of this estrangement from nature on the environmental crisis we face? It is hard to imagine that there is no connection between the devaluation and disregard of nature, on the one hand, and the maltreatment and shameful exploitation of nature on the other.

These considerations, for the most part historical and theoretical, are meant to suggest that a vital an`d relevant Judaism for our age must begin to reclaim seriously its nature heritage. Such a suggestion has, I think, much to support it, as evidenced by the way people do, in fact, respond to such reclamation. Let me cite a few examples.

For some four summers, we held Friday evening services outdoors at the Jewish Center of Princeton, weather permitting. The setting itself was the attractive lawn behind the sanctuary, flat but ringed by shrubs and bushes, with a number of older, substantial trees in view. The start of the service was made a bit earlier to take full advantage of sunset, twilight, and the late-summer dusk. Nature elements in the traditional service were emphasized; special readings appropriate to a natural setting were included in the service; periods of silence and meditation on trees and shrubs were part of the worship; and the varying qualities of the "twilights" (*aravim*) were also a focus of attention.

I can report that the reaction to this, among adults as well as young people, was almost universally favorable and often enthusiastic. Except for a few occasions when bugs were especially bothersome (no, we did *not* spray!), the out-of-doors services were deeply appreciated by nearly all involved.

Another practice that received a generally favorable response was connected with the morning service of Sabbaths and festivals. When there was no *bar mitzvah* and our numbers were not increased by people unfamiliar with the building, on bright days, temperature permitting, we would leave the sanctuary immediately after the *Barkhu* and head out of doors. There, under the skies and in the face of the sun, we would chant together that part of the service that celebrates the gift of light and the radiance of the luminaries. And on days when it was not possible to go out of doors, this part of the service was prefaced by a focusing of attention on the light streaming in through the many windows in the sanctuary. In both cases, the added power of this part of the service was quite perceptible.

Speaking to various groups, I have found that, for the most part, people have responded with considerable interest as nature elements in Judaism were brought to their attention. They often seemed eager to relate to more of these elements in their own lives, and were also extremely appreciative of the nature poetry I often read on such occasions.

I make no claim that such findings constitute a "scientific" survey of the total scene today. I am convinced, however, that they do represent the expression of a profoundly felt need among many people for a renewed relationship to *khey ha-olamim,* the Life of the Universe. I am also convinced that contemporary Judaism, if it is to be a living religion, must respond to this need by a renewed emphasis on those many nature elements that lie dormant, neglected, sublimated, and suppressed within the tradition.

At one period of history it may have been the proper task of Judaism to struggle against nature cults insofar as they represented human subjugation to nature. Over the centuries, however, the reverse has occurred, reaching a frightening climax in our age: the almost total alienation of human beings from nature. Consequently, one of the crucial religious tasks of our age is to work towards human integration with nature, with all that implies societally, psychically, and theologically.

The elements of religious renewal are many, and the paths to the Divine various. But for at least some of us in this age, the following expresses, far better than we could ourselves, how it appears to us:

> And if you ask me of God, my God,
>   "Where is He that in joy we may worship Him?"
> Here on earth too He lives, not in heaven alone,
>   And this earth He has given to man.
>
> A striking fir, a rich furrow, in them you will find His likeness,
>   His image incarnate in every high mountain.
> Wherever the feeling of life flows — in animals, plants,
>   In stones — there you will find Him embodied.
>
> And His household? All being: the gazelle, the turtle,
>   The shrub, the cloud pregnant with thunder;
> No God disembodied, mere spirit — He is God-In-Creation!
>   That is His name and that is His fame forever!
>
> Saul Tchernichovsky (c. 1900)
(translated by R. Cover, E. Gendler, and A. Porat)

From *The New Jews,* edited by James A. Sleeper and Alan L. Mintz, Vintage Books/Random House, 1971

A Time to Sow and a Time to Reap

Jewish Agricultural Time

The Jewish Almanac, *published in 1980, became a handbook for baby-boomer Jews who were bringing to their Judaism a feminist, ecological, and communal awareness, while seeking a progressive renewal of Jewish identity. In this essay, which appeared in that volume, Rabbi Gendler unpacked some elements of Judaism that mark it as the religion of an agricultural people.*

The Jews, living in "exile" for two thousand years, are not usually identified as farmers. However, from the earliest biblical account of Adam in the Garden until the "blooming deserts" of modern Israel, the land has served as the basis of the Israelite economy and Jewish religious rituals. Each of the three major pilgrimage festivals – Passover, Shavuot, and Sukkot – is based on the agricultural cycles. So precious was the land that there is an obligation to rest it every seven years, an agricultural Sabbath parallel to the Sabbath day. The Land of Israel is, in fact, a central figure in Jewish history: promised to Abraham, conquered by Joshua, it was from the Land that the Jews were exiled in 586 B.C.E. and 70 C.E., and it was for the Land that the Jews yearned during their many years of wandering. To this day, Israel is referred to simply as "*ha-aretz*" (the Land).

With such extensive connections, it is not surprising that an intimate knowledge of the ways of land developed within Judaism. From observations about the Moon to remedies for unsuccessful tree grafts, the literature is replete with commentaries on virtually every aspect of agricultural life. Many of these, as may be expected, are long out of date; others have withstood the test of time.

The following is a sampling of the wealth of agricultural knowledge amassed by the Jewish tradition. In it can be seen the intricate interconnections of Sun, Moon, wind, rain, seasons, cycles, human energy, and Divine blessing.

Agricultural Time

> His two months are olive harvest,
> His two months are planting grain,
> His two months are late planting;
> His month is hoeing up of flax,
> His month is harvest of barley,
> His month is wheat harvest and feasting;
> His two months are vine-tending,
> His month is summer fruit (figs).
>
> *Gezer Calendar, 10th century BCE*

This school exercise tablet, written on soft limestone and found among the excavations at Gezer, is the earliest written record of a Jewish enumeration of time. The young student is learning the names of the months in relation to the agricultural tasks of the seasons. From the beginning, it would appear, Jewish calculations of time were intimately linked with the life-sustaining sequence of the seasonal cycle.

Biblical names of the months used before the Babylonian Exile (6th century BCE) reflect this. *Aviv* (Exodus 13:4, 23:15, 34:18; Deuteronomy 16:1), usually translated as "spring," seems related to the Canaanite designation for "month of ears of grain." *Ziv* (1 Kings 6:1, 37) means "month in which only permanent water courses flow." Finally, *Bul* (1 Kings 6:38) means "month of the great rains."

Equally significant are the post-exilic, Babylonian-derived names of the Hebrew months, still in use today. A brief list shows connections with seasonal, astronomical and agricultural phenomena:

Nisan – Month when early blossoms appear in the land (Hebrew: *nitzan*).

Iyar – Month of brightness due to the proliferation of buds and flowers (Hebrew: *or*).

Sivan – Perhaps connected with the time of ripening produce; in Babylonia dedicated to the moon god, Sin.

Tammuz – Named after Dumuzu, the Akkadian analogue to Adonis, god of vegetation and plant life.

Av – Named after the wood and reeds from which shelters were erected in Babylonia.

Elul – Onomatopoetic derivative from the Akkadian for "women singing," in celebration of Tammuz's return from the netherworld and the consequent revival of vegetative growth after the burning heat of high summer.

Tishri – "First" month of the year in Akkadian; dedicated to the sun god, supreme judge of the Babylonian pantheon, whose "balance" is reestablished at the autumn equinox.

Marheshvan – Literally "the eighth month."

Kislev – Uncertain in origin, but some would connect it with *k'sil*, the biblical word for Orion (Sagittarius, the Archer), so prominent in the night sky at this time of year.

Tevet – "Drowned and submerged in mud," the rainiest of months in Babylonia (Hebrew: *tavua*).

Shevat – "Rod, staff, scepter," referring to the beating rains which descend so forcefully this month.

Adar – "Cloudy," referring to the heavens which are still overcast during this last month of the rainy season; or "threshing floor," *i.e.* the month during which the granaries are readied for the new crop.

THE SEASONS AND THE SOLAR-LUNAR CALENDAR

With such seasonal awareness embedded in the very nomenclature of the months, it is not surprising to find widespread rabbinic interest in astronomy, the calendar, and the seasons.

> R. Simeon b. Pazzi said in the name of R. Joshua b. Levi on the authority of Bar Kappara: He who knows how to calculate the cycles of the seasons and the courses of the planets, but does not, of him Scripture says, "They regard not the work of the Lord, neither have they considered the operation of his hands" (Isa. 5:12)
> *Shabbat 75a*

> Samuel said: I am familiar with the paths of heaven as with the streets of Nehardea, with the exception of the comet, about which I am ignorant.
> *Berakhot 58b*

Given this interest in astronomy, considerable attention is given to the complex relation of the solar to the lunar year.

> Samuel said: The lunar year consists of no fewer than 352, nor of more than 356 days.

> *Arakin 9b*
> The sun is called great while the moon is called small; the sun is called great because it exceeds the moon by eleven days.
> *Exodus Rabbah XV, 22*

> God created 365 windows in the firmament, 183 in the east and 182 in the west, some of them were created to serve the sun and some for the moon, which comes up and travels after it, save for eleven windows into which the moon does not enter.
> *Exodus Rabbah XV, 22*

> Said the Holy One . . . Twelve constellations have I created in the firmament, and for each constellation I have created thirty hosts, and for each host I have created thirty legions, and for each legion I have created thirty cohorts, and for each cohort I have created thirty maniples, and for each maniple have created thirty camps, and to each camp I have attached 365,000 myriads of stars, corresponding to the days of the solar year . . .
> *Berakhot 32b*

A myriad being 10,000, this is a total of 1,064,340,000,000,000,000 stars.

The Seasons and the Soil

The succession of the seasons and their agricultural consequences are of more direct concern than astronomy. Awareness of human dependence on the soil was established from the earliest of times:

> All the conversation of humankind concerns the earth:
> "Has the earth produced, or has the earth not produced?"
> And all humankind's prayers concern the earth:
> "Lord! May the earth yield fruit!"
> Or "Lord! May the earth be successful!"
> *Genesis Rabbah XIII, 2*

Not only commoners but kings are subject to this dependency, as is expressed in the following midrash:

> Even though he is a king and holds sway from one end of the world to the other, he is a "servant to the field," if the earth yields produce, he can accomplish something; if the earth does not yield, he is of no use whatever.
> *Leviticus Rabbah XXII, 1*

Small wonder, then, that the rabbis tend to construe seasonally and very specifically such passages as this one from Genesis 8:22: "While the earth remains, seedtime and harvest, and cold and heat, and summer and winter, and day and night shall not cease."

> "Seedtime" – this is autumn. "Harvest" – this is spring. "Cold" – this is winter. "Heat" – this is summer.
>
> Pirkei d'Rabbi Eliezer 8

> R. Simeon b. Gamaliel said on the authority of R. Meir, and R. Simeon b. Manasya said likewise: (The second) half of *Tishri, Marheshvan*, and the first half of *Kislev* is seed-time; (the second) half of *Kislev, Tevet*, and half *Shevat* are the winter months; (the second) half of *Shevat, Adar*, and (the first) half of *Sivan* is the period of harvests; (the second) half of *Sivan, Tammuz*, and the first half of *Av* are summer; the second half of *Av, Elul,* and the first half of *Tishri*, hot months. R. Judah counted (these periods) from (the beginning of) *Tishri*; R. Simeon, from *Marheshvan*.
>
> Baba Metzia 106b; cf. also Genesis Rabbah XXXIV, 11

The qualities of the seasons are strikingly portrayed in a play on the four words used to designate the Earth:

> R. Simeon b. Gamaliel said: It (the Earth) has four names: *eretz, tevel, adamah, arka*. The name *eretz* corresponds to the vernal equinox which forces up *(me-altzah)* the crops, *tevel* to the summer solstice which lends savor to *(me-tabbelet)* the crops; *adamah* to the autumn, when the ground consists of clods of earth (due to autumn rains moistening the heat-parched summer ground); *arka* corresponds to the winter which causes the crops to wither *(moreket)*.
>
> Genesis Rabbah XIII, 12

Their coordination with the path of the sun is also explicit:

> R. Nathan said: In summer the Sun travels in the heights of the heaven, therefore the whole world is hot while the wells (springs) are cold; in winter the Sun travels at the lower ends of the sky, therefore the whole world is cold while the wells are hot.
>
> Our rabbis taught: The Sun travels over four courses: (during) *Nisan, Iyar,* and *Sivan*, it travels over the mountains, in order to melt the snows; (in) *Tammuz, Av,* and *Elul,* over the inhabited world, to ripen the fruits (in) *Tishri, Marheshvan*, and *Kislev*, over seas, to dry up the rivers, in *Tevet, Shevat*, and *Adar*, through the wilderness, so as not to dry up the seeds (in the ground).
>
> Pesahim 94b

The results are evident:

> At the winter solstice there are no grapes on the vine and no figs on the fig-trees . . . But at the summer solstice there are grapes on the vine, figs on the fig-trees, and even the leaves are not withered.
>
> *Lamentations Rabbah I, 42*

The tradition also records that there are those so attuned to the solar sequence that they can identify the months without the pages of a calendar. Two examples from the Talmud follow:

> Three cowherds were standing conversing, and were overhead by some rabbis. One of them said: "If the early and late sowing sprout together, the month is *Adar*; if not, it is not *Adar*." The second said: "If, in the morning, frost is severe enough to injure an ox, and at midday the ox lies in the shade of the fig-tree and scratches its hide, then it is *Adar*; if not, it is not *Adar*." And the third said: "When a strong east wind is blowing and your breath can prevail against it, the month is *Adar*; if not, it is not *Adar*."
>
> *Sanhedrin 18B*

> "The rams have mounted the sheep and the valleys are covered with corn, they shout for joy, yea, they sing" (Psalm 65:14). R. Meir reasoned: "When do the rams mount the sheep? At the time when the valleys are covered over with corn. And when are the valleys covered over with corn? In *Adar*. The sheep conceive in *Adar* and bear in *Av*, and their New Year is in *Elul*.
>
> R. Eleazar and R. Simeon said: When do the rams mount the sheep? At the time when they (the ears of corn) shout for joy and sing. When do the ears of corn burst into song? In *Nisan*. They conceive in *Nisan* and bear in *Elul*, and their New Year is in *Tishri*.

THE SOLSTICES: AS THE WORLD TURNS

The seasons' effect on the growth cycle figures explicitly in determining when a year is to be intercalated (with the addition of a leap month) so that solar and lunar years remain in seasonal harmony. Writing to the communities of the Diaspora, R. Simeon b. Gamaliel is quoted as saying:

> We beg to inform you that the doves are still tender and the lambs still young, and the grain has not yet ripened. I have considered the matter, and thought it advisable to add thirty days to the year.
>
> *Sanhedrin 11a*

And the general rabbinic consensus?

> Our rabbis taught: A year may be intercalated on three grounds: on

> account of the premature state of the grain-crops; or that of the fruit-trees; or on account of the lateness of the *tekufah* (equinox). Any two of these reasons can justify intercalation, but not one alone. All, however, are glad when the state of the spring-crop is one of them.
>
> Sanhedrin 11b

As is clear in the consideration of *tekufah*, the turning point of the Sun in its course, it is critical that the movements of the Sun and its seasonal shifts be plotted precisely:

> Samuel stated: The vernal equinox occurs only at the beginning of one of the four quarters of the day, viz, either at the beginning of the day or at the beginning of the night or at midday or at midnight. The summer solstice only occurs either at the end of one and a half or at the end of seven and a half hours of the day or night. The autumnal equinox only occurs at the end of three or nine hours of the day or the night, and the winter solstice only occurs at the end of the four and half or ten and a half hours of the day or night. The duration of a season of the year is no longer than ninety-one days and seven and a half hours; and the beginning of one season is removed from that of the other by no more than one half of a planetary hour.
>
> Samuel further stated: The vernal equinox never begins under Jupiter but it breaks the trees, nor does the winter solstice begin under Jupiter but it dries up the seed. This, however, is the case only when the new moon occurred in the moon-hour or in the Jupiter-hour.
>
> Erubin 56a

David Abudraham of Seville, a 14th-century Judeo-Spanish commentator on the Jewish liturgy, cites another tradition:

> As each season of the year begins, the hours of daylight and darkness vary. At spring the day and night are equal; at summer the day is one half again as long as the night; at autumn they once again are equal; at winter the dark is half again as great as the day.

The observation of significant points in the growth cycle could not fail to elicit ritual responses too:

> Our rabbis taught: One who sees the Sun at its turning point (vernal equinox), the Moon in its power, the planets in their orbits, and the signs of the Zodiac in their orderly progress, should say, "Blessed be He who has wrought the work of Creation."
>
> Berakhot 59b

A curious custom of wearing clothing of particular colors at particular seasons is mentioned in one obscure apocryphal source, "The Throne and Hippodrome of Solomon the King":

> His students asked R. Jose: Why the different-colored clothing which particular groups of people wear?
>
> He replied: They wear different colors in response to the four seasons. In autumn the seas are blue, hence the blue garments. In winter the snows descend, hence people wear white. In spring the sea is green and good for crossing, therefore people wear green. In summer the fruits are ripening red, and so the people dress in red.

Especially interesting, among customs observed at the change of the seasons, is that of not drinking water at the hour of solstice or equinox. David Abudraham, whose commentaries contain considerable folkloric material, transmitted the custom in these terms:

> I have found written that one should take care, at each of the four seasons, not to drink water at the hour of equinox or solstice, for at such times there is danger of swelling and illness from drinking the water.
>
> For it was at vernal equinox that the waters of Egypt were turned to blood (cf. Exod. 7:19-25).
>
> It was at summer solstice that Moses and Aaron struck rather than spoke to the rock, and blood gushed forth (cf. Num. 20:8).
>
> It was at the turn of autumn that Abraham, binding his son Isaac upon the altar (cf. Gen. 22), shed some drops of Isaac's blood, which spread through all of the waters. And it was at winter solstice that Jeptha's daughter was sacrificed (cf. Judg, 11:29-c40), and all the world's waters were turned to blood.
>
> And so annually, at the turning of the seasons, the ancient contaminations recur. . . . Some call these divinations or old wives' tales. But others say that for each season a guardian is appointed over the waters. At each change of seasons comes a changing of the guards, and at the precise moment of the exchange, the waters are without protection.

While this may be an unconscious memory of seasonal sacrifices offered in the dim past, whose bloody traces persist in folk tradition, it is clear that the change of the seasons was highly visible to the common people. Two further customs developed, notes Abudraham:

> At these times [of seasonal changes] some place a piece of iron (barzel) upon the well covers, storage tanks, or buckets containing water, confident

that the Merits of the Mothers, of Bilhah, Rachel, Zilpah, and Leah will protect us all from harm.

Still others, in lieu of drinking water, eat sweets at these times, that the season to come be a sweet one. But I say that for the person who worships the One God, trusting in Him alone, each season will be sweet in its turn.

Ritualized responses to seasonal succession have their satisfactions — and their limitations. Agricultural uncertainties are a given, whatever rites humans may practice:

> If a person sows, it is uncertain that he will reap the harvest; only when a person reaps is there certainty that he will eat.
>
> *Sukkah 49b*

Ancient Weather Forecasting

Weather is a perpetual preoccupation of those who live on the land. Thus the existence of wind was gratefully acknowledged:

> R. Levi said: Even assuming that you have ploughed, sown, hoed, removed the thorns, reaped, made sheaves, threshed, and laid up corn in the granaries, if the Holy One, blessed be He, did not bring out a little wind for you to winnow, what would you live from?
>
> *Leviticus Rabbah XXVIII, 2*

> R. Phinehas said: In the ordinary way, when a man washes his cloak during the rainy season, how much trouble he must go through until he can dry it! Yet people sleep in their beds and the Holy One, blessed be He, brings out a little wind and dries the earth!
>
> *Leviticus Rabbah XXVIII, 2*

Even more important was rain, whose timely arrival was devoutly prayed for, and whose characteristics were carefully noted:

> When do we [begin to] make mention of the power of rain? R. Eliezer says: On the first day of the Feast of Sukkot.
>
> R. Joshua says: On the last day of the Feast.
>
> *Ta'anith 2a*

> The rabbis have taught: "And I will give you rains in their season." [This means that the soil shall be] neither soaked nor parched, but moderately rained upon. For whenever the rain is excessive it scours away the soil so that it yields no fruit.
>
> *Ta-anith 22b*

> How much rain must descend that it may suffice for fructification? As much as would fill a vessel of three handbreadths. This is R. Meir's opinion. R. Judah said: In hard [soil], one handbreadth; in average [soil], two; in humid [soil], three.
>
> *Genesis Rabbah XIII, 13*
>
> How much rain must fall for one to recite a blessing? R. Jose said in Rab Judah's name, and R. Jonah and Rab Judah said in Samuel's name: At the beginning as much as will fructify [the earth]; at the end, even just a little.
>
> *Genesis Rabbah XIII, 15*
>
> Rab Judah further said: Wind after rain is as beneficial as rain, clouds after rain as beneficial as rain, sunshine after rain as beneficial as twofold rain. What does this exclude? – The glow after sunset and sunshine between the clouds.
>
> Raba said: Snow is beneficial to the mountains as fivefold rain to the earth.
>
> Raba further said: Snow is beneficial to the mountains, heavy rain to the trees, gentle rain to the fruits of the field, drizzling rain ('urpila) even to the seeds under a hard clod.
>
> *Ta'anith 3b-4a*

Naturally, there were attempts to predict the weather for the growing season:

> R. Abba said to R. Ashi: We rely upon [the weather information] of R. Isaac b. Abdimi. For R. Isaac b. Abdimi said: [At] the termination of the last day of Tabernacles, all watched the smoke of the wood pile. [If] it inclined towards the north, the poor rejoiced and landowners were distressed because [that was an indication] that the yearly rains would be heavy and the crops would decay. [If] it inclined towards the south, the poor were distressed and landowners rejoiced because [that was an indication] that the yearly rains would be scanty and the crops could be preserved. [If] it inclined towards the east, all were glad; toward the west, all were distressed.
>
> *Baba Batra 147a*
>
> Abba Saul said: "Fine [weather at] the Festival of Pentecost is a good sign for all the year."
>
> R. Zebid said" If the first day of the New Year is warm, all the year will be warm; if cold, all the year will be cold."
>
> *Baba Batra 174a*

The directions on the compass had agricultural implications, as indicated in the following references:

> The west is the region of the storehouses of snow and those of hail and

cold and heat . . . The south is the source from which emanate the dews and rains that bring blessing to the world . . . The north is the region from whence the darkness goes forth to the world . . . The east is the source from which light goes forth into the world.

Numbers Rabbah III, 12

The east [wind] is always beneficial; the west [wind] is always harmful; the north wind is beneficial for wheat that reached [the stage of] a third [of its maturity], and harmful for olives in blossom; and the south wind is injurious for wheat that reached [the stage of] a third [of maturity], and beneficial for olives in blossom.

Baba Batra 147a

Our rabbis taught: [If] the weather on the Festival of Pentecost is fine, sow wheat.

Mar Zutra stated: It was said, "Cloudy."

The Nehardeans said in the name of R. Jacob: "Fine" [does] not [mean] absolutely fine, nor does "cloudy" mean completely overcast, but even [when it is] "cloudy" and the north wind blows [the clouds], it is regarded as "fine."

Baba Batra 147a

Farming Wisdom and Technique

There is no substitute for the accumulated wisdom of generations of farming practice, accompanied by a certain intuitive sense.

Already in biblical times the preferred hillside location for a vineyard was known, and due attention was paid to the need to clear stones:

> Let me sing of my well-beloved,
> A song of my beloved concerning his vineyard.
> My well-beloved had a vineyard
> In a very fruitful hill;
> And he digged it, and cleared it of stones,
> And planted it with the choicest vine,
> And built a watchtower in the midst of it,
> And also hewed out a vat therein;
> And he looked that it should bring forth grapes,
> And it brought forth wild grapes.
>
> *Isaiah 5:1-2*

Another passage from Isaiah clearly distinguishes the operations of planting, sowing, and threshing for herbs from those for grains, along with some general rules for laying out plots:

Does he who plows for sowing plow continually?
Does he continually open and harrow his ground?
When he has levelled its surface, does he not scatter dill,
   sow cumin, and put in wheat in rows
and barley in its proper place,
and spelt as the border?
For He instructs him aright,
His God teaches him.
Dill is not threshed with a threshing sledge,
nor is a cart wheel rolled over cumin;
but dill is beaten out with a stick, and cumin with a rod.
Does one crush bread grain?
No, one does not thresh it for ever,
Though the wheel of the wagon and its sharp edges move noisily,
he does not crush it.
This also comes from the Lord of hosts;
Wonderful is His counsel, and great His wisdom.

Isaiah 28:24-29

Rabbinic tradition contains detailed instructions on planting, pruning, cutting, and grafting trees; a technique of grafting to increase the timber yield of the tree is mentioned.

> R. Joshua of Siknin said in the name of R. Levi: All other plants, if you cover their roots at the time of planting, do well, and if not, they do not do well; but a nut-tree, if its roots are covered at the time of planting, does not do well.
>
> *Song of Songs Rabbah Vi, 11, 1*
>
> When a nut-tree is pruned, it is for its benefit, since it renews its branches like hair which grows more quickly for being shorn and like the nails which soon grow again after being pared.
>
> *Song of Songs Rabbah VI, 11, 1*
>
> R. Judah says: "Any grafting that has not taken root within three days will never do so."
>
> *Shebi'ith II, 6*
>
> . . . [A]re there fig-trees which do not produce fruit? Yes, as stated by Rahabah. For Rahabah said: "They bring white fig-trees and scrape them with a rope of date-tree bark on which seed is smeared, and they are then planted in alluvial soil, and they produce trunks but no fruit, and three branches of one will break down a bridge."
>
> *Tamid 29b-30a*
>
> A person who comes to cut down a tree: a man who is not an expert lops

off the branches, cutting down each branch separately and tiring himself out, but the clever man lays bare the roots and cuts down the tree.

Numbers Rabbah XX, 19

Hints of the psychic go beyond the purely physical:

R. Tanhuma said: There was once a palm-tree in Hammethan which would not bear fruit. They grafted it and still it would bear no fruit. A palm-gardener said to them: "She sees a palm-tree at Jericho and longs for it." So they brought a portion of the Jericho palm, grafted it, and forthwith the Hammethan palm bore fruit.

Numbers Rabbah, III, 1

The importance of a southern exposure for early ripening is noted, along with soil preparation:

They may bring the Omer-offering only from the fields in the south, and which had been broken up for the purpose, for upon these fields the sun rises and upon these the sun sets. How was [the field] prepared? In the first year it was broken up and in the second year it was ploughed twice, and it was sown seventy days before the Passover so that it might be close upon the [increasing strength of the] sun; thus it would bring forth stalks one span long and ears two spans long. It was then reaped, bound into sheaves, threshed, winnowed, cleansed, ground, and sifted, and then brought to the Temple-treasurer.

Menahot 85a

The root systems of plants and their means of obtaining water are examined:

R. Eleazar b. Simeon said: The earth drinks only as far as its upper layer. If so, what are the roots of the sycamore tree and the carob tree to do?

[Moreover,] R. Hanina b. Ikah and R. Berekiah in the name of R. Judah said: "The roots of wheat strike down fifty cubits into the earth; the soft roots of the fig-tree break through the rock.

Said R. Levi: Once in thirty days the deep ascends and waters it.

Genesis Rabbah XIII, 17

Interplanting was discussed in the tractate Kilayim ("diverse kinds"), a guide to permitted and prohibited "companion planting," and in other texts. Some regard the prohibition of mixing species as an incomprehensible and irrational ancient taboo; others consider it to be ancient agricultural wisdom. An interesting episode involves the rabbinic sage Samuel:

> Samuel's field laborer brought him some dates. As he partook of them he tasted wine in them. When he asked the laborer how that came about, he told him that the date trees were placed between the vines.
>
> He said to him: Since they are weakening the vines so much, bring me their roots tomorrow. When R. Hisda saw certain palms among the vines he said to his field laborers: "Remove them with their roots. Vines can easily buy palms but palms cannot buy vines."
>
> Baba Kamma 91b-92a

Along with secular procedures shared for ages with the other agriculturalists of the Mediterranean basin, there was a persistent awareness of special, Biblically ordained agricultural practices:

> R. Levi said: In all their doings Israel are different from the other nations – in their plowing, in their sowing, in their planting, in their reaping, in their sheaf-gathering, in their threshing, in their garnering, in their wine-gathering . . . In their plowing, as it says, "Thou shalt not plough with an ox and an ass together" (Deuteronomy 22:10). In their sowing, as it says, "Thou shalt not sow thy vineyard with two kinds of seed" (Deuteronomy 22:9). In their planting, as it says, "Then ye shall count the fruit thereof as forbidden" (Leviticus 19:23). In their reaping, as it says, "And when ye reap the harvest of your land, thou shalt not wholly reap the corner," etc. (Leviticus19:9). In their sheaf-gathering, as it says, "If thou forgettest a sheaf in the field," etc. (Deuteronomy 24:19.) In their corn-treading, as it says, "Thou shalt not muzzle the ox when he treadeth out the corn" (Deuteronomy 25:4). In their garnering and wine-gathering, as it says, "Thou shalt not delay to offer of the fullness of thy harvest, and out of the outflow of thy presses" (Exodus 22:28). And it is also written, "As the corn of the threshing floor and as the fullness of the wine-press" (Numbers 18:27). . . . [Further,] Israel reckons time by the moon and other nations by the sun.
>
> Song of Songs Rabbah V, 16, 5

In summary, Israelite agriculture was designed so that at no point in the cycle of the seasons could the farmer or shepherd forget that –

> The earth is the Lord's
> and the fullness thereof;
> The world,
> and that they dwell therein.
>
> Psalm 24:1

Sowing Spiritual Seeds

There were those who worried about the burdens connected with soil and seasons. Bar Yohal, a radical mystic whose meditative practices removed him, for a time, from sympathetic involvement with the life-sustaining procedures of the earth, worriedly asked:

> If a man plows in the plowing season, sows in the sowing season, reaps in the reaping season, threshes in the threshing season, and winnows in the season of the wind, what is to become of the Torah?
>
> *Berakhot 35b*

Others were confident that "for everything there is a season, and a time for every purpose under heaven" (Ecclesiastes 3:1). For example, there is the discussion among the rabbis concerning the early Hasidim, the pietists, each of whose three hours of daily prayers was surrounded by an introductory and a concluding hour of meditative silence:

> But seeing that they spend nine hours a day over prayer, how is their knowledge of Torah preserved, and how is their work done? Because they are pious, their Torah is preserved, and their work is blessed [and so with little effort they accomplish much].
>
> *Berakhot 32b*

Performed in the proper spirit, the life-sustaining tasks of the cycles of the seasons can connect the human being with *khay ha-olamim*, the Life of the universe and its Source. Thus the *avodah* that is "work" becomes simultaneously the *avodah* that is "worship." Pastures and hills, meadows and valleys truly "shout and sing together for joy" (Psalm 65:12-13). They join humankind in that spirit of celebration so beautifully expressed in a rabbinic "legalism," a catalog of prescribed blessings:

> R. Mesharsheya said: Over garden narcissus the blessing is "who created fragrant woods"; over wild narcissus, "who created fragrant herbs."
>
> R. Shesheth said: He who smells a citron or a quince should say, "Blessed be He who has given a sweet odor to fruits."
>
> Rab Judah says: If one goes walking in the days of Nisan [springtime] and sees the trees sprouting, he should say, "Blessed be He who has not left His world lacking in anything, and has created in it goodly creatures and goodly trees for the enjoyment of humankind."
>
> *Berakhot 43b*

From *The Jewish Almanac,* edited by
Richard Siegel and Carl Rheins, Bantam Books, 1980

The Life of His Beast

Our Kinship with Other Creatures

This sermon from 1967 anticipated contemporary concerns about factory farming and its impact on the creatures we 'process' into food – and on our own spiritual sensibility.

Charles Darwin was not the first human being to posit a close relation between human beings and the other animals. He may have put this particular notion to new theoretical use, and he may have made our sense of kinship with other animals function differently in this particular age from the way it did in the centuries preceding, but the fact is that man's sense of relatedness to other living creatures is a very ancient inheritance of the human species. The 104th Psalm and the 148th Psalm express clearly the Psalmist's close identification not only with human life but also with the entire life of the Universe, even as it expresses itself in the lives of the beasts of the field, the monsters of the deep, and the birds of the air.

Nor is this simply an accident of the Book of Psalms. Those familiar with the creation story in Genesis have perhaps noticed that the sea animals and the birds which fly receive the same blessings as men: "be fruitful and multiply" (1:22). One notices also that beasts of the earth as well as men are invited to the banquet provided by the herbs, fruits, and growths of the earth's surface (Genesis 1:30). One notices even that the important Hebrew term *nefesh khaya* – which means "a living being" or "a living soul" – is applied both to animals and to humans in the Creation story in Genesis (1:20, 21, 24). Granted, humans surpass the capacities of the animals in some respects; Genesis is explicit about this. But the basic relatedness is not lost sight of, even with the awareness of difference.

Nor is this sense of kinship confined simply to sentiments for singing on occasions of worship. The Five Books of Moses include a number of specific laws dealing with proper treatment of the other animals, for they, too, are creatures of the Divine and objects of His express concern. To mention a few of them: "you may not muzzle an ox as it threshes the grain" (Deuteronomy 25:4). The grain looks good to your ox? Let it eat! It must not be subjected to the frustration of facing food while it works and is itself muzzled. This was extended by rabbinic interpretation to other animals, even birds, working within sight of food (Rashi, citing Talmud Baba Metziah 94b in support).

Another example: Even at the time when the sacrificial cult was practiced, it was forbidden to take a newborn ox, sheep, or goat from the mother until it had at least seven days of warmth and nourishment directly from her (Leviticus 22:27). The idea that a newborn sacrifice is superior was rejected by the Bible, lest there be the immediate theft of the offspring from the warm suckling of the mother.

There are other provisions, including the commandment with which we're all familiar: "Remember the Sabbath day and keep it holy"(Exodus 20: 8). Less famous but even more significant is the follow-up in Exodus 23:12: "Six days you shall do you work, but on the seventh day you shall cease from labor, in order that your ox and your ass may rest, and that your bondman and the stranger may be refreshed." Here the Sabbath is proclaimed not only for the sake of people but for the sake of the animals as well!

All of this could be summed up in the saying in Proverbs 12:10: *yodea tzadik nefesh b'hemto*, "the decent man considers the life of the beast."

Nor is the notion confined in the West only to the Jewish tradition. One great figure of Western culture is surely Francisca of Assisi, called St. Francis by the Church, who was known for his great friendship with other creatures. St. Bonaventure, in *The Life of St. Francis* (Chapter VIII, Section 6), mentions that when Francis "bethought himself of the first beginning of all things, he was filled with a yet more overflowing charity, and would call the dumb animals, howsoever small, by the names of brother and sister, forasmuch as he recognized in them the same origin as in himself." And in the *Mirror of Perfection* (Section XII, Chapter CXIV), St. Francis urges the emperor "to make a law that men should make a good provision for birds and oxen and asses and the poor at Christmas-time," with a specification thereof.

It is against this background of Biblical and traditional Western religious concern for all living creates, then, that I want briefly to view so-called factory farming or intensive rearing. What do the terms mean? Not simply the use of machines in farming, nor the striving for efficiency as such, but rather the uncritical application of technology to animal rearing so that animals, admittedly useful to human beings, are not regarded as fellow creatures.

The effect of this enterprise on the observer is quite shocking. My own awareness of the development dates from a couple of years ago when my wife and I were in Maine, driving along a country road at night, and discovered time and again buildings, multistoried, with light shining from them, looking very much like urban apartment dwellings. Yet there were no signs of any other habitations around, no sizeable towns on the map, and it was very puzzling. A couple of days later, walking along a country road, we came upon one such building by daylight and discovered that a door was open. There was netting across the opening, making sure that none of the "contents" of the structure would spill out, and we saw crowded against the netting, piled on top of one another, countless numbers of chickens. From an elevated vantage point we were able to discern that this particular structure contained tens of hundreds of chickens, most of them in a semigloom, barely visible, obviously enclosed permanently. We were rather horrified by this imprisonment of beings who, however "low" on the evolutionary scale, are gifted with flesh, blood, and a sensory apparatus. For it is now the case that millions of animals spend their entire lives in darkness or semidarkness, without any free exposure to the natural elements, crowded together in pitiless fashion, subsisting but hardly living. As Ruth Harrison writes (in *Animal Machines* 1964, Vincent Street Ltd.):

> . . . day-old chicks are installed, eight or ten thousand at a time, sometimes more, in long, windowless houses punctuated only with extractor fans in surried rows along the ridge of the roofs, and air intake vents along the side walls. . . inside a house the impression is of a long, wide, dark tunnel disappearing into the gloom, the floor covered with chickens as far as the eye can see."
>
> And the results? . . . the battery chickens I have observed seem to lose their minds about the time they would normally be weaned by their mothers and off in the weeds chasing grasshoppers on their own account. Yes, literally, actually, the battery becomes a gallinaceous madhouse. The eyes of these chickens through the bars gleam like those of maniacs. Let your hand get within reach and it receives a dozen vicious pecks, not the love peck or the tentative peck of idle curiosity bestowed by the normal chicken, but a peck that means business, a peck for flesh and blood, for which in their madness they are thirsting. They eat feathers and nibble voraciously at the roots of the same for tiny blocks of flesh and blood that may adhere thereto.

Feather-pecking and cannibalism replace the normal "pecking order" of the farmyard. And the "solutions" to these technologically created problems? Not the establishment of living conditions considerate of the instinctual needs of these creatures, but debeaking, reduced light, the fitting of opaque "specs" that prevent the chicken from seeing directly in front of it, cages, etc.

I am not raising the issue of a few technological improvements, nor am I raising the issue of food production, though that is a consideration. Neither am I raising the question of the ultimate end of these animals, slaughter for human food, though that also is a question. I am rather asking that in the light of our religious heritage we face the question posed by Ruth Harrison in her book: "How far have we the right to take our domination of the animal world? Have we the right to rob them of all pleasures in life simply to make more money more quickly out of their carcasses? Have we the right to treat living creatures solely as food-converting machines? At what point do we acknowledge cruelty?" In the words of St. Francis, even while they live, how in fact are we treating our "brothers and sisters" who help sustain us? In the words of Proverbs, how are we regarding the lives of our beasts?

Listen to the terms we use now. As Ruth Harrison points out, animal terms "hens" and "chickens" have become changed to such terms as "capons," a marketably profitable result of hormonal distortion, or "broilers," a term descriptive of the end result of creatures whose living identity doesn't matter to us. Listen to this passage she quotes from a technical journal: "The modern layer is, after all, only a very efficient converting machine, changing the raw materials – feeding stuffs – into the finished product – the egg – less, of course, maintenance requirements." Such examples can be brought in relation to veal calves, milk cows, and other animals whose very animality is disregarded in this one-dimensional viewing of them as mere food machines.

Let's dispel a certain kind of technological provincialism. Technology has never before on this planet been developed to its present heights, but there was awareness long ago of the fact that if you let an animal run around, part of the energy which could go into eggs or milk or flesh for consumption is dissipated. There is a discussion by a medieval Jewish commentator in which he asks whether the provisions for resting the beast on the Sabbath mean that you simply rest the beast while being permitted to keep it enclosed, or whether this requires that the beast be permitted to graze freely on the farmland, nibbling the grass, etc. The opinion of the commentator is that because the Bible uses the term "that your beast enjoy," it is required that it be permitted free grazing (Rashi on Exodus 23:12). All of this suggests that the calculations we make and can act on with greater efficiency in our age are not unique to our age. The most significant difference between previous ages and our own may be that while they to some extent regarded the lives of their beasts, we seemingly manage to ignore them almost completely. Harrison writes:

> To some extent . . . farm animals have always been exploited by man in that he rears them specifically for food. But until recently they were individuals, allowed their birthright of green fields, sunlight, and fresh air; they were allowed to forage, to exercise, to watch the world go by, in fact to live. Even at its worst, with insufficient protection against inclement weather or poor supplementation of natural food, the animal had some enjoyment in life before it died. Today the exploitation has been taken to a degree which involves not only the elimination of all enjoyment, the frustration of almost all natural instincts, but its replacement with acute discomfort, boredom, and the actual denial of health. It has been taken to a degree where the animal is not allowed to live before it dies.

Let me suggest that if we were to look closely at the issue, it might even occur to us that the issue of respect for animals is really the issue of respect for life as such. Great seers such as Gandhi and Schweitzer also suggest that life is a continuum, and that one cannot make arbitrary cuts anywhere in the chain without doing injury at all levels. The least that Darwinism should mean for rational human beings is that, in a continuum, orientation toward one level of life will affect orientation toward all other levels of life. The issue of treatment of God's beasts is, I suspect, in a subtle way also the issue of the treatment of other human beings and ourselves as well.

There are those who have noticed that the sound of the planet is somewhat different now from what it used to be. St. Francis heard the songs of the beasts in praise of the Lord, and the psalmist recites his extravagant poetry with the accompanying sounds of all Creation praising Him, the Creator of all life. Our own ears seem to hear only the whir of machinery, not only as once in cities and factories, but now increasingly in the mangers of the beasts and the nests of the feathered ones – and this, I think, poses yet another part of the grave problem for us.

I want to conclude with a story about one of the Hasidic rabbis, Reb Zusya, as told by Martin Buber in *Tales of the Hasidim*, Volume I:

> Once Rabbi Zusya traveled cross-country collecting money to ransom prisoners. He came to an inn at a time when the innkeeper was not at home. He went through the rooms, according to his custom, and in one saw a large cage with all kinds of birds. And Zusya saw that the caged creatures wanted to fly through the spaces of the world and be free

birds again. He burned with pity for them and said to himself: "Here you are, Zusya, walking your feet off to ransom prisoners. But what greater ransoming of prisoners can there be than to free these birds from their prison?" Then he opened the cage, and the birds flew out into freedom.

When the innkeeper returned and saw the empty cage, he was very angry, and asked the people in the house who had done this to him. They answered: "A man is loitering about here and he looks like a fool. No one but he can have done this thing." The innkeeper shouted at Zusya: "You fool! How could you have the impudence to rob me of my birds and make worthless the good money I paid for them?" Zusya replied: "You have often read and repeated these words in the psalm: 'His tender mercies are over all His works.'" Then the innkeeper beat him until his hand grew tired and finally threw him out of the house. And Zusya went his way serenely.

The conditions of captivity are different, and the requirement for freeing the birds and other animals perhaps less radical, but their captors today will not initially smile at any attempt to reopen the cages, and those so concerned will seem, like Reb Zusya and St. Francis, rather strange and somewhat queer creatures. There will be verbal beatings, and out of many an agricultural establishment and academic department we are likely to be tossed unceremoniously. But I would nonetheless suggest that if ever again on this anguished planet we are to realize that His tender mercies do indeed extend over all His works, even human creatures; and if ever again we are to sing a full hymn of praise to the Creator of Life, then somehow all of us must ourselves regain, and help our society itself regain, some considerable regard for the lives of our beasts.

>
> Sermon preached at Penn State University, January 22, 1967
> Published in *The Jewish Vegetarian* and
> by the National Catholic Society for Animal Welfare

The Universal Chorus

Joy and Vegetarianism

This essay from a 1996 volume, Rabbis and Vegetarianism, *locates within Jewish texts and traditions the rhyme and reason for Jews to pursue vegetarian diets.*

In recent decades, many authors have presented many good reasons for adopting and following a vegetarian diet. Some of the reasons concern health: We'll be healthier if we avoid eating animal flesh and its derivatives. Other reasons stem from other ethical considerations: to reduce the total suffering on our planet by reducing the suffering of animals; to increase the availability of food for all humans by eating lower on the food chain; to help to assure the future of the earth by consuming fewer resources to sustain ourselves. These are compelling considerations, and they have persuaded many to adopt such a diet.

There is an additional consideration I'd like to share that derives from one possible answer to the basic question of our ultimate purpose in this life on this planet. Let me state very simply this sense of purpose, support it with some traditional Jewish sources, and suggest how a vegetarian diet makes it possible for us to fulfill this purpose with greater ease and enthusiasm.

Why are we here? To exult in Creation! To sing God's praises! To enjoy the gifts of our life here on earth with full awareness, and to give voice to this enjoyment with words of poetry, songs of praise, and sounds of joyous appreciation.

On first reading, this may seem a bit odd. Is God, then, the Cosmic Music Lover par excellence? Before dismissing the notion, consider how ancient and basic to human expression are rhythm and melody. If our creation in the Divine image means that there are at least some significant resemblances between the Divine and the human, then such a notion is, upon reflection, not at all far-fetched.

Eric Gill, a visionary modern craftsman, communitarian, and creative

Catholic thinker whose outlook was profoundly influenced by the Hebrew as well as the Christian Bible, put it vividly and even more radically: "The Lord is a singer; the work of creation is a song – the morning stars sang together. And in a song all things must sing . . . (God) is a singer. The created universe is a little song of his – a little song, but big enough and loud enough for us – we are notes in it. There is no other explanation of the universe or of us."

Gill's daring formulation strikes me as a wonderful summary-in-image of what many a verse from Psalms proclaims. To cite just a few verses from four psalms which are part of every Sabbath morning service (and three of the four are recited also in the daily morning service):

> Rejoice in the Lord, O you righteous,
> Praise befits the upright.
> Praise the Lord with the lyre;
> make melody to him with the harp of ten strings.
> Sing to him a new song;
> play skillfully amid shouts of joy (33:1-3).
>
> Sing to the Lord with thanksgiving;
> make melody to our God on the lyre (147:7).
>
> Praise the Lord!
> How good it is to sing praises to our God . . .
> Sing to the Lord with thanksgiving;
> make melody to our God on the lyre (149:1,7).
>
> Praise God with trumpet sound,
> praise him with lute and harp!
> Praise him with tambourine and dance;
> praise him with strings and pipe!
> Praise him with clanging cymbals;
> praise him with loud clashing cymbals (150:3-5).

Especially pertinent to this essay, however, is one additional psalm that is also part of every traditional morning service, weekdays, Sabbaths, and Festivals. Psalm 148 begins: "Praise the Lord!/ Praise the Lord from the heavens;/ Praise the Lord in the heights!"

Sun, moon, and stars of light are summoned to praise the Divine along with angels and hosts of heaven. It continues: "Praise the Lord from the Earth" — and summons to the praise of God "sea monsters and all deeps,/ fire and hail, snow and smoke/ stormy wind . . . / all mountains and hills,/ fruit trees and cedars,/ beasts and cattle,/ creeping things and winged birds," along with women and men both young and old, and persons from all stations of life. Clearly we are not the only singers in this chorus of praise to the Creator, but are to join in a universal chorus of praise whose members include all of creation, including all our fellow creatures with whom we share this earth.

This tradition is not confined to the Psalms, nor does it end with the Bible. The Song of the Three Jews, found in the Apocrypha as an addition to the Book of Daniel, and probably a Hebrew composition, also summons all the works of the Lord to sing God's praise with exaltation.

> Bless the Lord, all you works of the Lord,
> Sing God's praise and exalt God forever . . .
> Bless the Lord . . . whales and all that
> swim in the waters . . .
> all birds of the air . . . all beasts and cattle . . .
> all people on earth . . .

Once again we find our fellow animals included with us in this summons to praise the Source of all Creation.

Even more striking is the portrayal of all living creatures singing their individual songs in praise of the Creator. In *Perek Shira* ("A Chapter of Song"), a mystical hymn dating from the 5th to 7th century that even today is found in all complete traditional Hebrew prayer books, worded songs are ascribed specifically to land animals, winged creatures, insects, and residents of the waters. Cows, camels, horses, mules; roosters, chickens, doves, eagles; butterflies, locusts, spiders, flies; sea monsters, fish, frogs: all of these and many more offer Biblical words of praise in song to their Creator, filling the universe with hymns and songs.

If, indeed, our purpose is to join with all of sentient creation in songs of praise to the Creator; if, in fact, the universe resounds with sounds of singing from all its living creatures; if, in truth, we are members of a chorus, not isolated soloists – then harmony among the choristers is evidently desirable. The better the terms of our relations with our fellow chorus members, the more natural the singing and the more beautiful the blending of voices and sounds. To respect the life of our fellow choir members by not killing them and eating their corpses would seem an obviously desirable condition for choral collegiality. To see other animals as fellow celebrants of life rather than primarily as potential corpses awaiting our consumption would surely affect not only their singing, but ours as well.

To say this is not to sentimentalize our relations with other animals. Messianic visions of the peaceable kingdom are precisely that, messianic visions whose fulfillment awaits a radical transformation of life conditions on this earth. Until that time (or end of time), rivalries and competition between humans and other species seem destined to persist. Yet to recognize that we inhabit a planet where much of life is companionable as well as competitive, and could become more companionable, would surely have significant effects on how we feel and how we live. Indeed, to apply the famous verse of Psalm 137:4 to this rather different context – "How shall we sing the Lord's song in a foreign land?" – in a land in which we feel isolated and alien from the creatures who surround us, to discover (or perhaps recover) some sense of kinship with our fellow creatures might, over time, have effects on our lives quite beyond our imagining in the mere articulation of this notion.

But is this idea of singing our way through life with life really Jewish, one might ask? By way of a suggestive supplement to the verses earlier cited, let me conclude by transmitting a verse from Talmud that I learned from that remarkable and inspired ethicist, mystic, and music lover, the late Rabbi Abraham Joshua Heschel, whose memory is truly a blessing:

Rabbi Akiba said:
A song every day!
Chant every day!
Sanhedrin 99b

May that become our philosophy and our practice as well.

From *Rabbis and Vegetarianism: An Evolving Tradition,*
edited by Roberta Kalechofsky, Micah Publications, 1996

A Sentient Universe

The Underlying Mystery of Nature

Rabbi Gendler developed a reputation over the past several decades as a "zeyde," a grandfather, of Jewish environmentalism. This essay, published in a pioneering 1998 book, unveils some of the sources that shaped his thinking about sentience and nature.

> It is taught: R. Jose says:
> Alas for creatures who see but know not what they see,
> Who stand but know not upon what they stand.
> *Talmud, Hagigah 12B*

Moses saw the Divine face to face. Still, God had to remind him, "Remove the sandals from your feet, for the place on which you stand is holy ground" (Exodus 3:5). Considering that this greatest of all prophets did not fully comprehend the nature of the ground on which he stood, it is not surprising that we, too, remain oblivious to the underlying mystery of nature.

A tree stands in front of us. It appears solid, but the molecular physicist, examining it with utmost scrutiny, observes that there is more open space than substance in the tree. What else might we miss on first observation? This tree is clearly alive, but by ordinary human measure it is without will, desire, emotion, or spirit. Perhaps we lack adequate senses to perceive the nature of the tree's inner life. Does it 'feel' as we do? Consider the grass beneath our feet, or the stars overhead. Does sentience, or panpsychism, in any sense characterize the rest of the universe?

These terms need not alarm us. Sentience, though solemn sounding, simply means the capacity for sensing, feeling, having some degree of awareness. As for panpsychism, which is a near synonym for sentience, it is neither a New Age notion nor an ancient Greek practice connected with the god Pan. It is simply the idea, in the words of Thomas Nagel (*Mortal Questions,* Cambridge University Press, 1979), "that the basic physical constituents of the universe have mental properties whether or not they are parts of living organisms." In other words, every 'material' particle, however small, is not only 'matter' but to some degree 'mind,' even if it remains forever beyond our experience.

Everyone knows that the Bible does not claim that independent, distinct spirits or souls are found in nature. In this way, ancient Judaism differed from other faiths of its time. This does not mean, however, that Judaism understands nature as lifeless and lacking all spirit or feeling. After all, one can have spirit without spirits. In the Biblical account of Creation, God, while connected with nature, is not entirely limited to it. The Divine is, in some significant way, more than nature. Yet, this does not necessarily mean that Creation is lacking in spirit or mind. In fact, a fresh look at Genesis 9:8-17 will quickly confirm that the Bible itself presupposes some degree of sentience in Creation, even in the Earth itself (italics added):

And God said to Noah and to his sons with him, "I now establish my *covenant* with you and your offspring to come, and with every living thing that is with you – birds, cattle, and every wild beast as well – all that have come out of the ark, every living thing on Earth. I will maintain my *covenant* with you: never shall again flesh be cut off by the waters of a flood, and never again shall there be a flood to destroy the Earth."

God added, "This is the *sign* that I set for the *covenant* between Me and you, and every living creature with you, for all ages to come. I have set my bow in the clouds, and it shall serve as a *sign* of the *covenant* between Me and the Earth. When I bring clouds over the Earth, and the bow appears in the clouds, I will remember My *covenant* between Me and you and every living creature among all flesh, so that the waters shall never again become a flood to destroy all flesh. When the bow is in the clouds, I will see it and remember the everlasting covenant that I have established between Me and all flesh that is on Earth." Then God said to Noah, "This is the *sign* of the *covenant* that I have established between Me and all flesh that is on Earth."

In this passage, both the terms *brit*, "covenant," and *ot*, "sign," apply to all living creatures and to Earth, not only to humans. Upon first consideration, a reader who tends toward rationalism is likely to dismiss the wording as a mere figure of speech. Yet the sevenfold repetition of *brit* and the three-fold repetition of *ot* prevent easy dismissal. (Seven and three are, in many traditions, sacred numbers.) Their repeated use and their specific references to living creatures and the Earth imply that the notion of Divine covenant in relation to Earth and its life must be taken seriously. While the covenantal references do in four instances specify human beings, in those same four instances the other living creatures are included as well. Two covenantal references pertain generally to all living creatures, while the seventh speaks exclusively of God's covenant with the Earth.

To accept seriously God's covenant with other living creatures as well as with the Earth itself raises questions that are disconcerting yet exciting. A covenant is reciprocal. It involves an exchange of responsibilities and duties. What does this imply about the status of Earth and its living creatures? If the Earth can participate in a covenant, then the Earth has some qualities of a living being. Johannes Pedersen, one of the 20th century's greatest Biblical scholars, argues (in *Israel: Its Life and Culture,* Oxford University Press, 1959) that ". . . the Israelites do not acknowledge the distinction between the psychic and the corporeal. Earth and stones are alive, imbued with a soul, therefore able to receive mental subject-matter and bear the impress of it. The relation between the Earth and its owner . . . is a covenant-relation, a psychic community, and the owner does not solely prevail in the relation. The Earth has its nature, which makes itself felt and demands respect."

Therefore, according to Pedersen, the important thing is to "deal kindly with the Earth, to uphold its blessing and then take what it yields on its own accord."

When Pedersen uses the term "soul," he does not mean something immaterial and unrelated to the physical composition of an object or person; he means the collection of innate inclinations of that entity, what we would call its nature or character. "Earth and stones are alive," concludes Pedersen. They are "able to receive mental subject-matter." From this perspective, some element of the mental or spiritual characterizes all of Creation.

Similarly, Professor Monford Harris, a philosophy professor at Spertus College, argues (in "Ecology: a Covenental Approach," *CCAR Journal,* Summer 1976) that the natural world was alive for the ancient Hebrews. It could be used, it could be appropriated, but it could not be violated. "Man has covenantal relationship, community, with the natural world,"writes

Harris, adding that, using the terms of Martin Buber, an "I-Thou" approach to the natural world must complement and constrain our more ordinary, more instrumental "I-I" approach.

The fact that Earth and all living beings are bound by covenant to God implies that Judaism takes universal sentience for granted: all of Creation must be alive with feeling. Yet rarely do we think of the Bible as making such a claim. Why is this? How did we come to see all the world – except our species – as essentially inert, lifeless, and lacking sentience? We are not lonely soloists in this world, the only ones capable of experiencing and expressing. There is a vast symphony singing, if we could only hear. Grasses whisper and animals sing the praises of God. The Bible tells us this again and again: in Psalms19, 96:11-12, 98:7-9; in Isaiah 44: 23, 55:12; in Job 38:7 . . .

Psalm 148, which is included in the daily morning service of the Hebrew prayer book, is particularly rich in this regard. Observant Jews are instructed to recite it 365 times a year:

> Praise God, sun and moon;
> Praise God, all you shining stars!
> Praise God, you highest heavens,
> And you waters above the heavens! . . .
> Praise the Lord from the Earth,
> You sea monsters and all deeps;
> Fire and hail, snow and frost,
> Stormy wind fulfilling God's
> command!
>
> Mountains and all hills,
> fruit trees and cedars!
> Wild animals and all cattle,
> Creeping things and flying birds!
>
> Kings of the Earth and all peoples,
> Princes and all rulers of the Earth!
> Young men and women alike,
> Old and young together!
> Let them praise the name of the Lord . . .

Among those summoned to "praise the Lord" are sea monsters and the deeps of the oceans, fire and hail, snow and frost, and stormy wind. So, too, are mountains and hills, fruit trees and cedars, wild animals and cattle, creeping things and flying birds – together with kings, peoples, princes, rulers, men, and women. The wording of the Psalm is clear: the same praise asked of humans is asked of the other natural elements.

Yet, rarely do these words touch our hearts. First we tell ourselves that the Psalms are not referring to literal praise. Instead, the authors are implying that the orderly functioning of nature is itself a kind of praise for the Creator. What could be more of a hymn to God than the dance of crackling fire? Doesn't a hummingbird hail the Creator simply by hovering near a flower? Surely, nothing more than this is meant by the repeated phrase, "praise God."

Alternatively, we reason that to "praise God" is simply a figure of speech and need not be taken literally.

Why do we overlook what is written? Isn't such a denial of the simplest meaning of the text illogical? In fact, such a reading is contrary to the principles of Jewish scriptural interpretation.

If orderly functioning is all that the term "praise" implies, then it is superfluous to ask for such praise; it already exists. In Psalm 19:2-5, for example, the alternations of day and night, the regularity of the Sun's circuit, and the patterns of the heavens are deemed sufficient praise of their Creator, without words to embellish them:

> The heavens are telling the glory of God;
>   And the firmament proclaims His handiwork.
> Day to day pours forth speech,
>   And night to night declares knowledge.
> There is no speech, nor are there words;
>   Their voice is not heard;
> Yet their voice goes out through all the Earth,
>   And their words to the end of the world.

But Psalm 148 demands more. It asks for intentional praise of the Creator not only from humans but from all realms of nature. It asks for praise beyond simple existence. The Psalm presupposes a response from nature. Why ask for praise from something that is not capable of giving it?

As for dismissing the praises of nature as merely metaphorical, even Nahum Sarna, one of the most distinguished Biblical commentators of the 20th century, uses precisely this device to avoid the issue of sentience. Commenting (in *Songs of the Heart,* Schocken, 1993) on Psalm 19, in which "the poetic notion of nature's constituents [extol] their Maker," Sarna cites Psalm 148 and Job 38:7. He admits that in Psalm 148 all heavenly beings and objects are called upon to "rhapsodize God," and that in Job "we are told that at the creation of the world, 'The morning stars chanted in unison, and all divine beings shouted for joy.'" But Sarna then blunts the sharpness of the language by declaring, "We are dealing, of course, with figurative language."

"Of course" is hardly a compelling argument. It is no argument at all, simply an appeal to commonly held beliefs. Confident that the Psalmist and Job were either in error or carried away by emotion upon contact with "the timeless magnificence of the celestial scene," Sarna seeks to explain the dynamics underlying the figurative language. Obviously sensitive to "the inward, spiritual experience" that the starry skies can evoke in us, he can only suggest that the Psalmist "projects this situation onto the heavens and the heavenly bodies, which are now all personified." Thus Sarna, like many other commentators, succumbs to the post-Cartesian assertion of the radical distinction, the total difference, between minds and matter.

In fact, Sarna departs from the principles of traditional Jewish interpretation when he denies what the text is plainly saying. The Talmud says (Shabbat 63a): "A verse cannot depart from its plain meaning." Therefore, whatever interpretations the language may stimulate, there is a good reason to insist on the literal meaning of Psalm 148: Creation is being called to praise God.

It seems that the early rabbis also interpreted Psalm 148 literally, according to *The Student's Guide to the Talmud* by Z.H. Chajes (Philip Feldheim, 1960):

> As Scripture says, The Lord hath made everything to bear witness to His glory (Proverbs 16:4). He created the heavens to sing His praises, and so they sing them, as it is said, The Heavens declare the glory of God, and the firmament showeth His handiwork (Psalm 19:2). And even as the heavens all that is in them sing praises of God, so also the Earth and all that is in it sing His praises, as it is said, Praise the Lord from the Earth. . . .
>
> After God's praises are sung from the heavens, who ought to be the first on Earth to sing His praises? He that is larger than his fellow creatures. And who are the largest? The sea-monsters, of whom it is said And God created the great sea-monsters (Genesis 1:21). Therefore, the first on Earth to sing God's praises are the sea-monsters, to whom it is said, "Ye sea-monsters, and all deeps" (Psalm 148:7).

Here, the literal meaning presupposes that, to some degree, all of Creation is sentient, feeling, and able to respond to this encompassing cry of "Halleluyah, Praise the Lord!"

From Ecology and the Jewish Spirit: Where Nature and the Sacred Meet, *edited by Ellen Bernstein, Jewish Lights Publishing, 1998*

A Matter of Spirit

The Gift of Genesis

This 2007 essay, published for the first time here, explores how the Creation story of Genesis is replicated in our science, our spirituality, and our relationship to the Earth.

How did the world begin? Scientific exploration suggests that it began with a Big Bang. Why did the world begin? Biblical revelation proclaims that it began with a Vast Vision. The answers are different because the questions are different, yet the answers, although not identical, are compatible: They can comfortably coexist as ideas within our minds, and they can harmoniously join in expanding any mental narrowness that may entrap us.

Both introduce us to immensity: in one case, 15 to 20 billion years in time, with distances measured in dizzying digits of light years; in the other, a sweeping intention of Spirit that begins with matter at its chaotic inception and extends to the highest developments of conscious awareness in the human being.

Both abound in details. For science, discoveries of galaxies in rapid expansion, of helium in the universe, of infrared light at the furthermost reaches of space are heartening signs of confirmation for the current theory of how the universe came to be. Without such particulars, the theory would be vacuous, sadly empty of content. In the Biblical vision, details also abound, but the details are of a different kind. Whereas science occupies itself with understanding the material universe as it is, the primary concern for Biblical religion is the role of human beings, and especially Jews, in bringing about a universe that could be but is not yet fully realized. Understandably, then, most of the details that follow the account of Creation are narratives of the founders of the Jewish people, the relations of the leaders and the people to God, and the specific ways and spirit in which the people are to follow God's directives.

This later emphasis, however, should not distract us from the opening

Biblical affirmation. In its basic shaping, the world we know is Divinely directed by a purposeful Deity whose intention extends to and affects raw energy and primal matter. Thus from its earliest imaginable beginnings, that which we call matter is informed and infused by spirit, the Spirit of God.[1]

"In the beginning God created the heaven and the Earth. Now the Earth was unformed and void, and darkness was upon the face of the deep; and the spirit of God hovered over the face of the waters." This long-familiar translation of the opening verses of Genesis suggests that God alone existed before Creation, and asserts that God's spirit hovered over the unformed matter at its inception. Creation, this wondrously animated material world which is our daily delight and challenge, is preceded by spirit; is it thereby affected by spirit, informed by spirit, infused with spirit? A reading of Genesis that considers carefully the depiction of God's spirit at that formative moment invites an affirmative answer. The term "hover" (*m'rakhefet*), both in English and in Hebrew, refers to both the protective fluttering of a bird over its nest and also to the dam providing the warmth that hatches the brood.[2] On this reading, when what we call matter first is formed or shaped, spirit is in attendance, assisting. At the earliest imaginable beginning, Genesis introduces us to matter touched by spirit, to matter affected by spirit. The initial gift of Genesis is matter intimately connected with spirit.

But what if matter were somehow preexistent? This is a possible interpretation of the unusual combination of grammatical forms in the first two Hebrew words, and it is implicitly accepted in several recent translations: "When God began to create the heavens and the Earth, the Earth was a desolate waste . . ." "When God began to create heaven and Earth – the Earth being unformed and void . . ." "At the beginning of God's creating of the heavens and the Earth, when the Earth was wild and waste . . ." In each of these, there is the intimation that matter existed in inchoate form before the creative process initiated by God. However, even if these

---

1. "The Spirit of God" or "the spirit of God" is variously rendered in other translations as "a tempestuous wind," "a wind from God," "a mighty wind," "a wind from God," "God's spirit," "rushing-spirit of God." For *ruakh elohim,* as one can see, the consensus is that *elohim* designates God rather than simply a powerful, undefined force.

2. Cf. Deuteronomy 32:11: "As an eagle that stirreth up her nest,/ Hovereth over her young,/ Spreadeth abroad her wings, taketh them,/ Beareth them on her pinions . . ." The overtones of caring and hatching/warmth are attested by both Brown-Driver-Briggs and Kohler-Baumgartner.

versions may question or deny the ancient doctrine of *creatio ex nihilo*, creation out of nothing, they do not contest the hovering presence of the *ruakh elohim*, the Divine spirit. Was matter pre-existent? It matters not. Even on this understanding, spirit was present at the very beginning of the shaping of matter, when matter first assumed form. The philosophical and environmental importance of this Biblical vision will soon be noted.

Looking around at the Creation in which we are embedded, we see clearly that, whatever the case may be with plants (a point of some contention), all animals show discernible signs of feeling, and in the case of human beings, conscious awareness as well. Whether we think of them/us as mattered-spirit or spirited-matter, all visible and palpable creatures represent an unmistakable fusion of matter and spirit, difficulties of philosophical explanation notwithstanding. However it was at the beginning, now, as we consider what the matter-of-spirit has manifestly become, primordial matter is revealed as having had the capacity to become, or at least to accommodate, feeling, consciousness, and self-awareness.

This intimately interwoven, inextricable combination of spirited-matter or mattered-spirit, constitutes part of what we are accustomed to call "nature" or our "environment." Plant life, together with the inorganic and organic substances that are the physical grounds of our being, are the rest. How are these other, not-evidently-feeling things to be regarded? Descartes may have proposed a clear division into thinking and extended substances, but for the Bible there is no such absolute bifurcation. Does the Bible acknowledge the great variety of existent things? Of course, and it expresses clearly such contrasts as life and death, human and animal, strength and weakness. But the distinctions are never absolute, the contrasts never total. The commonly heard distinction between matter and spirit, between body and soul, is alien to the spirit of the Hebrew Bible.

The great Danish Biblical scholar, Johannes Pedersen (in *Israel: Its Life and Culture,* Oxford University Press, 1959), from a close reading of the Hebrew, depicts the essential unity of spirited-matter in these words: "Yahweh, as a potter, moulded man of clay or Earth, and into the moulded

---

3. Also interesting, but not germane to our inquiry, is the question of whether the creation account in Genesis suggests that chaotic matter already existed "at the beginning of God's creating," or whether it regards chaotic matter itself as the first of God's creative acts. In either case, what is essential is that God's Spirit did shape/form/inform/infuse matter at the very beginning of Creation.

image he breathed his breath, in which manner man became a living soul... The fragile corporeal substance... by the breath of God... was transformed and became a *nefesh*, a soul. It is not said that man was supplied with a *nefesh*, and so the relation between body and soul is quite different from what it is to us. Such as he is, man, in his total essence, is a soul."

This use of soul may seem peculiar, but Pedersen carefully explains that "the soul is a depth of forces... That which the Israelite understands by soul is, first and foremost, a totality with a peculiar stamp... The Israelite does not distinguish between a living and a lifeless nature. All is living which has its peculiarity and so also its faculties." Pedersen also extends this to what we, with little thought, usually call inanimate objects: "A stone is not merely a lump of material substance. It is, like all living things, an organism with peculiar forces of a certain mysterious capacity, only known to him who is familiar with it..." The "Earth itself is alive," he continues, "... imbued with a soul, and therefore able to receive mental subject-matter and bear the impress of it... The relation between the Earth and its owner is not that the Earth, like a dead mass, makes part of his psychic whole – an impossible thought. It is a covenant-relation, a psychic community, and the owner does not solely prevail in the relation. The Earth has its nature, which makes itself felt, and demands respect."

Can this assertion of a sentient universe, obviously important as the basis for an environmental outlook and ethic, be supported either philosophically or Judaically? From both perspectives, I would suggest, the answer is yes.

Philosophically, the world as we experience it is composed of physical objects and mental awareness, what Descartes famously called thinking and extended substances. Both are evident and undeniable realities; however, to account for their connection is a challenge both to philosophy and to science. Alfred North Whitehead and Charles Hartshorne are two of the most eminent modern philosophers who emphasize Process, Becoming rather than Being, as the basis of all observable phenomena in our world. They argue cogently that the most coherent account of reality is to discern or posit, at the very inception, some infinitesimal amount of whatever characteristics may appear later in more fully developed, more evident form. Thus in the case of mental phenomena – perception, feeling, consciousness – if some degree of sentience, however immeasurably small, is not present in the earliest and simplest forms of "matter," then at what point in the evolutionary unfolding of "matter" does it enter? Why at that point? From what source? By what means? This scrambling for an ad hoc explanation of the novel appearance, at some point in time, of sentience/awareness/consciousness, is inelegant and unconvincing. More logical is the existence of some germ of awareness at the very beginning of "matter." Whitehead expresses it in these words (in *Science and the Modern World,* 1925): "[A] dead nature can give no reasons. All ultimate reasons are in terms of aim at value. A dead nature aims at nothing. It is the essence of life that it exists for its own sake, as the intrinsic reaping of value."[4]

Whitehead's comprehensive portrayal of "actual occasions," real events rather than abstractions, illustrates the centrality of this incipient awareness, however rudimentary, for even the most simple occurrences. The coherence of this outlook with Pedersen's portrayal of the Biblical outlook is evident; the notion of a sentient universe is, indeed, profoundly Biblical.

This is surely the simplest, most convincing basis for understanding Psalm 148, with its universe-spanning, repeated urging of all God's creations – Sun, Moon, stars, heavens, mountains, deeps, fire, hail, snow, frost, wind, trees, and the list goes on – to "Praise God!" Attempts to deny this plain meaning through question-begging phrases such as "figurative language" notwithstanding, and however challenging to our usual ways of thinking, the idea that all of Creation is alive, endowed with at least some degree of feeling, is the clear presupposition of Psalm 148. As for the status of this psalm in Jewish tradition, by virtue of its early rabbinic inclusion as part of the "Verses of Song" (*P'sukey d'Zimra*) in the daily, Sabbath, and holiday morning prayers, it is recited 365 days each solar year by those who pray the full morning service – hardly a marginal expression of Jewish piety and worldview.

The argument for universal sentience, I believe, is thus both solidly grounded philosophically and reflective of a significant perspective among Jewish views of the world. Two further examples from Jewish tradition, whose greater liturgical use would enhance our own services, are "The Song of the Three" from the Apocrypha, and *"Perek Shirah,"* "A Chapter of Song," found in most traditional Hebrew prayer books.

"The Song of the Three" is an addition to the Apocryphal Book of Daniel, and dates probably from the second century BCE. It purports to be a prayer recited by Hananiah, Mishael, and Azariah from the fiery furnace

---

4. Two comprehensible introductions to theology based on Process Philosophy are *Process Theology* by John B. Cobb, Jr. and David Ray Griffin (1976) and *The Evolving God in Jewish Process Theology* by William E. Kaufman (1997).

into which they had been thrown for their refusal to bow to the idols of Nebuchadnezzar (Daniel 1:3). The prayer opens with words affirming the blessedness of God, and then asks all created things to bless the Lord:

> Bless the Lord, all you works of the Lord;
> Sing God's praise and exalt God for ever.
> Bless the Lord, you heavens;
> Sing God's praise and exalt God for ever . . .
> Bless the Lord, Sun and Moon;
> Sing God's praise and exalt God for ever.

The stirring hymn continues with calls to stars, rain, fire, wind, snow, mountains, plants, springs, whales, cattle, birds, and finally, humans, to Bless the Lord! Here, as with Psalm 148, this outpouring is most easily understood if one grants that all parts of the universe are to some degree sentient.

Perek Shirah is more easily found in traditional Hebrew prayer books than in most recent versions that come with translations, a situation that we should try to rectify. A mystical hymn dating probably from the 5th to 7th centuries, it ascribes various Biblical verses praising God to a wide range of natural elements. Heavens, the desert, rivers, cows, camels, serpents, snails, elephants, trees and grasses, frogs and fish: all these and more offer praise to their Creator in songs that fill the universe. It is a joyous, tumultuous celebration of Creation that rarely fails to evoke a smile from anyone who reads or recites these verses.

This textual and academic argument for panpsychism as a legitimate Jewish expression finds support, also, from tales that clearly reflect the view that all of nature is sentient. Let me cite, by way of example, this tale from *Sippurei Hasidim, Hasidic Stories*, arranged by the renowned scholar Rabbi Solomon Joseph Zevin to follow the weekly Torah portions (Tel Aviv, 1957). He selects it as illustration and application of the verse, "And this stone . . . shall become a house of God" (Genesis 28:22). I translate quite literally:

> In the city of Alisk [Aleksandriya?], whenever the foundation was laid for any building, they had to dig down a number of feet, until they reached virgin soil on which the foundation could be securely laid. When they built a synagogue there, they followed, of course, the same procedure. It happened to be on a Friday that they finished excavating for the southwestern foundation. At the completion of their digging, the builder sent a message to Rabbi Hanoch Hinich from Alisk, of blessed memory (son-in-law of Rabbi Shalom of Belz, of blessed memory), requesting that he climb down to place the omer-stone on the bottom layer of the foundation,

as was his custom.

The rabbi answered, "This time I won't go down, because I am afraid that the walls will cave in on me."

The builder listened with astonishment, then asked: "How is today different from yesterday? Have we not excavated meticulously, following every rule of proper construction? If there were even the slightest doubt about the safety of the excavation, I would never ask the rabbi to take the risk of laying the foundation stone, not for all the wealth in the world."

The rabbi wavered, then replied: "Even so, I will not climb down."

The builder implored the rabbi to reconsider, arguing that he couldn't afford the delay of all the workers standing idle while waiting to continue their work, a delay caused solely by the rabbi's obstinate refusal. But the rabbi refused to yield to the urgings of the builder, and said that he must first immerse himself in the mikvah. Almost immediately after he left, two of the walls collapsed completely, and it seemed a miracle.

When the rabbi returned from the mikvah, he said to the builder: "Do you wonder how I knew that this excavation would collapse? Because I had seen that at the very bottom of the excavation there lay a stone, which had prayed and pleaded before the Holy Blessed One, that it might be found worthy to be among the stones selected for the synagogue that we are building. And I understood that the prayers of the stone would have effect before God, may the Name be praised."

And so it was. When they removed the freshly fallen dirt from the hole, they discovered, at the very bottom, a boulder measuring more than an amah and a half, perfect for the foundation. They took the stone and built it into the foundation of the synagogue.

#77, Parshat Vayetze

Would that our *kavanah* were as effective as that which Reb Hanoch reported of the stone! Meanwhile, can't we easily imagine the authors of Psalm 148, "The Song of the Three," and *Perek Shirah* nodding their heads and smiling, as if to say: "So what else is new? Long ago we told you so, didn't we?"

At the same time, to reassure the doubting reader, I do want to acknowledge and affirm what is obvious to both our common sense and our common senses: Sentient or not, the natural world does not communicate with us through words. All of nature, not only the heavens, is "without speech, without words, their voices unheard," at least to our ears if not to God's.

The natural world is visible to our eyes and audible to our ears; we see its colors, its forms, its textures, its movements; we hear its sounds, its shrieks, its sighs, its songs; but not one of its secrets is conveyed to us by words. In mute contrast to Sinai and the words of the prophets, whatever nature may reveal to us of the Divine, its revelation is not by words.

Yet this fact does not preclude Nature from being, along with Scripture, a Divine text revelatory of the Giver of Life and of Guidance. Both Nature and Scripture are appropriately to be regarded as texts of revelation. Both are the garb of God, and like all clothing, they conceal and reveal. Each invites a more penetrating glance, a closer look, a lifting of the garment, perhaps an embrace. In obvious contrast to the centrality of the word in Scripture, in Nature the visible and the palpable hold sway. But to recognize the distinction is not to establish an absolute disjunction between these two sources of revelation. Judaism first strides onto the world scene with the sweeping combination of words and objects that is the opening chapter of Genesis. Nature's role in that stirring declaration makes it a strong candidate for designation as text.

Does this seem an exaggeration? Quite the contrary: it is literal truth. For what is a text, after all? The word is derived from the Latin; its literal meaning, says the *Oxford English Dictionary*, is "that which is woven, web, texture." While the word soon comes to designate the arrangement of words on a written page, and later the exact wording of Holy Scriptures, its origin in the weaving process makes it quite an appropriate term to refer us to the texture of Nature. In that respect, it hardly needs stating that for the authors of Psalms, Job, and the Wisdom tradition in general, the natural world gives convincing testimony of God's reality and presence, thereby serving quite literally as text.

The textual character of Nature finds echoes in later ages as well. Two examples, one Talmudic, one Hasidic, will illustrate:

> R. Simeon b. Pazzi said in the name of R. Joshua b. Levi on the authority of Bar Kappara: He who knows how to calculate the cycles of the seasons and the courses of the planets, but does not, of him Scripture says, "They regard not the work of the Lord, neither have they considered the operation of his hands." (Isaiah 5:12)
>
> *Shabbat 75a*

This passage of Isaiah begins with "Woe unto them," and condemns actions that distract people from recognition of the Divine, such as heavy drinking or late night partying with wild music. To this list Rabbis Simeon, Joshua, and Bar Kappara add the disregard of seasons and planets, of Earth and sky, as additional instances of human failure to discern the Divine. Whereas the original examples in Isaiah refer to distortions of human perception by unwise acts, the rabbis focus on our ignoring natural occurrences that could remind us of the workings of the Deity. For them, this failure to read the text of nature is as disruptive of our connections to God as drunken, riotous living.

The Hasidic example is from *Khidushei Ha-Rim* on Genesis (my translation):

> Rabbi Isaac Meir of Ger heard the Holy Yehudi ask Reb Bunam about his source of inspiration: "From where do you receive the inspiration to worship God?" Reb Bunam replied: "From the verse, 'Lift up your eyes on high,/And see: who hath created these?/ He that bringeth out their host by number,/ He calleth them all by name;/ By the greatness of His might, and for that He is strong in power,/Not one faileth." (Isaiah 40:26)
>
> The Yehudi responded: "The children of Israel don't need this verse. They have experienced the redemption from Egypt and that is sufficient. As R. Yitzhak said: There was no need to begin the Torah with the creation account; it should have begun with: 'This month shall be unto you the beginning of months.' (Exodus 12:2)"
>
> "But," continued the Gerer Rebbe, "despite the proof-text of the Yehudi, the words of Reb Bunam are also correct."[5]

Both Reb Bunam and Reb Isaac Meir affirm the capacity of Nature to inform, inspire, and invite the praise of God. Word-texts can hardly claim greater inspirational powers.

---

5. For example; Rashi's comment on the first verse of Genesis, found also in *Yalkut Shim'oni* on Exodus 12:1. Both cite Rabbi Isaac, who states that the Torah, insofar as it is a compendium of commandments for the Israelites, need not have begun with anything other than a commandment. Why, then, the universal reference? So that if anyone should question Israel's taking possession of the Land of Israel from the seven nations who originally inhabited it, there is this clear testimony: "All the earth belongs to the Blessed Holy One; He created it and He apportions it as He sees fit. By His will He gave it to them, and by His will He took it from them and gave it to us." While these commentators quickly turn the universal reference to a particular purpose, they first enunciate a clear recognition of the broad sweep of the opening of Genesis. Others, Nahmanides, for example, regard the Creation account as a necessary prelude to all that follows, "for it is the root of faith . . . and one who denies it has no Torah." In all these cases, the universality of the opening chapters of Genesis are acknowledged.

As we saw, traditional Jewish commentators have long recognized that the Bible begins with a cosmic, universal vision rather than with particular mandates to the Israelites. This later particularity itself, however, remains forever anchored in what we have called the initial Biblical affirmation: In its basic shaping, the world we know is Divinely directed by a purposeful Deity whose intention extends to and affects raw energy and primal matter. Christianity, by virtue of incorporating the Hebrew Bible as preface to the New Testament, naturally and necessarily inherits this view of Creation, and in contemporary Christian thought, the increasingly prominent Creation Theology speaks very much in terms derived from Genesis.

Muslims also affirm the initiating vision of Genesis, a world Divinely directed by a purposeful Deity. Unlike the Bible, however, the Qur'an does not begin with an account of Creation. In fact, as Fazlur Rahman puts it (in *Major Themes of the Qur'an*, 1980): "The Qur'anic cosmogony is minimal. Of the metaphysics of creation the Qur'an simply says that the world and whatever God decided to create in it came into existence by His sheer command: 'Be' (2:117; 3:47,59; 6:73; 16:40; 19:35; 36:82; 40:68). God is therefore the absolute possessor of the universe and its unquestioned commander, just as He is its merciful sustainer."

Both the spirit and also the wording of Genesis seem clearly present in that formulation. They are also reflected in Qur'anic references to the beginnings of the natural order, with repeated proclamations declaring God "the Originator of the heavens and the Earth . . ." "who has created the heavens and the Earth and never been wearied by their creation."[6] Thus Islam joins Judaism and Christianity in insisting that Creation is Divinity-determined.

Within this common affirmation, however, there is one subtle but significant difference that should be made explicit. As noted earlier, there is a grammatical peculiarity in the first verse of Genesis that does leave open the possibility of there having been some kind of pre-existent matter. In the Qur'an, such an idea finds no support and is hardly conceivable. In the Bible, however, not only is it grammatically supportable, but there are other passages suggesting that Creation was not quite so effortless a fiat as the Priestly account in Genesis asserts.

Precisely stated: to assert that God's intention extends to raw energy and primal matter is not to assert that the intention is totally realized; neither is it to claim that the dominion over *t'hom* (ocean/the deep/the abyss) was

---

6. Surahs 6:14, 46:33. Cf. Also 6:79, 12:101. 14:10, 21:56, 35:1, 39:46, 42:11, and others.

easily achieved. When we look at some other descriptions of Creation, the earliest imaginable state of our world, we hear a quite different tone, with emphasis on the mighty effort required of God in subduing Sea Monsters, the Dragon, and the Abyss.

> Yet, God, my king from the first,
> author of saving acts throughout the Earth,
> by your power you split the sea in two,
> and smashed the heads of monsters on the waters.
>
> You crushed Leviathan's heads,
> leaving him for wild animals to eat,
> you opened the spring, the torrent,
> you dried up inexhaustible rivers.
>
> You are master of day and night,
> you instituted light and Sun,
> you fixed the boundaries of the Earth,
> you created summer and winter.
>
> *Psalm 74:12-17*

The operative word here is *koah,* power, not *y'hi,* let there be; muscle and might, not mandate, determine the outcome. Similar passages could be cited from Psalm 89:9-11, Job (3:8, 7:12, 9:13, 26:12-13), and Isaiah (27:1, 51:9-10). Leviathan the Elusive Serpent, Leviathan the Twisting Serpent, the Dragon of the sea, Rahab: these are the formidable foes of God the Creator. The recalcitrance of matter is implied in the physical terms used to describe God's actions: crushed, smashed, scattered, split, punish, kill. Coercion, not persuasion is the mood of these verses. All of them affirm the final triumph of God over the forces of chaos and disorder, but the memories of primordial tumultuous struggles cast a shadow over the outcome.

This shadow is explored in penetrating and poignant fashion by Jon D. Levenson in *Creation and the Persistence of Evil* (1988). It may also cross our minds as we try to confront the theological implications of events such as earthquakes or tsunamis. Whence this restless shifting of the foundations of Earth? How is it that the Creator, whose benign natural gifts we rightly celebrate, seems also to have bequeathed some unfinished business? Are we here confronted with a theological challenge analogous to that presented, especially post-Holocaust, by the difficulty of reconciling God's Absolute Goodness with God's Absolute Omnipotence? For natural events whose results may include massive human dislocation and suffering, *tikkun olam,* improving the world by alleviating the human suffering, is assuredly a necessary and appropriate first response. But as we seek to understand more deeply the relation of God and the world, it seems to me that even as we read the triumphant Creation epic of Genesis 1:1-2:4, we should keep in mind the disturbing ambiguity of its opening three words. And to complete the sobering full creation story rather than the (perhaps incomplete) one to which we are most accustomed, we should also read the alternative strains given voice by Isaiah, Psalms, and Job.

What might this mean in application? We must, I think, seriously consider the possibility that inspiriting matter was no simple, easy task. Perhaps the currently emerging sense of a powerful and loving, but not totally powerful, God will be essential to our thoughtful efforts to formulate an honest, adequate conception of God. Confronting the societal horrors of the 20th century, some serious theologians have emphasized anew not only the compassion of God but also certain (perhaps logically entailed) limits to God's absolute power. It is conceivable to me that a parallel process will need to take place in the realm of spirited-matter or mattered-spirit that we call Nature or Creation. Whether God the Originator created this world out of nothing, or whether the Divine shaped and inspirited some kind of pre-existent matter, in either case there would appear to be an inherent recalcitrance in the material substratum, recognized and eloquently expressed by Job, the Psalmist, and Isaiah. If this be so, one of our tasks is to explore the implications of this qualification of Genesis for a realistic theology of nature. But that must wait for another occasion.

The Jewish tradition already offers mo'adim *(the "appointed times,"* that is, the Jewish festivals) that can be seen as opportunities for raising environmental awareness, and they should be explored and engaged in their full potential for this.[7] But why should we confine ourselves within these boundaries — particularly when, for Jewish communities living south of the equator, the seasonal scheme of the Bible is completely reversed: Sukkot comes in the spring, Pesakh in the fall! For these communities, I believe, extra-Biblical resources will be of special environmental value.

---

7. Hayyim Schauss, *The Jewish Festivals* (1938), and Theodor H. Gaster, *Festivals of the Jewish Year* (1952), remain for me the old reliables, never superseded and never surpassed. Of interpretive versions, I prefer Michael Strassfeld's *The Jewish Holidays* (1985) (and not, I trust, because a few of my comments appear in the margins).

Then there is Genesis, awaiting our engagement with its precious gifts. For this brief exposition, I'll be guided by four verses of Genesis that point to seed (1:11-12); Sun, Moon and stars (1:16); and the seasons (8:22).

The Mystery of the Seed: What is the first Biblical expression of wonder? I'd be inclined to answer, verses 11-12 of chapter 1. Although the term "wonder" is not used, the state of astonishment to which it refers seems to me the likeliest explanation for a stylistic peculiarity of this pericope. After the introductory, "And God said," there follow two verses, each of eighteen words, and each containing a three-fold repetition of "seed" –

> And God said, Let the Earth sprout forth with sprouting-growth, plants that seed forth seeds, fruit trees that yield fruit, after their kind, (and) in which is their seed, upon the Earth! It was so.
>
> The Earth brought forth sprouting-growth, plants that seed forth seeds, after their kind, trees that yield fruit, in which is their seed, after their kind. And God saw that it was good.
> *Genesis 1:11-12 (my translation)*

Why the repetition? It is surely not stuttering. To my eye and ear, the repetitive sounding of *zera,* seed, bespeaks wonder, amazement. From our vantage point, so dominated by technology, it is difficult to imagine the mental state of early humans when they slowly discovered the marvel of the seed, whether in cereal grain or in tree fruit. At the death of the producing crop, this was what remained; yet what it provided seemed almost miraculous. Eaten, it nourished humans; buried, it sprouted new life after its own kind. That grain was probably central to the ceremonies of the greatest of Greek mystery rites, the Eleusinian Mysteries is, on reflection, quite comprehensible. Like fruit and all edible herbage, it is simultaneously terrestrial and celestial, nourished by soil and Sun, an almost incomprehensible blending of death and life. Rilke captured beautifully this paradox and wonder of the seed in one of his sonnets.

> Banana, rounded apple, russet pear,
> gooseberry . . . Does not all this convey life and death into your mouth?
> . . . It's there! . . .
> Read it on a child's face any day,
> when it tastes them. What infinity!
> Can't you feel inside your mouth a growing
> mysteriousness, and, where words were, a flowing
> of suddenly released discovery?

> Dare to say what "apple" has implied!
> Sweetness, concentrated, self-repressing,
> slowly yielding to the tongue's caressing,
> growing awake, transparent, clarified,
> double-meaning'd, sunshine-full, terrestrial:
> O experience, feeling, joy, – celestial!
> "Sonnets to Orpheus," Part I, Sonnet XIII19

Agriculturally and, by extension, for the human psyche, seed bridges the chasm between death and life, between soil and Sun, between Earth and heaven, between planting and harvest, linking all of the seasons in the vegetational cycle of renewal. Zoologically, as sperm and egg, it connects past and future generations, parents and offspring. "Seed of Abraham" looks both backwards and forwards, towards progenitor and successor. By virtue of its agricultural and its zoological functions, seed also, at some level, connects the vegetational and the animal realms. And in both realms, it represents bounty, the promise of abundance. As an object of contemplation, it offers a measure of mystery and wonder not only to the ancient Greeks, but to us as well.

How can we accept this offering? How can we become more aware of, receive more fully, celebrate more joyously the wondrous gift of the *zera*, the seed? Two brief suggestions for a beginning.

1) A modified "rebbe's *tish*" (table).

2) Plant winter grain at Sukkot and begin regular cutting at Pesakh for omer-counting.

The mystique of the rebbe's *tish* is an example of what we know from a variety of sources: that the act of eating can have significance far beyond physical nutrition alone. Community is confirmed by sharing food, food can carry with it and evoke strong feelings, and reflective eating can nourish the spirit along with the body. How might these well known facts help our reappreciation of *zera*, the seed?

We could periodically, perhaps near each *t'kufah*/turning of the seasons, include in the service a special ceremonial eating focused on *zera*, the seed. Autumn, for example, could be marked at the end of Yom Kippur, when we begin preparing for Sukkot. At that time, winter rye or soft winter wheat grains begin to sprout. Coordinated with our sowing of such crops during Sukkot, the service could include *niggunim*, special poetry, and other readings that could help establish the proper atmosphere for seeing, tasting, and appreciating the rye or wheat sprouts.

Post-Pesakh, Spring could be marked by again sprouting the grains, this time related to the steady growth of the grain as numbered by the omer. Summer invites a comparable use of a ripening fruit, strawberries, for example, which can substitute for the gooseberries of the Rilke poem, and whose abundant edible seeds can further illustrate the point. Finally, for Winter, why not the pomegranate? It is readily available at this time of year in north-of-the-equator markets, and its striking color and abundant, succulently fleshed seeds draw attention to themselves without our additional words.

Alternatively, for a more text-oriented congregation or study group, the focus on *zera* could correspond to Biblical readings. The references to Sarah and Abraham's descendants as "seed," frequent in the blessings and promises of Genesis, could be moving occasions for the physical/psychological, material/mental exploration of the image. Deuteronomic references to the grain of the bounteous land provide other textual links. The pomegranate? Its role in priestly and sanctuary/temple decor offers many occasions for that focus. Other fruits of the land? Numbers and Deuteronomy can keep the congregation eating throughout those months of the year!

More examples could be provided, but for the moment, *dayenu*. As for those who protest, "Too much," an earnest plea: The words are not the experience. Please, *ta'amu ur'u,* taste and see, before passing final judgment.

Regarding the Sun, the Moon and the Stars, three examples here:

For stars, at favorable viewing times, integrate the telescopic observation of certain planets with a sense of *um'sader et hakokhavim b'mishm'rotehem barakia kir'-tzono* (setting the stars in their constellations by Divine will).

For the Moon, for our Rosh Hodesh/New Moon or Full Moon rituals, reconstruct what may have been the torch used in Mishnaic times to send fire signals from Jerusalem to other places, announcing the sighting of the New Moon.

For the Sun, in all of our synagogues and temples, illuminate our eternal lights by solar power. In every synagogue, above every ark, glows a *ner tamid,* an eternal light. It is a symbol of the eternity of God's endlessly dependable illumination and teachings.

Such symbols participate in the nature of that to which they refer. To be consistent and as effective as possible, a symbol of eternity should ideally embody something that is itself as eternal as any created thing can be. When eternal lights were fueled by olive oil, perpetually renewable because its solar collector, the olive tree, is perpetually renewed or replanted, they transmitted their message clearly. When they first became almost universally dependent on vanishing or polluting sources of electricity, fossil or nuclear, few of us realized this contradiction. Now that we are aware of our energy dilemma, however, we face a problem both symbolic and realistic. We could meaningfully address both aspects of the problem by working towards the conversion of all synagogue eternal lights to photo-voltaic, solar power before the next observance of *Birkhat Hakhama*, the Blessing of the Sun. At least one synagogue, Temple Emanuel of the Merrimack Valley, Lowell, Massachusetts, has installed photo-voltaic panels to provide electricity for its eternal light. This was done in 1979. Many years later, the assessment was positive on all counts: The financial cost was modest, the maintenance has been minimal, the inspiration of the light has continued undimmed, and energy awareness has remained ever-present.

Were this simple, low-cost, hands-on project to be adopted by congregations, the process itself could contribute vitality and excitement to the institutions. Members of ritual committees and building committees, and students in the religious school, would find themselves collaborating to learn details of their environment that were once common knowledge to all but have been lost to many. Times of sunrise and sunset, the angle of inclination of the Sun at various times of year, the difference between magnetic north and true north, hours of sunlight and hours of daylight at different times of year, energy requirements of different watt bulbs, how silicon (found in the sand of the desert) converts light to electricity, etc. All of these theoretical, academic questions suddenly become practical questions, with direct effects on the life of the synagogue. Within the synagogue, there are opportunities for experimentation, innovation, and the revitalization of an often hardly-noticed ritual object; in the larger religious community, there are opportunities for environmental collaboration with other traditions and institutions; and in the common life of our nation, there is the opportunity to contribute significantly to greater energy awareness and more responsible energy policies. Were any of this to happen, there is also ceremonial material available for both the dedication of a solar-powered eternal light and for its bar/bat mitzvah celebration – an offer hard to refuse, let us hope.

Finally, I would feel remiss without at least mentioning Jewish resources for marking the seasons.

> As long as all the days of the Earth –
> seedtime and harvest

and cold and heat
and summer and winter
and day and night
shall not cease.

Genesis 8:22 (Robert Alter translation)

Following the cataclysmic flood, this Divine gentle promise of continui-ty is especially poignant, with cradling rhythms that tenderly evoke the succession of the seasons. Many people, I find, are moved by the change of seasons, with increased sensitivity to the natural surroundings at such times.

There are resources within our tradition that could enhance these moments. To begin with the obvious: For those of us living in the Northern Hemisphere, the three Biblical Pilgrimage Festivals, closely linked to the Mediterranean agricultural cycles of grain and of grapes, correspond to the sequence of seasons where we now live. Sukkot falls at Autumn, Pesakh at Spring, and Shavuot at the height of the winter-grain harvest. Rather than emphasizing their historical origins in a different region, the Festivals' natural correspondences with our own here-and-now could be given more ritual and liturgical prominence in our services. Seasonal poetry from local or regional poets, appropriately selected, can blend harmoniously with our established prayers, at the same time providing a contemporary reference to familiar surroundings. Over the decades, I found that people very much appreciated

this *yikhud*, this unification of the traditional and the contemporary, of classical Judaism and classic American poetry, for example. Some said that it represented a pulling together of pieces of their lives that were too often separated from one another.

There is, in addition, a simple act that can bring us even closer to the seasonal rhythms and help us dance to their beat: planting barley or winter rye or winter wheat during Sukkot, beginning to cut it at the start of omer-counting, offering some of its sheaves as part of the Shavuot service, and at its final ripening (it matures more slowly in Massachusetts than in the Mediterranean), harvesting, threshing, and winnowing the grain. It is a sequence that fascinates both kids and adults, and it provides opportunities for contact with the soil (digging and sowing a small swatch of ground at the temple) as well as for creative music and movement ("elevating" or "lifting" the grain as part of the ritual offering; cf. Leviticus 23:11). The possibilities are far richer than can be conveyed in this brief sketch, and I hope that the sketchiness will invite further consideration rather than the immediate dismissal of the bare idea.

A fascinating additional Jewish custom at the *tekufot*, the seasonal turnings, distinct from the Pilgrimage Festivals and corresponding to the solstices and equinoxes, is reported by Avudraham. This involves water, wells, and seems to draw on mythic memories of the blood-pollution of rivers and streams at the liminal moments of seasonal turnings.

The Creation account in Genesis has been recognized as a gift not only to devout believers but to scientists also, for it encourages the basic trust that the observable physical universe behaves in accordance with discoverable laws. This basis for the development of the Western scientific outlook is a direct inheritance from the Hebrew Bible, with its confident assertion that God has established the rule of Divine law over primordial, chaotic matter. Johannes Pedersen, referring to the myth of God's triumph over Ocean and the Dragon, states the point succinctly: "The ocean which, as chaos, is a curse, is changed into a blessing by being subjected to the law; for from the ocean comes the life-giving water."

Many scriptural verses support this notion of nature as following an established rule of law, hence as regular, understandable, and predictable. The importance of this conviction for Western experimental science has been succinctly stated by such modern thinkers as Albert Einstein and Alfred North Whitehead, who wrote (in *Modes of Thought*, 1968): "This unquestioned belief in order . . . finally started the first phase of the modern world in the sixteenth century with the unquestioning presupposition that there is an order of nature which lies open in every detail to human understanding. This belief can be traced back to the initiation of Plato and the Jewish prophets."

In fact, Whitehead insists (in *Adventures of Ideas*, 1967), this trust in an order of nature is essential for science. "[T]here can be no living science unless there is a widespread instinctive conviction in the existence of an Order of

Things, and, in particular, of an Order of Nature. I have used the word instinctive advisedly. It does not matter what men say in words, so long as their activities are controlled by settled instincts. The words may ultimately destroy the instincts. But until this has occurred, words do not count."

Einstein speaks (in his 1949 essay, *The World as I See It*) of a "cosmic religious feeling" with beginnings that "already appear in earlier stages of development – *e.g.,* in many of the Psalms of David and in some of the Prophets. Buddhism . . . contains a much stronger element of it . . . I maintain that cosmic religious feeling is the strongest and noblest incitement to scientific research . . . What a deep conviction of the rationality of the universe and what a yearning to understand, were it but a feeble reflection of the mind revealed in this world, Kepler and Newton must have had to enable them to spend years of solitary labour in disentangling the principles of celestial mechanics . . . [T]he scientist['s] . . . religious feeling takes the form of a rapturous amazement at the harmony of natural law, which reveals an intelligence of such superiority that, compared with it, all the systematic thinking and acting of human beings is an utterly insignificant reflection."

Reciprocally, of course, the astonishing accomplishments of modem science provide support, although not proof, for the Biblical outlook that was its original foundation.

It is clear, then, that the gift of Genesis is not for religionists only. ❧

2007

Perek Shirah: Marginal or Mainstream?

Time to Reassess

Perek Shirah *is a medieval Jewish text that celebrates the sentience of all creatures by portraying them in the act of praising God. This 2006 essay, published for the first time here, urges its revival in the Jewish liturgy.*

Fifty years ago, when I was a rabbinical student, the sounds of *Perek Shirah* ("Chapter of Song") – a venerable text that dates back at least to the 10th century – were hardly audible in the general Jewish community. No translated prayerbook of which I knew included it, nor did many of the small, portable *siddurim*. Now, in 2005, at the annual convention of the Rabbinical Assembly, *Perek Shirah* is the focus of one of the study sessions offered by the dean of the Ziegler School of Rabbinical Studies, Bradley Shavit Artson. What a change from fifty years ago, and one that deserves attention.

Back in the 1950s, *Perek Shirah* was to be found in the scholarly *Avodat Yisrael,* but that seemed quite beyond the competence of those of us struggling with even simpler texts. True, those of us who were students of Heschel and followed his prayerbook recommendations did, in fact, have it on our shelves. *Siddur Otzar Ha-t'filot,* a two-volume compendium of prayers together with some valuable traditional commentaries from across the centuries, printed it in full just before "Laws upon Awakening" and "Introductory Morning Prayers." Included was a preface by Joseph Albo, a strong advocate of *Perek Shirah*'s value, who suggested ways to derive from it moral and spiritual guidance. Also included were introductory comments from the rabbis recommending its recitation, along with the cautionary tale of David's excessive pride in his praise of God, which was effectively deflated by the croaking reproof of a frog! In the world around us, however, no special attention was drawn to the Chapter of Song, and I imagine that most of us quite overlooked it as a liturgical resource.

The *Jewish Encyclopedia* had a full article on *Perek Shirah* by J.D.

Eisenstein, which listed the sources for all of the Biblical verses cited in the Song. Yet informative as it was, it hardly conveyed the exuberance and excitement of the Song's crescendo of voices from every part of the universe – plants and animals, stones and storm clouds, winds and seas – in praise of the Creator.

In 1980, twenty-five years later, a full translation appeared in English, perhaps for the first time. Credit for this goes to Richard Siegel and Carl Rheins, the compilers and editors of the endlessly fascinating *The Jewish Almanac,* and to Barry W. Holz, whose introduction and translation convey the excitement of this liturgical outpouring. Holtz characterizes it as "a mysterious and compelling vision of the entire world of God's creation, the entire cosmos, engaged in song. Every creature, every living and inanimate thing sings its own special song." In his introduction, Holtz cites the Israeli scholars Malachi Beit-Arie and provides a balanced view of the probably origins of the Song in Merkabah myticism.

This universal singing is the most distinctive feature of *Perek Shirah*. Other living creatures sing their songs, each citing an appropriate (though sometimes puzzling) Biblical verse.

Its appearance in Holtz's idiomatic English translation eased the task for those of us who felt moved to include parts of it in services, and for a few of us, selections were likely to be found in any service that we conducted out-of-doors. I cannot say, however, that it dominated the consciousness of Jewish middle America.

It was also of value for considerations of Jewish attitudes towards the environment. If, indeed, all elements of Creation were singing in praise of the Creator, what did this imply about the entire realm of nature? How did this affect our view of the human relation to the rest of Creation? What did it imply about universal sentience? The availability of *Perek Shirah* in English meant that we could refer to it in trying to respond to these questions. Even so, the Song remained a relatively unknown curiosity rather than a ready point of reference. There the matter seemed to rest – until this past decade, when three new publications of *Perek Shirah* have given it perhaps unprecedented prominence in the Jewish community.

In 1996, Facsimile Editions, the London publishing house responsible for a stunning series of facsimile reproductions of some of the most beautiful illuminated Jewish volumes in the great European libraries, issued an edition of *Perek Shirah* from the British Museum. This version, ascribed to

Aaron Schreiber Herlingen, an 18th-century artist residing in Pressburg, was issued in a limited edition of 550 copies by Michael and Linda Falter in celebration of the bar mitzvah of their eldest son Gideon. Although obviously not a mass-circulation item, the consummate artistry of the facsimile, together with the accompanying English volume authored by Malachi Beit-Arie, Jeremy Schonfield, and Emile Schrijver, testifies to the status of *Perek Shirah* as a significant and esteemed Jewish liturgical treasure.

In 1997, B. Klein in Brooklyn published *Sefer Perek Shirah*, a large collection in Hebrew of comments from the tradition about each identified singer of God's praise. This remarkable volume includes explanations of the quoted verse, the species, grammatical issues, questions of meaning, rabbinic sources for the verses, correspondences with the Tabernacle of Meeting and within the human being, etc. Its numerous citations from both Talmudic and mystical sources is impressive.

Most recently, in 2004, Art Scroll's Mesorah Publications in Brooklyn issued an oversize, richly illustrated volume, *Perek Shirah, the Song of the Universe*, edited by Rabbi Nosson Scherman. However one may assess some of the comments, the photographs are stunning, the layout attractive – and the publication represents quite an act of *teshuvah* for the omission of the Song from the standard editions of the Art Scroll *siddurim*. This validation of a great Jewish nature hymn from the heart of Orthodox tradition today strikes me as quite significant.

What are we to make of all this? It seems to me that the increasing audibility and visibility of *Perek Shira* answers to a profound need of our time, for further clarification of the Jewish attitude towards Creation. Important as are the theological and philosophical discussions of the natural order and the locus of the sacred, so is the availability of resources in our prayerbooks that celebrate the vitality and sanctity of Creation. *Perek Shirah*, of illustrious ascribed ancestry, David the King, and dating from at least a thousand years ago, surely meets this need.

Yet doubts beset this particular Song. Are they echoes of earlier controversies about its propriety within Jewish tradition? Do they reflect concern that its possible origins in Merkavah mystical circles somehow impugn its Jewish authenticity? This latter attitude can hardly withstand critical scrutiny, yet we remain with a problem that neither an English translation nor multiplying editions have yet resolved: What was the status of *Perek Shirah*? Was it a valid part of Jewish liturgy, to be cited as evidence for a genuinely Jewish view of the world, or was it a deviant and suspect expression of a point of view quite out of the Jewish mainstream? How shall we confront and banish the ghosts of "violent opposition, contempt, and accusations of forgery" that Beit-Arie reports characterized some earlier reactions to the Song? The answer is simple, I believe, and it lies within the heart of the Talmudic tradition itself.

There is a well-known passage from Avodah Zarah 24b reporting on various rabbinic interpretations of I Samuel 6:12, one verse in the portrayal of the extraordinary events connected with the return of the Ark of the Lord from the field of the Philistines to its proper resting place: "The cows went straight forward by the way to Beth Shemesh." The plain meaning of the verse is simple and descriptive, but immediately a question is raised:

> "What is the meaning of the word 'va-yish-shar-nah?' Said R. Johanan in the name of R. Meier: 'They sang a song' (from *shir,* a song). R. Zutra b. Tobiah said in the name of Rab: 'They directed their faces towards the Ark and rendered song.'
>
> "What was their song? Rabbi Johanan in the name of R. Meier said (Exodus 15:1), 'Then sang Moses' etc. R. Johanan himself, however, said (Isaiah 12:4), 'And ye shall say on that day, Give thanks unto the Lord, call on His name,' etc. R. Simeon b. Lakish said: They sang the orphan chapter (in which the author's name is not mentioned) (Psalm 98:1), 'Oh sing unto the Lord a new song; for He hath done marvelous things,' etc. R. Elazar said (Psalm 99:1), 'The Lord reigneth; let the people tremble.' R. Samuel b. Nachmani said (Psalm 93:1), 'The Lord reigneth; He is clothed in majesty.'
>
> "R. Isaac Nappaha said:
> 'Sing, O ark, in beauty shining;
> Thou adorned with chains of gold —
> Ever close the Word enshrining —
> Glittering with gems untold.' (S. Sekles in *Ein Yaakov*)

or

> 'Sing, o sing, acacia tree;
> Ascend in all thy gracefulness.
> With golden weave they cover thee,
> The sanctuary palace hears thy eulogy.
> With diverse jewels art thou adorned.' (Soncino)

or

> 'Rejoice, rejoice acacia . . .
> Stretch forth in the fullness of thy majesty
> Girdled in golden embroidery

> Praised in the recesses of the palace
> Resplendent in the finest of ornaments.' (Scholem)
>
> "R. Ashi taught the saying of R. Isaac Napakha in connection with this (Numbers 10:55), 'And it came to pass, when the ark set forward that Moses said,' etc. And what did Israel say? Whereupon R. Isaac said, 'Sing, O ark, in beauty shining,' etc."
>
> Avodah Zarah 24b

The richness of this passage is evident, and how tempted I feel to digress along any of the several interpretive paths to which it points! With firm resolve, however, I stick to the central issue. R. Johanan, R. Meir, Resh Lakish, R. Elazar, and R. Isaac Nappaha, among others, renowned scholars and highly respected, have their names associated with an interpretive tradition that, departing from the simple meaning of I Samuel 6:12, insists on explicitly ascribing to one set of animals *haparot*, verbal sounds of praise to the Creator. As Scholem finds warrant (in *Jewish Gnosticism, Merkabah Mysticism, and Talmudic Tradition*, 1960) in the particular wording of R. Isaac's citation for dating the *Hekhalot* hymns as early as the 3rd century, so would I argue that the entirety of this passage supports the contention that the ascription of verbal praise to the Creator by the non-human world accurately reflects a significant body of classical rabbinic opinion. Rather than *Perek Shirah* representing a "forgery," on the contrary, it affords us a vivid glimpse of another rabbinic attitude towards the non-human realms of the natural world. What we have in this passage is a clear affirmation that at least some animals are capable of singing praise to the Creator. And with this perforation of the purported absolute barrier between the human capacity to praise God and that of all the rest of Creation, there is now an opening for the appreciation of the praising capacities of all the realms of the created order. This development, given its full expression in *Perek Shirah*, is thus a quite consistent expansion of the authentic rabbinic outlook expressed in Avodah Zarah 24b.

But isn't this passage in itself a remarkably numinous passage, with the preternatural crackling all through it? And doesn't the Ark of the Lord represent a concentration of the Divine Power that is itself out of the ordinary? Was it not the sight of the Ark that set the cattle singing the verses of praise? Grant all that and we still have a clear rabbinic portrayal of animal instincts discerning some special power of the Divine within the surroundings, and responding to that perception. If that discernment is within the capacities of cattle, there is additional traditional support for this important rabbinic affirmation of the capacities of the non-human realm of nature to praise the Creator.

It is my conviction that the time is ripe for increased use of *Perek Shirah* in our theological, meditational, and liturgical initiatives. Not only do issues of the environment remain of deep concern to many of our fellow Jews, but there is increasing societal unease with the sometimes dogmatic scientific claim that the workings of evolution require the absence of any overarching purpose in the universe. This is a philosophical or theological proposition, not a scientific proposition, and it needs to be addressed in those terms. But in addressing this issue, we shall need to become increasingly clear and articulate about the range of normative Jewish views of nature that offer us insight into this profound life orientation. *Perek Shirah* is one such resource that invites further serious study and appropriation.

Along with the unavoidable questions of abstract thought, the growing interest in aids to religious meditation could be well addressed by *Perek Shirah*. How we sense the other realms of nature; whether or to what degree we regard them as sentient; how variously we might relate to them or use them depending on our answers: all of these surely invite our reflection. And beyond that, those especially sensitive to the religious inspiration of the natural world may well find elements in *Perek Shirah* that aid their fuller integration with this realm.

Finally, at the celebrative liturgical level, as our communities become ever more attuned to the inspiration of natural surroundings, *Perek Shirah* may well help us provide fresh ways in which to give voice to these often subverbal stirrings within. In this respect, some of the recent artistic and scholarly editions mentioned earlier may be of special value.

Perek Shirah is surely better known today in the Jewish community than at any time in recent decades. Even so, it is, at least for now, likely to be regarded as a somewhat peculiar and marginal piece of the tradition. That it is peculiar unto itself is surely so; but after all, what's wrong with being distinctive? As for its purported marginality, this calumny must not any longer hold sway. If its core notion enjoyed the approval of R. Johanan, R. Meir, R. Elazar, Resh Lakish, and R. Isaac Nappaha, it is surely time that we join them in affirming that, truly, the entire universe resounds with the praise of the Creator.

2006

Through the Zen Garden of the Hebrews

A Scriptural Stroll

Rabbi Gendler has enjoyed a long, cordial, and productive relationship with the Tibetan community-in-exile. This 2001 essay, published in the journal of the Reform rabbinate, links elements of Zen Buddhism with Judaism — from a perspective of his own personal spiritual yearning.

Seismic shifts in the ocean floor, unseen by our eyes, initiate the overwhelming wave we call a tsunami. Their invisibility leaves us quite unprepared for the shattering force of that unanticipated inundation. Looking back, I think that the religious wave that rolled in from the Far East shortly after World War II felt that way to a number of us who in those years were beachcombing on the religious shores of the West.

It did resemble events sixty years earlier, when Swami Vivekenanda had startled the 1893 Chicago World Parliament of Religions with his compelling presentation of the Vedanta outlook. As a result, Hinduism became a significant religious influence in the West, furthered by the literary contributions of Aldous Huxley and Christopher Isherwood, among others, and sustained by the various Vedanta centers subsequently established.

The new wave in the 1950s, by contrast, was Buddhist. There was no single public event that clearly marked its arrival. D. T. Suzuki, the preeminent Zen scholar, had earlier been writing learned essays to try to communicate the wordless insights of this elusive Buddhist approach to life. A talented Episcopal clergyman, Alan Watts, had left his previous theological and clerical commitments to lend an idiomatic Western voice to the expression of these new and fascinating insights into life and reality. No signal initiating event comparable to Vivekenanda's lectures had preceded the rising tide, however, and so the wave felt, indeed, like a tsunami, shaking both the foundations and the superstructures of Western religious communities.

This was, perhaps, especially the case for the U.S. Jewish community, where the Zen influence seemed to be strongly felt almost from the beginning. It was the now-deceased Columbia Professor Jacob Taubes, brilliant son of a distinguished Swiss rabbi, who as early as 1960 aptly coined the phrase "Zen Judaism" to characterize the syncretistic developments that he was observing within the Jewish community. Since those early years, of course, the Zen influence on many spiritually seeking Jews has been augmented by additional meditative and prayer elements from Vipassana and Tibetan traditions. But that fuller story is for another time and place.

In those earlier years, while intellectually I appreciated the aptness of Professor Taubes' *bon mot,* for me the issue was personal as well as intellectual. In retrospect, it seems to me clear that I was suffering from an acute case of a related phenomenon, "Zen envy," and the focus of my longing, the object of my envy, was quite specific: not the Zen suspicion of words, appealing as that was; not even the promise of *satori,* unmediated perception and recognition, desirable though that sounded. No, the desired end for me was the Zen garden!

How utterly winning it sounded, as Alan Watts characterized it (in *The Way of Zen,* 1959): "to suggest the general atmosphere of 'mountain and water' in a small space . . . to follow the 'intentionless intention' of the forms themselves . . . to prune, clip, weed, and train plants, but . . . in the spirit of being part of the garden . . . rather than a directing agent standing outside." The most famous of the sand and rock gardens at Kyoto "consists of five groups of rocks laid upon a rectangle of raked sand, backed by a low stone wall, and surrounded by trees. It suggests a wild beach, or perhaps a seascape with rocky islands . . . "

The rocks were often the result of "difficult expeditions to the seashore, to mountains and rivers, in search of rock forms which wind and water have shaped into asymmetrical, living contours. These are then carried to the garden site, and placed so as to look as if they had grown where they stand . . . The Zen monks liked also to cultivate gardens which took advantage of an existing natural setting – to arrange rocks and plants along the edges of a stream, creating a more informal atmosphere." Their reserve in the use of color contributed to the elemental effect, and the spare severity of the garden invited reflection on the most basic of matters.

Although obviously contrived and highly formalized, the garden nonetheless had a natural appearance, being composed from the natural elements of plants, trees, water, and stones, artfully arranged upon a carpet of sand. Of course, it was also wordless, thereby offering refuge from what at times seemed like a dizzying swirl of endless words surrounding me. The Zen garden was to be apprehended not by history or association, not by philology or memory or allusion, but simply by cool, cleansed, clear perception. It also represented the persistence of nature unvanquished, thus speaking to the deep desire of so many – at that time as now – for a proper balance between the naturally given and the humanly devised. In short, all the virtues in a single beckoning image!

Internally, I asked: Why did only Zen offer such a haven? Why was such a refuge absent from my inherited Jewish tradition? The question, for me, was as much accusatory as inquiring, yet another bit of substantiating evidence for the failure of Judaism to comprehend the natural realm. Too bad, but wasn't that rather to be expected? After all, hadn't the doyen of all of Jewish history, Salo Baron, assured us that the distinct contribution of the Hebrew Bible was the dominance of nature by history?

For me, there the matter rested for many years.

Even when the positive and influential existence of the natural within Judaism was being rediscovered and re-asserted beginning in the early '70s – a development in which I was much involved – my wish for the Zen garden lay quiescent, as do so many of our unfulfilled early loves. Nor was my by-then quite forgotten Zen-envy reawakened even by such a stimulating and traditions-spanning work as Mircea Eliade's *Patterns in Comparative Religion*. Despite the predominance of nature themes in that great work, I was not moved to renewed longing for the Zen garden. It was only decades later, when one of our daughters gave me a copy of Simon Schama's learned, engaging, and stimulating 1995 work, *Landscape and Memory*, that I noticed the three major divisions of his book were "Wood," "Water," and "Rock." These were followed by a final section that brought them all together. The elements and their combination suddenly reminded me of the pain I had once felt at the absence of the Zen garden or its equivalent within my own tradition.

So I had once thought, as obviously do so many other Jews as well: The hiking trails of the Himalayas, the ashrams and monasteries of the East, the Zen and Vipassana meditation centers East and West, are filled with Jews, both young and old, in serious search of natural surroundings and contemplative settings from which to view afresh the world in which we find ourselves. They think, as did I at one time, that such resources are absent from Judaism and must be sought elsewhere.

Yet as I followed the Torah cycle after becoming familiar with Schama's book, certain details of the natural settings of the patriarchal narratives, so familiar as to pass almost unnoticed, caught my attention for the first time. In each case, a different element figured in the account of the first revelation or promise of God to the mature patriarch. For Abraham it was trees; for Isaac it was water; for Jacob it was stones. Hmm, a familiar and suggestive triad. Nor should the prominence of these elements be lightly dismissed as "merely the setting." Their inclusion in episodes of such gravity indicates, I think, that they are significant. I suggest that the prominence of these elements in the initiatory revelation for each patriarch yields an equivalent-in-words of the Zen garden.

In the case of Abraham/Abram, following God's verbal command to leave land, kindred, and father's house, he went forth "as far as the Place of Shekhem, as far as the Mighty Tree of Moreh" (Genesis 12:6).[1] It was at this place that God first "appeared to/was seen by" Abram, and here for the first time the land was promised to his seed (12:7). Always in previous readings, my attention had been focused on the revelation rather than the surroundings, the promise rather than the setting. This time, however, my attention lingered on the Place of Shekhem and the Mighty Tree of Moreh. The word for place, *makom*, especially in this unique usage with the proper name Shekhem, has overtones of "sacred site." As for the Mighty Tree of Moreh, the latter term suggests "the sage/the teacher/the oracle giver." Here, then, was a sacred site with a tree so striking that near its trunk or beneath its branches, oracles were spoken, teachings transmitted. It was precisely here, within the numinous-field of this tree, that the first defining revelation to Abram was received.

In further passages about Abram, the tree motif returns. After some exploratory wandering, he "moved-his-tent and came and settled by the

---

1. The core translation is from the Everett Fox translation of *The Five Books of Moses*, New York, Schocken, 1995. The reading "Mighty Tree" is based on Koehler-Baumgartner: *Lexicon in Veteris Testamenti Libros*, Leiden, E.J. Brill, 1958. Cf. entries on *elah* and *elon*, where it is argued that the terms refer to "an undecided species of remarkably big trees . . . of religious significance . . . mighty . . ." etc.

2. Brown, Driver, Briggs: *A Hebrew and English Lexicon of the Old Testament*, Oxford, 1962, entry on *elah* I., p. 18, citing B. Stade: *Geschichte des Volkes Israel*.

Mighty Trees of Mamre, which are by Hevron" (13:18). Of such numinous quality are these trees that in the opinion of one 19th century German philologist,[2] *elon* or *elah,* mighty tree (usually translated as oak or terebinth), is derived from the designation for God, *el* or *elohim*.[2] Given that the first promise to Abram had been revealed in this sacred grove, and that Abram chooses to establish his permanent settlement beside these trees, it seems fair to say that there is a primary association of Abram/Abraham with trees. In short, one element of the Zen garden, the tree, is centrally present with Abraham our Ancestor.[3]

And if one asks: Isn't the Mighty Tree associated with Abraham different from the tree typically found in the Zen garden? – the answer is: Of course, Judaism is not Buddhism. The issue is not the kind of tree, but rather whether there is a tree at all. And assuredly there is a tree that comes into focus when we see Abraham in the fullness of his environment.

If we look, now, at Isaac the Patriarch through the same inclusive lens, we see water as the prominent natural feature. Abraham's servant, in quest of a wife for Isaac ,makes his way directly to Aram of-Two-Rivers (24:10), and stations himself with his camels "outside the town at the water well" (24:11). The test he devises to determine the proper maiden for Isaac centers on the water spring, the drawing of water, the lowering of the pitcher of water, and the giving of drink (24:13-14). In the verses immediately following (vv.15-22), the number of references to water – drawing water, the pitcher, the drinking trough, the act of drinking – is impressive: more than fifteen!

As for Isaac the adult, he first appears coming from "the Well of the Living One Who-Sees-Me" (24:62). And beyond his dealings within his family, the most extended narrative concerns his digging wells of water in the presence of the Philistines, and the quarrels that ensue. Four times Isaac digs wells (26:18, 19, 21, 22), seeking both the renewal of the wells that his father, Abraham, had dug (26:15) and space for his own fruitful expansion in the land (26:22). Isaac concludes: "Indeed, now YHWH has made space for us, so that we may bear fruit in the land! He went up from there to Be'er-Sheva," itself a well-site (26:22-23). In these two narratives involving Isaac as a mature agent, it seems fair to say that a second element of the Zen garden, water, is the prominent natural element.

Referring to Jacob's encounter with God in Genesis 28:10-22, Nahum

---

3. One notes, also, that following the covenant with Avimelekh at Be'er-Sheva, Abraham "planted a tamarisk in Be'er-Sheva and there he called out the name: YHWH God of the Ages" (21:33).

Sarna says (in the Jewish Publication Society's 1989 Torah commentary): "The biography of Jacob as an independent personality, a patriarch in his own right, now begins." When we look at this episode with attention to the natural object involved, it is a stone that we notice. After leaving Be'er-Sheva, Jacob "encountered a certain place" where he had to spend the night. "Now he took one of the stones of the place and set it at his head and lay down in that place. And he dreamt" (vv.11, 12). There follows the famous dream of the ladder set upon the earth, its top reaching the heavens, with angels or messengers of God going up and down on it. God promises Jacob that "The land on which you lie I give to you and to your seed" (v.13), and that "Your seed will be like the dust of the earth . . ." (v.14). When Jacob awakens the following morning, he is awestruck by the realization that this place "is none other than a house of God, and that is the gate of heaven!" (v.17). He then takes the stone upon which he had rested his head, sets it up as a standing-pillar, pours oil upon it, makes a vow, and declares that "this stone that I have set up as a standing-pillar shall become a house of God . . ." (v.22).

The narrative immediately following concerns a well in the field with a large stone on the mouth of the well (29:1-10). It is here that Jacob first encounters Rachel, reacting to the sight of her by single-handedly rolling from the well the massive stone, which generally required the massed strength of all the herdsmen. One immediately notices that the stone motif associated with Jacob does not exclude the presence of the water motif associated with Isaac. A full analysis (not possible here for reasons of space) would, in fact, show that both of the other natural elements are found in subordinate association with each patriarch. Yet in the case of Jacob, the centrality of the stone is incontestable when one recalls the stone pillar at Bet-El (31:13); the pact with Laban marked by the collecting of stones and the making of a mound and pillar (31:45-52); his "pillaring" of a slaughter-site and calling it "God, the God of Israel" (33:20); his erecting a pillar on the occasion of the changing of his name (35:14-15); his setting up a standing pillar over the burial place of Rachel (35:20); and his unique use of "the Stone of Israel" *(even Yisrael)* as a synonym for God (49:16).

Reading these patriarchal episodes with focus on backgrounds rather than foregrounds, settings rather than narratives, has yielded clear associations of trees with Abraham, water with Isaac, and stones with Jacob.

And the floor of the garden, often raked sand in the Zen tradition? For the Zen garden of the Hebrews, there are choices. Sand is certainly one possibility: Following the *Akedah*, Abraham is told, "indeed, I will bless you, bless you, I will make your seed many, yes, many, like the stars of the heavens and like the sand that is on the shore of the sea" (22:17).

Another possibility is dust: At the end of God's first appearance to the mature Jacob at Beth-El, the promise is made: "Your seed will be like the dust of the earth . . . All the clans of the soil will find blessing through you and through your seed!" (28:14). Nor should we overlook the further suggestion of a canopy above the garden: Both Abraham (22:17) and Isaac (26:4) are promised "many seed, like the stars of the heavens."

From this way of reading the text, the elements of a garden clearly emerge. But is there any warrant within Jewish tradition for such a way of reading the text? I think there is. Familiar from *Pirkei Avot* is the dictum of Ben Bag Bag (Avot 5:25): *"Hafokh bah v'hafokh bah d'kula bah. Uvah teheze."* The usual translation is found in *Gates of Prayer*: "Turn it (the Torah) over and over, for it contains everything. Keep your eyes riveted to it." But what does "turn it over and over" mean? Does it mean to ponder and reconsider it ceaselessly? Surely. But the force of *hafokh* is considerable, suggesting a total reversal of the usual sequence or order. One could, then, with equal validity, render *"hafokh bah"* as "reverse it, turn it upside down." So understood, the charge would be: "Reverse it (the Torah), reverse foreground and background, for it contains everything. Keep your eyes riveted to it." As applied to our analysis, the applied meaning would be: Look at the images, not only the narrative, the background, not only the foreground. Keep your eyes riveted upon it, and there, indeed, in clear succession, are the central elements of the Zen garden: trees, water, and stones!

Can discrete elements, verbally presented, yield a whole picture? Words, of course, are successive rather than simultaneous, and any images that they evoke will be separate rather than a unified picture. Unlike images, words must follow one another, be they written or oral; to attempt to present them all at once yields either a smudge to the eye or a cacophony to the ear. Although physically word must follow word in succession, however, once within our minds, their referents can be visualized simultaneously. In this way, the verbal can become visual, and a succession of discrete images, if simultaneously present to our minds' eyes, can become a whole picture.

Is this not an alternative way of understanding *"En muqdam um'uhar b'torah"* (Midrash Ecclesiastes Rabbah to verse 1:12)? While usually and appropriately translated as, "Scripture does not follow a strict chronological order," also admissible as a rendering is, "Words of Torah are not only sequential; they can also be simultaneous." A sequence of Scriptural images can be retained and unified in the mind of the reader to yield a fixed and full picture.

Reading Jewish Scripture by the light of these two principles, and considering the associations of trees, water, and stones with the initial revelatory experiences of Abraham, Isaac, and Jacob, a Zen garden of the Hebrews may not be so implausible after all. But one may wonder what it would look like, and whether it would be different from a Buddhist Zen garden.

My own response at this point is, yes, it would be different from a Buddhist Zen garden. After all, Hebrew tradition validates, emphasizes, and rejoices in associations and overtones. Hence the physical images of the Zen garden of the Hebrews are likely to evoke memories of the Divine appearances and Divine promises associated with those natural objects. Such memories and associations, however, need not in any way deny or depreciate the numinous value of the trees, the water, the stones, or the sand or dust of the floor.[4]

As for the appearance of the garden itself, how unseemly it would be to configure for others what may finally arrange itself in one's own mind. Apart from allowing for different configurations of the given elements in different minds, should not one also allow for shifting configurations within the same mind at different times? It is worth remembering that Zen tradition warns against confusing the pointing finger with that to which it is trying to point, just as Jewish tradition is wary of trying to describe or name the ineffable. Sufficient unto the garden are the elements thereof.

For a people destined to experience exile and suffer frequent prohibitions against owning land, was not this Hebraic Zen garden of the mind a potential source of continuous meditative connection with nature? Whether, in fact, it served such a function for our people through the centuries I do not know. Nor do I know if the late Professor Jacob Taubes had this in mind when he spoke of Zen Judaism some forty years ago. I am convinced, however, that among the "everything" that Torah contains is a Zen garden of the Hebrews.

Even if so, one may rightly ask, has this Scriptural stroll any environ-

---

4. It would be interesting and valuable, I think, to look comparatively at the whole question of landscapes and associations, or lack thereof, in the Zen garden, in the Hebraic garden-in-words, and in Schama's Arcadia, where wood, water, and rock are joined.

mental relevance or practical religious application to our situation today? I think it has. By way of illustration, let me offer one example. What if every synagogue were to set up a small meditation space, arranging trees, water, and stones upon sand or soil, as an explicitly contemplative space? Similar to the Zen garden, yet drawn from the most basic, formative narratives within Judaism, it could offer many Jews seeking nature and contemplation a haven within rather than outside of Judaism. Resembling, also, the Biblical gardens that have been established in some synagogues, this space would be less botanical, more explicitly meditative in intent. Derived from the Hebrew Bible, it would also remind us that the God of history has never departed residency from within the natural realm.

The Zen garden of the Hebrews awaits only our recognition for it to inform our spirits and infuse our lives anew with the redemptive vitality of *Khey Ha-olamim*, the Life of the Universe.

Published in *CCAR Journal: The Reform Jewish Quarterly*, Winter 2001

The Solar-Powered Eternal Light

"See My Works!"

Rabbi Gendler's synagogue in Lowell, Massachusetts was the first to install a solar-powered eternal light. This article, adapted from an interview in Genesis 2, *describes its inspiration, design, and impact.*

In 1979, my synagogue community, Temple Emanuel in Lowell, Massachusetts, installed above our ark a *ner tamid* (eternal light) powered by solar energy — the only one of its kind at the time. It was a process that began in the autumn, on a particularly beautiful day, when I could see and feel the shortening of the daylight. I was musing at the temple, thinking about Psalm 19, with its celebration of the Sun:

> In the heavens God has pitched a tent for the sun.
> It is like a bridegroom coming out of his chamber,
> like a champion rejoicing to run his course.
> It rises at one end of the heavens
> and makes its circuit to the other;
> nothing is deprived of its warmth.

I began thinking about the Sun as a symbol of the Divine, so inferior to yet derivative of the great Source. It struck me: My God, here was this reality of enormous power, yet the energy for our *ner tamid* was mediated by such questionable and lethal sources of power – either fossil fuels, coal or oil, or nuclear power. Such sources of power for the eternal light were incredibly inferior to the beautiful solar collector which is the olive tree and its olive oil. I managed to resist the temptation to declare, "Abolish all electified eternal lights and return to olive oil!" – but that was my first thought.

I had heard about photovoltaic cells. Symbolically, at the spiritual level, how beautiful it would be if the light above the Torah directly derived from the Sun. What a contribution to all our awareness of the energy question at a practical, societal level.

The panel was installed, and a year later, on the anniversary of our *ner tamid* going solar, we added the internal lights of the ark to the same unit. We had an astronomer, a friend of the congregation, come with slides and talk about the Sun.

Our celebration of Tammuz and the beginning of the summer was also quite special. We had a mathematician from Northeastern come speak on ethics, energy, and the solar transition.

We're now quite attuned to the Sun in our *shul*, which means that seasonal shifts and energy questions come in for more explicit consideration. But the impact of going solar has been more than that: It really touches people at a very deep level. We've become more spiritually alive and not so flabby.

This planet Earth was created as a kind of life experiment, and we are part of it. Everything we do has to be measured against maintaining its inhabitability. One of my favorite *midrashim* is from Ecclesiates Rabbah (7:13), as translated here by Nachum Glatzer (in *Hammer on the Rock*):

> In the hour when the Holy One, blessed be He, created the first man, He took him and let him pass before all the trees of the Garden of Eden, and said to him: See My works, how fine and excellent they are! Now all that I have created, for you have I created. Think upon this, and do not corrupt and desolate My world: for if you corrupt it, there is no one to set it right after you.

Any source of energy that we use has to conform to the mandate of this *midrash*. It has to operate in a way that doesn't threaten the possibility of future life continuing on the Earth and doesn't assume that someone else will clean up the mess after us. Insofar as any source of energy violates these rules, to that extent it seems to me to be invalid and has to be ruled out.

Conservation at the individual and institutional levels is important, for what we demand of society we must demand of ourselves. It's no coincidence that renewable sources of energy tend also to be decentralized. Policies that put a premium on small, local units offer greater community independence and self-determination, and less massive, centralized bureaucracy, and are therefore much more in the spirit of what I think is the decentralism of "proclaim liberty throughout the land," from Leviticus, the Jubilee proclamation that is written on our unrung Liberty Bell. ❧

Adapted from an interview in *Genesis 2,* May, 1980

Our Environment: Study and Action

Judaism's Festival Rituals

This 1990 essay describes creative, seasonally-linked observances of Sukkot, Pesakh, and Shavuot, Judaism's cycle of agriculturally linked holy days.

From the very early times, Judaism has placed at its center the goal of an Earth fit for life and habitation. Isaiah 45:18 proclaims it quite stirringly:

> For thus said the Lord,
> The Creator of heaven who alone is God,
> Who formed the Earth and made it,
> Who alone established it —
> Who did not create it a waste,
> But formed it for habitation:
> I am the Lord, and there is none else.

An earlier text (Genesis 8:22) nicely connects this preservation of the Earth with natural rhythms of the universe:

> So long as the Earth endures,
> Seedtime and harvest,
> Cold and heat,
> Summer and winter,
> Day and night,
> Shall not cease.

Numerous other verses and teachings further emphasize the environmental concern of Judaism. The most basic is Deuteronomy 20:10-20, from whose interpretation comes the rabbinic principle *bal tashkhit*, do not waste.

Yet there are some today who argue that a verse from Genesis (1:28) invites or permits human exploitation of the rest of Creation, and that many of our environmental problems can be traced to the attitude of this verse:

> Be fertile and increase, fill the earth and master it; and rule the fish of the

sea, the birds of the sky, and all living things that creep on earth.

But notice, this verse is followed immediately by a limitation: In verse 29, the human is given seed-bearing plants and seed-bearing trees for food, and in verse 30, the very same green plants are given for food to all the animals, birds, and creeping things on Earth "in which there is the breath of life." Nahum Sarna points out (in the *JPS Torah Commentary: Genesis*) that while the terms "master" and "rule" express the "coercive power of the monarch," in "the model of kingship here presupposed . . . the monarch does not possess unrestrained power and authority; the limits of his rule are carefully defined and circumscribed by divine law, so that kingship is to be exercised with responsibility and is subject to accountability . . . man . . . although he 'rules' the animal world . . . is not here permitted to eat flesh." And in the account in Genesis 2, Sarna adds, the human is placed in the Garden "to till it and tend it," the terms having distinct overtones of "responsibility to nurture and conserve the pristine perfection of the Garden." Attempting to blame this verse from Genesis for our present problems is to misread and distort the meaning of the text.

Simeon ben Gamaliel taught: "Not just study, but the practice of mitzvot is essential" (Avot 1:17). It is important that we consider ways in which some of these environmental issues might be practiced as well as preached, implemented as well as investigated. A good point of departure is the text from Genesis 8. Are there ways, for example, that we might make "seedtime and harvest . . . summer and winter" more than simply words of texts? What are some resources within Judaism that might help us bring alive the notions of the growth cycle and the succession of the seasons?

For the past fifteen years at our temple, we have adapted a traditional ritual that links Sukkot, Pesakh, and Shavuot while simultaneously increasing students' awareness of the cycle of seedtime and harvest. On the intermediate Sunday of Sukkot (this could also be done during the week), all students are taken, class by class, out to the *sukkah*. There we recite the blessing over the *lulav* and *etrog*, which each student in turn waves in the

four directions, beginning eastward, then clockwise towards the south, west, north, and finally up and down. Questions and discussion easily produce the realization in our students that this traditional waving, in effect, draws an outline of our earth and its axis.

Next, each student has something to drink and eat in the *sukkah*. Then comes something a bit different. Having just enjoyed the fruits of a harvest, we now move as a class to a small section of ground previously dug and prepared for planting. Each student receives a handful of winter rye or winter wheat, and broadcasts the grains upon the prepared plot; the soil is lightly raked to cover the seeds. The lesson is immediately evident: with the enjoyment of the previous year's harvest comes the responsibility to plant for the year to come.

But there is more to be learned. Within a couple of weeks, the grains sprout, and some growth is visible. With the coming of winter in our climate, this growth looks rather forlorn and gets covered with ice and snow, and we give little thought to it until early spring and Pesakh. At this point, beginning with the communal seder the second night of Pesakh, and continuing Friday nights and Sunday mornings, we count the omer (cf. Leviticus 23:15-16), using each time a recently cut handful of the growing wheat or rye. (It is convenient to wrap this at the bottom with a bit of aluminum foil to hold the blades together.) Each week, the development of the grain progresses visibly, and most students are quite fascinated as the stalks form the new grains. We count seven times seven over the next seven weeks. Shavuot arrives, and the students easily grasp its character as a Feast of Fruits as well as a Festival of Revelation.

The entire process invites discussion of the wonders of the growth cycle: the miracle of seeds, the life-out-of-death that planting has always suggested to human beings, the process of wintering-over, the need to care for and conserve our precious topsoil, the problems of acid rain, drought, food and hunger in our world today, and more. Beyond discussions, celebrating the early grain harvest with music and dance is also a natural activity. By this simple act of planting a winter grain crop at Sukkot, three Jewish pilgrimage festivals are visibly linked, a parallel to the vegetation cycle is provided, basic preservation issues of our planet are raised concretely and naturally, and our curriculum encompasses both the study and the practice of *mitzvot* that Simeon ben Gamaliel so esteemed. ❧

From *Compass,* Vol. 13, No. 1, 1990

Sustaining the Soil, Sustaining the Spirit

Gardening as a Jewish Spiritual Practice

This 2003 essay anticipated the burgeoning movement of young Jewish farmers and gardeners who are combining their concerns about sustainable agriculture and meaningful spiritual practice.

Gardening is an ancient activity that has brought deep satisfactions to millions of human beings over the centuries. It probably dates as far back as the discovery of the mysterious reproductive power of the seed. This event marked the beginning of the momentous shift in human food dependency from hunter-gatherers to cultivators of the soil. Both the Greek Eleusinian Mysteries, one of the most notable celebrations in classical Greece, and the astonished repetitions of "*zera*/seed" as noun and verb in Genesis 1:11-12, testify to the significance of this discovery.

The calming solace of gardening surely underlies Voltaire's resolution of Candide's plight when he portrays the protagonist as turning to his garden. Even though agriculture has become more massive and mechanized in our age, hundreds of thousands of individuals maintain their direct, enlivening contact with the vegetative growth cycle, continuing to garden for the sensual satisfactions and spiritual rewards of this ancient practice. This is surely reason enough for its continuation, and I doubt that most gardeners ask more.

There may be some, however, who would welcome a way to connect this deeply rewarding personal practice with a broader worldview – in this case, with a conception of Creation as the foundation for the cultivation and tending of plant life that so enhances our earth. For them, the following thoughts may enrich and expand their personal gardening experiences.

Agriculture is a Jewish spiritual practice. This simple yet startling proposition seems to me a core affirmation of Judaism. What does it mean?

Agriculture is tillage of the land, the science and art of cultivating the soil. Spiritual practice is a set of acts or a discipline that draws our attention to the Divine. For the modern mind, this association of soil with soul or spirit may seem strange. For the Bible, the connection is Divinely natural: "The Eternal God formed the human of dust from the soil, and breathed into its nostrils the breath of life, and the human became a living soul" (Genesis 2:7). Soil and soul eternally embrace in the composition of the human being.

To become aware of this Divine interweaving of heaven and earth is not automatic or easy, and often we live our entire lives without ever feeling it emotionally. Hence the importance of agriculture as spiritual practice.

Which means, first of all, the recognition that we belong to the land, not the land to us, and that both of us belong to the Source from which we derive our being. As Ecclesiastes pointedly remarks: "The advantage of land is paramount; even a king is subject to the soil" (Robert Gordis translation of the enigmatic verse 5:8). It also means coming to know the teeming life and intricate complexity of soil, and finding ways to sustain and strengthen it. It means humility in the face of that tiny miracle at the juncture of death and life, the seed, which preserves the life of the vegetation cycle just ended so that it can be reborn in the cycle to come.

These truths have become vivid in the informed, mindful, daily agricultural practices at such exemplary institutions as Isabella Freedman in Connecticut and Urban Adamah in Oakland, California. Each of these has established an atmosphere of prayer and Jewish learning related to the land.

In turn, agricultural procedures establish a background that is ideal for sustaining and strengthening traditional Jewish practices such as prayer. Look at some of the key words in one of the great bodies of devotional literature, the Psalms: shepherd, green pastures, still waters, hills, trees of the forest, breakers of the sea, rivers, streams, dew, rain, Sun, moon, stars. These religious inspirations are clearly not the products of fingers on laptops in enclosed office spaces! What a contribution to their renewal is the daily drudgery/enlivening activity of tilling the soil and tending the flocks.

Another aspect of the Divine presence that is written into the charter of Jewish agriculture is *tzedek*, justice. The corners of the field, the dropped gleanings, tithing: The Torah proclaims that the bounty is to be shared equitably. Community Supported Agriculture, food distribution to disadvantaged sections of our cities, the quiet concern for the silent, unseen rural poverty – these are among the modern social justice equivalents that we need to cultivate along with soil. Soil, soul, justice: This threefold cord can be a lifeline for anchorage in a too-rapidly-changing age.

For those of us whose gardening is individual, not communal, are there additional resources from Jewish tradition that might help us feel this broader connection and give us, also, a grasp of that lifeline?

As most know, Jewish tradition has a number of names designating the Divine: Lord, God, the Eternal One, the Holy One, the Name, the Place. In Jewish mystical tradition, there are additional "names," some of them numerical, that point towards the Divine. Two of these I have found valuable in reminding me, each time I step into my garden, that the living soil, with which I cooperate in helping food grow, is itself a gift from the Author of the Works of Creation.

There is a 42-letter name of God associated with the potential of Creation becoming realized, with the world assuming a material substance and shape. In this view, the world was waiting to be "written" into existence, and the ink for the writing was "clinging" to the point of the pen. It was the 42-letter name of God that freed the ink so that the "writing" of Creation could continue. What is this name? It cannot be seen or uttered. There is, however, an intimation of its existence in the prayer *Ana B'koakh*, which consists of seven lines, each of six words, totaling forty-two.

There is also a 72-letter name of God, in Jewish mystical thought, concealed in three consecutive verses from Exodus (14:19-21), each consisting of 72 Hebrew letters. These verses are protective in tone, describing the presence of the angel of God both before and behind the camp of the Israelites as they emerged from bondage in Egypt. Present, also, is the pillar of cloud by day and of light by night, along with the wind that preserves the dry land from inundation.

Why not, then, measure your garden so that it is 42 by 72, whether in feet or inches – or in the Biblical measures of a cubit *(amah)* or a span *(zeret)* or a handbreadth *(tefah)* or a finger *(etzba)*? (Equivalents in inches are roughly 18, 9, 3, and $3/4$.) One or another of these should permit you to measure out 42 by 72 to remind yourself that the productive soil is a gift, an inheritance of Creation preserved by previous generations, not just a possession validated by a title deed.

For each of these dimensions, you might select passages from the Jewish tradition that can be posted near the entrance to your garden or at the corner. For the dimension of forty-two, I have used a succinct introduction by the great British kabbalistic scholar, A. E. Waite, a classic verse from the Zohar:

> "And the earth was void and without form." This describes the original state — as it were, the dregs of ink clinging to the point of the pen — in which there was no subsistence, until the world was graven with forty-two letters, all of which are the ornamentation of the Holy Name.
> Zohar 1, 30a

There is also the Hebrew prayer associated with the 42-letter Name:

> By the great power of Thy right hand, O set the captive free.
> Revered God, accept Thy people's prayer; strengthen us, cleanse us.
> Almighty God, guard as the apple of Thy eye those who seek Thee.
> Bless them, cleanse them, pity them; ever grant them Thy truth.
> Mighty, holy God, in Thy abundant grace, guide Thy people.
> Exalted God, turn to Thy people who proclaim Thy holiness.
> Accept our prayer, hear our cry, Thou who knowest secret thoughts.
> Blessed be the name of His glorious majesty forever and ever.
> Rabbi Jonathan Sacks translation

For the 72-letter Name, the three verses from Exodus are quoted, along with a classic validating statement of derivation from the great medieval commentator Ibn Ezra. Covered in plastic and posted on a small piece of exterior plywood, these pages have served me as a helpful, unobtrusive reminder of the potential for Divine connections while tending the garden. I urge you to create your own.

A seed, as mentioned earlier, is itself notable for encapsulating the moment where death and life meet, embrace, and by that embrace enable life to continue. The marvel of the seed is attested, as mentioned earlier, by the repetition of the Hebrew root, *zera,* in Genesis 1:11-12, six times in two verses! Indeed, "And God saw that it was good."

One aid for recapturing this primal wonder is watching the actual sprouting of a seed. Keep it moist but not too wet — a seed sprouting device is ideal, but a wet paper towel, carefully tended, also serves very well. Slowly the tiny seed, or corn or grain kernel, puts out, before our eyes, all the elements needed for drawing sustenance from the soil, energy from the Sun, and transmitting the product of photosynthesis to the developing plant. From time to time it is good to have a fresh look at this unfolding. It is really quite amazing, and I, for one, am in danger of forgetting just how miraculous it all is.

Finally, in scholarly support of this approach to the earth that we cultivate, let me mention the work of the Harvard Biblical scholar, Theodore Hiebert. His well-documented volume, *The Yahwist's Landscape,* argues convincingly that the J version of the Creation story, beginning with Genesis 2:4 and for the rest of the chapter, has "as its central feature . . . arable land . . . *adama,* fertile soil that can be cultivated. "This adama or cultivable soil," Hiebert writes, ". . . is the setting for human society. . . . The first human, Adam, is described as the cultivator of *adama* . . . He is fashioned by God out of the land he farms . . . *Adama* is the beginning and the end of human life . . ."

And of crucial importance is the presence of God in this garden: "J's God[1] . . . lives a very earthly life . . . J views the world of nature as a single metaphysical reality, the central and defining feature of which is *adama,* arable land. . . . However one might wish to define or explain the ontological difference between God and humanity in J's epic . . . it can hardly be put in the categorical terms of the absolute transcendence of nature customarily employed for the Bible's God . . . J's deity is primarily a participant in the same agrarian realm inhabited by all other life."

Hiebert's scholarship suggests that claiming agriculture was *a* Jewish spiritual practice may be an understatement. Instead, we might convincingly argue that originally agriculture was *the* Jewish spiritual practice! If this be so, it is surely time to reclaim and develop, without apology, the cultivation of the soil as a recognized and recommended Jewish spiritual practice. ❧

2003, modified 2011 for Camp Isabella Freedman

---

1. This is a reference, of course, to the Yahwist or "J" source of Biblical narrative, one of the four strands that Biblical scholars have identified in the Pentateuch.

Haystacks and Haybales, Pumpkins and Seeds

On the Transmission of Legacies

Rabbi Gendler spent his childhood in the farmlands of Iowa. This essay from 2000 recalls how the agricultural landscape shaped his aesthetic, his Judaism, his creative leadership as a rabbi, and his sense of wonder.

Wonder precedes words. Can we doubt this simple assertion? Not if we observe an infant or a very young child sitting for minutes at a time, perhaps staring fixedly at something out of reach, perhaps engrossed in touching-feeling-manipulating something within reach. The intent look, the persistent fondling, the brightness of the eyes, the puckered lips all testify eloquently to the presence of the child's wonder long before she/he has any words with which to communicate verbally that felt response to the surrounding world.

Wonder precedes words. Might the transmission of childhood wonders from the environment, then, be aided by actions as well as words? Perhaps the doing rather than the saying, or at least the doing along with the saying, would help us share some of our fondly remembered childhood wonders with those yet to come. Or, to the contrary, might this intrusion of reality by the doing, not just the saying or imagining, in practice impede the transmission of the fondly remembered childhood treasures?

These thoughts and questions come to mind as I sit remembering some precious experiences of earlier years, when our two daughters, Naomi and Tamar, were quite young – 5 and 8 – and Sean, the little lad across the street, was only 4. Although I was hardly conscious of it at the time, I realize now that a variety of activities involving haystacks, haybales, pumpkins, and seeds were my attempts to share with posterity a legacy that I had cherished since childhood, a sharing that I thought might be assisted by doing as well as hearing or imagining.

Was this the case? The answers vary with the specifics. Two of the attempts were informal, in natural settings; two were formal, in structured religious-educational settings. All were rewarding, each was instructive. Of special significance for environmental education, I think, are the religious settings. Much in the Bible offers natural connections with our natural surroundings, and we might do well to develop this religious resource for environmental awareness.

For now, however, let us turn to the telling of the tales.

As I was growing up in a small Iowa town, five architectural forms punctuated the surrounding landscape: houses, barns, silos, water towers, and haystacks. While all of them interested me, it was the haystacks – long before I had ever known of Monet – that most attracted me. How various they were: some squat, some tall, some round, some elliptical. And how mysterious. Take lawn clippings and try piling them high: a couple of feet up, and down they come. Yet all through the rolling Iowa fields stood these great pillars of grass, and they didn't come tumbling down! Seven, eight, nine, even ten feet high, and there they stood, resistant to downpours, blizzards, and severe winds. What protected them from the weather? Why didn't they rot over the winter? Why didn't they collapse or blow away? This mystery of childhood remained unsolved, and was soon forgotten when we moved to the city.

Decades later, now married and with two daughters, I moved to a three-acre parcel in a then-rural part of Andover, Massachusetts. The site, except for the lawns surrounding our house, was mostly rough and wooded, and our garden area, although sizable, enjoyed/suffered considerable shading from the surrounding trees. A couple of years later, however, we were able to purchase from Mr. Boutwell, our back-fence neighbor, a two-acre hay field to augment our original land, thus providing a more suitable, sunny garden spot along with plenty of hay for mulching the garden. And not surprisingly, that hay field released in me a flood of memories long dammed up behind the dike of adult amnesia.

Along with the memories came the mysteries as well. How did those haystacks stand? Why didn't they collapse into unsightly heaps? Happily for me, a repository of such traditional knowledge, Scott Nearing, was still alive and vigorous in his eighties, and having been close to him and Helen for many years, our family went for a hands-and-feet-on practical tutorial in proper haystack making. Given Scott's predilections and procedures, our daughters were too young at the time to do more than observe the tutelage from a safe distance. As for Mary (my wife) and me, the fresh climate of Maine in early summer, with breezes from the Penobscot Bay moderating the mild heat of mid-day, provided the loveliest imaginable classroom for our crash course in the vanishing skill of haystack construction. Instructed, invigorated, and inspired, we headed back to Andover to apply the newly acquired knowledge.

Vintage equipment was offered by Mr. Boutwell, now in his eighties but looking youthful compared with the ancient sickle-bar mower, the tether, the hay-rake, the cart, and the tractor in his barn. Nevertheless, they did their jobs despite highly audible wheezing, sputtering, and squeaking. Unlike the conditions in Maine, however, the Sun which shone upon our hay-making was not moderated by fair breezes from the ocean bay, the temperature reached towards the nineties, and the relative humidity followed in hot pursuit. The family, looking like figures from a Breughel painting, bravely took to the field, I pitching the hay, Mary arranging it, Tamar and Naomi stomping it down. Ever so slowly, the stack grew taller; meanwhile, the workers grew sweatier and sneezier as the pollen, the chaff, the seeds and the dirt stuck to their skins, filled their nostrils, and covered their eyes. Sunglasses, kerchiefs, bandannas – all were futile as protective agents against the all-pervasive dust.

At last the height of the stack exceeded my pitching capacity, and so it was declared completed. The day's ordeal – the unseen precondition of those romantic haystacks of my childhood – did not endear the haystack to its current builders, nor did the prospect of building one more the following day. "Maybe we can do it earlier tomorrow, Daddy, before it gets so hot?" "Alas, dear daughters, the dew lasts late, I'm afraid we have no choice."

The next day was like the previous, except that both temperature and humidity reached the mid-nineties! Despite such deterrence, the doughty crew reluctantly returned, and a second haystack joined the first in companionable proximity. When friends came over to play, our daughters did take them up to the field, pointed with pride to their towering achievements, and clambered up with cheerful determination. When finally on top of the haystacks, they stretched out their hands in triumphal gestures, and regally surveyed the close-cropped fields whence came the hay for their fancy foot work.

The following year, alas, reluctance rose to resistance at the prospect

of a repeat of the previous year's ordeal; memories had obviously not captivated the captive work crew. Rather like Frank Morgan as the Wizard of Oz – haggard and hassled as he emerged from behind the controls responsible for the lovely effects on the other side of the curtain – these reconstructors of my childhood icons had experienced more weariness than wonder building them. It was only the generous nature and physical stamina of a sturdy neighbor down the road that made possible the construction of that year's stacks. The temperature and humidity, I need hardly report, surpassed the highs of the previous year by several degrees and percentage points, and the defectors felt fully vindicated, perhaps even divinely liberated.

The next year was terminal for haystacks reconstructed. My faithful neighbor, Ted, in real life a skilled technician for Massachusetts Electric, found that during periods of electrical overloads and brownouts, he was on 24-hour emergency call. These periods – caused by the heavy use of indoor air conditioners – coincided, of course, with prime time for outdoor haying, and so my last ally was conscripted for service on a different front. There was now no alternative to enlisting the help of the hay-baler.

The prospect of the hay-baler put me in a grumpy mood. I did, however, retain some perspective. Even while I complained audibly about the unending clanking noises of the baler, it did occur to me that such sounds were, perhaps, less inhumane than the sighs, the sneezes, and the sniffles of the long-suffering human serfs of that earlier summer. I was also realistic enough to recognize that Mr. Boutwell's advancing years and physical decline were not only matched but exceeded by the plummeting physical condition of his haying equipment. That machinery, after all, had been neither smooth nor silent during its functioning those previous years. So, then, let the hay-baler enter the garden.

The operator of the new machinery was experienced, and his equipment was up-to-the-minute. A rotary cutter, a revolving tether, rake and baler combined: Never had this hayfield known such treatment. Still put off by the mechanical efficiency of it all, I was piling the bales when Sean, the youngster from across the street, came up our hill and approached the scene of the action. How would he react, I wondered, to these mechanically-gathered, string-tied bundles of recently cut, thoroughly dried grass? Could these hay-bricks, uniform, identical, substitute for the unpredictable loose hay that in earlier years had been pitched and tromped into distinctive, individual shapes? His answer to my unasked question was not long in coming.

"Mr. Gendler," he exclaimed excitedly, "it's a mountain!" His face all aglow, he could hardly wait for the stacking to be finished so that he could scale the newly erected heights.

A mountain? Of course. How could I not have seen it? And a veritable ziggurat besides, I mused to myself, as images of the ancient near-Eastern step-like shapes came traipsing past my mind. Having piled it with ascending, step-like bales on each side, I could imagine the legendary Hanging Gardens of Babylon atop this West Andover replica of classical Mesopotamian forms.

"Yes, Sean, it is a mountain, and maybe a special tower besides. Do you remember the story of the Tower of Babel?"

"Of course, my Mommy teaches Christian School every Sunday. You know that."

"Well, scholars think that the Tower of Babel may have looked like this. It was much taller, of course, and made of Sun-baked bricks, but its shape may have been like our stack of haybales. Isn't that interesting?"

Sean smiled at the idea that his mountain might be a three-dimensional replica of his mother's Bible story, and resumed his ascent of the mountain/the Tower with even greater enthusiasm. Who knows what inner imaginings may have fueled his final climb to the top of that mountain? And who knows what associations may cross his mind now if he, grown up and living elsewhere, happens across stacks of haybales in old country farm yards?

As I reflect on these memories from long ago and longer ago, several thoughts occur to me. First of all, duplication of form does not necessarily yield duplication of effect. Reproducing the haystacks with the help of our daughters did not reproduce for them the effects that haystacks had for me in my childhood. How fared this attempt to transmit a natural legacy to posterity by doing it? As our fax machine sometimes succinctly says, "Transmission error." Monet's haunting paintings of haystacks, shimmering and mysterious in the varied light of various hours from dawn to dusk, requiring only viewing by the viewer, not doing by the doer, are surely more effective, more reliable transmitters of the inherent or associative wonder of haystacks.

Secondly, to my surprise – though it should not have been – the transmission of legacies is not unidirectional. Sean, for example, transmitted to me the latent wonder of the stack of haybales. This strikes me as significant for our consideration of the relations of legacy and posterity, especially in a world so rapidly changing. For a generation now exposed to the uniform but imposing sights of large, circular shapes dotting the hayfields, those very figures may, in striking light or against the proper background, be themselves occasions for fresh wonder. Happily, it seems that wonder may emerge whenever the human imagination, if its freshness and individuality be unimpaired, encounters a natural object. As William Blake expressed it:

> Great things are done when Men & Mountains meet;
> This is not done by Jostling in the Street.

Thus wonder itself is wondrously unpredictable.

The national and the natural sometimes stand in sharp opposition. What is thought to be good for America is not necessarily good for the environment, and vice versa. However, this tension is reassuringly resolved by the existence of the pumpkin. Can one imagine a more glowing natural embodiment of autumn's bounty than this bright orange product of lengthy, leafy vines? And except, perhaps, for apple pie and the flag, can one think of a more widely recognized national embodiment of America than this denizen of autumn? Celebrated by patriotic poets from James Whitcomb Riley to Carl Sandburg, the national and the natural are reconciled in warm embrace by grace of this fetching fruit of the earth.

Such musings were far from my consciousness when pumpkins first caught my attention as a child. Suddenly visible as the surrounding corn stalks were toppled during harvesting, "orange and tawny gold clusters" did, indeed, "spot the hills with yellow balls" and "light the prairie cornfields" (Sandburg's words). Even when isolated and few in number, they were striking to behold in the rolling fields that stretched for miles, just beyond the railroad bridge near our house on an unpaved street in my Iowa home town.

Quite unforgettable, however, and splendid beyond description, was their mass assemblage each autumn at Pumpkin Center, Missouri. Not incorporated and too tiny to receive even a pinpoint on a map, Pumpkin Center was physically nondescript: a few large, tin-sided, tin-roofed sheds, some trampled, dusty fields in between, with a filling station and a sprinkling of houses nearby. Its cartographic nonexistence, however, did not preclude its being a pilgrimage center for me in my youth. On a highway not far from a rail line, it was the receiving station for tens of thousands of pumpkins produced annually in the favorable growing conditions of northwestern Missouri's Nodaway County. At high season, out they poured from haywagons, pickup trucks, cattle carriers and flat beds, awaiting shipment to their final destinations. Spread on the ground nearly as far as a child's eye could see, that vast carpet of yellow and orange shimmered even in clouds and rain; in full sunlight, the brightness and the brilliance were almost more than my tender eyes could tolerate. Although a good hundred miles from our home, now in Des Moines, my father managed to take me at least once each autumn to see that wondrous sight, and it has remained aglow in my memory through all the passing decades.

How to share that sight? How to transmit that wonder? Although not formulated in words, it may have been my unconscious effort to answer such a question that set loose a rollicking stream of associations one bright autumn day while I was at temple. Jack O'Lantern . . . hmm, why not Jacob Lantern? And why should that golden glow be confined to doorsteps and house windows? Why not adorn the altar of the temple as well with the luminosity of a Jacob/Jack O'Lantern, truly an inspired conflate of light and vegetation? As for timing, late in the harvest season felt appropriate, with declining hours of daylight, and night arriving earlier and earlier. Ah-ha, the last Friday night service of October would directly precede the weekend termination of Daylight Savings Time; and immediately after, darkness would invade mid-afternoon and vanquish the light well before evening. And if some of the mysterious aura of Halloween were also to hover, what harm could there be in that? The return of the ancestral spirits at the end of the harvest season is also attested in Jewish tradition by the ceremony of *ushpizin*, our invitation to the spirits of Biblical figures to join us in the *sukkah*, the harvest hut prescribed in Biblical tradition.

An announcement in our Temple Emanuel bulletin invited members to bring appropriately carved pumpkins to grace the altar the last Friday night in October; at the service, candles would be provided for the Jacob Lanterns, that their glow enhance and illuminate our own Sabbath worship. Among the distinguishing features of this service were appropriate selections of poetry, special music, and a period of meditative darkness during which the only illumination was the massed light of the Jacob Lanterns; the reactions of the worshippers, old as well as young, were immediately positive. Over the years, attendance steadily increased, with more than fifty pumpkins annually present along with twice that number of worshippers! In a small congregation of fewer than a hundred families, where the usual number attending Friday evenings was around twenty-five, this response was quite extraordinary.

How might it be explained? There are probably many elements at work: the novelty, the reawakening of the child in all of us, the invitation to creativity in carving and decorating the pumpkins, the simple enjoyment of these innocent delights, the awe-engendering darkness suffused by streams of golden light. Each of these contributes, I suspect, to the popularity of this annual service. But at the heart of it, I am convinced, is that dashing, decorative, natural image of growth, fruition, sunlight and ripening, the eye-engaging, mystery-evoking, nourishment-promising pumpkin. How we hunger spiritually for connection with the earth! And when such fare is offered, great is the response.

But is this "environmental education," one might ask? The question is appropriate, the answer only tentative. It seems to me, however, that fascination with what comes from the earth and appreciation of its wonder do incline us to work for its preservation. If the presence of pumpkins can excite and delight us, we'll be all the readier to guard earth from harm.

*Personal success with sowing seeds was not part of my childhood ex*perience; amazement and envy of those who succeeded was. In neither of my childhood homes was the garden area hospitable to gardening; planting the seeds and burying them were sadly indistinguishable operations. But how they sprouted, thrived, and towered in the nearby corn fields and sunnier-sited home gardens! What secrets did those planters possess that were denied me? Not only seeds but the conditions of their growth were impenetrable mysteries in my childhood.

Later, of course, I learned some practical answers, and my envy disappeared, but not my wonder at the mystery of seeds. Despite my increasing knowledge of successful cultivation, the sight of seeds germinating and bursting through the soil has never lost its excitement. A brief poem, "Fueled," by Marcie Hans from the 1960s expresses it nicely:

> Fueled by a million man-made wings of fire
> the rocket tore a tunnel through the sky
> and everybody cheered.
> Fueled
> only by a thought from God
> the seedling
> urged its way
> through the thickness of black
> and as it pierced
> the heavy ceiling of the soil
> and launched itself
> up into outer space
> no
> one
> even
> clapped.

How to share this legacy and transmit some of this excitement? One autumn day during Sukkot, the Festival of Booths – the great harvest celebration dating from Biblical times and still observed in Jewish tradition – an idea came to me. The Biblical holidays at autumn and spring are agriculturally connected by autumnal planting and spring reaping. The major grape and produce harvest at Sukkot occurs just before the rainy season, and is immediately followed by the fall sowing of winter barley and wheat typical of the Mediterranean basin; the spring festivals, Passover and Pentecost, mark the beginning and the culmination of those grain harvests. (Cf. Exodus 23:14-18 and 34:18, 22; Leviticus 23:4-6, 9-11, 15-16, 33-34, 39-43; Deuteronomy 16:1-17.) During the Passover-to-Pentecost period of seven weeks the following spring, freshly cut grain was raised high each day and waved about in a dance-like offering at the altar.

What, then, if at our temple we were to plant a small patch of winter barley or rye or wheat during the harvest celebration? The following spring we would have the wintered-over grain steadily developing, and starting with Passover, before each Friday evening service we could cut a handful to lift high and wave at that part in the service where the particular day is numbered.

And so the following year, just before Sukkot began, we dug up a small patch of the lawn that was directly in front of the south-facing wall of the temple building. On the intermediate Sunday of the holiday, class by class the children of our religious school came out of doors to wave ceremonially the palm frond, willow, myrtle and citron prescribed in Leviticus; they ate grapes and drank cider in the *sukkah* (the autumnal harvest booth); then they walked in ritual procession to the small patch of prepared soil, and each one broadcast a handful of the wheat or rye or barley grains, thus sowing the future harvest. The kids loved it, and without weighty words a message was also delivered: no planting, no harvest; without some human tending, the earth will not provide the bounty upon which our lives depend.

The grain germinated from the residual summer warmth of the soil, but the onset of winter soon arrested any further growth. Then, as the Sun climbed higher with the approach of spring, the grain resumed its growth, growth all the more rapid because the south-facing stone wall absorbed the heat of the Sun. Adults as well as children regularly checked outside to see how the grain was growing, and the inherent drama of winter dormancy to spring revival was newly appreciated by all. Each week we cut some of this developing grain for the Friday evening service, then waved it ceremonially as we proclaimed the number of that particular day. We kept the sheaves from the previous weeks, and so the new growth was easily seen. Some weeks, chilly and rainy, there would be little visible increase; on sunny weeks the stalks seemed to add height as if propelled by a rocket. And each week everyone could see the development of the grain as the spikelets filled out and grew plump. Thus harvest became seedtime, seedtime harvest, and the wonder of the seed was powerfully experienced.

This, in turn, presented new opportunities for environmental education and awareness. An obvious issue to explore was the dangerous decline and disappearance of seed varieties, with the attendant threats to agriculture. An irresistible reaction to explore was the excitement at the discovery of the seed. In the Creation story of Genesis, Chapter 1, verses 11-12 speak of the earth putting forth "vegetation: plants yielding seed, and fruit trees of every kind on earth that bear fruit with the seed in it." What the English translation does not convey is that in those two short verses, the root form of "seed" occurs six times; "yielding seed" is literally to be rendered, "seeding seed" *(mazria zera)*. It is as if the discoverer of the power of the seed to reproduce cannot stop exclaiming in wonder, *seed, seed, seed!*

These were some of the childhood treasures that I wanted to bequeath to posterity. Obviously, this legacy is not subject to inheritance taxes; it does, however, require appropriate and effective transmission, and this can be rather taxing if also joyous. The best ways to achieve the desired transmission are not obvious. How much doing, how much saying, how much showing, how much telling? But even if the process of transmission is challenging, each opportunity is irresistibly inviting, deeply rewarding, and leads us to an occasion of wonder, an opportunity for amazement at the marvels surrounding us.

It is the quality of this encounter which ultimately validates our work in the world. Rabbi Abraham Joshua Heschel, late professor of ethics and mysticism at the Jewish Theological Seminary, expressed it in these words: "As civilization advances, the sense of wonder declines. Such decline is an alarming symptom of our state of mind. Mankind will not perish for want of information, but only for want of appreciation."

Or as the West Coast poet of the 1950s, Lawrence Ferlinghetti, repeatedly cried out in his short poem, "I Am Waiting" (in *A Coney Island of the Mind*):

> and I am perpetually awaiting
> a rebirth of wonder . . .
> a rebirth of wonder . . .
> and I am awaiting
> perpetually and forever
> a renaissance of wonder

Is it not the burden and blessing, the challenge and calling, of environmental education to serve as midwife for this rebirth of wonder?

From *Whole Terrain, Reflective Environmental Practice,*

Part Two

Issues of War, Peace, and Community

Not by military might, and not by destructive violence,
But by My Spirit, says God, Commander of the Heavenly Legions.
—Zechariah 4:6

War and the Jewish Tradition

"Just Wars" and the Issue of Conscience

In this 1968 essay, written smack in the middle of the Vietnam War, Rabbi Gendler, a pacifist for much of his adult life, explores Jewish teachings about the limits placed on military violence and the grounds for conscientious objection to war.

At the outset, two source-problems of some seriousness confront any Jewish approach to the issues of "just war" doctrine, individual conscience, and selective conscientious objection.

The first of these problems Professor Julius Kravetz has called (in *CCAR Journal*, 1968), an "embarrassment of poverty." For reasons easily enough understood, there is not great corpus of Biblical and rabbinic legislation dealing directly with these issues. Augustine and Aquinas may have fancied that their findings about just and unjust wars would have application to the body politic of Christendom, represented by the Christian kings. The rabbinic fathers had no such hopes that Roman emperors would seek their religious findings, nor could Maimonides and other Jewish medieval scholars expect their halakhic deliverances to be heeded by regnant powers. Naturally, then, there was no felt urgency to formulate anything so directive of the use of power as a fully elaborated "just war" doctrine, and the elements we do have are somewhat incomplete and unsystematic. As for the Biblical material, it, too, is somewhat limited in extent, and its locus classicus in Deuteronomy places it, documentarily at least, well after the period of the Conquest of the Land. Nevertheless, as I will indicate, there are quite valuable elements in both the Biblical and rabbinic material, however limited in quantity and comprehensiveness this material may be.

The second problem is the application of such source material as we have to present circumstances. The social, political, religious, and human context of the material differs considerably from both our present self-understanding and our present situations, and these differences must be kept clearly in mind. Even within the same historical and social setting, the application of rules to cases is often difficult, as the workings of any legal system indicate. When there are additional differences, the difficulties are compounded.

These two source problems do not, of course, dictate that the grave issues confronting us should be avoided, nor do they render the source material inapplicable. They do, however, urge upon us a constant appreciation that, combined with the felt sense of the present urgency of the issue, may yield certain findings which are both fair to the sources and relevant to our own times.

One last introductory caution: The following material, while hopefully an accurate presentation of some major teachings of the Jewish tradition in these areas, does not pretend to be comprehensive. A comprehensive treatment would necessarily extend far beyond the limits of an essay, developing many points that are only alluded to here.

1. BIBLICAL MATERIAL

Most discussions of the Biblical material focus on the specific regulations of Deuteronomy 20, and these will be considered. However, without some preliminary indication of the variety of communal contexts within which armies were mobilized in Biblical times, there is great danger that invalid analogies will be drawn with our own times. To reduce this danger, a brief summary of some parts of Roland de Vaux's fine survey of Israelite Military Institutions will be helpful.[1]

• *Recruitment of fighting men*: Details of the nomadic period are scanty, but it seems reasonable to assume that "there is no distinction between the army and the people." By the period of the Judges, however, there is more information, some of it of particular relevance for us. Most significant are the following findings:

a. During this period, individual tribes and families decided within their own intimate groupings whether or not to respond to the general call to arms. "During the period of the Judges," writes de Vaux, "the response to these appeals depended on each group, which made its own decision. The Song of Deborah twice insists on this freedom to fight or not to fight (Judges 5:2 and 9), and expresses nothing stronger than reproach or regret

---

1. Roland de Vaux, *Ancient Israel: Its Life and Institutions* (New York: McGraw-Hill, 1961), especially pp. 213-267.

about the tribes which chose to stand aside (Judges 5:15-17)."

b. "The units of the army were based on those of society. The unit was the clan (*mishpakhah*) . . ."

c. The voluntarism extended to individuals within the clan and tribal groups. "Gideon's action against the Midianites is even more typical; of the 32,000 men who answered his call, he sent home all who had no heart to fight, and only 10,000 remained; of these, he chose 300 . . ."

d. "From time to time, two enemy forces would agree to settle the issue by single combat."

e. "[I]t must not be forgotten, even now, that the warriors of Israel were upheld by their firm belief that Yahweh fought with them and that he could grant them victory whatever the odds against them (I Samuel 14:6; 17:47)."

This period of small group autonomy and individual voluntarism was succeeded by a period of professional armies with mercenaries and chariotry, "the work of the first kings of Israel," and still later (and at times simultaneously) by conscript labor forces and conscript armies as well.

These latter developments were ambivalently regarded within the Biblical literature. On the one hand there is a stream of thought distinctly favorable to the monarchy (I Samuel 9 and 11, praise of the Davidic dynasty, etc.). On the other hand, there is a strong current severely critical of the monarchy and its implications for the life of the people, as in I Samuel 8:4-18:

> Then all the elders of Israel gathered together and came to Samuel at Ramah, and they said to him, "Consider, you have become old and your sons do not follow in your footsteps. Now set up for us a king to judge us like all the nations."
>
> But the thing was evil in the sight of Samuel, when they said, "Give us a king to judge us."
>
> Nevertheless Samuel prayed earnestly unto the LORD; and the LORD said to Samuel, "Listen to the voice of the people according to all that they say to you; for they have not rejected you, but they have rejected me from being king over them. Like all the deeds which they have done to me from the day I brought them up from Egypt even to this day, inasmuch as they have forsaken me and served other gods, so they are also doing to you. Now therefore listen to their utterance, expect that you shall certainly warn them, and show them the procedure of the king who shall reign over them."
>
> Then Samuel told all the words of the LORD to the people who were asking of him a king; and he said, "This will be the procedure of the king who shall

reign over you: he will take your sons and appoint them for himself for his chariots and for his horsemen; and they shall run before his chariots; and he will appoint for himself commanders of thousands and commanders of hundreds, and some to do his plowing and to reap his harvests and make his implements of war and equipment of his chariots. He will take your daughters for perfumers, for cooks, and for bakers. He will take the best of your fields and your vineyards and your olive orchards, and give them to his servants. He will take the tenth of your grain crops and of your vineyards and give it to his eunuchs and to his servants. He will take your male and female slaves, and the best of your cattle and your asses, and make use of them for his work. He will take a tenth of your flocks; and you yourselves will become his slaves. Then you will cry out on that day because of your king whom you will have chosen for yourselves; but the LORD will not answer you on that day."

The legislation restricting the king in Deuteronomy 17:14-20, and passages from Hosea (7:3-7, 8:4, 13:9-11) reveal the continuation of suspicion and hostility toward the king as divine surrogate and usurper. In this latter respect, the attitude toward the census of the people for military purposes is especially significant (II Samuel 24:1-10):

> Now the LORD was again angered against Israel, and he incited David against them, saying, "Go number Israel and Judah!"
>
> So the king said to Joab and the commanders of the army which was with him, "Go about now throughout all the tribes of Israel, from Dan even to Beersheba, and take a census of the people that I may know the number of the people."
>
> Joab said to the king, "May the LORD your God add to the people a hundred times as many as they are, while the eyes of my lord the king look on! But why does my lord the king take delight in this thing?'
>
> But the word of the king prevailed over Joab and the commanders of the army. Therefore Joab and the commanders of the army went out from the king's presence to take the census of the people of Israel. They crossed the Jordan and started from Aroer, and from the city that is in the midst of the torrent valley, toward Gad and on to Jazer. Then they came to Gilead and to the land of Hittites, to Kadesh; and they came to Dan, and from Dan they went around to Sidon, and came to the fortress of Tyre and all the cities of the Hivvites, and of the Canaanites; and they went forth to the Negeb of Judah at Beersheba. When they had gone about through the whole land they came to Jerusalem at the end of nine months and twenty days; and Joab gave the number of the census of the people to the king, and Israel consisted of eight hundred thousand able-bodied men who drew sword, and the men of Judah were five hundred thousand.

> But David's conscience smote him after he had numbered the people. Then David said to the LORD, "I have sinned exceedingly in what I have done. But now, O LORD, take away, I pray thee, the iniquity of thy servant, for I have done very foolishly."

In the words of de Vaux: "Thus the tradition of a people under arms persisted, but the mass response to a call from a leader inspired by God had given place to mobilization organized by the royal administration. The first indication of this development can be seen as early as David's reign: his census had a military purpose and was equivalent to drawing up a register for conscription, but this step was condemned as an abandonment of the rules of a holy war, and a profanation (cf. verses 3 and 10)."

- *Varieties of Biblical wars*: Scholarly classifications of Biblical wars tend to coincide. Thus Kaufmann distinguishes three main types: wars of conquest, wars of liberation, and wars of empire, with one intermediate type, wars of tribute.[2] De Vaux's division into wars of conquest, defensive wars, and wars of expansion, is essentially the same. The basic Biblical legislative differentiation is, however, confined to the distinction between wars with "towns that lie very far from you" and wars with "towns that belong to nations hereabout," as in Deuteronomy 20:10-18:

> When you invest a city, you must offer it terms of peace. If it agrees to make peace with you, and surrenders to you, then all the people to be found in it shall become forced laborers for you, and serve you. But if it will not make peace with you, but wages war with you, you are to besiege it, and when the LORD your God delivers it up to you, you must put every male in it to the sword; but the women and children and livestock and everything that is in the city, that is, all its spoil, you may take as your booty, and yourselves use the spoil of your enemies which the LORD your God gives you. So shall you treat all the cities that are very far away from you, that do not belong to the cities of the nations here. However, in the cities of the peoples here, which the LORD your God is giving you as a heritage, you must not spare a living soul; but you must be sure to exterminate them, Hittites, Amorites, Canaanites, Perizzites, Hivvites, and Jebusites, as the LORD your God commanded you, so that they may not teach you to imitate all the abominable practices that they have carried on for their gods, and so sin against the LORD your God.

---

2. Yehezkel Kaufmann, "Traditions Concerning Early Israelite History in Canaan," pp. 304-309, in *Scripta Hierosolymitana, Volume VIII*. Jerusalem, 1961.

The primary characteristics of wars of conquest, the *herem*, "the anathema carried out on the vanquished enemy and his goods," was understood to be by the express command of God, applied only to the "seven nations" inhabiting the promised land (cf. Deuteronomy 7:2), and characterized these wars only and no others. "The characterized quality of the wars of conquest," writes Kaufmann, "is that they are exclusively Canaanite . . . Ammon, Moab, Edom, and Aram, whose lands were never promised to Israel, are excluded from these wars" (p. 304). From the Biblical text itself it is clear that the *herem*, the total destruction of persons and goods, is limited in application to a single category of conflict: the wars of conquest of the promised land. Any additional instances, such as the total destruction of the Amalekites, were exceptions and understood to be only at the direct instigation of God, not by inferential human discretion.

There is one other characteristic, common to all the varieties of Biblical wars, which requires some clarification: the holy or sacred character of the wars. De Vaux uses the term "holy war," a term which appears to suggest what we might designate an ideological conflict, but de Vaux is emphatic in rejecting such an identification. To attempt to spread one's faith by force of arms was utterly foreign to Israel, and until the time of Maccabees the concept of a war of religion had not appeared. "Israel did not fight for its faith, but for its existence." War was indeed "a sacred action, with its own particular ideology and rites," but so were many other actions and activities, and the religious character of Biblical war was quite distinct from those distortions that we designate as medieval religious or modern ideological "crusades." De Vaux summarizes the meaning of this in the following words: "This is the principal fact: it was Yahweh who fought for Israel, not Israel which fought for its God. The holy war, in Israel, was not a war of religion."

The sacred character of Biblical war was reflected in such acts as sacrifices prior to marching to battle (I Samuel 7:9; 13:9, 12), the consultation with Yahweh by means of the *Urim* and *Tumim* oracles (I Samuel 23:9 f.; 30:7 f.), requirements of ritual cleanliness for combatants (Joshua 3:4) and for the camp (Deuteronomy 23:10-15), and the frequent presence of the Ark (Numbers 10:35-36).

Most important for our considerations, however, are the implications for the combatants of the sacred character of Biblical war. "Faith," writes De Vaux, "was an indispensable condition: they had to have faith and to be without fear (Joshua 8:1, 10:8, 25). Those who were afraid did not have the necessary religious dispositions and were to be sent away (Judges 7:3; cf. Deuteronomy 20:8, where the dismissal of such men is explained by a psychological reason, which was not the original reason for the custom)."

With the establishment of the monarchy, ". . . this strictly sacred character of war disappeared with the advent of the monarchy and the establishment of a professional army. It is no longer Yahweh who marches ahead of his people to fight the Wars of Yahweh, but the king who leads his people out and fights its wars (I Sam. 8:20). The combatants are no longer warriors who volunteer to fight, but professionals in the pay of the king, or conscripts recruited by his officials."

De Vaux traces this "profanation" of war as it became the state's concern; adduces prophetic retentions of the original idea which serve as the bases for criticism of the later secular wars of the Jewish state; and analyzes the reappearance of certain elements of the holy war in the Maccabees (which do not, however, make theirs a holy war in the older sense, but rather a "war of religion": "The Maccabees and their men are not inspired by God; God did not order the war and he does not intervene directly in it"). He makes very clear, in short, the non-transferable nature of the "holy war" and so enables us to guard against that fearful tendency to identify our own impulses and ideologies with the sacred as such.

- *Specific Biblical regulations*: The major remaining, though sketchy, Biblical regulations concerning the waging of war find their classic formulation in Deuteronomy 20:

> When you go out to battle against your enemies, and see horses, and chariots, forces greater than your own, you must not be afraid of them; for the LORD your God who brought you up from the land of Egypt is on your side. When you are on the eve of a battle, a priest must come up and speak to the people. He shall say to them, "Listen, O Israel; today you are on the eve of a battle against your enemies; do not be faint-hearted, nor afraid, nor alarmed, nor stand in dread of them; for the LORD your God is going with you, to fight for you against your enemies and give you the victory." Then the officers shall say to the people, "Whoever has built a new house, but has not dedicated it, may leave and return home lest he die in the battle, and another dedicate it. Whoever has planted a vineyard, but has not had the use of it, may leave and return home, lest he die in the battle, and another get the use of it. Whoever has betrothed a wife, but has not married her, may leave and return home, lest he die in the battle and another marry her." The officers shall say further to the people, "Whoever is afraid and faint-hearted must leave and return home, so that his fellows may not become faint-hearted like him." As soon as the

officers have finished addressing the people, the army commanders shall place themselves at the head of the people (20:10-18).

> When you have to besiege a city a long time in your war on it in order to capture it, you must not destroy its trees by taking an ax to them, because you can eat their fruit; you must not cut them down; for are trees in the field men to be besieged by you? It is only trees which you know are not fruit trees that you may destroy and cut down for the construction of siegeworks against the city that is waging war with you, until it is razed. (20:19-20)

Of these provisions, those respecting the morale functions of the priest and the officers can be well understood in the light of de Vaux's discussion of the role of faith in the rallying of men to combat. One also notes the necessity of individual consent, as it were (verse 8), a provision highly significant for our own considerations.

In the case of siege warfare outside the Promised Land, peace terms must first be offered, and if the population accepts, it may be subjected to forced labor but to nothing else (verses 10-11, cited above). If it refuses, the possibilities are specified in verses 12-15, including the execution of the males and appropriation of the remaining persons and property.

The *herem* provisions of verses 16-18 have already been discussed above, leaving two final elements for comment: rules of exemption (verses 5-7) and limitations on destruction (verses 19-20). In both cases, the penetrating comments of Johannes Pedersen are especially illuminating.[3]

With respect to personal exemptions or deferments, Pedersen suggests that the following profound human consideration is at work: " . . . the army should only admit to its ranks men who can be entirely merged in the whole and act as part of it. In the military laws of Deuteronomy we find the following passage (verses 5-7). In these tree laws we find the same considerate spirit which prevails in many of the laws of Deuteronomy and which is generally characterized by the honorable name 'humane.' A close inspection will show, however, that the laws are not considering casual instances, but something greater and more profound. In all three cases a man has started a new, important undertaking without having finished it yet. In such a case something has been created, which is greater than the man himself, a new totality has come into existence. To make a breach in

---

3. Johannes Pederson, *Israel: Its Life and Culture, Vol. III-IV* (Oxford University Press, London, 1959).

his prematurely, that is to say, before it has attained maturity or has been finished, involves a serious risk of sin. This risk must be avoided for the sake of the cause itself, and the man who came to the army after committing such a breach might mean a danger much more than a help in the psychic whole constituted by the army" (pp. 9-10).

As for the law requiring that the enemy's trees be spared to some extent, Pedersen writes: "Here there is a demand for the moderation characteristic of the old time. Life is to be respected, it must not be entirely destroyed ... Reduction is allowed, but not extermination" (pp. 23, 24).

Or in the beautiful summary of this spirit by Isaiah (45:18):

> ... the Lord Who created the heavens
> (He is God!),
> Who formed the earth and made it
> (He established it),
> He did not create it a wasteland,
> He formed it to be inhabited!

2. RABBINIC MATERIAL

As I have noted, one does not find ready-at-hand a fully developed rabbinic formulation of a "just war" doctrine, and the problem of the application is further increased by the fact that much of the legislation presupposes the existence of a divinely established state in the Holy Land. Further, since such a state was regarded as divinely ordained, it is especially perilous to extrapolate from permissions granted it to any other situation.

Neither does one find a systematic elaboration of the individual moral considerations for determining individual participation in any given conflict. Yet there is, scattered throughout the classical rabbinic writings, significant teachings relating to these questions. Much of it is Biblically based, though it often goes beyond the Biblical texts, sometimes expanding, sometimes modifying, sometimes applying them. I will attempt to show that some selections from these teachings are pertinent to the specific issues confronting us.

The traditional rabbinic classification of wars distinguishes three types: *milhemet hovah* (obligatory), *milhemet mitzvah* (mandatory), and *milhemet reshut* (discretionary) (Talmud Sotah 44b). For almost all practical purposes, however, the first two categories are one, leaving in effect the distinction between mandatory and discretionary wars (*mitzvah* and *reshut*).

Which specific wars fall into these categories? Although there are some points at issue, it is widely agreed among rabbinic authorities that man-datory wars obtained in only two or possibly three Biblical instances: a) Joshua's war of conquest against the seven Canaanite nations (directly commanded by God); b) the campaign against Amalek (directly commanded by God); c) a war of clear and immediate defense against an attack already launched (including by Maimonides but not classical rabbinic).[4]

Instances of discretionary war (*reshut*) include the following: a) expanding the boundaries (perhaps to strengthen one's strategic position); b) increasing one's power or prestige.[5] In the opinion of all, such wars anticipatory of future power-political problems are at best discretionary (*reshut*), even in the case of the divinely ordained state, and thus subject to the checks and limitations to be indicated below.

Especially significant with respect to classification is one particular case, that of "preventive" or "preemptive" attack. In the classic statement of the issue in the Talmud, Raba, discussing a difference of opinion between the Rabbis and R. Judah, says the following (Sotah 44b):

> The wars waged by Joshua to conquer Canaan were mandatory (*mitzvah*) in the opinion of all; the wars waged by the House of David for territorial expansion were discretionary (*reshut*) in the opinion of all; where they differ is with regard to wars against heathens so that these should not march against them. One calls them mandatory (*mitzvah*) and the other discretionary (*reshut*) . . .

Or, in the wording of the Talmud Jerushalmi: "Rabbi Judah designated discretionary (*reshut*) a war in which we attacked them, and obligatory (*hovah*) a war in which they attacked us."

In short, the majority opinion of Talmudic thinking is that a war "preemptive of future danger . . . is at best a *milhemet reshut*."[6]

In evaluating these classifications, it is well to keep in mind that they are largely theoretical findings after the fact, and further that subsequent authoritative opinions tend to reduce severely the range of "discretion" in the case of *milhemet reshut*. Thus Maimonides forbids the waging of

---

4. Cf. Maimonides *Code*, "Laws Concerning Kings and Wars," Chapter 5, Law 1.

5. *Ibid.*

6. Cf. the sensitive article by Prof. Irving Greenberg of Yeshiva University on "Judaism and the Dilemmas of War," in *Judaism and World Peace: Focus Viet Nam* (Synagogue Council of America, New York, NY).

war against any nation before peace offers are made to it, and insists that even in the case of a supposed *milhemet mitzvah* (mandatory war), "if the inhabitants make peace, accept the seven Noahide commandments, and submit to certain conditions of taxation and service, one may not kill a single person."[7]

There is also evident among Jewish authorities a strong tendency to emphasize limitations on the so-called "discretionary" wars. Thus Rabbi David S. Shapiro, in a learned and well-documented essay, states the following:

> The category of *milhemet reshut* includes wars against the avowed enemies of Israel, nations that flagrantly violate the Seven Commandments and recognize no international obligations. This kind of war may be declared only after the *sanhedrin* of seventy-one, the highest tribunal in Israel, the king of Israel, and the high-priest through the *Urim* and *Tumim* have given their approval. Its purpose may not be conquest, plunder, or destruction. It may be waged only for the protection of Israel and for the sanctification of the name of God, that is the imposition of the Seven Commandments.
>
> . . . No war may be waged against a nation that has not attacked Israel, or that lives up to the fundamental of the Universal Religion. Even Edom, Ammon, and Moab, who had throughout their history displayed hostility to Israel, were not to be attacked, not to speak of those nations who were not bellicose. It would seem that the *milhemet reshut* was limited by the ideal boundaries of the Holy Land.[8]

And the eminent Israeli halakhist, Rabbi Shelomo Yosef Zavin, suggests that "in fact a war of attack, though designated a *milhemet reshut* (discretionary war), is forbidden to the nations of the world."[9]

With this caution in mind, it will now be of value to consider briefly the traditional significance of these distinctions among wars. In the three cases of *milhemet mitzvah*, it is the rabbinic view that such wars may be initiated by the king without his consulting the Court of Seventy-One, that the claim of conscription applies to all, even those specifically exempted by the provisions in Deuteronomy 20:8 and 24:5, and that all may be coerced to participate. It is interesting (and ironic) that Maimonides takes those critical threats in I Samuel, cited above, and reads them as sanctions for such

---

7. Maimonides, *op. cit.*, Ch. 6, Law 1.

8. David S. Shapiro, "The Jewish Attitude Towards War and Peace," in Leo Jung, ed., *Israel of Tomorrow* (N.Y., 1946), p. 237.

9. Rabbi Shelomo Yosef Zavin: L'or Hahalacha (Tel Aviv, 5717), p. 17.

acts by the ruling power!

On the other hand, in instances of discretionary wars (*reshut*), it is rabbinic opinion that the king may not involve the people without the sanction of the Court of Seventy-One and of the *Urim* and *Tumim* consulted by the high priest, and that the various exemptions do indeed apply. While reducing in some respects the application of Biblical exemptions, the rabbinic authorities in other respects extend them. Relying on Deuteronomy 24:5, "When a man is newly married, he is not to go out with the army, nor be counted with it for any duty; he is to be free at home for one year, to enjoy himself with his wife whom he has married," the rabbis apply it as follows:

> The following do not move from their place (to join the army and then claim exemption): He who built a new house and dedicated it, planted a vineyard and uses its fruit, married his betrothed, or took home to his brother's childless widow . . . These do not even supply water or food or repair the roads (for the army).
>
> Mishnah Sotah 8:4

The exemption in such cases is thus total.

We further note in passing that the provision of *rakh levav* ("tender of heart") in all opinions applies to all cases of discretionary war, a fact of some import since no war today can be regarded as either *hovah* or *mitzvah*.[10]

Other elements of rabbinic teachings are relevant to our current considerations – for example, attempts to limit destruction of resources during war. Among the provisions from the classical rabbinic tradition attempting to limit the destructive consequences of war, the following are clearly relevant to our own age:

> It is forbidden to cut down fruit-bearing trees outside a (besieged) city,

---

10. Such a statement may appear doubtful today given the strong feelings concerning the value, perhaps even the sanctity, of the reestablished State of Israel. Without entering into the question of any of the specific wars involving the modern State of Israel, it is surely clear that in the strict sense of the terms they cannot be regarded as anything more than *reshut*. As recently as 1946, before the establishment of the State of Israel, Rabbi Shapiro could plainly state: "Since the destruction of its state, Israel can no longer wage wars, for its war-declaring agencies are no longer in operation. All attempts at armed reconquest of the Holy Land are expressly forbidden. God has imposed an oath upon Israel to that effect. The Land of Israel will be restored to its people in God's own good time" (*op. cit., ibid*). It must also be remembered that so inspired a teacher as Jeremiah raised serious questions about particular wars involving the ancient Jewish State, that very State established by Divine edict according to the Biblical tradition. To insist that all wars today are at most *reshut* is simply to insist that every single one must be subject to serious moral evaluation, and that no claims of sanctity can serve to exempt any conflict whatsoever from this moral judgment.

nor may a water channel by deflected from them so that they whither, as it is said: "Though shalt not destroy the trees thereof" (Deuteronomy 20:19). Whoever cuts down a fruit-bearing tree is flogged. This penalty is imposed not only for cutting it down during a siege; whenever a fruit-yielding tree is cut down with destructive intent, flogging is incurred. It may be cut down, however, if it cases damage to other trees or to a field belonging to another man or if its value for other purposes is greater (than that of the fruit it produces). The law forbids only wanton destruction.

Maimonides Code, "Laws of Kings and Wars," Chapter 6, Law 8

Not only one who cuts down (fruit-producing) trees, but also one who smashes household goods, tears clothes, demolishes a building, stops up a spring, or destroys articles of food with destructive intent, transgresses the command "Thou shalt not destroy." He is not flogged, but is administered a disciplinary beating imposed by the Rabbis.

Ibid., Law 10

It was after these things and this loyalty [cf. Hezekiah], that Sennacherib, king of Assyria, came and invaded Judah, and besieged the fortified cities and expected to take them. When Hezekiah saw that Sennacherib had come determined to attack Jerusalem, he decided in council with his princes and his leading men to stop the water of the fountains that were outside the city, and they helped him. Indeed a great crowd of people collected and stopped up all the fountains and the torrent that coursed through the midst of the land, saying, "Why should the kings of Assyria come and find abundant water?"

II Chronicles 32:1-4

It was Hezekiah who stopped the upper springs of Gihon and directed the waters straight down on the west side of the city of David.

II Chronicles 32:30

Our Rabbis taught: Six things King Hezekiah did; in three they (the Sages) agreed with him, and in three they did not agree with him . . . and he closed up the waters of Upper Gihon, and they did not agree with him . . ."

Pesahim 56a

Other teachings are directly applicable to traditional attempts to limit injury of persons during war. The rabbinic tendency to modify the Biblical meaning of certain texts toward what we might designate "humane ends" was noted above with Maimonides' insistence that even the "seven nations" were first to be offered peace rather than *herem*, and that such acceptance meant that "not one person was then to be slain." The attempt to prevent unnecessary injuries and deaths during conflict, especially among noncombatants, is expressed in a number of rabbinic rulings:

> When siege is laid to a city for the purpose of capture, it may not be surrounded on all four sides but only on three in order to give an opportunity for escape to those who would flee to save their lives, as it is said: And they warred against Midian, as the Lord commanded Moses (Num. 31:7). It has been learned by tradition that that was instruction given to Moses.
> *Maimonides, op. cit., Ch. 6, Law 7*

> One should not sell them (gentiles, during their festivals) bears, lions, or anything which may injure the many.
> *Mishnah Avodah Zarah 1:7*

> The reason is because they may injure the many.
> *Talmud Avodah Zarah 16 a,b*

Maimonides spells out more fully the implications of this dictum: "It is forbidden," he writes, "to sell to idolaters any weapons of war. Neither may one sharpen their weapons nor make available to them knives, chains, barbed chains, bears, lions, or anything which might cause widespread injury. One may sell to them shields or shutters which are purely defensive" (Maimonides Code, "Laws of Murder and Defense," Ch. 12, Law 12).

One notices, incidentally, that the nature of the weapons themselves, and not the purported intentions of their users, determines the prohibitions!

In further treating this provision, Maimonides extends the principle to include indirect supplying of such material, and makes clear that the prohibition applies to Jewish brigands as well: "That which is prohibited for sale to idolaters is also prohibited for sale to Jews who are suspected of then selling such materials to idolaters. Likewise, it is forbidden to sell such weapons to Jewish brigands (*listim*)" (Maimonides Code, "Law of Idolatry," Ch. 9, Law 8).

Zavin, relying on Maimonides, states the following principle as well: "In all cases of *milhemet reshut* (discretionary war), it is forbidden to kill women and children" (Zavin, op. cit., p. 44).

There is no developed rabbinic doctrine on the scale or dimensions of any given conflict, although some of the previously indicated limitations suggest that in practice any war had to be rigorously bounded. Two further remarks on this specific question should be cited, however: 1) "R. Eleazar said: Every war which is waged with more than sixty thousand men is waged in disorder (*milhemet irbuviah*, a chaotic war)" (Song of Songs Rabbah, IV, 4). 2) "Samuel said: A government which kills up to one out of six (by going to war) is not punished . . ." (Talmud Shevuoth 35b) – implying, of course, that beyond this such a government is liable to punishment. From Rashi's comment, this would seem to apply to those conscripted by the king, and would refer to the casualty rate among the soldiers themselves. From the current text reading, however, it would appear to apply to the nations attacked. In either case, however, it clearly excludes a war of "attrition" or a war of mutual extirpation.

Rabbi Immanuel Jakobovits, addressing himself to the issue in modern terms, states emphatically:

> A major source in the Torah for the law of self-defense is the provision exonerating from guilt a potential victim of robbery with possible violence if in self-defense he struck down and, if necessary, even killed the attacker before he committed any crime (Ex. 22:1). Hence, in the words of the rabbis, 'if a man comes to slay you, forestall by slaying him!' (Rashi; Sanhedrin 72a). Now this law confers the right of self-defense only if the victim will thereby forestall the anticipated attack and save his own life at the expense of the aggressor's. But the defender would certainly not be entitled to frustrate the attack if this could be done only at the cost of both lives; for instance, by blowing up the house in which he and the robber encounter each other. Presumably the victim would then have to submit to the robbery and even to death by violence at the hands of the attacker rather than take 'preventive' action which would be sure to cause two deaths.
>
> In view of this vital limitation of the law of self-defense, it would appear that a defensive war likely endanger the survival of the attacking and the defending nations alike, if not indeed of the entire human race, can never be justified. On the assumption, then, that the choice posed by a threatened nuclear attack would be either complete mutual destruction or surrender, only the second alternative may be morally vindicated.[11]

Besides such regulations dealing with the body politics and its policies, there are a number of rabbinic teachings which deal with considerations of conscience for the individual facing a situation of war. Most significant is the fact that in these life-and-death confrontations, restraint, limitations, and scruples are explicitly affirmed as appropriate. This is so in both individual and collective confrontations.

---

11. In *Tradition: A Journal of Orthodox Jewish Thought*, Vol. 4. No. 2, Spring, 1962, p. 202. Cf. Also the American Jewish Congress paper by Morris Laub: "Maimonides on War and Peace (with Special Application to Vietnam)."

> It has been taught by Rabbi Jonathan ben Saul: If one was pursuing his fellow to slay him, and the pursued could have saved himself by maiming a limb of the pursuer, but instead killed his pursuer, the pursued is subject to execution on that account.
>
> *Sanhedrin 74a*

Especially revealing are the classical rabbinic comments on the anticipation of war between Jacob and Esau, deriving from the following verse in Genesis (32:8): "Then Jacob was greatly afraid and was distressed."

> R. Judah b. R. Ilai said: Are not fear and distress identical? The meaning, however, is that "he was afraid" lest he should be slain, "and was distressed" lest he should slay. For Jacob thought: If he prevails against me, will he not slay me; while if I am stronger than he, will I not slay him?
>
> *Genesis Rabbah 76:2*

Another rabbinic comment ascribes to Jacob the following sentiment: "If he overpowers me, that is bad, and if I overpower him, that is bad!"[12]

There are also two classical statements, referring to the same verse in Genesis, which affirm explicitly that murder (*shefikhut damim*) is a category applicable to armed conflict:

> "And Jacob was greatly afraid and was distressed." One might think that Jacob was literally afraid of Esau, fearing that he might not he able to defeat him; but this is not the case. Why, then, was Jacob afraid of Esau? Because Jacob took seriously the prohibition against murder. And so Jacob reasoned as follows: If I succeed and kill him, behold, I have transgressed the commandment "thou shalt not murder." And if he kills me, woe is my lot! Hence it is written: "And Jacob was greatly afraid and was distressed."[13]

Even more remarkable is the comment of Rabbi Shabetai Bass, compiler of *Sifte Hahamim,* the classic subcommentary on the commentary of Rashi. Bass takes explicit note of the Talmudic permission to defend oneself, yet suggests that murder is still an issue, even in a situation of armed combat!

> . . . Yet one might argue that Jacob surely should have had no qualms about killing Esau, for it states explicitly, "If one come to slay thee, forestall it by slaying him" (Talmud Sanhedrin 72a; Berachot 58a and 62b).

---

12. Lekach Tov, cited in *Torah Shlemah*, edited by M. Kasher, Vol. 6, page 1266, footnote 49.

13. Schechter Genizah Manuscript on an early edition of Midrash Tanhuma, cited in *Torah Shlemah, ibid.*

> Nonetheless, Jacob did indeed have qualms, fearing that in the fray he might kill some of Esau's men, who were not intent on killing Jacob (for only Esau had this intention) but merely fighting against Jacob's men. And even though Esau's men were pursuing Jacob's men, and every person has the right to save the life of the pursued at the cost of the life of the pursuer, nonetheless that provision applies which states: "if the pursued could have been saved by maiming a limb of the pursuer, but instead the rescuer killed the pursuer, the rescuer is liable to capital punishment on that account." Hence Jacob rightly feared lest, in the confusion of the battle, he kill some of Esau's men outright when he might instead have restrained them by merely inflicting injury upon their limbs.[14]

Thus Bass, whose subcommentary Louis Ginsberg describes (in *The Jewish Encyclopedia*) as a summary of "the best work of his fifteen predecessors who had commented on Rashi," relays the opinion that even in an actual combat situation, the principle does obtain that the least possible and least injurious force should be applied, even to combatants!

Rabbinic comments on Abram's participation in the War of the Kings (Genesis 14) sustain the validity of this concern:

> After these things the word of the Lord came unto Abram in a vision, saying: "Fear not, Abram . . ." (Genesis 15:1). This related to the verses from Proverbs: "Fortunate is the man who fears perpetually; But he who hardens his conscience shall fall into evil" (Prov. 28:14); and "A wise man is fearful and turns away from evil, but a fool is overbearing and careless" (14:16). Who is the wise and fortunate man alluded to? Abraham. And of whom was he afraid? Of Shem, for he killed in battle Chedarlaomer, King of Elam, and his three sons, descendants of Shem . . . Thus Abram was afraid, saying: "I have killed the sons of a righteous man, and now he will curse me and I shall die . . ."
>
> *Midrash Tanhuma on Lech L'cha*, 19, ed. Buber

Even more telling is the further speculation in Midrash Tanhuma: "Still another reason for Abraham's fear after killing the kings in the battle was his sudden realization: 'Perhaps I violated the Divine commandment that the Holy One, Blessed be He, commanded all men, "Thou shalt not shed human blood" (Gen. 9:6). Yet how many people I killed in battle!'" For this reason, too, the Midrash imagines Abram needing divine reassurance.

Among other explanations of the grounds for Abram's fear, R. Levi suggests the following:

---

14. *Sifte Hahamim* on Geneses 32:8.

> Abraham was filled with misgiving, thinking to himself, Maybe there was a righteous or God-fearing man among those troops which I slew . . .
> *Midrash Rabbah on Genesis, 44:4*

There are, of course, other explanations that take Abram's fear in the most self-concerned sense: that he feared for his life when the avengers of the dead would set out for him. Yet the interjection of scruples about killing in the midst of conflict is highly significant for our considerations, and that Abram needed direct divine reassurance indicates that the bloodshed consequent upon warfare was not to be lightly regarded.

The provision in Deuteronomy 20:8, which provides exemption from combat for one who is "fearful and/or tender-hearted," has received comment from the rabbinic tradition also:

> R. Akiba says: "Fearful and tender-hearted" is to be understood literally, viz., He is unable to stand in the battle-ranks and see a drawn sword. R. Jose the Galilean says: "Fearful and faint-hearted" alludes to one who is afraid because of the transgressions he had committed . . .
> *Sotah 44a*

Lest Rabbi Akiba's interpretation be understood in purely "medical" or "psychological" terms, the Tosefta cites Akiba's position in these words: "Why are both terms, 'fearful' and 'tender-hearted,' specified? To indicate that even the most physically fit and courageous, if he be a *rakhman* (compassionate, gentle), should be exempted . . ."

There are, further, teachings which concern obedience to established authority.

• The respect which Judaism accords the law is well-known, and this respect extends to the civil laws of the secular state. Frequently cited is the rabbinic dictum: *dina d'malkhuta dina,* "the law of the government is the law." Not so often cited, however, are the precise conditions in which this dictum is asserted. The four Talmudic instances concern: the validation of a deed of sale, the method of acquisition of real property, tax collectors exceeding their authority, and extortioners, official oppressors, or tax-farmers behaving illegally.

All four cases involve monetary matters or matters of civil procedures, not matters of life and death. Furthermore, in the two cases where officials exceed their rightful authority, the dictum does not determine the issue, but rather tax-refusal/resistance/evasion is countenanced! (Cf. Talmud Gittin

10b-11a, Baba Batra 54b, Baba Kama 113a, Nedarim 27b-28a.)

- In the Talmud, a discussion is recorded between Resh Lakish and R. Johanan concerning the respect that should be shown a king. At issue is a legend that Moses struck Pharoah in contempt and anger just before stalking out. While one of the rabbis is of the opinion that no matter what the ruler's nature, respect must be accorded him because of his office, the other maintains that a ruler's wickedness should call forth contemptuous behavior in his presence! Thus, it is not at all certain the man in office is to be accorded the respect due the office if he, in that office, violates the dignity of the office itself.

- There is on record a specific case in which constituted authority commands an act contrary to the most basic moral teaching of Judaism. In such a case, the Talmud and later rabbinic tradition are at one in counseling refusal no matter what the personal consequence. "In every other law of the Torah," says Talmud Sanhedrin 74a, "if a man is commanded, 'Transgress and suffer not death,' he may transgress and not suffer death, excepting idolatry, incest, and shedding blood . . . Even as one who came before Raba and said to him, 'The governor of my town has ordered me, "Go and kill so and so; if not, I will slay thee."' Raba answered him, 'Let him rather slay you than that you should commit murder; who knows that your blood is redder? Perhaps his blood is redder.'"

- Many instances could be cited of disobedience to established authority, whether Jewish or non-Jewish, where such authority violated the basic moral and religious convictions of Judaism. Abraham, Moses, Elijah, Jeremiah, Shimon bar Yochai, Jochanan ben Zakkai, etc., are the heroes of numerous tales and legends lauding their refusals to obey illicit authority and unjust laws.

It should be mentioned, finally, that a well-established principle of Talmudic law is: "There is no agent for a sinful act." This is held to mean that a responsible adult cannot evade the legal consequences of the act committed by pleading that he was "merely following orders."

More precisely, in the opinion of the Talmud he is guilty of following the wrong orders: "If there is a conflict between the words of the Master (God) and the words of the student (man), whose are to be obeyed?" (Talmud Baba Metzia 10b; Kiddushin 42b, 43a.)

The foregoing selections should already have suggested some direct im-plications, both negative and positive, for our own situation. It is clear that the Biblical period prior to the establishment of the monarchy was characterized by intimate family and tribal groupings, considerable local autonomy, and a high degree of voluntarism with respect to recruitment of fighting men. Professional armies and conscription of individuals by the central monarchy seemed to some of the prophets a serious violation of divine intent. The first Biblical record of monarchical conscription receives unqualified condemnation.

It should be evident from these facts that any attempt to validate a centralized and bureaucratized system of mass conscription on the basis of early Biblical practice and later prophetic evaluation is a serious misreading of the meaning of that tradition.[15] Inferences from an intimate community to a mass society are extremely dubious, to say the least.

It is further evident from the Biblical materials that there were distinctions among categories of wars; that "ideological wars" have no Biblical basis; that individual willingness to participate in war was an indispensable condition; that a premature breach in a man's involvement in life was explicitly prohibited; and finally, except for the limited specific cases of the wars of conquest (from which no analogies to modern times can be drawn in any respect), a war which destroys the bases of human existence, i.e., a war of scorched earth or extermination, is strictly prohibited.

One further detail should be made explicit. There were two occasions on which exemptions were granted: before conscription (Deuteronomy 24:5) and after entering the ranks (Deuteronomy 20:5-8). This option did not apply once a force went off to battle, but it did apply during what we might call the training period, when the implications of war became evident to the person. It is, in fact, precisely to such a situation that the provision of *rakh-levav* (tender of heart) applies.

The rabbinic material, though not a complete statement of a "permissible war" doctrine, evidently supplies significant criteria for determining whether or not one should participate in a given conflict. It is further evident that individual scruples were regarded as appropriate to war situations, that obedience to established authority was not sufficient justification for participation, and that individual responsibility for actions could not be evaded by appeal to superior human authority.

---

15. Cf. the outrage expressed by Rabbi Aaron Samuel Tamaret as early as 1905 at the violation of individual existence by modern collective nationalist demands (in *Judaism*, Vol. 12, No. 1, Winter, 1963, especially pp. 42-46).

It seems evident from the foregoing that Judaism cannot be characterized, in the strict sense of the term, as a "pacifist" tradition. It seems equally evident that Judaism does not regard every war as permissible, nor does it regard every means of prosecuting war as permissible. It is further evident that while Judaism is highly respectful of duly constituted authority, this does not absolve the individual from the duty of making responsible moral decisions. Neither these moral decisions nor their bases are delegated to human authority in any unchallengeable way.

If the above can be an accurate rending of an essential part of the Jewish tradition, it would appear that "selective" conscientious objection on moral grounds is a fundamental teaching of Judaism and a fundamental demand of its adherents.

> From *A Conflict of Loyalties: The Case for Selective Conscientious Objection*, edited by James Finn, 1968

Can a Jew Be a Conscientious Objector?

Jewish Teachings and Military Violence

This essay for the Jewish Peace Fellowship was addressed directly to young Jews contemplating draft resistance or conscientious objection during the Vietnam War.

The fact that you bother to read this article says something about you. It suggests that you, like so many others, are troubled by modern war: the weapons used, the destruction wrought, the human beings killed, the resources wasted, the threat of world annihilation. It suggests that at some level of your being you balk at lending your talents, your abilities, your very self to this activity of the modern nation-state.

You balk, yet you are uncertain. On the one hand, you are aware of the satisfactions of constructive activity, of feelings of love and compassion, of a desire to build a better world, of a reluctance to kill. On the other hand, you know the demand of nation-states today: that you make yourself available for military service and, in the name of human values, be willing to kill and destroy if so ordered.

It is a painful conflict. Certainly, all of us appreciate the importance of social organization for human welfare, all of us learn to respect the nation for its potential and actual contributions to human welfare, all of us want to be good citizens. But at the same time, we know that within us are elements we must also respect: those deep deliverances of conscience, which forbid us to kill or injure our fellow human beings; those stirring feelings of compassion and sympathy for our fellow creatures; and the powerful urge to preserve and build a better world through constructive activity.

How, then, shall we resolve this conflict?

It is interesting, and a great credit to the United States, that the Selective Service regulations take note of this dilemma in Title I of the Universal Military Training and Service Act:

> Nothing contained in this title shall be construed to require any person to be subject to combatant training and service in the armed forces of the United States who, by reason of religious training and belief, is conscientiously opposed to participation in war in any form. Religious training and belief in this connection means an individual's belief in a relation to a Supreme Being involving duties superior to those arising from any human relation, but does not include essentially political, sociological, or philosophical views or a merely personal moral code.[1]

That is to say: If you find, after an honest inspection of your deepest commitments and after a careful consideration of your own religious tradition, that you cannot in good conscience respond to your nation's needs by serving in the military, your nation recognizes your legal right to present this claim before your local draft board.

> Any person claiming exemption from combatant training and service because of such conscientious objections whose claim is sustained by the local board shall, if he is inducted into the armed forces under this title, be assigned to noncombatant service as defined by the President, or shall, if he is found to be conscientiously opposed to participation in such noncombatant service, in lieu of such induction, be ordered by his local board, subject to such regulations as the President may prescribe, to perform for a period equal to the period prescribed in section 4(b) such civilian work contributing to the maintenance of the national health, safety, or interest as the local board may deem appropriate.

What do you say? In this brief essay, it is not possible to offer specific guidance for you in the important work of discovering and expressing your own basic religious value commitments. And in a non-dogmatic tradition such as Judaism, there is much room indeed for individual intuition and understanding. In this area, you might find it helpful to talk with your rabbi, or some other teacher of religion whom you respect.

It is possible, however, to share some of the teachings of the Jewish tradition that provide the basis for many of those Jews who are conscientious objectors today. For while Judaism is not in any absolute sense a "pacifist" tradition, some of its basic teachings, when applied to what we know of

---

1. In an historic decision broadening the Selective Service Act, the Supreme Court on March 8, 1965 ruled in part: "The test of belief 'in a relation to a Supreme Being' is whether a given belief that is sincere and meaningful occupies a place in the life of its possessor parallel to that filled by the orthodox belief in God of one who clearly qualifies for the exemption. Where such beliefs have parallel positions in the lives of their respective holders we cannot say that one is 'in a relation to a Supreme Being' and the other is not."

modern war, raise grave doubts about the permissibility of participation in war today.

Well known is the fact that already in the Biblical period, Judaism regarded the achievement of peace as the most divine of man's accomplishments.

> It shall come to pass in days to come . . . that they shall beat their swords into plowshares and their spears into pruning-hooks. Nation shall not lift up sword against nation, neither shall they learn war any more . . . There will be no harm or destruction in all My holy mountain; for the land shall be full of the knowledge of the Lord as the waters cover the sea.
> *Isaiah 2:2,4; 11:9*

This attitude, so basic to Judaism, was strikingly reaffirmed in the classical rabbinic period.

> Great is peace, for all blessings are contained in it . . . Great is peace, for God's name is peace . . .
>
> It is written, "Seek peace and pursue it" (Psalm 34:15). The Law does not command you to run after or pursue the other commandments, but only to fulfill them upon the appropriate occasion. But peace you must seek in your own place and pursue it even to another place as well.
> *Leviticus Rabbah, Tzav, IX, 9; Numbers Rabbah, Hukkat, XIX, 27*

But the tradition did not rest content merely with general statements of ideals. It was very specific about what it understood to be the application of these ideals to daily life with all its conflicts.

Thus, for example, while Judaism does recognize the duty of a person to preserve his own life and defend others, it is very specific in *prohibiting the shedding of innocent blood:*

> In every other law of the Torah, if a man is commanded, "Transgress and suffer not death," he may transgress and suffer not death, excepting idolatry, incest, and shedding blood . . . Murder may not be practiced to save one's life . . . Even as one who came before Raba and said to him, "The governor of my town has ordered me, 'Go, and kill so and so; if not, I will slay thee.'" Raba answered him, "Let him rather slay you than that you should commit murder; who knows that your blood is redder? Perhaps his blood is redder."
> *Sanhedrin 74a*

Judaism further insists that even in the most clearcut case of self-defense against a precisely identified assailant, the use of excessive violence is not to be sanctioned.

> It has been taught by Rabbi Jonathan ben Saul: If one was pursuing his fellow to slay him, and the pursued could have saved himself by maiming a limb of the pursuer, but instead killed his pursuer, the pursued is subject to execution on that account.
>
> Sanhedrin 74a

The same limitation, incidentally, applied also to a bystander who, witnessing such a murderous pursuit, is enjoined to intervene on behalf of the pursued. He, too, if he needlessly slay rather than maim the assailant, is regarded as subject to execution because of that excess.

Nor should one think that Judaism, while insisting on the scrupulous limitation of violence in individual cases, was willing to forget such scruples in the case of war itself. Even when war was fought for the most legitimate reasons, it was recognized that killing was an offense before God, and a sin offering was made by all soldiers.

Here, also, the tradition was specific in declaring certain strategies impermissible no matter what ends were being sought.

> When siege is laid to a city for the purpose of capture, it may not be surrounded on all four sides but only on three in order to give an opportunity for escape to those who would flee to save their lives . . .
>
> Maimonides Code, "Treatise on Kings and Wars," Chapter VII, Law 7

> When in your war against a city you have to besiege it a long time in order to capture it, you must not destroy its trees, wielding the ax against them. You may eat of them, but you must not cut them down. Are trees of the field human to withdraw before you under siege? Only trees which you know do not yield food may be destroyed . . .
>
> Deuteronomy 20:19-20

The strict limitation of violence, no matter what the end sought by such means, is one of the most basic of all Jewish ethical teachings. With the power of modern weapons, the impersonal nature of long-range warfare (do we really know whom we are killing?), and the complexity of issues being fought about, can you imagine that a tradition so scrupulous about shedding innocent blood and so scrupulous about limiting destruction could possibly sanction war today, whether nuclear or "conventional"?

On first consideration, such a rejection of war may seem irresponsible. After all, haven't we certain responsibilities for others and to ourselves? Are we simply to remain passive before tyranny and injustice? Shall we not defend human values when they are threatened?

Such questions are reasonable, and the conscientious objector has no easy answers. (Neither has the military, it should be noted, for it is not perfectly clear that proposed military solutions to these problems are relevant.) But even here the tradition has something to suggest that we, in our age, may be able to understand and apply with new insight. Knowing as we do what Gandhi and Martin Luther King, Jr. achieved by nonviolent means, does not Isaiah speak in terms that are strategic as well as sentimental (30:15): "For thus saith the Lord God, the Holy One of Israel: In turning and stillness shall you be saved, in tranquility and trust shall be your strength . . ."

And when we consider what Rabbi Yokhanan ben Zakai accomplished nonviolently in the face of Roman military might, or when we read in Josephus the stirring report of the successful nonviolent resistance to the Emperor Caligula by our people, we realize how harmonious with the Jewish tradition modern experiments with nonviolence really are.

Though far from fully understood or developed, such nonviolent techniques seem to offer more genuine hope for the future than any means currently available for defending human values. The pacifist position, then, which compels us to intensify this search for effective nonviolent alternatives, asserts that at this critical period in human history, to say "no" to war is to say "yes" to a slowly developing but vital mode of human struggle, and that, in fact, the apparently irresponsible negation of military service may be the most deeply responsible affirmation of all that we would truly fight for. ❧

Published by the Jewish Peace Fellowship, 1968

"... Therefore Choose Life"

In the Face of Nuclear Annihilation

"Pacem in Terris," a 1963 encyclical by Pope John XXIII, "urgently demand[ed] that the arms race should cease, that the [nuclear] stockpiles which exist in various countries should be reduced equally and simultaneously . . . that nuclear weapons should be banned, and finally that all come to an agreement on a fitting program of disarmament . . ." This 1963 essay by Rabbi Gendler was a response to that encyclical.

As recently as ten years ago, I can recall conversations among seminary students who found themselves wondering if traditional religion had anything really to say to the modern scene. Was there anything in the Biblical and rabbinic tradition that, applied today, was more than a truism, a generality, a statement of the obvious? In those youthfully naive days, when nuclear delivery time was still measured in hours rather than minutes, we had not yet realized how ancient statements of the obvious would soon come to be recognized as penetrating and radical.

How should we have imagined then, not so many years ago, that a simple call to trust one another would sound so revolutionary? That to declare the mass killing of hundreds of millions of human beings "no possible instrument of justice" would sound so radical? That to assert basic human rights and dignity should prove so critical of social organization on this Earth?

It is now painfully clear to us: The once-obvious is no longer obvious. Values once taken for granted, limitations once readily assumed, are no longer to be taken for granted or assumed. This is the singular religious and ethical fact of our age. It was to this that the much loved Pope John XXIII spoke in "Pacem in Terris," and it is to this condition that each of us also must now speak. The reassertion of simple things is today a radical task.

Where shall we begin? Clearly with our sense of cosmic purpose, for it is only within that larger scheme that our own limited place can be ascertained and appreciated. Two brief statements, one Biblical and one rabbinic, help to gain some idea of where we are and what it is all about:

> . . . the Lord Who created the heavens (He is God!), Who formed the Earth and made it (He established it), He did not create it a chaos, He formed it to be inhabited!
>
> *Isaiah 45:18*

> In the hour when the Holy One, blessed be He, created the first man, He took him and let him pass before all the trees of the garden of Eden, and said to him: See My works, how fine and excellent they are! Now all that I have created, for you have I created. Think upon this, and do not corrupt and desolate My world: for if you corrupt it, there is no one to set it right after you.
>
> *Ecclesiastes Rabbah 7*

How simple and obvious! The Earth is meant to be inhabited, cared for, and enjoyed! Can anyone, in tranquil moments of the spirit, not know this? Yet the din of daily pursuits somehow drowns out this plain proclamation, and it is only at moments of keen hearing that we reawaken to the appalling fact that the military means by which we now seek to attain certain ends jeopardize the very existence of human life on this planet so precious to us.

It is true that violence was resorted to and war waged throughout history, often with religious sanction, but classical Judaism, simultaneously with its sanction, bounded the permissible range of destructiveness. In both individual and collective instances, Judaism was quite specific in limiting the application of violence for human ends, for it was well aware, even in those technologically primitive times, of the tragic tendency of violence to become indiscriminate and unbounded.

> However mighty the man, once the arrow leaves his hand he cannot make it come back . . . However mighty the man, once frenzy and power take hold, even his father, even his mother, and even his nearest of kin he strikes as he moves in his wrath.
>
> *Mekhilta of Rabbi Ishmael, Shirata 4*

It is well known that Judaism recognized the preservation of one's own life as a primary duty. Less well known is the clear rabbinic limitation set upon violations of the religious code in accomplishing this.

> In every other law of the Torah, if a man is commanded, "Transgress and suffer not death," he may transgress and not suffer death, excepting idolatry, incest, and shedding blood. . . . Murder may not be practiced to save one's life . . .
>
> *Sanhedrin 74a*

It is also well known that Judaism recognizes the right of a person to defend himself against an attacker to the point of killing him if necessary. Not so often noted, however, is the strict limitation of means imposed even upon this plain act of self-defense.

> It has been taught by Rabbi Jonathan bar Saul: If one was pursuing his fellow to slay him, and the pursued could have saved himself by maiming the limb of the pursuer, but instead killed his pursuer, the pursued should be executed on that account.
>
> *Sanhedrin 74a, cf. Maimonides Code, Laws of Homicide, Chapter 1, Law 13*

The same limitation applies also to a bystander who, witnessing such a murderous pursuit, is enjoined to intervene on behalf of the pursued. If he needlessly slays rather than maims the assailant, he is regarded as deserving execution because of that excess.

The same insistence upon limitation characterizes authoritative Biblical and rabbinic rulings concerning the waging of war. Massive destruction of populations and resources may have been thinkable but was clearly unacceptable within traditional Judaism. Cities under siege were to be surrounded only on three sides, to give residents opportunity for escape, teaches Maimonides in his "Treatise on Kings and War." Food-bearing trees were not to be cut down by the besieging army, declares Deuteronomy 20:19-20. Can one imagine such a religious tradition sanctioning modern nuclear war or even modern "conventional" warfare? I cannot imagine it sanctioning even the "mere" act of preparing for such modes of conflict. Genuine preparation, after all, is predicated upon the possibility of use in extreme circumstances, "credibility" being essential to a possibility of deterrence – but if the use is quite outside the bounds of permissibility in any circumstances whatsoever, the preparation itself is also illicit.

> Resh Lakish said: He who lifts his hand against his neighbor, even if he did not strike him, is called a wicked man.
>
> *Sanhedrin 58b*

Pope John found it "impossible to imagine that in the nuclear era war could be used as an instrument of justice." Yet to learn that modern war, together with its preparation, no longer lies within the boundaries of religious permissibility is frightening. For millennia we have – perhaps reluctantly, but with much religious sanction, reasonably clear consciences, and reasonable expectations of survival – put our trust in armed might, at least as the ultimte arbiter of human conflict. And suddenly, almost in spite of us, it is removed from the scene as a possible instrument of life both by conscience and by consequences. Had we deliberately, through trust and intent, abolished war by moral effort and human growth, how glorious a prospect the future should present. But it was not we who managed to put an end to war as an agency of human arbitration. In fact, war as a life option *has been abolished;* it remains now only as a death option. But its abolition in this sense has been accomplished more by technology than by our own intentions. And so we find ourselves naked and seemingly defenseless in a world fraught with terror and enmity.

We are terrified and understandably so. But we are also liberated; never before have we been quite so free. Until now, we have acted on insufficiently generous assumptions about human beings, and we have failed. We now find ourselves free to try far more generous assumptions about both others and ourselves. In a sense, everything is now permitted: everything, that is, which flows from generosity and largeness of spirit; everything, that is, which flows from the love and appreciation of humanity and our Divine possibilities.

> Rabbi Akiba used to say: "Beloved is man, for he was created in the image of God. Extraordinary is that love which made known to him that he was created in the image of God."
>
> *Avot 3:18*

We belong, and likewise all other human beings, to that universal human association, the Fellowship of the Beloved. For centuries, circumstances permitted us to forget; they now require that we remember.

> A gentile who occupies himself with the study of the moral law equals in status the High Priest.
>
> *Bava Kama 28a*

Nor is membership confined to the righteous alone:

> Whenever destruction of the wicked takes palce, there is grief for them above.
>
> *Zohar I, 576*

It is no simple matter to take such a teaching to heart and live by it. It requires that we stop playing the outmoded game of "friend-foe" in which the object is to defeat or destroy the "foe." We shall have to enlist all our religious and educative forces in freeing us fully for a radically different game.

> There were once some lawless men in the neighborhood of Rabbi Meir

who caused him a great deal of trouble. Rabbi Meier accordingly prayed that they should die. His wife Beruriah said to him: "How can you think that such a prayer is permitted? . . . When sins will cease there will be no more wicked men! Rather pray for them that they turn from their ways, and they will be no more wicked." He did pray on their behalf and they did turn from evil.

Berakhot 10a

There are many ways in which we are already free to help people turn from evil.

> When Aaron would walk along the road and meet an evil or wicked man, he would greet him . . .
>
> *Avot de Rabbi Natan 12*
>
> For the sake of peace, one greets idolaters and inquires after their welfare.
>
> *Mishnah Shevit 4:3*

Direct communication must not cease among people, however greatly they may differ in outlook. And knowing that all of us are members of that Fellowship of the Beloved, we should neither scorn nor despair of that mediation that appeals to the not-yet-actual but in-principle-possible.

> When two men had quarreled with each other, Aaron would go and sit down with one of them and say to him, "My son, mark what the fellow is saying! He beats his breast and tears his clothing, saying, 'Woe unto me! How shall I lift my eyes and look upon my fellow! I am ashamed before him, for it is I who treated him foully.'" He would sit with him until he had removed all rancor from his heart, and then Aaron would go and sit with the other one and say to him, "My son, mark what the fellow is saying! He beats his breast and tears his clothing, saying, 'Woe unto me! How shall I lift my eyes and look upon my fellow! I am ashamed before him, for it is I who treated him foully.'" He would sit with him until he had removed all rancor from his heart. And when the two men met each other, they would embrace and kiss each other.
>
> *Avot de Rabbi Natan 12*

Neither should we forget our unusual freedom to contend with that source of strife so succinctly portrayed in the Talmudic proverb: "When the barley is gone from the pitcher, strife comes knocking at the door" (Bava Metzia 59a). We are blessed with unprecedented resources to devote to this aspect of peacemaking; the traditional pittance for poverty will no longer do.

> Rabbi Simeon used to say: Note how different from the ways of God are the ways of men. When a human king goes to war he goes with multitudes

and legions, but when he goes on a peaceful mission he goes alone. Not so the Holy One, blessed be He. When He goes on a mission of peace, He goes forth with multitudes and legions.

Numbers Rabbah 2

It would be tragic indeed if we failed to make use of our exceptional freedom to "imitate God" by allocating a generous share of our world's resources for the alleviation of worldwide poverty.

By remembering that all people are members of the Fellowship of the Beloved, we should also find some terrors diminished. There are certain representations of "the enemy" – specters of unmitigated monolithic evil – that are more caricatures than portrayals of reality. Yet these distortions of perspective haunt us severely.

"He stood, measured the Earth, and beheld . . ." What did He behold? He beheld that the seven [basic moral] commandments* were accepted by all the descendants of Noah . . .

Bava Kama 38a

Although these natural intuitions of morality have often enough been disobeyed by all peoples (the "good" also, not only the "wicked"), the fact remains that in all human beings is planted that from which decency may spring forth. To see this is to see in some small measure as He sees; to see that from within the worst of tyranny goodness may arise – if there but be life.

Remembering that we are members of the Fellowship of the Beloved should not blind us to another fact that is all too evident: We simultaneously find ourselves members of that equally universal human society, the Fellowship of the Imperfect. As the High Holy Day liturgy puts it, "In Thy sight no one is wholly righteous . . . We have all sinned." Hence, honest criticism is very much in order, toward ourselves as well as toward others. The great demand to criticize the power centers and politics of one's own nation, felt so keenly by the prophets of Israel, should now be felt by every person, as in Numbers 11:29: "Would that all the Lord's people were prophets!"

The sobering awareness of our common imperfection also makes clear the fact that struggle will continue to be a necessary part of human existence.

---

1. According to the rabbinic tradition, the seven commandments, six enjoined upon Adam and one added after the flood, are: 1) not to worship idols, 2) not to blaspheme the name of God, 3) to establish courts of justice, 4) not to shed blood, 5) not to commit incest, 6) not to rob, 7) not to cut flesh or limb from a living animal.

But by the same token we must make certain that the instruments of the struggle are appropriate to our imperfect state. Modern weapons of mass destruction are plainly not. And so, freed as never before from the constraints of traditional military strategy, we must now investigate thoroughly the power of nonviolence as a means both for the defense and for the attainment of human values. The accomplishment of Gandhi and Martin Luther King, Jr. suggest that Isaiah's dictum (30:15) is not so much sentimentalism as it is *realpolitik* of the spirit:

> For thus said the Lord God, the Holy One of Israel: In turning and stillness shall you be saved. In tranquility and trust shall be your strength.

There is a tone of muted messianism in these brief paragraphs, but how dare there not be at this stage of human history? Read dispassionately, and from a distance, the emphases of "Pacem in Terris" on coexistence, disarmament, trust, and world fraternity also sound somewhat messianic. And precisely in that muted messianism lie the power, strength, realism, and relevance of that stirring encyclical.

> If you see the great powers contending with one another, anticipate the footsteps of the messiah.
>
> *Genesis Rabbah 42*

Here, too, the once fanciful has become hard fact, and the world will long admire and cherish the late Pope John XXIII for enunciating so that all the world might hear.

One does not expect that full personal perfection from which peace would automatically result, nor does one anticipate the full knowledge of the Lord, which would banish all hurt from among us (Isaiah 11:1-9). Rather, to expect and insist that our unprecedented situation today be recognized and responded to in unprecedented and daring ways – that is both our privilege and our mandate!

> I call Heaven and Earth to witness against you this day, that I have set before you life and death, the blessing and the curse; therefore choose life, that you may live, you and your seed.
>
> *Deuteronomy 30:19*

Excerpts published in *Saturday Review,* 1963; full text published by Center for the Study of Democratic Institutions, 1963 and *Reconciliation International,* April, 1987

Teaching *Shalom* in the Shadow of Tibet

Nonviolent Resistance for National Survival

Written with Mary Gendler

Everett and Mary Gendler have for years been involved with the exiled Tibetan community in Dharamsala, India. In this 1998 essay they describe conversations they have had with thousands of people of that community about the mobilization of non-violence as a tool of cultural survival and resistance in a condition of exile.

"Why are you talking to us about nonviolence?" we were asked again and again by the bright, eager, incredibly patient Tibetan youngsters seated on the hard floor of their unheated assembly hall in Dharamsala. They had kept us there for hours, plying us with questions about the efficacy of nonviolent struggle, to which they gave lip service because of their reverence for their beloved Dalai Lama, but about which they had grave doubts. "Isn't it clear that nonviolence doesn't work? Shouldn't we turn to other means?" they asked. "Why are you here? Why do you want to help us?"

Why, indeed, had we come to this former British hill-station, seat of the Tibetan government-in-exile and temporary home of the Dalai Lama, which, at 6,000 feet, becomes bone-chilling in winter? "We're here because we're Jewish," we replied without hesitation. Then, realizing that these Buddhist young people, tucked away in a remote corner of the Himilayas in northern India, might not understand what we meant – indeed, might not even know who Jews are – we explained:

"For thousands of years our people have been persecuted and oppressed. Only fifty years ago, we suffered a terrible genocide when the Nazis murdered six million Jews. And yet we have survived. Our religion has instructed us to 'hate evil and love what is good' and to work for justice. It has also taught us: 'You shall not stand idle while your neighbor bleeds.' What the Chinese are doing to the Tibetans is evil and unjust. Your people are being injured; they are suffering. We admire the Dalai Lama's determination to save your people and your culture by nonviolent means. We would like to help by talking to you about how to make nonviolent struggle even more effective."

A shy but determined Tibetan boy of about 16 remained doubtful. "People say the Tibetans and Jews are alike. I have read *O Jerusalem* and I don't think we are alike at all."

"Why do you think that we are not alike?" Everett asked.

"Because the Jews were brave and fought for their country. We Tibetans are not brave. We do not fight. And look what the Chinese are doing to Tibet."

Here it was: the big question. Inevitable, even welcome, but still a challenge. Had we not discussed these same issues a thousand times at home with friends? Were there alternatives to violence in the final stages of the struggle for Israel? What if the efforts to regain the land had been attempted through nonviolent means, would independence have taken longer? Almost certainly, but might not the terrible situation today, the enmity between two peoples and the persistent bloodshed, have been avoided? Where does our own community stand in relation to the insistent teachings of *shalom*, of nonviolence, of swords into plowshares, which are clearly present as powerful, if sometimes ignored, dictums of our tradition?

The Reform movement has played an important role in increasing the visibility of our commitment to peaceful conflict resolution. The founders and earliest leaders of the Jewish Peace Fellowship, back in the 1930s, included Rabbi Abraham Cronbach of the Hebrew Union College and Jane Evans of the National Federation of Temple Sisterhoods, both of whom encouraged us to affirm Psalm 34-15: "Seek peace and pursue it." As it says in Numbers Rabbah 19:16: "The Torah does not order you to run after or pursue the commandments, but only to fulfill them when the appropriate occasion comes . . . But peace: you must 'seek peace' in your own place and 'pursue it' in another."

Today, memories of the Holocaust make it hard for us to place our trust in anything but weapons for our defense, even though we know that in the long run "a king is not saved by his great army; the war horse is vain hope for victory" (Psalm 33:16-17). But in a moment of crisis, who can think of the long run?

The assembled Tibetan students politely awaited our response. "Yes, certainly, I can understand why it looks that way to you," Everett said. "But let me assure you that nonviolence does not mean simply being passive and not fighting; it doesn't mean that you are not brave; it doesn't mean that you cannot win. Active, strategic nonviolent resistance takes much more courage than you think, and it is often far more effective than violence. The Indians whose heads were cracked by the British during the salt march were certainly brave; they were also effective. Keep in mind that the British never recovered their self-respect after that event, and their hold on India was quietly but permanently weakened. Consider the dramatic overthrow of the Marcos regimes in the Philippines in 1986, and the success of the Latvian independence struggle against the USSR in 1989. Also, the man who stood in front of the Chinese tank in Tienanman Square displayed enormous courage. Perhaps if you knew more about the various strategies and the power of active nonviolent struggle, you would feel differently."

"Yes, you are right," the ever-polite Tibetan boy responded, "but I think the Chinese are different. The man who stood in front of the tank was brave, but look what they did to their own people, their own students. That proves nonviolence will not work with them."

"It is true that the Chinese authorities can be brutal and ruthless. Yet even in such situations there can be surprises. As you know, it was the policy of Nazi Germany to exterminate all Jews. But something amazing happened in 1943. The Gestapo arrested several hundred Jewish husbands of non-Jewish German wives. The wives descended upon Gestapo headquarters. Facing Nazi machine guns, they refused to leave. Day after day they confronted the German authorities without violence, and within a week they had obtained their husbands' release. Most of these Jewish men survived the war, living with their non-Jewish wives in Berlin, Hitler's capital! Let's keep this episode in mind before we decide that nonviolence can never work against murderous regimes. Maybe the powerful are not as all-powerful as we fear, and nonviolence is more powerful than we might imagine."

"Doesn't violence get more attention?" another student asked. "We've been trying nonviolence for a long time and no one notices. Perhaps if we did something violent, the world would listen."

"Actually, I don't think you realize how much you have gained by following the nonviolent path," responded Mary. "If you abandon this way, you might get attention for a few days, but you will become just one more violent struggle, and no one would really care. By following the Dalai Lama, your people have gained the sympathy and support of many peoples, even if their governments are not responding the way they should. This soul force which Gandhi spoke of is more powerful than you think. What you need to learn now is how to use it more effectively."

"But we can't even get the Chinese to listen to us," another youngster protested. "They do and take what they want. They don't need to talk because they're so much stronger. We have nothing and can do nothing."

"Here's where active, nonviolent struggle comes in," said Mary. "Of course the Chinese are not going to give you anything so long as they feel they have all the power. But they do not have all the power. You also have power, more than you realize."

"But we don't have time for nonviolence. We've been trying for thirty-seven years already and nothing has happened. Our people and our culture are being destroyed. You've gotten back your homeland, and we haven't!" We could hear the pain and anguish in the voice of this young teacher, who could barely speak through her tears.

"It is true that our people have recovered our homeland," we conceded, "but our wait lasted a lot longer." Many of the students nodded in acknowledgment of their impatience.

In addition, Everett said, although a military struggle helped effect our return to Zion, it had been preceded by centuries of spiritual resistance and renewal. "About two thousand years ago," he explained, "the Jews revolted

against the Roman occupation, taking up arms, preventing all Jews from leaving the city, and insisting that everyone fight the Romans, although many Jews warned that armed struggle would surely lead to disaster. Disagreeing with the zealots, a rabbi named Yokhanan ben Zakkai made a daring escape from the besieged city of Jerusalem and negotiated an agreement with the Roman enemy: He would continue to oppose the armed rebellion if the Romans would allow him to set up a school in the town of Javneh. Some Jews called Rabbi Yokhanan a coward; others accused him of treason. The Romans crushed the Jewish fighters, slaughtered or exiled the remaining Jews, and destroyed the Temple. Had Yokhanan not established the school at Javneh, our people might have disappeared. Thanks to that school, we learned how to live in exile, and, as you can see, we are still here. Does any of this remind you of someone?"

Smiles of recognition abounded. The parallel between Yokhanan ben Zakkai and the Dalai Lama was obvious to all.

But there are also obvious differences. In recent decades, the scientific study of nonviolence has become a recognized academic discipline as well as a practical strategy for achieving social change. As committed as the Dalai Lama is to imparting the traditional Buddhist teaching of *ahimsa* (non-harm), he is equally and eagerly open to learning about its active, practical, political application as a tool for liberation from the Chinese.

There have already been efforts to share the methods of nonviolent resistance with Tibetan leaders. Thirty highly placed Tibetans recently completed a seminar on strategic, active nonviolence taught by Dr. Gene Sharp of the Albert Einstein Institution in Cambridge, Massachusetts and retired Colonel Robert Helvey, a former instructor at Fort Benning, Georgia, who has become intrigued with the possibilities of nonviolence as an effective alternative to violent struggle. Helvey put the Tibetans through demanding strategic analyses of their situation. He explained that nonviolent and military strategic planning begin the same way – with an assessment of strengths and weaknesses on each side. In the case of Tibet, the Chinese military presence is the occupying force's main pillar of support. As an occupying rather than combat force, it is subject to special vulnerabilities. Stationed far from home in inhospitable surroundings, soldiers frequently suffer problems of morale due to the radical change of climate and the perceived hostility of the occupied population. Often the recruits come from disadvantaged sectors of their own society and harbor latent resentment toward their superior offices and their entire government apparatus; they may recognize that they, like their Tibetan subjects, are themselves victims of an exploitative regime. Effective interactions may lead to soldiers' deliberately overlooking prohibited Tibetan activities, reluctantly and haphazardly obeying instructions, and, in the end, perhaps even refusing to follow orders. Strategically speaking, this is equivalent to disabling a unit through armed combat; in both cases, the unit needs to be replaced.

Another area of vulnerability, Helvey noted, is the local civil administration of the Chinese occupying forces, which, with proper handling, might be induced to compromise the accuracy of Chinese records and impair the transmission of directives, procedures, and policies. In addition, a more self-confident and aware local Tibetan populace could be developed through a classic Constructive Works Program, similar to the one so effectively devised by Gandhi in the Indian independence struggle. Tibetans who have studied in India and returned could serve as teachers in a literacy campaign; others trained in simple paramedical techniques might improve the health and consequently the energy of the local Tibetans; others with some business training could help Tibetans organize their own local enterprises and extend marketing operations. All of these activities would strengthen a people and increase its possibilities for carrying on a persistent and ultimately effective struggle for self-determination.

And so the discussions continued. During the three months we spent in Dharamsala, we spoke to more than three thousand students, teachers, youth leaders, administrators, monks, and nuns. Were those inquisitive and skeptical listeners immediately convinced by our arguments and illustrations? Although the energy, excitement, and hope generated by our talks and the Sharp-Helvey seminar were palpable, we know well that the effort to educate and convince people of the moral superiority and efficacy of nonviolent struggle is neither quick nor easy. We have no illusions that a few hours of talking with each group resulted in instant conversion or ongoing commitment. Like all of us in the world today, they are surrounded by a popular culture which offers a thousand exciting, Rambo-style images of violence to every one Gandhian image of effective nonviolence. And if we in the Jewish community, despite our centuries-long tradition of *shalom*, have more trust in a military rather than a nonviolent approach to struggle and security, it is not surprising that the Tibetans are hesitant to put their full trust in nonviolence. The searching questions of the Tibetan students give voice to that skepticism and doubt felt by many. At the same time, they are open to learning how nonviolent struggle can be successful.

Is there any hope for the success of this approach? With a billion Chinese for their six million to confront, the Tibetans have a tough struggle no matter what means they choose. On the other hand, the "soul force" about which Gandhi spoke is real, and once mobilized and combined with hard-headed strategies, it becomes a formidable power. We have only to remember the astonishing recent transformations in the Philippines, Eastern Europe, and the former Soviet Union, where nonviolence played a much larger role than violence against these brutal regimes.

Many thoughtful observers of Tibet's struggle for survival believe that the Prophet Zechariah's vision – "Not by might, not by power, but by My spirit, says the Lord of Hosts" – is the best path to liberation. If they are right, and the Tibetans recommit themselves to active nonviolence, perhaps our biblical teachings will have come full circle, and we Jews will learn anew from our Tibetan brothers and sisters about the power of shalom.

From *Reform Judaism*, Fall 1998

Universal Nonviolence Training

A Moral Equivalent of Universal Military Training

Written with Mary Gendler

This 1999 essay, reflective of the Gendlers' rich involvement over the course of years with the Tibetan community in exile in Dharamsala, India, proposes the institution of Universal Nonviolence Training in the Tibetan high school system, and details some elements of what that training might comprise.

Professor Samdhong Rinpoche has managed to combine in his life both professional dedication to scholarship and personal involvement in affairs of the world. His editing of classical manuscripts has not precluded his envisioning a not-yet-achieved nonviolent society, nor did his distinguished directorship of the Central Institute for Higher Tibetan Studies prevent his assuming numerous responsibilities as speaker of the Tibetan Parliament-in-Exile and then as the first popularly elected *kalön tripa* (prime minister) within the Central Tibetan Administration. It is not often that vision and practicality are so harmoniously joined, and it is to this rare and redemptive combination that we should like to offer a few thoughts about one aspect of the practical realization of Professor Samdhong Rinpoche's goal: the establishment of a nonviolence training program for a nonviolent society coming into being.

There are some who dismiss this nonviolent society as quite unachievable. We are not among them. We note with appreciation Professor Rinpoche's earlier exploration of a *satyagraha* project and his continuing investigation of the pragmatic possibilities of strategic nonviolent struggle towards this end. When one considers the improbable and unanticipated variety of nonviolent achievements during the past bloodiest century in recorded human history, it would be presumptuous, indeed, to insist that His Holiness' vision of Tibet as a Zone of Peace and Rinpoche's version of such a society cannot possibly come into being on this planet. The struggle to achieve this will be neither easy nor quick, but do join us in granting the theoretical possibility that it can happen.

How to bring into existence a nonviolent Zone of Peace in Tibet and, once it is established, how to defend it, are interrelated concerns. Once in existence, of course, the challenges would not end, for it would take its place in a world composed of nation-states that are neither nonviolent nor necessarily benign. And insofar as its own residents will be human beings, not saints, it will surely have within it persons and groups of diverse and conflicting interests. Hence it will be faced with the dual challenges of defending itself against both potential foreign aggression and possible internal threats to its democratic institutions and values. How might it do this?

For traditional nation-states, the answer is easy: Armies and police forces exist and are trained for precisely such purposes. Some countries have universal military training for all their youth who reach a certain age; others limit such training to those who will serve as soldiers. For policing functions, the training is almost always specialized and limited to those who will then occupy such posts in the society. As for the anticipated nonviolent society, since it will confront similar problems, must it not devise appropriate analogous methods and train its youth to perform these functions?

The more immediate question, however, is how to struggle to bring about a Zone of Peace in Tibet in the face of the present Chinese opposition. How can the Tibetan people become more effective in their nonviolent struggle to establish such a Tibet? How can they retain hope, raise morale, and at the same time prepare themselves individually and communally for the eventuality of such a society? Most urgently, how can they respond now to understandable impatience and increasing frustration, especially among the youth?

Our proposal is a simple one. The Tibetan government-in-exile should institute as soon as possible a program of Universal Nonviolence Training for all Tibetan youth during their grades 10+2 studies in schools throughout the Tibetan diaspora. Analogous to universal military training for the youth in nation-states with traditional armies, yet different in significant ways, this Universal Nonviolence Training would provide every Tibetan young person with both a theoretical understanding and a practical experience of preparation for serious, sustained, and disciplined nonviolent action on behalf of their country. Scheduled for the months before or immediately following graduation, this program would not delay those continuing on to college, others entering the work force, still others joining the Special

Frontier Force. It would, however, send an unmistakable message, both to the Tibetans and to the Chinese, of a new level of dedication and determination on the part of the Tibetan people that their struggle shall continue into the foreseeable future. By institutionalizing in this way the teachings of the Dalai Lama concerning nonviolent struggle, the continuity of this effort would be ensured for generations to come.

The goals of this proposed program refer to the near future, the far future, and the immediate present. In the near future, a Universal Nonviolence Training Program would help young Tibetans become fuller participants in the communal effort to preserve their traditions and culture, and would train them in new methods and techniques that could be used in the ongoing struggle to achieve a Free Tibet. Looking further ahead to the realization of that goal, the community would, at that time, find itself with citizens trained in peaceful, cooperative, democratic procedures, hence ready to take their place and function knowingly in the brave new nonviolent society. This aspect should, of course, be integrated with the general plan of civic education currently presented in the Tibetan school system-in-exile. And in the immediate present, it would offer energetic, eager, and frustrated Tibetan young people the opportunity to become actively and constructively engaged in the struggle of their people, thereby restoring hope and moderating both their frustration and their impatience.

What might such a program look like? Two general observations need to be made at the beginning. First, although serving a function analogous to that served by universal military training, Universal Nonviolence Training will differ from the latter in a fundamental respect: It will strive to cultivate discipline without demanding uncritical obedience – at the same time, however, rejecting the anarchy of each person "doing his / her own thing." While it will insist that strategic decisions be followed, it will involve the participants themselves in devising such strategies. Tried and true formulas, handed down from above by experts, will not be the way nonviolence moves into action at this stage of history. Instead, for each situation there will need to be an assessment of the circumstances, the creative imagining by all those participating of ways to proceed, and the devising of alternative responses to various possible reactions by the opponent. This will be a middle path between the sometimes endless communal attempts at complete consensus and simply following authoritarian orders from above.

The second preliminary observation recognizes that particular projects and individual undertakings need to be part of a larger, overall plan that reflects the considered aims and aspirations of the community as a whole. Such a grand strategy should emerge from thoughtful consultations and careful planning by all agencies of the Tibetan exile community, both governmental and non-governmental. Insofar as possible, it would also benefit from expressions of aims and aspirations by Tibetans living under occupation. The clear formulation of the basic goal for Tibet – independence, autonomy, or a unique, yet-to-be defined status – together with intermediate goals leading towards that end; the selection of particular areas and projects for action; the kinds of means to be employed: these must affect the tone, the emphasis, and the details of the nonviolent training, for such training will have as its aim the realization of those community goals.

In a short essay, there is not space for a complete, detailed program for such nonviolent training. Yet a general outline can be offered, including six essential training categories. While these six categories can be distinguished for explanation and clarification, the reader will quickly discern that each relates to and intertwines with the others. Since such a program of Universal Nonviolence Training has few if any precedents, we shall try to make it concrete and comprehensible by giving at least a few examples from each category.

Spiritual Elements: Along with an appreciation and cultivation of the spiritual for its own sake, major religious traditions have always been interested in some of the potential practical effects of the spiritual. The Hebrew prophet Isaiah is one of the earliest to suggest that faith, trust, silence and stillness may contribute to personal strength, which can have important political consequences (cf. Isaiah 30:15). In our past troubled and turbulent century, M.K. Gandhi in South Africa and India, and Martin Luther King, Jr., in the United States provided stirring examples of this faith-based power. Given the centrality of religious teachings in the Tibetan tradition, it seems most appropriate, then, to begin by mentioning certain aspects of Buddhist teaching that could directly contribute to effective nonviolent actions. To speak in pragmatic terms is in no way to devalue pure spiritual practices which have no external motivations or purposes; such purity of approach, of course, is fully respected. In the present context, however, it is also appropriate to illustrate briefly some ways in which these practices could contribute to a nonviolent struggle.

Tibetan Buddhist meditation cultivates the ability to see the world clearly, unclouded by wishful thinking. It also offers guidance for overcoming fear and for gaining a sense of balance and equilibrium. Are these not valuable practical assets for those engaged in active nonviolent struggle?

The discussion and comprehension of ideas and teachings about universal compassion for all sentient beings is another feature of traditional Buddhist practice. What might this mean if it were seriously applied to the Chinese? Here, besides facing the personal obstacles to such compassion and the difficulties of its cultivation in the present political situation, one would look at some of the possible effects of such an attitude were it effectively communicated to those Chinese with whom Tibetans are in contact. Obviously, strong emotions will be raised by this issue, and these would become one focus for the category of emotional elements discussed below. One would also want to raise the question of how Tibetans should treat those Chinese who chose to remain in Tibet after the Tibetans achieved their independence or autonomy.

Physical Elements: Physical exercises can strengthen and give tone to the bodies of the young people. These should include both standard conditioning exercises, elements of basic military training designed to strengthen the body, and any traditional Tibetan movements and practices intended to develop physical poise and balance.

Disciplined drills in marching formations, with music, will give practice in cooperative movement, provide an outlet for the energy of young people, and permit the preparation of morale-building and community-building pageantry to be shared with the Tibetan populace at large (cf. the marching bands and formations which are seen at the Tibetan Children's Village annual celebration).

Also valuable would be instruction in self-protection when facing a brutal adversary. These would include ways of protecting the skull, the face, the groin, etc.

Training in basic health and hygiene should also be a part of the program. This should include information about cleanliness, diet, and exercise, as well as about the hazards to health of drugs, alcohol, smoking, poor eating and sleeping habits, etc. Young people should learn that failure to take care of the body is a form of violence to oneself. An unhealthy population will be less able to defend itself either violently or nonviolently.

Intellectual Elements: Theoretical, historical, and pragmatic elements need to be addressed here.

For beginning the theoretical, one would want a simple yet accurate introduction to the basic theories of power and obedience that have made pragmatic nonviolence an effective force politically. For this, Gene Sharp's *From Dictatorship to Democracy*, available in both English and Tibetan versions, could serve admirably. Of special interest is the idea of pillars of support: those social institutions and groupings that enable a society to function. These include schools, monasteries, armies, police, merchants, farmers, nomads, the press, etc. One would also encourage students to use this scheme to analyze and comprehend the strengths and weaknesses of the Tibetans and the Chinese in occupied Tibet. A further dispassionate factual analysis of China today – its strengths, its weaknesses, its accomplishments, and its problems in the social, political, economic, military, and religious areas of life – would also be valuable.

The historical could begin by providing a brief review of how this method of struggle was developed and employed by Mahatma Gandhi in South Africa and India, and Dr. King in the United States. In addition to these well-known and much-studied campaigns, some lesser known nonviolent struggles against ruthless totalitarian regimes and brutal opponents should be studied. These case studies provide examples of other peoples, in other places and at other times, struggling with issues similar to those facing the Tibetans today. Significant cases might include: the 1942 Norwegian teachers' strike against the attempted Nazi cultural infiltration and ideo-logical domination of the schools; the Czech resistance to the Warsaw Pact invasion of 1968, in which the Czechs found ways to reduce the morale of invading troops and make them increasingly unwilling to carry out orders from Moscow; the 1986 overthrow of President Marcos in the Philippines by an unarmed citizenry which faced a ruthless dictator who had overwhelming military superiority; Latvia, 1989, where Russian settlement over the decades had resulted in the Latvians having become a numerical minority in their own country, yet the Latvians were able to gain independence from Russia using nonviolent means, and to set up an independent nation-state.

The pragmatist would ask the students to apply strategies learned from these theories and case studies to the Tibetan situation today. Two examples can illustrate. As mentioned above, the Czechs succeeded in demoralizing many of the invading soldiers, whose willingness to carry out orders was consequently diminished. How were they able to do this? Students would try to answer this question on the basis of historical accounts: how the Czechs communicated with or refused to speak to the soldiers, what they said, how the soldiers reacted, and so on. The students would then try to imagine, and perhaps role-play, how Tibetans in Tibet might work to reduce the willingness of Chinese soldiers to follow orders from Beijing.

Another crucial area is the economic. Here reference would be made to Gandhi's constructive program, with its central symbol, the spinning wheel, its dedication to *sarvodaya*, working towards the well-being and basic equality of all members of the society, and its community-based, cooperative economic orientation. With respect to the Tibetans today, one might pose the following question for strategic consideration: "Imagine that you are in occupied Tibet, where you suffer many economic disadvantages in relation to the Chinese. What concrete actions can you think of that would help improve the economic situation now for you and other members of the Tibetan community?"

In this way, practical exercises and relevant simulations of nonviolent strategies for the Tibetan cause would naturally develop from the theoretical, the historical, and the pragmatic study of nonviolent actions in this century. The intellectual element, however, approached in this way, would lead quickly and directly to the emotional.

Emotional Elements: It is almost indisputable that once Tibet is regained, many Chinese will remain. It is therefore crucial that Tibetans and Chinese learn to see each other as people and find ways to coexist peacefully. This is not always so easy, and will involve much hard work on both sides.

In any conflict, indeed in almost any human situation, emotions play an important role not only in how we feel but also in how we think and react. It is important to anticipate and find ways to deal with some of the powerful negative emotions bound to arise in relation to the Chinese and in nonviolent resistance. Among the most challenging of these feelings are fear, anger, hatred, and the desire for revenge.

Fear: Any time one is in a situation perceived to be dangerous, it is normal to feel fear, for fear alerts us to danger. Soldiers engaged in violent struggles are trained to recognize both the physical signs – sweaty palms, shaking, shortness of breath – and emotional cues – a desire to flee or to fight. These are all perfectly normal, instinctive reactions to danger. Those engaged in serious nonviolent resistance will sometimes find themselves in dangerous situations; they must be trained to deal with their fear.

The first step is to learn to recognize these cues and to accept them as useful warnings. The second step is to learn and practice ways of overcoming fear. These can range widely, and their success depends both on the situation and on the psychology of the person involved. Staying close to or in some sort of contact with other people is a major antidote to fear; reciting mantras, chanting, singing, breathing deeply, humor, are other ways. A belief that the cause is worthy of the risk is crucial for developing the courage and determination to overcome fear.

Anger: When someone has harmed you or someone you love, or has taken something from you unfairly, or has injured you in some other way, anger is an emotion which naturally arises. Within the Tibetan Buddhist tradition, much emphasis has been put on learning to overcome anger, and we would urge that these traditional methods be taught and practiced during this training. Western approaches are somewhat different in emphasis, and focus more on first recognizing and accepting the anger, then finding alternative ways of expressing and focusing the energy which is behind it, rather than lashing out verbally or physically.

Hatred, Desire for Revenge: It could be said that these two emotions are extensions of anger in its more extreme form. As with fear and anger, they are normal and understandable responses to abusive situations. This, however, does not make them useful emotions, and so, as with anger, ways need to be found to get past them. Again, a Western approach would include recognizing and acknowledging the feelings, talking about the situation(s) which gave rise to them, and trying to figure out ways to turn the negative energy into positive.

Tibetan Buddhist teachings emphasize compassion. A fine example of the value of this teaching is a true story told to us by a Tibetan teacher whose family had fled Tibet to India many years ago. Traumatized as a young woman by her escape from Tibet, the mother passed her fears on to her young daughter (the teacher), who reported having had, throughout her childhood, recurring nightmares that she would be captured and harmed by the Chinese. These fears and nightmares followed her into young womanhood. It was not until years later, when she was in a hospital in Nepal visiting her sister, that she saw her first Chinese person, a young girl who was all alone in the next bed. At first all she could feel was the hatred instilled in her by her mother, and she refused to talk to the Chinese girl despite her obvious misery. Finally, the woman's own feelings of compassion won out, and she comforted the girl. From that moment on her nightmares and feelings of hatred ceased.

Both Western and Tibetan means of confronting these emotions might be taught and practiced. Role-playing the Chinese view of the problem to gain an emotional comprehension of how it feels to them could also be a useful way of getting past some of these emotions. How does it feel as a Chinese soldier or business person or administrator when confronted with a Tibetan protester? How might it feel as a Tibetan in free Tibet when confronted with a Chinese protestor? How can the situation be humanized? This approach could aid in finding ways to approach the Chinese that would take into full account their humanity while still advancing the Tibetan cause.

Social Elements: The experience of living and working together in community is, in itself, valuable training for nonviolent resistance. Cooperation, consideration, discipline, are all important elements in a successful nonviolent campaign as well as in living together in a nonviolent community. Spending some time on self-consciously understanding and developing ways to develop a better community would be a helpful way to bring these social elements to the awareness and experience of the young people. For example, how we resolve disputes and settle arguments among ourselves can provide clues for how to handle such problems at a larger political level. This is valuable training in how to be good citizens in a peaceable, democratic society.

Affinity groups have been an integral part of nonviolence training for many years. These are small groups that meet regularly so that their members come to know one another personally, learn how to communicate effectively with one another, and slowly develop strong bonds of mutual trust and respect. Such close interaction helps form a cohesive bond that remains with the members even when separated by time and geography. The sense of closeness is valuable in reducing fear and alienation. Over the years, the common experience of the training program should help create a cohesive nonviolent society with a sense of shared purpose and commitment. Linked to the larger community and reflecting its purposes, the affinity groups are like cells in a biological organism, ready to act when signals from the central nervous system, the Central Tibetan Administration, so direct them. And if communications are impaired, the affinity groups, like cells in the body, have become imprinted with the purposes of the organism and so can function as self-directed entities, working independently yet in harmony with other such groups.

Cultural Elements: Instruction in traditional Tibetan arts, culture, and religion would be an important part of the training. Along with the political struggle, these elements are crucial to ensuring the continuity of an identifiable Tibetan people by creating a sense of social solidarity extending into the remote past and towards an unbounded future. Cultural elements transmit social and religious values that bind members of the community to one another and give them definition as a people. No longer living in their traditional land, therefore without the unifying effects of shared territory, Tibetans' need for these artistic, cultural, and religious traditions is all the greater.

The instruction might take the form of activities, such as presentations of Tibetan song, dance and drama; making posters using traditional Tibetan symbols; learning old stories and folk tales; and making up plays about important historical events. All of this would be even more effective if ways were developed to integrate traditional cultural symbols and forms of expression into the understandings and expressions of nonviolent struggle and defense. For example, the youngsters might make up a play about an historical encounter between Tibetans and some invading foe in the past. They could show how this encounter might have looked and turned out if the Tibetans at that time had employed nonviolent rather than violent defense.

Obviously, the above represents only a bare sketch of the focus and possibilities of such a Universal Nonviolence Training Program. It would surely evolve and change over time as many people add their thoughts and ideas and as experience accumulates. Not discussed here are the practical problems associated with mounting a training program of this scale, including personnel, logistics, planning, and money.

The challenges here are increased by the fact that, so far as we know, such a program for training its citizenry in nonviolent struggle and defense has never before been attempted by an entire people with a well-organized governmental structure. The closest previous approximation may have been Khan Abdul Ghaffar Khan's Khudai Khidmatgar in the early 1930s, organized in the Northwest Frontier of India in a Muslim setting, and inspired by Gandhi. Details of that program in its particulars, however, are few.

Despite the special challenges of such an undertaking, it also presents special opportunities that seem especially appropriate as we humans enter the 21st century. The Universal Nonviolence Training Program here envisioned combines elements of traditional Buddhist teachings of universal compassion with Biblically-inspired Western and Gandhi-inspired Eastern social activism, and joins contemplative Buddhist meditation with practical Western pragmatism in harmonious mutual reinforcement. Perhaps such an example can serve all humankind as we hopefully take another halting yet necessary step towards the fulfilling future that is the ultimate promise of all our most cherished moral traditions. ❦

> Published by the Active Nonviolence Education Center
> in Dharamsala, India, 2009
> Originally published in a 60th birthday tribute
> to Samdhong Rinpoche by Central Institute for Higher Tibetan
> Studies, Sarnath/Varanasi, India, 1999

The Loving Rebuke

Personal Confrontation and Human Harmony

Judaism provides not only a blueprint for relations between human beings and the Divine, but for human conduct between individuals and within community. This 1982 essay offers guidance for reckoning both privately and publicly with anger, hurt, or concern about the behavior of others.

A loving rebuke? On first hearing, the phrase sounds strange to the ear. We ordinarily associate love with consensus, harmony, seeing things alike. Discord? Dissent? Disagreement? These dire D's are linked in our minds with something contrary to love, whatever it may be.

This is understandable, since an ideal of friendship and a desired outcome of love is *"ahavah v'akhvah, shalom v'reut"* (love and harmony, peace and companionship), to quote the beautiful words of blessing from the traditional Jewish wedding ceremony. And what vision do the words usually conjure? Perhaps one of amity and agreement, of like-sightedness and like-mindedness.

This is surely part of a loving relationship between two persons, and its existence is to be celebrated and cherished. At the same time, however, at least equal weight must be given to personal differences, both of preferences and of perceptions. We don't all want the same things; we don't all see things identically. Neither do we assess or evaluate situations in the same ways. Amidst the most profound of harmonies important differences persist. This is part of what it means to be a human being, each one of us "stamped in the mold of the first human being, yet not one of us resembling his/her fellow. 'How great are Thy works, O Lord!'"[1]

This is part of what it means to be an individual, distinctive and different from all others. Such differences are interpersonally, organizationally, and societally enriching. They are also challenging, difficult, and at times

---

1. Seder Eliayahu Rabba II, cited in N.N. Glatzer, *Hammer on the Rock*.

threatening, for differences often create tensions, disagreements, feelings of personal hurt, and disappointment in others.

How can one deal with them? Various strategies have been recommended and tried through the ages. The ancient Egyptian Wisdom tradition regularly contrasts the "passionate man" and the "silent man," according to Ernest G. Wright (*The Old Testament Against Its Environment*, 1951). The latter is the successful man because he is always calm and never a disturber of the established order. The former, on the other hand, is the bad man because his passionate self-assertiveness "destroys that harmonious integration in the existing order which alone is effective."

The message? Whether faced with personal irritation or issues of social injustice, the word is "Shah! Shtill! Don't make waves!"

As strategies go, this one has its problems. On the societal level, acquiescence before "realities" and quiet resignation are the likely outcome of following such advice. It is small wonder, therefore, that all polytheisms tend to be religions of the status quo and that none of them, as Wright notes, has ever produced a thoroughgoing social revolution based upon a high concept of social justice.

At the personal level, if such an orientation toward resolution of differences is followed to its limit, sycophancy is the likely result in relation to those perceived as more powerful than oneself.

> If thou art one of those sitting at the table of one greater than thyself ... let thy face be cast down until he addresses thee, and thou shouldst speak (only) when he addresses thee. Laugh after he laughs, and it will be very pleasing to his heart and what thou mayest do will be pleasing to the heart. No one can know what is in the heart.[2]

While this mode of interaction should not be regarded as the total advice of the ancient Egyptian Wisdom tradition,[3] it is representative of one recommended way of relating to other human beings in our lives with one another.

---

2. James B. Pritchard, editor, *Ancient Near Eastern Texts Relating to the Old Testament*, Princeton, 1955, p. 412, "The Instruction of the Vizier Ptah-Hotep," translated by John A. Wilson.

3. R.B.Y. Scott in *The Anchor Bible: Proverbs and Ecclesiastes* (Garden City, New York, 1965) emphasizes an aspect of this Wisdom tradition that values justice, and he places the Biblical Book of Proverbs in closer relation to the Egyptian tradition. Henri Frankfort's *Ancient Egyptian Religion*, also provides a fuller and more nuanced view of this ancient Egyptian Wisdom tradition.

In striking contrast to this strategy of silence stands the example of the Hebrew prophets. In Ahab's accusatory words of greeting to Elijah, the early prophets were "troublers of Israel" (I Kings 18:17). Nor were the later, literary prophets better-behaved. Amos was ordered deported from the Northern Kingdom for conspiracy against the royal household;

> Then Amaziah the priest of Bethel sent to Jeroboam king of Israel, saying: "Amos hath conspired against thee in the midst of the house of Israel; the land is not able to bear all his words. For thus Amos saith: 'Jeroboam shall die by the sword, And Israel shall surely be led away captive out of his land.'"
>
> And Amaziah said unto Amos: "O thou seer, go, flee thee away into the land of Judah, and there eat bread, and prophesy there; but prophesy not again any more at Beth-el for it is the king's sanctuary, and it is a royal house."
>
> Amos 7:10-13

Jeremiah was beaten, imprisoned, and nearly lost his life for purported treason:

> The word that came to Jeremiah from the Lord, saying: Stand in the gate of the Lord's house, and proclaim there this word, and say: . . .
>
> Thus saith the Lord of hosts, the God of Israel: Amend your ways and your doings, and I will cause you to dwell in this place. Trust ye not in lying words, saying: The temple of the Lord, the temple of the Lord . . . Behold, ye trust in lying words, that cannot profit. Will ye steal, murder, and commit adultery, and swear falsely, and offer unto Baal, and walk after other gods whom ye have not known, and come and stand before Me in this house, and say: "We are delivered" . . . For go ye now unto My place which was in Shiloh, where I caused My name to dwell at the first, and see what I did to it for the wickedness of My people Israel.
>
> Jeremiah 7:127

"Throughout the Bible," wrote Abraham Joshua Heschel in *The Prophets*, "the prophets faithfully challenge the status quo: They make much ado about paltry things, lavishing excessive language upon trifling subjects. What if somewhere in ancient Palestine poor people have not been treated properly by the rich? . . . Why such immoderate excitement? Why such intense indignation? The things that horrified the prophets are even now daily occurrences all over the world."

Truly, it would seem, they came "to root out and to pull down, and to destroy and to overthrow; to build, and to plant" (Jeremiah 1:10). If there lived a group of truly "passionate men," the Biblical prophets were such human beings.

Confronted by these two extremes, the supremely silent and the pre-eminently passionate, where do we middlers fit? How do we choose between these limiting cases? On first consideration it might seem simple. Given the alternatives of ancient Egyptian conformity or prophetic challenge, how could we not side with the latter?

But it isn't quite that simple. First of all, we're not prophets. Secondly, even within the Biblical tradition there is advice recommending silence as a virtue: "A man of discernment holdeth his peace"(Proverbs 11:12). "In too much talk there is sure to be some error. So a shrewd man holds his tongue" (Proverbs 10:19). Clearly there is some truth to those cautionary words. All of us know how irritating loudmouths can be, and how counterproductive harsh and accusatory words may be at times.

How, then, in our interpersonal, our organizational, and our political lives shall we reach a balance of silence and words, of acquiescence and challenge, of acceptance and protest?

No formula can yield a full answer, and general rules also require a careful inspection of each particular situation. On the other hand, a thoughtful formula and sensitive general rules can help us determine how best to respond to particular situations in particular circumstances. Not surprisingly, Judaism has material aplenty to impart, beginning with the Bible and continuing through the ages. The material is especially relevant to the interpersonal, but it has organizational and societal applications as well.

> Thou shalt not hate thy brother in thy heart; thou shalt surely rebuke thy fellow, and not bear sin because of him. Thou shalt not take vengeance, nor bear any grudge against the children of thy people, but thou shalt love thy neighbor as thyself: I am the Lord.
> *Leviticus 19:17-18*

This basic Biblical statement is concise, and its sequence reads like a wish fulfillment. Starting with hate, it ends with love – an outcome to be wished for devoutly. But how do we attain such an end? To state the goal is not the same as telling how to reach it; the how is what we need.

On closer inspection, the Biblical statement is more than merely a statement of an end. Its implications were elaborated by later Jewish tradition into some specific suggestions about the means which can assist the reaching of such an end.

1) Recognize and admit any resentment or hostility you are feeling toward another person. Feeling angry or irritated about something? Don't pretend you are not feeling angry. Don't sit on it. Don't keep it in.

What may happen if you dissemble or try to suppress the feelings? Resentment may build, misunderstanding increase, with a resultant explosion far more injurious than had the feeling of anger or hurt or disappointment been shared while at a lesser intensity. The first principle of practice, then, is out with it!

The classical Biblical instance of suppression of feelings of injury and resentment, cited by later tradition, is Absalom's absolute silence toward Amnon after the latter's seduction and heartless abandonment of Absalom's sister. "And Absalom spoke unto Amnon neither good nor bad, for Absalom hated Amnon . . ." (II Samuel 13:22). Beneath the silence, resentment smoldered: "And it came to pass after two full years" that Absalom engineered the slaying of Amnon.

This is an unusually dramatic and extreme example of suppressing the expression of feelings of having been wronged, but its very extremity invites attention to lesser cases of smoldering resentment, where suddenly, and at times almost incomprehensibly, clashes occur between persons for no apparent reason. As Maimonides wrote in the *Mishneh Torah* (Hilkhot Deot, 6:6), "When a person wrongs another, the aggrieved must not hate the offender while keeping silent . . . Rather he ought to inform the offender by saying, 'Why did you do this to me? Why did you wrong me in this instance?' As it is said: 'Thou shalt surely rebuke thy neighbor.'"

2) On the other hand, don't imagine you ought to feel resentment if such feelings don't come naturally. There are, after all, numerous cases of minor slights or trivial injuries which we can well afford to overlook or ignore. If you feel so inclined, by all means indulge the inclination! Again Maimonides: "If one is wronged by another person and feels disinclined to rebuke the offender because the latter was either uncomprehending or confused, then one need not administer a rebuke so long as the feeling of forgiveness is genuine. Such generous behavior is commendable since the Torah wants only to prevent persistent hatred" (*Mishneh Torah,* Hilkhot Deot, 6:9). But be quite sure that no resentment lingers, for if it does, one might well "take vengeance" or "bear a grudge." The difference between the two? According to the Talmud (Yoma 23), as quoted in the J.H. Hertz Chumash: "If a man says, I will not lend you the tool you require, because

you did not lend it to me when I asked for it – that is vengeance. If a man says, I will lend you the tool, although you refused to lend it when I asked for it – that is bearing a grudge."

But suppose feelings of resentment persist, which is often the case. What then? How shall one rebuke another? In what spirit? Here again there are interesting suggestions from tradition, and they are best begun by listing several things not to do:

1) Do not talk about the person to others. "Thou shalt not go up and down as a talebearer among thy people" is a classic Jewish teaching, found in the same above-quoted section of Leviticus that urges us to rebuke lovingly our neighbor. The juxtaposition of the commandments makes clear the overwhelming preference of Judaism for direct confrontation rather than spreading rumors, relaying gossip, or disseminating one's dissatisfaction with the behavior of another. Violation of the traditional prohibition against speaking evil of others (*lashon hara*) offers little toward effecting reconciliation between two disputants, and will most likely aggravate the dispute and exacerbate the ill feelings. Much preferable is speaking directly to the person, for from such honest confrontations mutual understanding may result.

2) If possible, do not confront the person when you are most angry. The negativity associated with anger tends to be destructive. Maimonides recommends that since anger "is an exceedingly negative quality . . . one should make every effort to keep far from it. One should learn how not to yield to anger even when anger might be appropriate to a situation . . . If a person wants to impress members of his immediate family or the community by expressing anger, it is best that this anger be a simulation, proceeding from inner calm" (Hilkhot Deot, 2:3).

This advice is difficult to live out, since we often do feel angry. In such cases, what shall we do? Obviously, admit the anger! No pretending or fooling oneself: Make the anger explicit to yourself, bring it fully to your own attention, look carefully at it. One might even ask a few questions about the anger, especially questions directed at the issues in relation to oneself, for often we become most angry about traits or characteristics or actions which have a special inner connection with ourselves:

> Rabbi Nathan said: Don't reproach your neighbor for an imperfection which you yourself have.
>
> *Baba Metzia 59b*

> Said Resh Lakish: First correct yourself, then correct others.
>
> *Baba Metzia 107b*

3) In interpersonal matters, avoid harsh words or epithets or painful personal references that would embarrass or hurt the other. Such an appeal will only aggravate the bad feelings between the two of you, and such infliction of hurt is specifically forbidden by the tradition.

4) Above all, in interpersonal matters, do not deal with the issue publicly. Any public embarrassment of another is considered by Rabbinic tradition to be a form of bloodshed, "whitening the face" of the other. In any case, it makes all the more difficult the achievement of mutual understanding, since each person tends to become locked in his/her public posture.

In addition to these four negative "*mitzvot*" are positive actions to take in reconciliation:

1) First and perhaps most important of all, take time to recognize and reaffirm the deeper connectedness of the two of you. At times of dispute, we often focus on differences and lose sight of the important sharings which still exist. Hence, it might be helpful to ask such questions as: What do we share, despite our differences? On what do we agree, despite our disagreements? Could I imagine myself having done something similar to what was done? Have I, perhaps, at some point in my life, done something similar? For what reasons? Struggling with such questions, however distracting they may feel at the moment, will help maintain some perspective.

Such perspective is important. Noticing that the injunction to rebuke uses three distinct terms for one's fellow human being – *akhikha* (brother/sister), *amitekha* (fellow), and *reakha* (neighbor) – Samson Raphael Hirsch remarked: "Hate not thy brother in thy heart – Our Torah here chose the term 'brother' to remind us that even if one human wrongs another, so that the person cannot really be designated a true neighbor or fellow, nevertheless, the person remains 'thy brother,' and this designation persists under all conditions and cannot be annulled."[4]

2) Speak as calmly, as softly, as lovingly as possible. In this way the persistence of your caring for the other person will not be doubted, and your words will be more easily heard.

> It is related that when Reb Aharon Leib of Primishlan saw from the face of a person that the latter had committed a wrong, he would ask the

---

4. Cited in *Iturei Torah*, edited by A.Y. Greenberg, Volume 4, p.111.

person to meet with him privately. Then, after kind and reassuring words to the person, Reb Aharon would begin his loving rebuke. When asked why he proceeded in such a manner, he replied: In Psalm 51 it is written:

> "A Psalm, A Song of David, when Nathan the prophet came unto him just as he had gone into Bathsheba." What do the words mean? Note them well, for they convey an important teaching. Had Nathan come to David in a judgmental spirit, rebuking him angrily in public, it is possible that he would have failed to achieve his end. Perhaps David would have hardened his heart and closed his ears to the prophets plea for repentance. But Nathan came to David lovingly and privately, just as David had gone in to Bathsheba. Thus the prophet's words entered David's heart and he immediately uttered this Psalm of repentance."[5]

3) Focus on the deed, not the doer; criticize the act, not the actor; respect the person even while rebuking his/her transgression.

This distinction between deed and doer, person and behavior is not, of course, absolute. Personal responsibility implies a connection between the two, but connection is not identity, and it can be quite destructive to confuse the two.

When young children misbehave, we try to avoid such expressions as "bad Jimmy, naughty Jane." Instead we might say, "Nice Jimmy did a bad thing, nice Jane made a nasty mistake." What effect has such a distinction? It affirms the basic decency and potential of the child for better behavior. It makes possible the hearing of criticism or correction without feeling personally condemned. It singles out and strengthens the ability to act differently which lies within the child. Thus it encourages change of behavior and positive growth rather than guilt and despair.

Such a distinction is helpful for adults as well. We, too, need assistance and encouragement, support and affirmation as we try to live more responsibly, more thoughtfully, and more considerately of our fellow human beings and our planet. It is not surprising, then, to find this distinction between deed and doer clearly articulated in Jewish tradition.

> It says, 'Thou shalt not hate thy brother . . .' By 'brother' it intends to say that even when a person transgresses, it is not appropriate to hate the person, but only to hate his/her deeds, and the rebuke should be administered in order that the person return to the good.[6]

---

5. *Ibid.*, p. 112.

6. Don Isaac Abarbanel, *Perush Hatorah* on Leviticus 19:17.

Or, in Beruriah's still earlier classic formulation:

> There were once some lawless men in the neighborhood of Rabbi Meir who caused him a great deal of trouble. Rabbi Meir accordingly prayed that they should die. His wife Beruriah said to him: "How can you think that such a prayer is permitted? . . . When sins will cease there will be no more wicked men! Rather pray for them that they turn from their ways, and there will be no more wicked." He did pray on their behalf and they did turn from evil.[7]

4) If you feel the need, raise issues of personal preference as well as of principle. While the latter may be of greater weight and consequence, the former are not to be ignored. The overlooking or disregarding of our personal preferences by others is a source of considerable interpersonal resentment, and often needs airing.

Nachmanides applies the injunction to rebuke to instances of personal desire as well as matters of right and wrong.

> "Thou shalt not hate thy brother in thy heart" refers also to his doing to you something contrary to your wishes. In such a case, do rebuke him, saying, 'Why did you do thus and such to me?' . . . By your not concealing your resentment but instead speaking openly to him, he is likely to make amends.[8]

When airing personal grievances, be sure to maintain perspective. Remember that personal preferences are not matters of principle, and they must not be elevated to such status. On the other hand, they well may need stating.

5) Learn to accept as well as to administer reproof. "'Tis more blessed to give than to receive" should not be applied too hastily, or without qualification, to the matter of rebuke. Concerned as was the tradition that reproof be administered when appropriate, it was comparably concerned that reproof also be accepted. As Rabbi Tarfon said in the 1st century CE (Arakhin 16b): "I wonder whether there is anyone in this generation who accepts reproof, for if one says to another: Remove the mote from between your eyes, the other answers, Remove the beam from between your own eyes!"

The non-defensive acceptance of reproof is perhaps as rare today as in the days of Rabbi Tarfon. To cultivate this art of acceptance remains both

---

7. Talmud, Berachot 10a. Beruriah's opinion vocalizes the second printed word of the verse to read "sins," not "sinners."

8. Nachmanides, Commentary on Leviticus 19:17 in *Mikraot G'dolot*.

desideratum and a challenge.

It is not easy, after all, to hear criticism of one's actions, however gently spoken. At best it is hard to avoid internal feelings of unworthiness or guilt; we often identify ourselves closely with our actions. It is also usually the case that reproof is given harshly rather than gently, from anger rather than from understanding. As Rabbi Eleazer ben Azariah put it (Arakhin 16b), "I wonder whether there is anyone in this generation who knows how to reproach!"

It is not surprising that hearing reproof is not a highly developed capacity among us. Yet it is important. Here again, perhaps the key is the ability to distinguish ourselves from the errors we commit and the injuries we inflict – accepting our responsibility for, but not our total identity with, such actions. Maintaining an appropriate measure of self-esteem may aid our hearing personal rebuke and turning it to positive use.

But suppose the quiet approach and the gentle appeal fail? Suppose what seems to be a grievous moral wrong, not simply a discretionary difference of approach, remains the practice of an individual with whom you have significant contact? In such a case, the tradition does allow for public rebuke if all other means have been tried. Maimonides writes: "In matters of Divine duties, if a private rebuke fails to effect a change in the person, then open public discussion must ensue, with full focus on the misdeed of the person and sufficient condemnation until the person changes for the better. This was the procedure of all the prophets of Israel" (*Mishneh Torah, Hilkhot Deot,* 6:8).

According to Maimonides, the prophetic tradition of public rebuke does have some claim upon us. If one is convinced that the issue is truly one of important principle, not merely personal preference, and if one has already employed private rebuke sincerely and caringly, with self-scrutiny and self-criticism, then public rebuke is called for. Such public rebuke should follow the cautions and recommendations for private rebuke except for its being openly audible and visible.

Performed in the right spirit, avoiding personal attack, and focusing on the deed or policy in question, public rebuke may even enlist public sanction to support the positive tendencies in the wrongdoer. In this way it may ultimately enlist his/her energies on behalf of the more appropriate policy or action. When employed, public rebuke should have as its goal the positive reincorporation of the wrongdoer into the community rather than his/her exclusion.

Up to what point shall one keep trying? How long shall a person persist in such efforts? Here opinions vary.

> To what point shall one carry reproof? Rab said: Until the reprover be beaten. Samuel said: Until he be cursed. Rabbi Yohanon said: Until he be rebuked. The same point was at issue between tannaim. R. Eliezer said: Until he be beaten. R. Joshua said: Until he be cursed. Ben Azzai said: Until he be rebuked.
>
> *Arakhin 16b*

In short, the question discussed by *tannaim*, the rabbis of the Mishnaic period, around 100 C.E., was still under discussion by the *amoraim*, the rabbis of the Talmud, 150 years later, without consensus!

Maimonides (*Hilkhot Deot* 6:7) is of the opinion that one should persist either until he is struck or until the reproved person states unequivocally: "I will not hear it." On the other hand, one commentator on the *Shulhan Arukh* cites an opinion that one should not reprove a person who will retaliate by seeking to injure the reprover:

> As one is commanded to say that which will be obeyed, so one is commanded not to say that which will not be obeyed . . . "Reprove not a scorner lest he hate thee" (Proverbs 9:8)
>
> *Yevamot 65b*

Where does that leave us? With the necessity of deciding just how far we will pursue a given issue with a particular person. Somewhere between not trying at all and persisting beyond reasonable limits lies the appropriate path, and each of us must try to locate that path for each situation.

The value of the loving rebuke for interpersonal relations seems quite clear. Does it apply to wider, more public situations as well? The tradition thought so, and was explicit about it:

> If one could have influenced his/her household and failed to speak out, one is implicated in household misdeeds. In the case of one's city, the same holds true: could one have influenced by speaking out but instead maintained silence, she/he is implicated in communal misdeeds.
>
> *Shabbat 54b-55a*

What might this mean for organizations? In this sphere the applications

---

9. *Magen Avraham* on *Orah Hayyim* 608.

seem fairly evident. Important issues must certainly be raised publicly. Yet if an issue becomes especially sharp between two persons, there is much warrant for applying some of the personal criteria to this situation. Directly addressing the person with whom you have a disagreement, doing so privately and in a gentle spirit, avoiding abusive or insulting language and focusing on the issue, not the person, should make for a more harmonious and constructive resolution of differences and disagreements within any organization.

On the other hand, some disagreements must be further discussed publicly, at meetings, in newsletters, at conferences. In such circumstances, the principles of gentle and respectful speech are to be scrupulously followed. Perhaps most important of all is to remind yourself of those who differ with you. Presumably everyone is seeking the welfare of the organization; presumably everyone is seeking wider values as well. You merely see the issue in different terms. To remember at each stage of the debate that you remain kindred, dedicated to common purposes despite the differences, will help insure that at no point does the discussion deteriorate to attacks against the personhood of others. Here the distinction between the person and his/her proposal or position is crucial. Remembering and applying this principle, analogous to the distinction between doer and deed discussed above, may make a significant difference to the discussion and its harmonious outcome.

In our organizations and communities we are in direct personal contact with one another. Here we can practice the principles previously enunciated with some hope of their having salutary effects on our immediate surroundings.

Yet our responsibilities do not end with our immediate communities. The Talmudic quotation above (in section F) continues:

> With public officials the same holds true: by acquiescence through silence one bears responsibility. Yet further to the ends of the earth itself, this responsibility extends: that ever we attempt, by clear and forthright speech and action, to prevent that from happening which ought not to happen.
> *Shabbat 55a*

This, needless to say, is a very extensive responsibility, and its challenge is compounded by what we sometimes experience as the hierarchical and impersonal nature of our world as a whole. Local injustices often seem connected with persons and policies far out of reach.

> If you see in a province the poor oppressed and justice and right violently

> taken away, do not be amazed at the matter; for the high official is watched by a higher, and there are yet higher ones over them.
>
> Ecclesiastes 5:7 (5:8 n RSV)

Given such complexity and remoteness, how can we begin to approach and deal with such political or institutional arrangements and those who administer them? First of all, and perhaps most important, don't give up without a struggle! Such a lesson is stated very early in Jewish tradition:

> R. Zera said to R. Simeon, Let the Master rebuke the members of the Exilarch's administration. They will not accept it from me, he replied. Though they will not accept it from you, he replied, yet you should rebuke them.
>
> Shabbat 55a

And in a legendary conversation (Shabbat 55a) between the Holy One, Blessed be He, and the Attribute of Justice (Midat HaDin), the Attribute of Justice objected to the designation of certain persons as wholly righteous because "they had the power to protest but did not. . . . God replied: 'It was fully known that had they protested they would not have been heeded.' 'Sovereign of the Universe,' replied Midat RaDin, 'even if it was known to You, was it known to them?' (And God conceded the argument.)"

No matter how poor the odds may appear, one can never know what the outcome may finally be.

Second, make sure to apply the earlier rules of loving reproof. Avoid harsh personal words or epithets, speak from calm conviction rather than from agitated anger; focus on the deeds in question, not the doer, remember always the common humanity which is our common human inheritance, the *"tzelem Elohim,"* the Divine Image, "that of God in every person," to which appeal can be made. Observing these rules will substantially increase the possibility of a satisfactory resolution of conflicts, as illustrated in our own century by the remarkable work of Mohandas K. Gandhi in India and Martin Luther King, Jr., in the United States. Both of these figures operated in a spirit akin to that articulated in the Levitical tradition of the loving rebuke, and their accomplishments afford significant confirmation of the efficacy of this approach.

All the while, keep in mind two differences that apply to matters of public policy. First of all, since the public is involved, issues of principle and policy should be aired publicly. Where there are unrepented misdeeds that violate basic religious or moral precepts, those who perpetrate them and refuse to heed private appeals for rectification must be denounced publicly until a change of policy results. In cases of injustice, the prophetic example ought to be followed even if those denounced suffer public embarrassment. In the final analysis, the demands of justice may not be denied out of undue consideration for the personalities of those perpetrating injustices.

Third, talk about a public functionary is appropriate within limits. Even the classic prohibitions against derogatory speech (*lashon hara*) and tale-bearing (*r'khilut*) permit such speech if it is for beneficial or constructive purposes or if the pertinent derogatory information will prevent a significant loss to another person. Thus one may criticize the craftsmanship of an artisan where such criticism may prevent loss to another; one may inquire and receive specific information about a potential partner in a business enterprise, even if the information be derogatory. In these and similar instances, critical words about another person are appropriate when substantiated, carefully limited to specifics, and of direct relevance in preventing loss to another.

In the realm of public policy such considerations surely apply with even greater force, for a great deal is at stake for all members of society. The character and reliability of those who propose policies, the likely or possible deleterious effects of such policies, and the broader vision of the society which they imply – all of these are appropriate for careful, limited, but searching comment and criticism, even of a derogatory nature.[10]

It is not appropriate, however, for the derogatory to deteriorate to the defamatory, to generalized character assassination. It is also incumbent upon the listener to listen with caution and not accept what is heard as the absolute truth. A measure of cautious skepticism as well as some "benefit of the doubt" should be exercised concerning criticism of public figures and their policies.[11]

Approaching the end of this sketch of the praxis of the loving rebuke, it might be worth making explicit three basic assumptions which seem to underlie this approach to human tension and disharmony.

1) The world as we know it is imperfect; it stands in need of correction.

---

10. See Rabbi Zelig Pliskin, *Guard Your Tongue,* "A practical guide to the laws of *lashon hara* based on Chofetz Chayim," pp. 32, 54, 77-79.

11. *Ibid.,* p. 83.

"A profound disharmony exists between the will of God and the existing social order," writes Ernest G. Wright. Hence our constructive criticism is needed, our involvement in *tikun haolam*, the improvement of the world, is asked.

2) There is that of God in every person, the *tzlem Elohim*, the Divine Image, to which appeal can and must be made.

3) The practice of the loving rebuke is both a sign of human caring and concern and a contribution toward a more genuine human harmony.

> Rabbi Yose bar Hanina said:
> Reproof leads to a state of love . . .
> Love without reproof is not true love.
> Resh Lakish said:
> Reproof leads to a state of peace . . .
> Peace without reproof is not true peace.
> *Genesis Rabba 54*

From the National Jewish Resource Center, 1982

Rabbi Nachman's *"Od"*

An Ode of Human Redemption

The famous storytelling rabbi, Nachman of Breslov (1772-1810), offered paths to personal emotional healing through engaged living and relationship-building with the natural world. This 2011 essay contextualizes Nachman's insights about good and evil within the transformational views of Mahatma Gandhi, Martin Luther King, Jr., and the Dalai Lama.

> Know that one must judge every human being favorably, even one who seems wholly wicked. One must search to find some bit of goodness in that person, to locate the small portion that is not evil. For by finding that bit of goodness and judging the person favorably, one thereby truly elevates that person to a state of merit from which s/he can turn in repentance. Thus the meaning of Psalm 37:10 is: This *"od m'at,"* this touch of goodness, can initiate the process of redemption for the wicked; hence when you look at the place previously occupied by a wicked person, no wicked person is to be found. No matter how evil the person appears, you must search ceaselessly for that bit of goodness that is not tainted by evil. For after all, how is it possible that any existing person shall not have done at least one good deed during those years of existence? Because you so insistently search to find that touch of goodness untainted by evil, and because you judge him/her favorably, you thereby elevate the person to a state of goodness from which full repentance follows. Thus, however diligently you may search, there is no wicked person now to be found in that place where previously a wicked person could be found.
>
> *Hasidei Bretzlaver: Likutei Moharan, 5736, #282*

Both in English and in Hebrew, the word-sound ode/*od* is a simple monosyllable. Small in sound, it is large in significance. In English, the word first denoted a poem intended or adapted to be sung, and later a rhymed lyric, often in the form of an address, generally dignified or exalted. From Pindar to Keats to Wordsworth to Tate, ever so many odes come to mind. In Hebrew, the word connotes duration, persistence, continuity, surplus. Here, too, numerous examples could be cited.

Let's focus on two: in Psalm 37:10, *"v'od m'at,"* and in Psalm 104:33 and Psalm 146:2, *"b'odi."* The former is regularly translated "and yet a little while"; the latter, "while I live," or "while I have being." Those are plain meanings and not to be denied, but they are not the only possible meanings. If one were to construe *od* as a noun, a noun that points to a pure part of a human being, that draws our attention to a meritorious aspect of a human being, then suddenly these phrases assume a different meaning. *"V'od m'at"* of Psalm 37:10 now means "a little merit," and *"b'odi"* in Psalms 104:33 and 146:2 means, "with the meritorious part of my being." Unlike any previous commentator that I know of, this is Rabbi Nachman's startling rendering of *"od,"* with spiritual consequences that we shall now consider.

Especially worth noting is the context that Psalm 37 provides Rabbi Nachman for his approach to the eradication of evil amongst humans. The psalm is often characterized as a meditation on the problem of evil, the painful fact that, all too often, the wicked prosper on this earth while the pious suffer and languish. The psalmist appears to counsel patient waiting, repeatedly assuring the meek, the humble, the wholehearted, the righteous, that in the course of time God will insure their future while cutting off the seed of the wicked. Those who faithfully hope/wait for God will ultimately be vindicated, while the wicked will perish. The psalm includes the verse in the Grace after Meals that we whisper or sing ever so softly: "I have been young, and now am old; yet have I not seen the righteous forsaken, nor his/her seed begging bread." Sometimes referred to as a psalm expressive of "*anavim* piety," the faithful, patient waiting of the poor and the meek for God's justice to appear, the psalm appears to recommend quietism rather than activism in relation to the world's woes.

Rabbi Nachman startlingly changes this scenario. By his interpretation, *od m'at*, human activity, can intervene to change the state of affairs. By identifying the barely visible hint of goodness hidden among the evident evil deeds of the wicked, then actively appealing to that element of goodness, a fellow human being can initiate the process of personal transformation so that, in truth, when one looks anew for the wicked person in his/her former location, one sees not a wicked but a decent human being. "Yea, thou shalt look well at his place, and (the wicked) is not" (Psalm 37: 10).

A few contemporary examples should help us grasp the vast implications of this teaching. I find one vivid, lived example of Rabbi Nachman's approach in practice in Martin Luther King Jr.'s stirring words (in *Strength to Love*, 1963), addressed to recalcitrant resisters of equal justice for all:

> To our most bitter opponents we say: "We shall match your capacity to inflict suffering by our capacity to endure suffering. We shall meet your physical force with soul force. Do to us what you will, and we shall continue to love you. We cannot in all good conscience obey your unjust laws, because non-cooperation with evil is as much a moral obligation as is cooperation with good. Throw us in jail, and we shall still love you. Bomb our homes and threaten our children, and we shall still love you. Send your hooded perpetrators of violence into our community at the midnight hour and beat us and leave us half dead, and we shall still love you. But be assured that we will wear you down by our capacity to suffer. One day we shall win freedom, but not only for ourselves. We shall so appeal to your heart and conscience that we shall win you in the process, and our victory will be double victory."

King is here referring to love as *agape*, selfless concern for the other, "understanding and creative, redemptive goodwill for all men." This stands in contrast to *eros*, esthetic or romantic love, and *philia*, "a reciprocal love and the intimate affection and friendship between friends." King's articulation of the power of *agape* includes, also, a strong emphasis on the transformative power of self-suffering. I cannot say whether this voluntary self-suffering motif is prominent in Rabbi Nachman's teachings; such "redemptive suffering" seems different from Rabbi Nachman's own depressive suffering (see Rabbi Arthur Green's *Tormented Master*, 1979). Yet without claiming Rabbi Nachman as a nonviolent activist in the modern sense of the term, I do think that we can best understand the practical implications of his teaching by examining examples of the work of such modern figures as Gandhi, King, and the Dalai Lama.

Decades before King, Gandhi insisted that we must always distinguish the person from the deed. "Whereas a good deed should call forth approbation and a wicked deed disapprobation, the doer of the deed, whether good or wicked, always deserves respect or pity, as the case may be," he wrote (in *My Experiments with Truth*, 1927). "'Hate the sin and not the sinner' is a precept which, though easy enough to understand, is rarely practiced, and that is why the poison of hatred spreads in the world. . . . It is quite proper to resist and attack a system, but to resist and attack its author is tantamount to resisting and attacking oneself."

Along with this principle, which Rabbi Nachman would surely recognize as akin to his, both Gandhi and King did, of course, use many other nonviolent techniques to coerce as well as persuade the opponent. Yet for each of them, the ultimate goal was that *agape*, selfless love, successfully address and draw into action the capacity for decency in every human being, so very like Rabbi Nachman seeking the *od m'at*, the element of goodness in even the greatest sinner.

The Dalai Lama also exemplifies this approach of Rabbi Nachman. His emphasis on compassion translates into advice such as this (in *Ancient Wisdom, Modern World,* 2000): "The appropriate response to someone who causes us to suffer . . . is to recognize that in harming us, ultimately they lose their peace of mind, their inner balance, and thereby their happiness. And we do best if we have compassion for them, especially since a simple wish to see them hurt cannot actually harm them. It will certainly harm us, though."

The three of them would concur, I believe, with Rabbi Nachman: By appealing to the latent, hidden decency in every human being, the errant human being can be so moved towards goodness that we, looking for the sinner previously seen, are startled to discover that now "*ein ra-sha,*" there is no sinner" (Psalm 37:10), so effective has been the appeal to the "od m'at."

The profound societal implications of this teaching demand further consideration. Do not all religions contain this teaching in some significant form? How far can this principle be applied? Are there limiting cases, such as Scarpia in Puccini's *Tosca*, or in the real world, Hitler or Stalin?

Following his remarks about looking for the good in others, Rabbi Nachman now asks, what about the self? Shouldn't this approach apply to every individual, including myself? His answer (*Likutei Moharan,* "*Mikketz,*" #54) is the following:

> Just as one should judge others charitably, even the wicked, finding in them certain good points, and by these truly bringing them from culpability to worthiness, as in the cited verse . . . exactly so with the person him/herself: one must judge oneself charitably, to find an existing good point, thereby strengthening the self so that one does not despair completely, God forbid. All the more should the person revive himself by rejoicing in the bit of good which she finds in herself: a good act, a commandment properly fulfilled. Then the person should seek additional examples of goodness within the self, even if they are mixed with unworthy elements as well. And as this process of gathering examples of goodness proceeds, and the good is distinguished and extracted from the evil, melodies are made... melodies and songs exalted and holy . . . These melodies and songs prevent one from succumbing to despair, and so the person revives

... and is again able to pray and sing praises to God . . . and again feel near, not distant from the Divine.

This attention to the self is not surprising for one who suffered such constant inner pain from feelings of personal unworthiness as did Rabbi Nachman. Hence the importance of the above formula *(etza)* for overcoming feelings of personal unworthiness that lead to depression and despair. Introspection, serious self-searching, though essential for fully aware and responsible living, can be demoralizing. In the process, we are likely to identify with Jeremiah's pained cry (17:9): "The heart is deceitful above all things,/ And it is exceedingly weak – who can know it?"

Mixtures of motives, doubts about intentions, and the ultimate unknowability of ourselves can indeed unnerve us. If not Rabbi Nachman's despair, vertigo, at the least, is likely to be our reaction as we contemplate the depths of our being. In Georg Buchner's words: "Every human being is an abyss,/ it makes one dizzy/ to look down into it."[1]

Or as Gerard Manley Hopkins vividly portrays our plight (in *Poems and Prose*, 1956):

O the mind, mind has mountains; cliffs of fall
Frightful, sheer, no-man-fathomed. Hold them cheap
May who ne'er hung there.

Small wonder that Rabbi Nachman searches with equal zeal for the *"od,"* the goodness within oneself. To find that is to find footing against what could otherwise be a precipitous, despairing plunge into depression or despair.

Rabbi Nachman now finds support for his interpretation in another Psalm where *"od"* can be construed as substantive, Psalm 146:2. Usually translated, "I will sing praises unto my God while I have my being" (see also Psalm 104:33), Nachman renders it, "by means of my merit *('od')* that I find within myself," as in the previously cited, "just a bit of merit and there is no wicked." Hence Psalm 146:2/104:33 is best understood as: "I am able to sing praises to my God because I have discovered that bit of merit, of goodness, within me." And "I will sing" is to be taken literally, referring to the liturgical songs and wordless melodies that emerge from collecting those elements of goodness."

---

1. Georg Buchner, *Wozzeck: "Der mensch ist ein Abgrund,/ es schwindelt Einem/wenn man hinunterschaut."*

Based on his own experience in overcoming despair, Nachman is confident that the natural human reaction to feelings of self-worth will be an overflow of gratitude to the Creator, expressed in heartfelt words of praise and melodies of exaltation.

> And our rabbi was very insistent that we follow this teaching ("Torah"), for it is the fundamental basis for anyone who wants to approach the Divine ... For the majority of human beings who feel remote from the Divine, the essential cause is despair, depression, bitterness of spirit due to feelings of worthlessness. They see within themselves the corruption that taints their deeds; they feel heart-broken. And from this follow the feelings of worthlessness that prevent their praying or doing whatever of value they might otherwise be doing. Therefore each person must be vigilant not to succumb to those dark, bitter feelings. Instead all must follow this teaching of searching for, and finding, the element of goodness that assuredly exists within each person. Encouraged by this, each should then find and collect additional elements of goodness within. And so each person comes to life again, feels joy, and can once more anticipate redemption. And in that state of morale, the person can truly utter heartfelt prayers of gratitude. Thus is fulfilled the meaning of, "I will sing praises to my God by virtue of my 'od', the worthiness that I find within me."

While this may appear repetitious to us, the recorder here is following Rabbi Nachman's explicit instruction to reemphasize this fundamental method for overcoming despair and avoiding depression.

Rabbi Nachman's prescription should not be confused with facile, just-feel-good-about-yourself nostrums. His advice emerges from the depths of having experienced the very despair that he is eager to help us counter. Critical self-scrutiny is an essential part of worthy living. That such introspection be constructive, not destructive, uplifting, not depressing, is Rabbi Nachman's goal; the repeated teaching is his urgent recommendation for achieving this positive outcome.

Ever since I happened upon this passage ever so many years ago, *"azamer lelohai b'odi,"* "I will sing praises to my God with my *'od"* – recited daily in traditional morning prayers as well as weekly on Sabbath afternoons between Sukkot and Pesakh – has reverberated with the overtones sounded by Rabbi Nachman. His profound expansion of the meaning of *od* has, at the same time, freed me to understand *od* in its plain, simple sense of "more, additional." More what? As applied to the human being, I suggest that aspect of ourselves that appears to further the life-ascent of all creatures: consciousness, self-awareness. We cannot, with certainty, deny this quality to other animals; which of us, after all, has successfully entered the mind of a fellow creature? Yet we do comprehend that our natural endowments exceed those necessary for simply staying alive. Imagination and creativity, artistry in all its forms, accumulated learning and scholarship: simple survival does not require these, yet they are prominent features of our existence. They represent, indeed an *od*, a "more," an addition, a surplus. It is from this abundance that we play, pray, sing, dance, draw, design, think and build. Perhaps this superfluous endowment is the God-like quality called *"tzelem elohim,"* the Divine image, in the great Creation epic of Genesis.

Might this personal extension of Rabbi Nachman's teaching be faithful to the spirit of his comments? Robinson Jeffers, a most improbable witness, quite independently affirms this quality as God-like in his poem, "The Excesses of God" (from *Selected Poems,* 1965):

> It is not by his high superfluousness we know
> Our God? For to be equal a need
> Is natural, animal, mineral: but to fling
> Rainbows over the rain
> And beauty above the moon, and secret rainbows
> On the domes of deep sea-shells,
> And make the necessary embrace of breeding
> Beautiful also as fire,
> Not even the weeds to multiply without blossom
> Nor the birds without music:
> There is the great humaneness at the heart of things,
> The extravagant kindness, the fountain
> Humanity can understand, and would flow likewise
> If power and desire were perch-mates.

This, perhaps, is another way of articulating the underpinning and ultimate source for the *od* of which Rabbi Nachman so movingly speaks. We, too, might see ourselves as recipients of that "extravagant kindness." Rabbi Akiba implies something of the sort, I believe, when he remarks in *Pirkei Avot* (3:18): "Beloved is the human being, for s/he was created in the image of God. It is yet greater Divine love that makes known to us that we are created in the image of God."

This, too, is an *od*, an addition to our being, isn't it? In ever so many areas of our lives, recognition of the *od* may, indeed, revive our morale and rejoice our spirits.

Ode/*od*: a single syllable both in English and in Hebrew. Yet what vast horizons it can open, and what profound introspection it invites. With that ode/*od* on our tongues, perhaps we, too, shall be able to sing, with renewed conviction and intensity, the fullness of God's praises.

Ken y'hi ratzon. Be this God's will.

> From *Jewish Mysticism and the Spiritual Life*, edited by Lawrence Fine, Eitan Fishbane, Or N. Rose, 2011

Community/*Kehillah*

Keystone of the Jewish Tradition

From Contemporary Jewish Religious Thought, *the enduring 1988 volume of essays by modern Jewish thinkers and doers, this brief essay provides textual and historical evidence for the centrality of community as a concept and a reality in Jewish life.*

*K**ehillah* (community) refers to the organized communal units of Jewish existence. Widely used in the Bible, the word's root designates the act of convoking an assembly. Such an assembly might be especially summoned for a specific purpose: for religious matters such as fasting, feasting, worshipping, or hearing the words of the Torah, or for civic matters such as rebellion or war. Such an assembly might, on the other hand, stand as an organized body or congregation; in this latter usage the term usually refers to the entire community of Israel.[1]

Closely related to the concept of *kehillah* in the Biblical schema are *mishpakhah* (clan or family), *bet av* (the father's house), and *am* (people). The presupposition of family is the union of man and woman, a union on which, at the time of creation, in the words of Johannes Pedersen (*Israel, Its Life and Culture*, 1959), "was laid the blessing to which later generations owe their existence." Family, deriving from this union, implies common ancestry and kinship. At the same time it has a fluid boundary. Again Pedersen: "The family extends as far as the feeling of unity makes itself felt . . . wherever there is a whole bearing the impress of a common character." Connecting the household with the tribe, family thus makes possible the further formation of a community, a people.

Like family, community is at first defined by blood: "Every community

---

1. Cf. Frances Brown, S.R. Driver, and Charles Briggs, *Hebrew and English Lexicon of the Old Testament* (1962); Ludwig Koehler and Walter Baumgartner, *Lexicon in Veteris Testamenti Libros* (1948).

is a community of kinsmen with a common ancestor." Yet two separate communities may become one by virtue of joining, living together, and coming to share common characteristics. Thus the foundation is laid for the inclusion of others, for the development of a community whose basis of unity transcends the biological.

From the Biblical perspective, community is also the essential background for the individual. "When we look at the soul," Pedersen writes, "we always see a community rising behind it. What it is, it is by virtue of others . . . it must live in community, because it is its nature to communicate itself to others, to share blessing with them."

This profound reading of the Biblical evidence helps in understanding the dynamics of *kehillah* as organic or organized Jewish communal units. There is also an essential theological dimension to the historical persistence of Jewish community in a wide variety of forms and settings.

Theologically, human community may be characterized as the divinely initiated counterpoise to solitude, both for human beings and for the Divine. For humans, this is evident already in the emphasis on companionability found in the J account of creation: "The Lord God said: 'It is not good for man to be alone; I will make him a fitting helper for him'" (Gen. 2:18).

That the human community in turn provides companionship, as it were, for the Divine is supported by both Biblical and classical rabbinic tradition. The language of the creation account in Genesis 1 suggests that a new quality informs the world with the advent of the human being. All previous creations came about by solitary divine fiat: "And God said"; and "And God made"; "And God saw"; "And God blessed." With human beings, the language shifts to the plural: "And God said, 'Let us make man in our image, after our likeness.'"

The classical rabbinic tradition asked: "With whom did God consult?" Several answers were proposed: "With the prior works of heaven and earth"; "with the prior works of each day"; "with Himself"; "with the angels." Most remarkable, however, was that which asserted divine consultation with human beings: "With the souls of the righteous He consulted" (Gen. R. 8:3-4, 6).

The motivation for divine-human communality in creation is expounded in another midrash, quoted by Abraham Joshua Heschel in *Between God and Man* (1965): "From the first day of creation the Holy One, blessed be He, longed to enter into partnership with the terrestrial world, to dwell with His creatures within the terrestrial world" (Num. R. 13:6).

It is by virtue of this divine involvement that Jewish community, Biblically understood, comes into existence. The common ancestor, Abram (along with Sarai), is called by God (Genesis 12) and, as Abraham (along with Sarah), enters into covenant with God (Genesis 17). Their descendants, already in Egypt designated an *am*, a people (Exodus 1:9), are soon to become that special community that shall make visible God's active involvement in and concern for human beings in history. "And the Egyptians shall know that I am the Lord, when I stretch out My hand over Egypt, and bring out the Israelites from their midst." (Exodus 7:5).

At Sinai the word is proclaimed that, contingent upon the keeping of the covenant, "you shall be to Me a kingdom of priests and a holy nation" (Exodus 19:5-6), thus reaffirming, at Israel's most solemn moment of encounter with the Divine, the communal dimension of this covenant. In fact, the specific content of the Decalogue itself has been persuasively interpreted by Martin Buber (in *Moses*, 1958) as addressing, in three parts, "the God of the community . . . the time, the one-after-the-other of the community . . . the space, the one-with-the-other of the community."

The Abramamic covenant, the Exodus, and Sinai intertwined to form a cord both strong and elastic. On the one hand, its strength was sufficient to link the Divine in history with the fate of the Jewish community, while at the same time shaping and unifying that people – and its elasticity was sufficient to permit the community to assume, through the centuries and throughout the world, diverse yet functionally comparable forms. This is evidenced in the numerous agencies and institutions each community developed to afford its members religious, educational, judicial, financial, and social welfare services that reflected the sense of covenant as expressed in *halakhah*.

In the self-contained patterns of Diaspora Jewish living, individual community structures become all the more important as the authority of Palestinian patriarchs and Babylonian exilarchs receded with the passage of time and the further dispersion of the people. In the words of Salo Baron (in *A Social and Religious History of the Jews*, 1952), "Jewish autonomous life became ever more decentralized in favor of the basic unit, the community."

Until the French Revolution, Jewish communal life continued largely self-contained, its morale maintained by an ever-renewed sense of covenant and sacred history transmitted by the structures and practices of the community. "The small-town Jewish community of Eastern Europe – the *shtetl*," write Mark Zborowski and Elizabeth Herzog in *Life Is With People* (1952), "traces its line of march directly back to Creation. The Exodus from Egypt, the giving of the Law on Mount Sinai, are seen as steps along the way, historical events no less real than the Spanish Inquisition or the Russian Revolution." Thus personal identity was "supported, reaffirmed, 'nurtured' in interactions with others," write Brigitte Berger and Peter L. Berger in *The War Over the Family* (1983), while "the overall framework of meaning within which the individual can make sense of life" was provided.

As a result of emancipation and the Jewish entrance into modernity, both the identity- and meaning-functions of the community were seriously affected. As individual Jews related directly to the surrounding culture and state rather than through the established *kehillah*, Jewish community lost these long-standing functions. A further reduction in community cohesion has resulted from such technical developments as the automobile, highways, and rapid surface transportation, which have made possible the dispersion of population, with the consequent reduction in the number and strength of once distinctive, tradition-sustaining, and identity-nurturing Jewish neighborhoods.

A further development in the Western democracies, whose full implications are yet to be assessed, is the increase in intermarriage. On the one hand, the given biological or kinship basis of community is weakened by intermarriage; on the other hand, as non-Jews choose to become Jews, the covenantal and commitment factors may become increasingly determinative of Jewish life among the identified.

Two other developments, both especially evident in the United States, should be mentioned. One is the quest for styles of community leadership that will facilitate communal self-direction and growth. Drawing from Mordecai M. Kaplan's definition of Judaism as an "evolving religious civilization" and most visible in the *khavurah* movement, participants seek small-group intimacy and active involvement as equals in religious and social expression.

Often combined with this quest is the reassertion of the feminine in Jewish life today. Socially, women are assuming new leadership roles, a development both validated and advanced by the fact that the Reform, Reconstructionist, and Conservative seminaries now accept women as candidates for rabbinic ordination. Theologically, searching questions are being asked concerning the possible overmasculinization of God in traditional

Jewish portrayals of the Divine, a likely consequence of which will be considerable revision of the former "overall framework of meaning within which the individual can make sense of his life."

Indeed, for Jewish communities throughout the world, the "overall framework of meaning" has suffered severe challenges in the modern age, perhaps exceeding the earlier theological questions raised by Spinoza, the textual questions propounded by Bible critics, and the *weltanschauung* issues posed by modern science. In this century, fundamental questions concerning God's relationship with the Jewish community have been painfully intensified by two world wars, by the use and further development of nuclear weapons, and, especially for the Jewish community, by the advent of the modern State of Israel – a cause for rejoicing among most Jews and a focus of Jewish concern everywhere. Apart from thorny issues of defining the relation of the diaspora to Israel, it is also unclear how the ideal of Zion, embodied in a modern political unit of power, the nation-state, can escape secularization, "normalization," a disturbing reenactment of certain elements of the earlier conquest of the land, and reduction to becoming "like all the nations" (I Samuel 8). Such a reduction would effectively nullify the redemptive function of the Jewish people and the injunctions that stand both at this community's inception – "and you shall be a blessing . . . the families of the earth shall bless themselves by you" (Genesis 12:2-3) – and at one of its prophetic peaks:

> I the Lord have called you in righteousness,
> And I have grasped you by the hand.
> I created you, and appointed you
> A convenant-people, a light of nations.
>
> *Isaiah 42:6*

To reintegrate the covenantal with the organic and to reaffirm universality with particularity may well be the central challenges to Jewish communal existence today.

From *Contemporary Jewish Religious Thought*,
edited by Arthur A. Cohen and Paul Mendes-Flohr, 1988

Reflections on Cuba

An Eyewitness Report

In the late 1960s, as the Cuban Revolution – and U.S. hostilities, including the embargo – ripened, Rabbi Gendler made a series of visits to the island and its shrinking but hardy Jewish community. What follows is a compression of four different essays that Rabbi Gendler wrote as an eyewitness.

1968

Cuba is far, very far, from the United States or Mexico, even farther than the necessities of Cuban visas, special State Department authorization for travel, or Mexican reentry permits would suggest. On reflection, though, such diplomatic hurdles seem like good preparation for a trip to that far-yet-near island; they suggest that one is about to enter a very different world, which is indeed the case.

Imagine, for example, leaving a Mexican airport where every hand is outstretched, and arriving at another where tips are not accepted! Imagine leaving a land where consumer products and stunning buildings abound, but appalling gaps between classes have increased markedly in recent years, and entering another where scarcities are the rule, products are in short supply, and there is an astonishing feeling of egalitarian camaraderie!

Or imagine leaving a land where attempts at remedial tutoring projects have been largely depressing failures, and entering another where outstanding nationwide gains in literacy and educational levels have been made by precisely such tutoring programs. Imagine leaving a land where vast resources have been unable to affect the hostility and bitterness of the dispossessed, and entering a poor land where hostility and bitterness, though they exist, pale beside the glow of cooperation, dedication, and mutual effort.

The shock of such contrasts could not have been fully prepared for in advance, no matter what reading I might have done, nor could any preparation have been adequate for the slowly accumulating realization. Here in this conversation, here in this relationship, nothing more is expected simply than what is shared between persons – no tips, no favors, no supplications; an exchange in dignity, nothing more, nothing less.

That feeling that gnaws at one all through Latin America – *why do I have while this person lacks? how can I rectify the imbalance? what does all this amiable chatter really mean when the stark necessities of the other's life are so persistent, so obvious, and so without hope?* – was palpable in its absence in Cuba.

Not that affluence confronts one. Hardly. The restaurant lines in Havana were long, the varieties of food in the shops severely limited (though nutritionally adequate), the availability of coffee insufficient for the constant tropical demand. There was impatience at times; there were barbed comments when freshly-brewed coffee ran out before all had gotten their sips; there were memories of the days of plenty when from Florida shores food flowed southward in exceeding quantities. Not in sufficient quantities for the peasants, true, not for the poor in Havana, but for the well off? Those were the days.

No, affluence does not confront one, nor plenty. What does confront one is the sharing, the equality, the considered and considerate dividing of that which is available. And somehow, given basic sufficiency, even though there is not plenty, there is enough. Ration cards are supplemented by cafeterias at places of work, by lunch rooms at schools, by resident schools for hundreds of thousands of youth, and so there is not plenty, but enough. Thus one sees people living a hard but not a miserable existence, and one meets another with understanding, with recognition of dignity, and without that demeaning commiseration that is the necessary and appropriate accompaniment of encounter elsewhere in Latin America today.

This general dignity and affirmative spirit of Cuba confirms itself institutionally as well. Everyone finds kibbutz-like projects, hard, invigorating, and inspiring. Work-study units exist, groups of youth from all over the Republic assembled in camp-like settings, working some hours each day and studying at other hours of the day or evenings. *Internados*, residence schools for children, especially in rural areas, house and feed the children from Monday morning to Saturday noon, providing bus service as well to and from their houses.

Such schools, besides meeting the problem of educational deprivation for rural youth, provide relevant and integrated curricula of academic subjects, supervised practice in the planting and tending of crops, music, crafts, sports, etc. More than 150,000 *becados,* full-scholarship resident-students from all over Cuba, now reside in the vacated mansions of the Marianao section of Havana, lending a beauty of use to these structures that could hardly have been the case before the revolution.

Scattered throughout the countryside are nuclei of new settlements: rural health clinics, people's farms, area schools, recreation centers, and new towns. Even from Havana, thousands of urbanites go regularly to the fields, participating in the *cordón* project, a green-belt-to-be surrounding the city and consisting of reservoirs, citrus groves, coffee plants, *gandul* (bean) bushes, sugarcane, useful and decorative trees, and fruits and other vegetables for local consumption. In these, as in other ways, Cuba is trying to address effectively the worldwide problem of over-urbanization and under-ruralization.

While positive impressions predominate, there are also some less attractive features. The press, for example, does not reflect much diversity or dissent in its presentation of national and international affairs, even though varieties of opinion are to be heard among the people. There is also some uncertainty about due process as we understand it, and an emphasis at times on official interpretations of revolutionary goals that do not contribute to a maximally libertarian atmosphere for personal opinion.

It is amidst this general atmosphere, intensified by the frequent and often inspiring speeches by Fidel Castro, that some 1,200 out of a pre-revolutionary Jewish population of 10,000, live their present lives and maintain their communal institutions. As can be imagined, there are difficulties, though not necessarily those that first come to mind.

Surprisingly, there is almost no direct conflict between the official Communist policy of the government and the Jewish – or, for that matter, other – religious institutions. That singular experiment that is the Cuban *proceso revolucionario,* while it has its principles and its affirmations, has also its breadths and flexibilities.

Whatever may be the official Marxist-Leninist attitudes toward religion, they have not affected the practice of religion in Cuba directly. Thus the Papal representative is well-received by Communist Party officials, full diplomatic relations with Israel exist despite Cuban "third world" rhetoric, a sympathetic member of the Central Committee of the Cuban Communist Party has among his other duties the coordination of particular religious needs with government policies, and among both church and synagogue leaders and members of the Party there seems to exist a mutual respect and accommodation that is encouraging.

What this means in practice can readily be seen by a survey of existing Jewish institutions. First of all, there are, as before the revolution, five functioning synagogues in Havana. All hold services on the High Holy Days, all have Sukkot celebrations, some hold regular Sabbath services, and one maintains a daily *minyan* mornings and evenings.

The diversity is considerable. One synagogue, for example, uses the Union Prayer Book (Reform), has page announcements in Spanish, the service in Hebrew and English, a full Torah reading, men and women seated together, and *kippot* (skull caps) worn by all male worshippers.

Another recites the service entirely in Hebrew and maintains a *mehitza* (separation between men and women) complete with curtains behind which the women sit, and the praying is thoroughly traditional in every respect. A third uses a Sephardic prayer book printed in Italy, following the Turkish *minhag* (custom), and is distinguished by the fine chanted responses of the congregants, women included. Yet a fourth, also Sephardic, is characterized by the distinctive responsive shouting of verses from the *piyuttim* (hymns) by various members, disciplined yet wild in mood and procedure. And the fifth, Ashkenazic-traditional in orientation, depends like the others entirely on its educated and devoted laymen for the continuation of organized Jewish religious services in Havana.

This diversity of mood and practice, a diversity to be savored and cherished, happily does not result in a sharply divided community – at least not now. Perhaps it is the reduced numbers, perhaps rather a genuine feeling that transcends particular differences. Whatever the explanation, I observed that members of any one congregation could be seen attending the services of another at times; that the young people, few in number now, met together despite differences in their synagogue affiliations; and that at the community-wide meals during the two days of Rosh Hashanah and at the conclusion of Yom Kippur, there seemed to be a fair amount of mingling among members of the various communities.

The community meals, held in the ample facilities of the Patronato de la Communidad Hebrea, are presently a prominent feature of Jewish life in Havana, and reflect both the attitude of the government and the general situation of life today in Cuba. As mentioned earlier, food is strictly rationed at this point, and supplements to the diet either at work or in restaurants are much sought. In the case of the Jewish community, kosher meat – available to individual Jews at all times in quantities at least equal to the general meat ration – is allotted so that the kitchen of the Patronato can serve at least one large meat meal each week.

In addition, for the various holidays extra rations are provided, and so all members of the Jewish community can join in an especially festive communal meal, celebrative both of the holiday itself and of the additional fare. From my vegetarian vantage point, I noticed that the meals this time included *gefilte* fish, chopped liver, chicken soup with *kreplakh*, chicken, farfel, *kugel*, vegetables, etc. – adequate anywhere and positively abundant in Havana at this time.

Another interesting feature of Havana Jewish life is the education of the children. With the nationalization of all schools some years ago, the Albert Einstein Jewish Day School, like all private schools, became a state school. In this case also, however, the government has displayed considerable understanding of Jewish religious needs. Any Jewish child in Havana may attend this particular school if he or she wishes, and special bus service is provided to and from school by the government.

At school, Jewish children take all classes with the neighborhood children of their age who now attend the school. Then, beginning with the 3:30 p.m. activity and sports period, all Jewish children who wish to pursue Jewish studies are excused from the activities, and from 3:30 to 5 p.m. they study with two teachers provided by the Jewish community. Altogether, there are about forty children between the ages of 6 and 14 who take advantage of this opportunity, the number being nearly the total of Jewish children of these ages in Havana.

As far as the curriculum is concerned, I discussed this with the Hebrew teachers and discovered the following: Religious instruction is not permitted in the public (state) schools any longer, being regarded as the proper function of home and church and synagogue. However, cultural subjects such as Hebrew, Yiddish, Jewish history, etc. are not regarded as objectionable, so only these are taught. "Only!" exclaimed one of the teachers. "If only the children learned all we try to teach!"

After class I was introduced to the principal of the school, a bright and cordial woman who seemed friendly both to the Hebrew teachers and to me. During a discussion afterwards with the teachers, one of them summed up by saying that "as far as Jews and Judaism are concerned, this government is *lifnim mishurat ha-din*" – considerate beyond what could strictly be asked.

One other interesting point of institutional contact between the revolutionary government and the Jewish community occurred with the nationalization of all cemeteries and the decree that burial without cost was one of the basic rights of all Cuban citizens. I learned what this meant in practice from the very devoted voluntary head of the Jewish cemetery.

Before, he said, he ran the cemetery effectively; now, he runs the cemetery effectively. Before, Jewish religious scruples were heeded; now, Jewish religious scruples are heeded. The difference? "If we need something, we let the government man in charge of cemeteries know of it, and he sees that it is taken care of. It runs just as before – except that I have no financial worries and nobody in the community has to pay anything."

Nonetheless many Jews have left Cuba, and while among those who remain there are some with genuine dedication to the revolutionary interpretations of the goal of a just, brotherly and equal Communist society, there are others who, despite monthly payments from the government in compensation for nationalized shops or industries, are waiting for the chance to leave.

It is not hard to understand their reasons. Those who did leave had their reasons. The advent of a social system that declared invalid the means by which a living was to be had previously was surely a shock to many, and the resulting dislocations could hardly have endeared the new system to those who felt penalized by it.

Furthermore, the growing estrangement from their chief point of reference, the United States, must have caused great anxiety to many, and those with family or friends felt a stronger desire to join them. Increasing difficulties of life in Cuba – due partly to a more equal distribution of resources, partly to difficulties and errors of the change of system, partly to the flight of trained personnel, and partly to the U.S blockade – were also felt, especially by those formerly well off.

All these factors, plus the negative associations with the word "communism" and a perceived arbitrariness of the new regime, help account for the large numbers of Jews who have left Cuba during these past ten years, and for those smaller numbers who still hope to leave. They are very human reasons and not hard to understand.

On the other hand, I must confess that after three weeks on that remarkable island, I am especially impressed by those Jews who have chosen to remain. Some, I know, have sacrificed much in material comforts, while others have known the bitter loneliness of friends and family leaving. Yet they stay. Why?

For some, it is primarily the feeling that Cuba is their home whatever the form of government, that there they belong and there they will remain. For others, there are special reasons. One man, for example, has been active in a congregation since its earliest days. To leave now, he feels, especially when so many have already left, would be to turn his back on all that this particular congregation has meant to the lives of several generations of Jews. So he remains, and with great devotion works to maintain the congregation at some level of functioning in spite of the departure of so many.

There is another group that remains for special reasons: those Jews, not many in number but passionate in their dedication, who regard the revolution as struggling to achieve such genuinely religious ideals as justice, equality, brotherhood, the cessation of exploitation, the better utilization of resources, and a concern for the basic needs of all citizens.

For them, there is a religious quality to their participation in the effort to provide for the basic medical and nutritional needs of all, to instruct every Cuban in reading, writing, and social ideals of cooperation, to provide every person with the chance for a feeling of human dignity and usefulness through participation in work of social value, and to create a new society in which, through sharing and contributing freely to one another, people will feel the idea of human interconnection to be a fact, not a fancy.

For such Jews, this period of severe trial is the Desert Experience of our people; the material deprivation remind them of scarcities in the desert; longing recollections of good times are like memories of the fleshpots of Egypt; and the goal, the transformation of a mass of recently emancipated semi-slaves into a people of profound dedication to social ideals with dignity for each one, reflects the goal of Moses during the desert trek.

Idolatry? Not necessarily. Fidel may be admired and esteemed, but he is hardly deified. A grievous error of understanding? Not necessarily. Our own crisis-ridden societies, East as well as West, hardly validate the methods and judgments we have applied to social problems, nor is the distribution of wealth between so-called developed and so-called underdeveloped countries any great tribute to the moral superiority of the former.

Altogether, some considerable humility would seem to me the most appropriate stance for us to assume before a significant and basically idealistic social experiment with such aims of human character and morale transformation, whatever its errors and excesses (and it surely has such). For as Robert Heilbroner pertinently expresses it (in *Harper's*, September, 1968), speaking of Cuba along with only a few other underdeveloped nations: ". . . a new and genuine spirit of idealism and endeavor is to be found among the young . . . I would insist on one central achievement whose importance it is impossible to overstate. It is that these nations *have* succeeded in touching and bringing to life the deadened humanity that is the despair of the underdeveloped world. Even if they fail now, they have opened the way for a future assault that can succeed. One may fault the Communist nations on many grounds, not least that of morality . . . but one must also admit that they have brought hope, enthusiasm and effort to the common people of their lands. *Of how many backward nations can this be said?*"

Even apart from such human considerations, which surely address our religious and ethical commitments, there is a further importance that the Cuban experiment has for us as Jews. The harsh fact is that poverty and demoralization are widespread in Latin America today, and the contributions of our favored U.S. palliatives, such as the Alliance for Progress, toward the solutions of these problems are hardly discernible.

Certainly no transformation of morale or attitude on the part of the masses has been seen. Heilbroner may again be correct when he emphasizes: "In many countries of the underdeveloped world only revolutionary activity will rescue the populace from its unending misery."

If this be true – and there is much evidence to support it – it probably means that the basis for a decent existence for hundreds of millions of human beings will require radical and social change, perhaps of the Cuban type, perhaps of a different type. In either case, the continued existence of Jewish communities in such countries will require the ability to adapt to such economic and social circumstances.

Can this be done, or is Judaism in Latin America for the most part dependent on the existence of social and economic systems that are, in many cases, an affront to human dignity?

If in a system change such as Cuba's, where there is no anti-Semitism, no official hostility to organized religion, and little Marxist-Leninist rigidity on such matters, a Jewish community cannot or will not exist, what does this imply for the Jewish future elsewhere in Latin America? It is a question that must not be slighted.

The many Jews who, along with some 300,000 non-Jewish Cubans, have left Cuba have done so for reasons that invite our understanding. At the same time, some of those Jews who remain may, with proper awareness and leadership, help lay the foundations for a Judaism that can exist not only amidst the cruel and exploitative social conditions of Latin America today but in new and more decent surroundings as well. If this be their calling and it be fulfilled, our debt to them may be considerable.

From *Israel Horizons,* December 1968

1969

The most striking feature of the religious situation in Cuba today is the attitude of the revolutionary government toward traditional institutional religion. Except for Jehovah's Witnesses, whose anti-government stance seems as unacceptable to Cubans as to us in the United States, the prac-ticing denominations are at least tolerated, perhaps respected, and always treated with consideration by the government. Evidence of this is everywhere.

Churches and synagogues are functioning and are about as well maintained as most other kinds of buildings in Cuba today. Although construction materials are not plentiful and waiting is the rule, supplies for church and synagogue repairs are usually provided in due course. In some cases the government has helped to keep in operation religious institutions whose work was jeopardized by the loss of many members.

Beyond this, the government gives considerable attention to the specific needs of religious groups. For example, while food is strictly rationed, kosher meat is available to Orthodox Jews, and special rations are supplied to the Jewish community for such occasions as Rosh Hashanah, Yom Kippur and Passover. This spring, when the continuing U.S. blockade, combined with the dock strike and other shipping difficulties, threatened to prevent the arrival of the Passover *matzot* (from Israel via England!) in time for the first seder, the government exerted itself to expedite delivery.

Again, the government recently licensed the importation of six new Volkswagens for Christian clergymen (nine were requested). It is true that, on the whole, Cuba's public transportation functions rather well. Still, because of the severe gasoline shortages and the lack of material for repairs, the *guaguas* (buses) do not always run on schedule and are usually crowded, so that it is extremely difficult to get around. Hence the significance of permitting the import of automobiles for clergymen should not be underestimated.

Two more examples. Last fall (for Rosh Hashanah, Yom Kippur and Sukkot) and again this spring (for Passover), I met at synagogue a young soldier – under the Castro regime military service is compulsory – who had been granted leave from his unit so that he might celebrate these holy days with his family. At the Passover services I also met a devout Jew who told me that when his small factory was nationalized, he was asked whether he would like to continue working there. "Fine with me," he told the government, "but I observe the Sabbaths and all the Jewish holidays, and that means I don't work on those days. Do you still want me under those conditions?" The government replied in the affirmative, and during the past several years, the man assured me, there has never been the slightest pressure on him to work on these days, not even at times of most intensive mobilization for extra hours of voluntary labor in factories or fields. His is but one of a number of similar cases.

All this is not to suggest, of course, that Cuba's general atmosphere supports traditional institutional religion. Last year, I was told, the children's carnival (the climax of the annual *Semana Infantil* or "Children's Week") was celebrated on Good Friday – whether by accident or design I do not know, though I suspect is was the latter. This year, however, there was no such conflict, and it was announced that henceforth Children's Week will coincide with celebration of the Victory of Playa Giron (the defeat of the U.S.-backed invasion in 1961) and will not compete with Holy Week.

Then there is the question whether those who "hold religious beliefs" may function in such roles as that of guide in the *Union de Pioneros de Cuba* – the equivalent of our Boy and Girl Scouts, but communist in orientation. This question is, I suppose, somewhat analogous to that of the "atheistic teacher" in certain areas of the U.S. Be that as it may, I gather that the Cuban answer varies from place to place and seems to depend to some degree on the person involved. Thus an active and dedicated community worker, whatever his or her religious beliefs, would probably not be refused such a position – unless by "sectarian" communists, who appear to be outnumbered by "liberal" communists. Even so, the issue is troubling.

As for downright anti-religious indoctrination, there seems to be little of it. One churchman whose children have been members of the *Pioneros* for quite a few years told me that he has yet to hear of any antireligious teaching at *Pioneros* meetings – "and my kids tell me plenty!" There are no "museums of atheism" in Cuba, and at present apparently no publications directly attacking religion as such.

On the whole, then, I think that organized religion is accorded non-repressive and even respectful treatment in Cuba today. How can we account for this situation, when Cuba describes itself as a Marxist-Leninist state? One factor may be the comparative weakness of religion in pre-revolutionary Cuba; thus the government does not find it necessary to combat institutional religion as an organized force. Also, thanks to the remarkable breadth of Fidel Castro's non-doctrinaire approach to many issues, the Cuban experiment is still open-ended in its search for solutions appropriate to Cuba.

Interestingly enough, however, deeper considerations are also at work here – considerations set forth by Lenin himself in 1905-1909. Let me summarize Lenin's approach to religion in relation to the state and to "the Party of the Socialist Proleteriat." I base my analysis on *Acerca de la religion, a* compilation of articles on religion selected from the fourth Russian edition of Lenin's works, translated into Spanish and published in Moscow by *Editorial Progreso,* 1968. (Translations into English are mine.) Says Lenin: ". . . religion must be a private matter . . . The State should have nothing to do with religion, and religious associations should not be based on the power of the State. Every person should have full freedom to profess whatever religion he prefers, or none at all . . . It is absolutely intolerable that any difference in the rights of citizens should be dependent on their religious beliefs." In this connection, Lenin points out that Engels regarded the idea of prohibiting religion in the socialist society as "pseudo-revolutionary" and utterly condemnable.

However, Lenin continues, insofar as the party is concerned religion is a different matter. The party "neither can nor should remain indifferent to unawareness, ignorance, or obscurantism in the form of religious beliefs." While the power of the state is not to be enlisted either for or against religion, "our press and our word" must combat "the religious fog" ideologically.

Yet this kind of ideological effort must not be overdone, says Lenin. Again citing Engels in support of his position, Lenin takes issue with those who would launch a primarily educational campaign against religion and clericalism. He labels them "adventurers" who, adopting the false approach of "the bourgeois progressive, the bourgeois radical, or the bourgeois materialist," wrongly attribute religious belief among backward people to "ignorance"; whereas true "dialectical materialism" sees that "the social oppression of the working masses, their apparent total impotence before the blind forces of capitalism" is "the most profound root of religion in our times." Therefore the genuine Marxist must "not place the fight against religion in the purely theoretical realm of abstractions and preachings, but concretely, based upon the class struggle, which in deed liberates and instructs the masses more effectively than any other mode." And this is not mere "Marxist moderation" for "tactical reasons," but rather – according to Lenin – a position which derives from the essence of Marxism.

As for "denying Christians or believers membership in our Party," this Lenin opposes for several reasons. First, such a denial would, as noted, make religion the primary rather than the secondary problem it really is. Second, it would divide "the forces of the true revolutionary struggle" without adequate reason, for "economic servitude is the authentic source of religious deception." "We should not only admit but try to attract to the Social-Democratic Party all those workers who maintain faith in God; we are unconditional enemies of the least offense to their religious beliefs."

Nor, Lenin adds, may priests be categorically denied membership in the party. The role of religion in western Europe, he insisted, must be carefully differentiated from its role in Czarist Russia, and in his view a priest who became a party member might contribute with integrity to the work of the party. In short, Lenin is opposed to the exclusion of any individual, even a priest, solely because of his personal religious beliefs.

It is precisely on these opinions of Lenin's that the Cuban Communist Party bases it attitude toward religion. The Russian's approach to religion as a general phenomenon and his emphasis on allowing for individual historical and cultural circumstances help, I think, to account for the atmosphere one senses in Cuba today.

Perhaps the best word to describe the party's attitude toward religious institutions is "challenging." Save regarding certain incidents of counter-revolutionary activity emanating from churches – and there have been few of such in recent years – I found no overt hostility to religious attitudes or outlook. Incomprehension of what traditional religion may mean in an increasingly scientific and technological society, yes; confidence that the religious residue will in time dissolve by itself, yes; but open hostility, coercion or repression, no.

There is a sense, however, in which the Castro government challenges religion at a deeper, existential level. In important ways Cuba's "mobilization system" – I borrow the term from an essay by David E. Apter (in *Old Societies and New States,* edited by Clifford Geertz) – betokens a prophetic concern for justice which pays attention both to the overall social structure and to the individual. A speech delivered by Fidel Castro on July 26, 1968 (and published in full in the magazine *Gramma* of the same date), describes this aspect of the Cuban experiment. What, Castro asked, is the "great task" of the revolution? He answers (I translate from the Spanish): "To form the new man . . . the man of truly revolutionary . . . truly socialist, conscience, truly communist conscience . . . No human society has yet achieved communism . . . A communist society . . . means that the human being has become capable of living that level of understanding, friendship and brotherhood which on occasion has been realized in the intimate family circle. To live in a communist society is to live without egotism . . . as though . . . every one of our fellow citizens were our most beloved brother."

The way to achieve this truly communist society, Castro insists, is by "translation of conscience into wealth," rather than the reverse: "[T]o stimulate a man by money that he fulfills his duties more completely is to acquire conscience with money. To give men collectively more wealth because they have fulfilled their responsibilities and produced more and created more for the entire society, that is to convert conscience into wealth. Communism certainly cannot be established . . . unless wealth is created in abundance. But the path, in our judgment, is . . . to create . . . always more collective wealth by means of more collective conscientiousness."

He spells out the meaning of these statements: societal responsibility for adequate housing, food, medical care and education for every citizen; full pensions for the sick and elderly; increasing equalization of wages, etc. (In fact, many of these ideas are already operative even under present conditions of scarcities.)

As for those "capitalist or socialist" devotees of the science of "pure economics" who insist that the revolution will fail by this path, Castro said, "There is another science, a more profound science, the truly revolutionary science; the science of consciousness, the science of trust in . . . human beings. If one believes that man . . . can march forward only be egotism, that man is incapable of learning [or of] developing his conscience, then the 'judicious' economists are right: the revolution will fail when it confronts the laws of economics."

Surely all this has a religious ring. Despite misgivings about the dictatorial nature of the Cuban regime (a different though significant question), one can scarcely miss the prophetic character of speech.

What, now, has been the response of organized religion in Cuba to the government's attitude and action? Until recently, one might have sketched that response as follows: Immediately after the triumph of the rebellion, sympathetic expectation; with the radicalization of the revolution, growing doubts, culminating in vocal opposition and some overt counter-revolutionary activity; increasing losses of church and synagogue members as many middle- and upper-class people left the island; then a long period of comparative silence on the part of the churches – a depressingly static situation, unaffected by the currents of religious renewal that were sweeping over the rest of the world (though there were always a few church leaders who combatted this apathy). In short, the churches tended to be "refuges for reactionaries," for those who identified the "old days" with religious rectitude.

But today storms are blowing in a new wind of change. A few months ago, a number of ministers affiliated with the Council of the Evangelical Churches of Cuba, dissatisfied with the council's failure to speak out strongly on Vietnam, issued in their own names a "Declaration of Cuban Christians Concerning Vietnam." They made three demands: unconditional cessation of U.S. bombings and attacks on the Democratic Republic of Vietnam; U.S. withdrawal of its occupying forces from South Vietnam; and negotiations by all parties to the conflict to create the conditions which would make possible fulfillment of the Geneva agreements and the reunification of Vietnam.

Some of the signers delivered a copy of this declaration to representatives of the National Liberation Front in Havana. It was, they reported, a moving occasion, which gave rise to a profound sense of religious concern and human fellowship. Unfortunately, since then some churchmen, apparently ignoring or unaware of the fact that this was a statement signed by individuals, have resigned from the council. One may hope that the break is only temporary.

On the Catholic side also there are signs of renewed concern for social conditions. In April of this year, Cuba's Catholic bishops issued a pastoral letter – *"Comunicado de la Conferencia Episcopal de Cuba a Nuestros Sacerdotes y Fideles"* – to be read to the faithful at all masses on Sunday April 20 and to be distributed in printed form the following Sunday. I am told that this was the first such communication to be made in seven years. Certainly it differs markedly in content from the anti-government pastoral letters of the early 1960s.

Their aim, the bishops say, is to "translate into practical norms the general principles of renewal" articulated at last year's Eucharistic Congress in Colombia. Referring to Pope Paul's encyclical *Populorum Progressio,* they declare that the church must concern itself with the unrest in developing nations and must inspire and educate the faithful to "perceive the responsibilities of their faith in their personal and social life." They continue: "A merely individual ethic is not sufficient; neither is a purely social ethic which places almost exclusive emphasis on the use of external things; what is rather needed is a social ethic which, while not neglecting the objective reality, nonetheless takes as its starting point the human person with his calling of integral development."

Speaking then of "the importance of work from the perspective of the renewed ethic of development," the bishops cite a passage from the encyclical which strikes one as especially applicable to Cuba, with its massive mobilization of all strata of society for common work in the fields: "Living together, sharing one hope, one suffering, one goal and one joy, such work unites the wills, brings near the spirits, and fuses the hearts; by participating in it, men discover that they are brothers." There follow two paragraphs directly addressing themselves to the situation in Cuba today, a situation of hard work, great effort, some errors and excesses, many scarcities, and some signs of progress. They are worth quoting at length:

> . . . [H]ow many excesses are due to the concrete situation of isolation in which we have found ourselves for so many years! Who can ignore the difficulties which obstruct the way to development? Internal difficulties, arising from the novelty of the problems and the technical complexities, though due also to the deficiencies and sins of men; but, equally, external difficulties, connected with the complexity which characterizes relations among nations, unjustly disadvantageous for small, weak, underdeveloped nations. Is this not the case with the economic blockade to which our people have been subjected, and whose automatic prolongation imposes still more difficulties upon our country? – difficulties which fall principally upon our workers in city and country, upon our housewives, upon our growing children and youth, upon our sick. . .
>
> Seeking the well-being of our people and faithful to the service of the poorest, in accordance with the mandate of Jesus Christ and with the promise renewed in Medellin, we denounce the unjust situation of the

> blockade which contributes to much unnecessary suffering and makes more difficult our search for development. We therefore appeal to all who are in a position to do so to take decisive and effective action to bring about the cessation of this measure.

According, as it does, at least a modicum of recognition and even worth to the Castro regime, this Episcopal letter certainly marks a milestone in the official church attitude toward the revolutionary government of Cuba.

Today, then, signs of a new spirit are evident in Cuba's churches. They are hardly sufficient to place religion in the vanguard of Cuban society, but their importance should not be underestimated. No longer confined to a few individual clergymen, these stirrings of the spirit are perceptible within religious institutions. While their leaders' views may still be well ahead of their laity's, these institutions bid fair to contribute significantly to the integration of some rather remote religious elements into the larger Cuban society.

At the same time, at least a few of the younger clergy are beginning to see that the times demand a kind of activity different from the established clerical ways. For example, I know one seminarian (there are Catholic and Protestant seminaries functioning in Cuba) who goes everywhere by public transportation, meets with people in non-church settings whenever possible, and does a great deal of voluntary work in the fields. He is convinced that only through such "worker-priest" witnessing can his ministry reach persons.

The future of religion in Cuba is hard to predict. I have described the various initiatives that have been taken. What will come of them? What should be the content of the institutional religious message in this new societal context? The nature of the specifically "religious" function is far from clear. Despite institutional problems and depleted numbers of communicants, however, a sense of anticipation, even excitement, pervades Cuba's churches and synagogues.

Many socialist regimes are oppressively antireligious. Cuba's, however, seems as open to religion as Leninism will allow. At the least, it abides by reasonably sporting rules of the game. Possibly the Cuban challenge to traditional religion will even prove purifying. All this remains to be seen. But of one fact there can be little doubt: The religious response to the Cuban challenge will be instructive and significant far beyond the borders of that remarkable island.

From *The Christian Century*, July, 1969

The U.S. Bicentennial and the Jubilee Year

The Right We Must Reclaim

The Biblical proclamation of the Jubilee – the dissolving of debt and redistribution of land every half century – is engraved on the unrung Liberty Bell in Philadelphia. This 1976 essay, published in the journal of the Reform rabbinate, seeks to ring the bell by applying the radical principles and the promise of the Jubilee to modern American society in its 200th year of independence.

En route to our bicentennial celebration, we Americans seem neither a happy nor a confident people. The promise of 1776 has not been fulfilled, and we know it clearly. Previous generations could nourish false hopes and sustain illusions; we, called upon to celebrate something that had potential elements of authentic greatness and glory, are today confronted by some sobering realities that recent events have made all the more evident.

Moving toward our bicentennial observance, we find ourselves societally in a triple bind, and "a triple cord is not so quickly broken" (Ecclesiastes 4:12). Our triple bind, in brief, is an unprecedented concentration of wealth in a period of combined economic recession and inflation, and an unprecedented concentration of human population. This triple concentration threatens not only our American political system and its values but the human enterprise itself, and the threat is both physical and psycho-spiritual.

The nuclear alert of not so long ago, with its attendant anxieties, was a pointed reminder that we live with centralized destructive power unparalleled in human history. Never before has destructive force been so concentrated and so available that it could threaten the destruction of all human beings everywhere on our planet. Such a situation is both physically dangerous and psychically demoralizing.

This loss of confidence in the future, posed by the existence of nuclear weapons that could destroy all mankind, seriously erodes one foundation-stone of Biblical religion – the messianic expectation of time fulfilled – and with it another major pillar of Western civilization as well. Without significant time expectation, neither the life of individuals nor of the species can continue as heretofore – a factor in our contemporary personal despair and social disorientation that deserves the most serious attention.

Related to the concentration of military power is the accumulation and exercise of concentrated political power in America. It is tempting to cite Watergate as the single case in point and rest content with that evidence, but such a treatment would be both superficial and sanguine. Watergate may be the most widely publicized and most visible example, but even a cursory review of developments in the United States since World War II reveals striking and consistent departures from democratic theory and practice.

Permanent peacetime conscription, a form of involuntary servitude once abhorred in this country, has become taken for granted, and registration continues even though inductions are presently suspended. President Kennedy's Bay of Pigs invasion and the Cuban missile crisis; the same president's assignment of "civilian advisers" to Vietnam in the early 1960s; raids by American-directed troops into North Vietnam before the latter was militarily engaged in South Vietnam; President Johnson's post-election escalation of direct United States involvement in sharp contradiction of his pre-election rhetoric and promises; President Nixon's Laos and Cambodian incursions, and his later escalations of the air war; CIA-directed coups against various governments which American citizens learn about years later, if at all – these acts are by now so much a part of common political practice that their denial of basic democratic values and procedures is hardly noticed. Enormous amounts of power are "there," waiting to be applied at the discretion of a few key figures.

Meanwhile, the surveillance apparatus, military and civilian, has been busy domestically as well as internationally. Military dossiers on citizens and congressmen, electronic listening devices, computerized data files – and who knows what else – provide central authority with unprecedented means for invading the privacy of citizens of this land, founded on the principle of rigorous safeguards against precisely such invasion.

One must re-read Samuel's warning about the consequences of a king – accurate even to the burdens of taxation (cf. I Samuel 8:11-18) – to find an ancient and strikingly accurate anticipation of our politically disturbed society today. Mistrust of the political process and a sense of personal powerlessness are widespread. It is a combination which affords neither strength for the present nor hope for the future.

The amassing of economic wealth is also immense and perhaps unprecedented in this period of history. Energy resources accumulated over millions of earth-years are being tapped at an accelerating and reckless pace. Fossil fuels are burned as never before, other sources of energy are sought, and the rate of increase has been dazzling. Productivity has been relatively high, whatever the case with quality, and since the basic economic-value distinction argued by Ruskin – that between "wealth" and "illth" – is almost universally disregarded, we live with the appearance, if not the reality, of prosperity, although the recent economic recession with its attendant sufferings has made clear how precarious our economic health is.

In any case, the distribution of wealth is appallingly unbalanced, especially between the so-called developed and the so-called developing nations. One valuable indicator is that of fossil fuel consumption. The Director of Statistics for the National Coal Board of Great Britain, Dr. E. F. Schumacher, wrote in 1969: "Let us define as 'rich' all populations in countries with an average fuel consumption – in 1966 – of more than one metric ton of coal equivalent (c.e.) per head, and as 'poor' all those below this level. On these definitions we can draw up the following table (using United Nations figures throughout):

	Rich (percent)	Poor (percent)	World (percent)
Population (millions)	1,060 (31)	2,284 (69)	3,344 (100)
Fuel consumption (mill. tons c.e.)	4,788 (87)	721 (13)	5,509 (100)
Fuel consumption per head (tons c.e.)	4.52	0.32	1.65

"The average fuel consumption per head of the 'poor,'" Schumacher concludes, "is . . . roughly one-fourteenth that of the 'rich' . . ."

Even allowing for the fact that fuel requirements for heating are lower in warmer parts of the globe, the difference is frightfully large. All projections indicate that this gap is increasing, not decreasing. The specter of a small group of over-privileged people living amidst appalling poverty afflicting billions of human beings becomes more a reality each day.

Nor are the inequalities of distribution of wealth merely international. Within the United States itself, the materially wealthiest of the world's nations, the inequalities are striking. With depressing regularity, the Congressional committees have discovered hunger and malnutrition due to poverty within America, and it is distressing to think of the nutritional effects on the poor of the present inflationary rise in food prices. Even before the present round of increases, the prestigious Brookings Institution, basing its findings on the 1970 Census, reported that the lowest 20 percent of American families in income received only about 3.2 percent of the annual income in the United States, while the highest 20 percent obtained 45.8 percent. Nor was this simply a problem on a comparative scale; the absolute figures were shocking: in 1970 the lowest 20 percent of families had an income range below $3,070 annually. Another 20 percent subsisted on income between $3,070 and $5,890 annually, and these combined 40 percent of American families received less than 14 percent of the annual income. Meanwhile, the top 5 percent, with incomes over $17,840, received 19.1 percent of the total annual income, while the top 1 percent, with incomes exceeding $33,330 annually, got twice the income of all 20 percent of the families at the bottom of the scale! Domestically we are not doing at all well by the standards of Amos or Isaiah.

It is a mistake, however, to imagine that such inequalities affect only the poor. The moderately well-to-do also feel the effects. As economic power becomes more and more concentrated and fewer economic opportunities exist outside the large corporate structures, individual citizens have less and less say about their economic lives. As remote conglomerates buy up more and more local resources, jobs are created or destroyed by corporate officers who may live hundreds or thousands of miles away and who share none of the consequences their decisions may bring to the life of the local community. Thus, in still another area of their lives, people find their effective personal power and independence reduced. As with the growth of military-political power, here, too, it appears that the massive increase in power at the industrial level has been purchased at the price of the effective economic power and independence of human beings who have been reduced to mere cogs in a vast, interlocking machine.

The third concentration, also unprecedented in history, is that of pop-ulation. Urbanization has been the constant trend in this century, and since World War II it has accelerated both worldwide and in the United States. Over the globe, 133 cities had populations of one million or more in 1971, 29 more than in 1960; among these, many cities have grown to massive, sprawling areas. In the U.S., meanwhile, less than 6 percent of the population is engaged in agriculture, and the movement away from the land has been a continuous one. The combination of an increase in population and the urbanizing trend has yielded unprecedented concentrations of people. The advantages of this have been more than fully appreciated and loudly proclaimed; at this point, the serious and increasingly threatening problems are coming into clearer view.

First of all, there are growing problems with both trash and human waste disposal. Secondly, when 95 percent of a population is dependent on 5 percent for its food, the latter can produce the requisite quantities only through fuel-costly mechanization and one-crop agriculture with heavy use of chemical fertilizers and pesticides. The threat that pesticides pose to general ecological well-being, including man as well as the other animals, is by now widely recognized. The problems that purely chemical agriculture pose for long-term soil fertility are only beginning to receive attention, while the excessive use of fossil fuels in highly mechanized production is already a critical issue.

Thirdly, there is some evidence (cf. the work of Leopold Kohr) that beyond an optimum size, which is well below that of all our major metropolitan areas today, higher and higher proportions of resources must go toward merely keeping the system functioning. Increasing the speed of surface travel at first seems to "save time," but as people live farther away from their work, the additional distances traveled quickly consume the time "saved." Congestion then increases the time expenditure, and so the time saved is soon surpassed by time spent in travel. Additionally, not only human time but precious and irreplaceable natural resources are used up in simply keeping abreast of the increased velocity of life.

Beyond such practical problems, however, lies another set of difficulties that affects the deepest levels of the human psyche. One result of heaping people together is an assault on the nervous system, which invites a tuning out of stimuli. Small wonder that in very large cities, open assaults on the street, even in broad daylight, often induce an avoidance response on the part of the passerby. Out of corners of their eyes, people may see a fight or even a murderous assault; nevertheless, they pretend not to notice, look the other way, and move a bit faster as they scurry past the possible demand on their time, compassion, and courage. What must this reaction do to such critical human feelings as responsibility, trust, and concern for others? How must this magnify the level of anxiety as well as the painful sense of human isolation?

Further, when 95 percent of the population depends on 5 percent for such a daily necessity of life as food, how does this situation affect people's feelings about themselves? Without falling prey to illusions of absolute independence, those who grow their own food or build or tend their own dwelling places are likely to have a much healthier sense both of their own capacities and of their own need for others than is the case with those whose necessities of life are obtained exclusively through the medium of money-exchange. Not to make, or cultivate, or tend, or produce directly any necessity of one's life must finally diminish a person's sense of independence, if not his feeling of basic human capability.

Beyond this, when we live our lives cut off from the sustaining cycle of natural growth – seed-time and harvest, with the wonders of sprouting, blossoming, fruiting, and ripening in between, and the yielding and decomposition at the end, which help prepare the seed-bed for new life – our primary experiences of development are mostly intellectual, mechanical, or organizational. Are these conducive to our own personal growth and maturation in the way that involvement with the vegetation cycle has so often been reported to be? I doubt it. Nor can we overlook the invigorating physical challenge of the non-human in nature, where so many human feelings may find fruitful expression without increasing the level of often over-loaded, interpersonal nervous excitement. Cutting, chopping, digging – these are natural releases for healthy aggression. Sowing, watering, transplanting – these are beneficial extensions of natural caring. What are the social consequences of the damming up of these once widely available outlets for human feelings? Hardly positive, I suspect.

We are in a triple bind, faced with unprecedented concentrations of military-political power, economic wealth, and human population. The enormous concentration of military-political power, summarized in nuclear, chemical, and biological weapons, threatens the entirety of historical time; the enormous concentration of economic wealth, summarized in growing extremes of luxury and deprivation, threatens the entire social order; the enormous concentrations of people, exemplified in environmentally disastrous megalopolitan sprawls, threaten the natural order.

Is it any wonder that en route to our bicentennial celebration, we, the people, seem neither happy nor confident?

Each strand of the three-fold cord is itself formidable. Twisted together in contemporary complexity, they make Gordian's knot seem rather like a child's bow. Consequently, there is no value in pretending that an easy or simple solution is at hand.

At the same time, if our considerable human abilities and resources are to be applied to unraveling the terrible tangle, we need at least some sense of direction, some indication of which way to move. If pretension to pat solutions is inappropriate, so is bewildered aimlessness.

Neither of these is necessary. What strikes me as a clear indication of direction is engraved upon a central symbol of our independence as a people, the Liberty Bell: "Proclaim liberty throughout the land unto all the inhabitants thereof" (Leviticus, 24:10). This verse and its context speak with remarkable directness to our triple bind today.

It is not a fully sketched solution. What is? On the other hand, it is worth remembering that the Bible is both a radical and sophisticated document of the ancient world, and that it reflects, albeit in simpler form, some experience of problems similar to, if not identical with, our own.

Frightening concentration of political power? I Samuel 8:11-18 is worth many a volume of political-power analysis, and supplemented by Dr. Seuss' *Yertle the Turtle,* is as good a brief guide as can be found to the actualities of many a nation-state today. Land monopolization? Read Isaiah 5:8-10, where declining soil fertility may also be alluded to. Control of raw materials and prices? Exploitation of the poor? Amos 5:11 or 8:4-6 speak eloquently to the issues. Luxury amidst poverty? For directness, Amos 4:1 and 6:4-6 have yet to be surpassed. Persistent debts, loss of land by the poor, poverty inherited from one generation to the next? Nehemiah 5:1-19 is painful testimony.

In extent our problems are unprecedented, but in essence they date from very ancient times. And it is toward the solution of these problems that the Sabbatical and Jubilee legislation was directed – that set of specific regulations which is the context of the verse engraved on the Liberty Bell and which defines the meaning of that "liberty" which was to be proclaimed "throughout the land to all the inhabitants thereof."

Ideals may be reduced to mere words, empty slogans, if there is no attempt to give them definition. However, to define them is also to invite controversy, for there can hardly be an application of an ideal to a social or personal reality which does not provoke discomfort or disagreement. Might this be the reason for the introduction to Chapter 25 of Leviticus?

> The Lord spoke to Moses on Mount Sinai and said,
> Speak to the Israelites in these words:
> When you enter the land which I give you,
> The land shall keep Sabbaths to the Lord.

A famous rabbinic question asks: "Why is this matter of the Sabbatical and Jubilee Years specifically mentioned in connection with the giving of the Torah at Mount Sinai?" After all, it is a traditional presupposition that all of the laws were given by God at Mount Sinai. Why, then, the singling out of these particular laws? My own conjecture is that there were surely those in the community of Israel, most likely the wealthy and powerful, who were less than pleased with these regulations. Very likely, then as now, the specific application of the principle of greater socioeconomic equality met with considerable resistance from established interest groups. Hence the need to re-affirm that idealistic general propositions inherently included some concrete means for effecting them. ("General principles were proclaimed at Sinai, and detailed laws in the Tabernacle" – Sotah 37b.)

What, then, are the specifics of these "Sabbaths" that the land shall keep to the Lord? "For six years you may sow your land and gather its produce; but in the seventh year you shall let it lie fallow and leave it alone. It shall provide food for the poor of your people; and what they leave, the wild animals may eat. You shall do likewise with your vineyard and your olive grove . . ." (Exodus 23:10-11).

Every seventh year, the fields are to be fallow and uncultivated. The soil shall replenish itself, and those in need shall come and take; the have-nots shall share fully with the haves.

"At the end of every seventh year you shall make a remission of debts. This is how the remission shall be made: everyone who holds a pledge shall remit the pledge of anyone indebted to him. He shall not press a fellow countryman for repayment, for the Lord's year of remission has been declared" (Deuteronomy 12:1-2). Every seventh year debts are to be canceled so that the economic race is off to a fresh start. No one is to inherit poverty because of the failures of those who came before him or her, nor is anyone to be permanently at a disadvantage. It is a basic human right to have regularly a fresh chance to succeed, without being forever weighed down by the past.

But seven years is a long time to wait for one who is hungry or in need. The Bible urges us, therefore, not to neglect the disadvantaged in the period between Sabbaticals. "When one of your fellow-countrymen in any of your settlements in the land which the Lord your God is giving you becomes poor, do not be hard-hearted or close-fisted with your countryman in his need. Be open-handed towards him and lend him on pledge as much as he needs. See that you not harbour iniquitous thoughts when you find that the seventh year, the year of remission, is near, and look askance at your needy countryman and give him nothing. If you do, he will appeal to the Lord against you, and you will be found guilty of sin. Give freely to him and do not begrudge him your bounty, because it is for this very bounty that the Lord your God will bless you in everything you do or undertake. The poor will always be with you in the land, and for that reason I command you to be open-handed with your countrymen, both poor and distressed, in your own land" (Deuteronomy 15:7-11). And we are not to shame them. Some form of sharing that respects the dignity of the needy is demanded. "When a fellow-Hebrew, man or woman, sells himself to you as a slave, he shall serve you for six years and in the seventh year you shall set him free. But when you set him free, do not let him go empty-handed. Give to him lavishly from your flock, from your threshing-floor and your wine-press. Be generous to him because the Lord your God has blessed you . . . Remember that you were slaves in Egypt and the Lord your God redeemed you; that is why I am giving you this command today" (Deuteronomy 15:12-15).

This provision speaks of those who, because of debts, had to sell themselves as slaves in order to work off their debts. There is a strict limit to such a term of servitude, and generous compensation on release from slavery was also part of the Sabbatical Year provisions.

In summary, land-release, personal debt-release, poverty-relief with dignity, and indentured-slave release with funds for a fresh start were the basic legal provisions of the Sabbatical Year. Their purpose might be understood as the redistribution of accumulated wealth, so that more widespread sharing and greater human equality would result. In this way, human beings would experience both stronger feelings of human fellowship and a keener awareness of God's redemptive activity in human history.

"No land shall be sold outright, because the land is mine, and you are coming into it as aliens and settlers. Throughout the whole land of your patrimony, you shall allow land which has been sold to be redeemed" (Leviticus 25:23-24). No land, instructs the Bible, may be permanently taken from those whose ancestral subsistence base it was; those who originally owned and worked it always retain rights to it. Come the half-century Jubilee Year, that person or his descendants receive without cost and with conditions their traditional plot of land, from which they should be able to supply their basic needs.

"You should count seven sabbaths of years," instructs Leviticus (25:8-10), "that is seven times seven years, forty-nine years, and in the seventh month on the tenth day of the month, on the Day of Atonement, you shall send the ram's horn round. You shall send it through all your land to sound a blast, and shall you hallow the fiftieth year and proclaim liberation in the land for all its inhabitants" (the more common translation is "Proclaim liberty throughout the land unto all the inhabitants thereof"). "You shall make this your year of Jubilee. Every man of you shall return to his patrimony, every man to his family."

The Jubilee Year, like the Sabbatical, has specific regulations. At its basis is the notion of ancestral subsistence land, that small holding where each man could dwell "under his own vine, under his own fig-tree, undisturbed" (cf. Micah 4:1-4; Isaiah 2:1-4; Zachariah 3:10; Kings 5:5; II Kings 18:31).

If someone had to sell his ancestral land, his source of subsistence, during the preceding years, it is now his again, free and clear. If someone had to leave his family and sell himself into debt-bondage, his enslavement is now ended. No matter what the remainder of the indebtedness or contract, he is now clear of all debts and free to return to his family and to his ancestral land. Free and clear: that is the heart of the Jubilee legislation, and still further provisions seek to insure the possibility of its realization.

Yet if seven years was a long time, forty-nine years was a longer time. Hence a further provision for social justice: "When one of you is reduced to poverty and sells part of his patrimony, his next-of-kin who has the duty of redemption shall come and redeem what his kinsman has sold. When a man has no such next-of-kin and himself becomes able to afford its redemption, he shall take into account the years since the sale and pay the purchaser the balance up to the Jubilee. Then he may return to his patrimony. But if the man cannot afford to buy back the property, it shall remain in the hands of the purchaser till the year of the Jubilee. It shall revert to the original owner, and he shall return to his patrimony" (Leviticus 25:25-28). In other words, the more immediate the action to relieve the economic distress, the better. If someone is in economic difficulty of a fundamental kind, help him now, not later. Do not wait. But if you permit him to wait, he must not pass on poverty to his children and his children's children. Whatever your preference, come the fiftieth year, that land is his or his descendants'.

Meanwhile, if during that interim he finds himself able to re-purchase the land, he had the right to do so, taking into account the years yet to run to the Jubilee. "When a man sells a dwelling-house in a walled town, he shall retain the right of redemption till the end of the year of the sale; for a time he shall have the right of redemption. If it is not redeemed before a full year is out, the house in the walled town shall vest in perpetuity in the buyer and his descendants; it shall not revert at the Jubilee. Houses in unwalled hamlets shall be treated as property in the open country: the right of redemption shall hold food, and in any case the house shall revert at the Jubilee" (Leviticus 25:29-31).

There is a lesser right of redemption of houses in a walled city, extending only one year. However, houses in unwalled hamlets are subject to the full provisions of the Jubilee legislation: the right of redemption at any time, and full reversion at the Jubilee year. Why the difference? S.H. Kellog writes (in *The Expositor's Bible,* 1903): "The obvious reason to exempting houses in the cities . . . is that the law has to do only with land such as may be used in a pastoral or agricultural way for man's support. And this explains why, on the other hand, it is next ordered (verse 31) that in the case of houses in unwalled villages the law of redemption and reversion in the Jubilee shall apply as well as to the land. For the inhabitants of the villages were the herdsmen and cultivators of the soil: and the house was regarded rightly as a necessary attachment to the land, without which its use would not be possible."

Again the point is clear. Not only shall the person have a piece of land that can produce his livelihood; he must also have easy access to it. Take away his house in the village, and where can he live? What good will the land be to him if he cannot get to it to work it? The intent of the law must be insured by protective provisions so that every man may have a real opportunity to support himself and his family with dignity and independence.

These, briefly, are the chief provisions of the Sabbatical and the Jubilee legislation. What they might mean for our own situation today must now be explored. To do so is to court obvious dangers, however. On the one hand, a literal transfer of particulars from the ancient to the modern can fail to take account of the differentia of the present; on the other hand, a loose disregard of particulars can yield empty generalities with little applicability to any situation, past or present. Somewhere in between lies the desideratum, and it is toward this end that I should like to indicate what seems to me the major illumination shed by the Sabbatical and Jubilee legislation on our plight today.

How might the central element of the Biblical legislation be characterized? It is, I believe, the ideal of a relatively independent, economically secure basis for the life of the (extended) family unit. This relative independence and security are to be achieved through the assurance of access to a means of fundamental subsistence which cannot suffer permanent alienation. This means is a small holding of land, sufficient for basic family needs, which is not liable to permanent sale or possession by another.

Clearly, then, what we have is a small-holder, decentralized, agriculture-based model from Biblical times. This model was already subject to severe challenge and strain by the political and economic-commercial development of the Roman period. (The prosbul of Hillel, which restricted application of these Biblical laws of debt-relief, reflects this strain.) For many centuries thereafter, in fact, until very recently, the Biblical model was not taken seriously as a pattern for any further social development, except perhaps by a very small number of millenarian movements. This, however, is no longer so. The Roman model for social development has indeed fulfilled itself in our age, and where do we find ourselves? In a triple bind from which we must extricate ourselves – and soon!

Can one read any serious study of environmental problems today and feel confident about the future of cities as we know them? Can one suffer rush-hour congestion in any major city and then sing with conviction the praises of this form of population distribution? Can one read projections of non-renewable resource depletion or energy requirements and maintain confidence in the future of a civilization which consumes as riotously and recklessly as we do? Can one take seriously the epidemic of degenerative disease that afflicts our civilization and still place faith in present methods of food production and processing?

Can one visit an inner-city ghetto or a depressed rural area and retain confidence in the justice of our present method of allocating resources? Can one visit with open eyes any capital city in Latin America, see the areas of mass misery which surround the central tourist and upper-class glitter, and rest content with our level expenditures, compared with the rest of the planet? How can we, descendants of Amos, Micah, and Isaiah, continue to support such social systems?

Can one take to heart worker demoralization as revealed in such incidents as the Lordstown, Ohio labor dispute (cf. Barbara Garson's article, "Luddites in Lordstown," *Harpers*, June, 1972) and be so sure that it is just fine that stockholders, not workers, "own" the jobs? Can one explore the implications of the widely noted decline in the quality of products and continue to insist that our present system of incentives and modes of production is respectful either of people or products?

Can one subscribe to the Biblical-rabbinic affirmation of the value of every human being and support the possibility of mass-destruction that is the ultimate resort of present strategies of "national defense"? Can we rest content in a civilization whose economic functioning and well-being seem increasingly linked to the continuation of a monstrous mechanism of military power?

In short, a strong case can be made that present trends toward increasing concentrations of population, wealth, and military-political might are both self-destructive and constitute basic denials of all that our most cherished moral teachings and finer human feelings have urged upon us. There is no longer reason to presume in favor of present structures, and every reason to consider alternatives!

The Biblical model, in eclipse for some centuries now, may deserve another look. The proclamation engraved on the Liberty Bell, neglected for many decades now, may also merit renewed consideration.

Let us imagine how one element of the United States bicentennial social policy might look if the Jubilee context of the Liberty Bell proclamation were applied in one particular throughout the country. The heart of this application would be the attempt to make available to seriously interested persons viable subsistence plots of land, along with assistance for the development of small-scale communally controlled facilities and enterprises.

How might such a plan be effected? First of all, there would have to be a widely-shared public commitment to the renewal of small-scale, rural or semi-rural opportunities as a significant aspect of present social policy. Such a commitment would, I believe, flow naturally from a genuine confrontation of our present plight combined with some attention to the Jubilee ideal and earlier American policies such as the Homestead Act of 1862. Given such a commitment, one might anticipate the allocation of substantial public funds for the purchase of available farmland and for the encouragement of work, educational, medical, religious, cultural, and recreational opportunities in areas outside the present overcrowded concentrations of population.

Where should such land be purchased and such development funds be directed? At least two possibilities suggest themselves. One is the purchase of rather sizable tracts of land where entirely new villages might grow, agriculturally based but with a potential for small-scale industry as well.

The other is the purchase of smaller tracts of land near already established smaller towns and villages, but well outside present concentrations of population. Which possibility should be selected would depend on a number of considerations, among them the preferences of those who might respond to such opportunities, as well as the attitudes of already existing smaller communities.

Who, might we anticipate, will manifest interest in such opportunities? First of all, there are literally hundreds of thousands of city residents today who are there largely through force of circumstances than through free choice. Many who came from rural areas have expressed longings for the life they once knew, and might welcome an opportunity to return to comparable settings under more favorable life circumstances.

Interest in moving away from present urban centers is not confined to those who once lived in rural surroundings. There are highly trained technicians, engineers, and scientists who find themselves presently unemployed or who are dissatisfied with the uses to which their talents and training are being directed. There are physicians, some already established, others just out of medical school, who are looking for alternatives to the inhumanly scaled health-care facilities of large cities, and who would welcome the chance to practice medicine part-time in a smaller community setting while also engaged in some amount of food growing. There are teachers, both old and young, who are looking for new environments and more variety than their rigidly defined professional lives have afford them until now. There are artists, dramatists, and musicians who value the communicative function of their callings and who would welcome the chance to relate to a surrounding community in terms other than those of purchased tickets at large concert halls. Not to mention, of course, the increasing numbers of young persons looking for land, young persons who are often well-educated and in search of socially responsible and personally satisfying ways of living.

The impression that such interest is widely shared is supported by the findings of public opinion polls. Martin E. Marty reports in *The Christian Century* (January 3, 1973): "According to figures of a recent Gallup poll, if they had a choice, 13 percent of the American people would live in the city, 31 percent in the suburbs, 32 percent in small towns, and 23 percent on farms. A Unidex poll taken in Autumn, 1972, revealed that among the 18-to-24-year-old group, 13.5 percent would choose the city, 20 percent the suburbs, 38 percent small cities or towns, and 28 percent rural life."

More recent reports further support such findings. For every forty openings for a full-time, year-round forest ranger with the National Park Service, one thousand people apply. And for six thousand summer jobs in the United States Forest Service each year, one hundred thousand applications are received. The New Hampshire Office of Comprehensive Planning reports that people coming from out-of-state are taking pay cuts in order to live in that relatively "undeveloped" state, and that the areas of attraction are no longer simply the southern parts but the northern as well (cited in *The Christian Science Monitor,* November 28, 1973).

Opportunities are far fewer than seekers. Yet the existence of such widely attested interest means that there is in America the beginning of a strong impulse to reverse the population flow away from the cities and back toward the land. Nor should this be surprising, for creatures formed from earth are not likely to lose totally their urge to remain in touch with earth so long as earth persists and "seedtime and harvest, and cold and heat, and summer and winter, and day and night shall not cease" (Genesis 8:22). Healthy urges are still asserting themselves in our society, urges that can provide the motive force for voluntary yet significant social change. The crucial question is whether we can respond, as a society, adequately and appropriately to these healthy impulses.

Further thought should now be given to the social response to these urges. The first question, as mentioned above, is the location of the land for public purchase. One possibility is the purchase of medium-sized (under five hundred acres) tracts of land near already established smaller towns and villages. The other is the purchase of large tracts of land (one thousand acres and over, perhaps) where completely new villages might grow. What could help determine such a choice?

Other things being equal, preference ought probably to be shown to already existent entities, such as smaller towns and villages that have been suffering a steady loss of younger persons to cities. Some such localities are hostile to the entry of newcomers; others would like to attract additional residents. A nationwide survey could help ascertain which places would like to attract new persons to their areas. Those which seem receptive might become the nuclei for the public purchase of available surrounding farmland. Land in viable subsistence plots (perhaps five acres) could be made available for distribution to urban residents.

In such a situation, those moving into the area would find possibilities of relating to already established institutions and industries in the town or village, as well as opportunities to develop new ones. I could imagine both the local residents and the newcomers mutually benefiting from the influx of fresh talent. If those with technical, industrial, and crafts backgrounds were invited to put them to use, additional local industries and crafts, democratically controlled, could surely develop, especially if funds were allocated to foster such development. Hopefully, small-scale productive units would focus on high-quality, durable items of a necessary, not a luxury, nature, with preference for resources drawn from, processed, and used in the region itself, insofar as this is possible. Such productive facilities, locally controlled though independent, would be a significant step toward making real, in terms of our age, the Jubilee ideal of every person having some direct access to means for basic subsistence with dignity. In addition, such revitalization of small communities might well attract physicians, engineers, teachers, and others who presently tend to avoid these places.

Moreover, were such projects undertaken with vision and human appreciation, those who moved to such communities would find themselves considerably enriched by contact with local residents. Food-growing for the family would benefit greatly from the experience of those who have lived in an area for many years, and mutually helpful contacts might be expected to develop quite naturally. Traditional arts of preserving, canning, baking, and hand-crafting might be of considerable interest to those whose lives are in process of becoming rebalanced. Here again the technically proficient, highly educated city dwellers would find much to learn from those unencumbered with academic degrees. The awareness of such possibilities of interchange would do much to reduce the threat of a subtle form of intellectual or cultural imperialism, and could also reduce the resentment which might otherwise be felt by local residents as a one-way imposition from the outside.

The other possibility, that of the purchase of sizable tracts of land where entirely new settlements might develop, agriculturally-based but with potential for the same development of small-scale local productive facilities, would offer similar opportunities. Here again, some funding for the encouragement of other social necessities, such as educational, cultural, medical, and religious facilities, seems essential.

What about the costs to the public? Even the considerable land costs might well be substantially less than the economic costs of making life livable for comparable numbers of persons in cities as presently constituted. The environmental costs would be far below those of maintaining cities of our present size. The costs of finding out who might wish to take advantage of such opportunities should be minimal if use is made of already established agencies for registration purposes. Social service agencies, for example, might prove most helpful. Costs for encouraging the development of work and community facilities would not be negligible, but such agencies as the Intermediate Technology Development Group might be drawn on for their experience with low-cost, small-scale, low-fossil-energy, labor-intensive development plans. In addition, the School for Living, the International Independence Institute, and the New Alchemists (to cite three of many) have much to share in the way of economical development plans and possibilities.

On the matter of costs, one further consideration should be borne in mind. The appropriation of public funds for widely dispersed land purchases and development opportunities would partially meet the understandable and growing resentment felt by many throughout the U.S. who perceive their hard labor as being unfairly taxed for remote cities with whose massive populations they have little human connection. A plan such as has been sketched above would hopefully distribute both social wealth and social benefits far more widely than is presently the case.

The foregoing, suggestive rather the prescriptive, is one attempt to sketch with a minimum of detail the application of one central feature of the Biblical Jubilee legislation to our present society. It is not intended to preclude other applications of such ideals; rather, it is an attempt to fill out what might otherwise have been merely an empty abstraction.

From such a modest proposal one must beware of claiming too much. Yet it does, I think, point in the right direction: toward areas of lower population density in order to help create semi-independent, human-scaled, environmentally respectful communities that can offer some satisfactions for the present and hope for the future. Greater economic and political sharing; less restrictive definition and functioning of human beings in narrow professional or status terms; some direct involvement in laboring for basic human necessities; an invitation to exercise both minds and muscles, to utilize both thinking and feeling faculties; role despecialization of a kind which would return "absentee fathers" to their homes while providing both parents with opportunities to express themselves and earn in the large world of compensated work; the family reconstituted as a functional unit in this modified homestead arrangement; renewed feelings of greater control over personal destiny and social decisions, with a stronger sense of independent citizenry – all these and more are among the possible benefits of the proposed sketches here.

Again, a word of caution. The triple bind in which we find ourselves will not easily be untangled. Yet there is, it seems to me, a marked convergence of a Biblical insight, a traditional American ideal, and a pressing contemporary need. Together they seem to point in the same direction.

Does this direction deserve some serious consideration on the eve of our bicentennial? Not since 1776, perhaps, has there been a greater need to

> Proclaim Liberty throughout the land
> unto all the inhabitants thereof.

From CCAR Journal
(Central Conference of American Rabbis), Summer, 1975

Part Three

Israel and Diaspora

The true locus and center of Judaism is within the heart . . . of flesh, not of stone.
Wherever on all this earth such a Jew is found, there is the true place of Judaism.
—Rabbi Aaron Samuel Tamaret (1869-1931)

To Be a Jew in the Diaspora

An Affirmation

This 1975 essay affirms the authenticity, integrity, and value for the Jewish people of a strong Jewish presence in lands outside of Israel.

For many centuries following the Exile, which began with the destruction of Jerusalem in 70-135 CE, Zion served as a point of spiritual reference for the Jew. Prayers sought mercy for Zion, psalms were recited singing its praises, the imagination of Jews outside of Israel was stirred by the very word, "Zion."

Yet throughout those centuries, Jewish life for the most part had its effective centers in the places where Jews actually lived. Jews prayed, studied, celebrated, and organized their communities where they happened to be. The ideal of Zion may have hovered over those various places, but as an ideal unrealized it served as the spatial analogue to the messianic temporal expectation. At once an anticipation of the future and the embodiment of present ideals, it served well to concretize aspirations. A memory from the past projected into the future, its non-realization throughout those centuries prevented its becoming a substitute for the day-to-day life that Jews lived in other places. At no time during that long stretch of time was Zion treated as a particular place offering vicarious experiences for Jews elsewhere. As messianic expectation did not fall prey to other-worldliness, the hope for Zion did not succumb to other-placeness.

Neither did Zion as an ideal decide among varying interpretations and understandings of Jewish values and traditions. By virtue of being an ideal, an anticipation of a situation yet to be, it could be invoked on behalf of various ideals and could encompass many of them. The exact shape that Zion was to assume in its realization was also open and indeterminate, here too offering a wide range of options.

With the coming of modern political Zionism, much of this began to change, and with the establishment of the State of Israel, a radical transformation occurred. The State of Israel became widely identified with Zion, and the consequences were several.

First of all, the power-political unit Israel inherited a religious aura from the repository of ideals long associated with Zion, though it is far from clear that those ideals were intended to issue in a modern nation-state established by military-political means. Secondly, by identifying the State of Israel with Zion, other interpretations of what it might mean for Zion to be approximated within time and space were foreclosed. Non-nationalist visions of Zion, for example, were widely dismissed, even though their claims to standing within the Jewish tradition had hardly been addressed, let alone refuted. Finally, Zion now purportedly realized, a particular political community in a particular place could claim to serve as the focus for the lives of Jews everywhere, thereby inviting the kind of vicarious Jewish living that has been one characteristic of diaspora-Israel relations in recent years.

The further effects of these developments have been far-reaching. The first, the religious aura surrounding the State of Israel, has tended to make many Jews, both in and outside of Israel, less critical of particular policies of the Israeli state than they might otherwise be. Giving full weight to the genuine concern for Jews in Israel that has muted some criticism, there are still signs of religious associations making possible widespread acquiescence in policies that otherwise would have been subjected to severe questioning. Seizure of Arab lands, purportedly on the basis of scriptural sanction, is one example.

The second, the reduction of various interpretations of Zion to but one, the modern nation-state called Israel, both distorts the past and limits the future. Rarely do history books remind us of even recent facts such as the significant proportion of the *yishuv* (the Jewish population of then-Palestine), fully 40 percent, who as late as 1947 opposed political partition and the establishment of an ethnically defined Jewish state. Not that the clock can be turned back, but by such omissions options for the future are thereby reduced, and the present Middle East political impasse is made all the more difficult to resolve. Additionally, the forgetting of things past has contributed to a steady narrowing of the Jewish religious understanding of what messianic fulfillment might mean, and there has been some tendency to identify the true aim of Judaism as the establishment of the State of Israel.

It is the third consequence, however, the vicarious living through Israel by

Jews elsewhere, on which I should like to focus, for it is in this area that some serious negative results of recent developments can be most clearly seen.

There has been in recent years a tendency to undervalue diaspora Jewish experiences and to overvalue Israeli Jewish experiences, and this has worked out badly both for Israeli and for diaspora Jews. Israeli Jews often complain that diaspora Jews expect too much of Israel and its Jews, and in many cases that is true. But that should come as no surprise given the present mood.

To Israeli Zionists, I would suggest the following consideration: If you insist on regarding lightly our diaspora lives and experiences, then expect your own to become correspondingly heavy, burdened by *our* expectations and hopes, which *you* ideologically insist cannot find fulfillment in our lives here where we live. If you want to maintain such claims, then either expect critical rejection by those of us who esteem our lives in many particular places throughout this world that God has created, or burdensome acceptance by those who look to *you* to provide vicariously the satisfactions that you tell them they cannot possibly know in diaspora.

The real tragedy, of course, is that both the undervaluation and over-valuation may well be false. Tendencies to such facile comparisons ought to be resisted, and it is as a contribution to such resistance that I want to devote the remainder of this essay. I regret that in places it may appear defensive of diaspora experience, but since diaspora experience has been called into question in recent years, there may be some value in defending that realm of experience from its detractors.

There is a presumption in the category, "diaspora," that the most significant Jewish fact of my life is my *not* living in Israel. Subjectively, however, I find that this fact hardly matters at all. I live my Jewish life in *this* place at *this* time. It is constituted by a series of specific experiences that involve and are informed by cultural and religious considerations, but these are quite different from the ideological abstraction of the term "diaspora." Since specifics seem to me to reveal the essence of life, let me now be specific.

We (my wife, our two young daughters, and I) live on a small acreage in a town of 20,000 about forty minutes north of Boston, in the Northeast of the United States. Five synagogues are found in the two small cities near us (population about 100,000), and the usual U.S. educational, medical, industrial, and cultural facilities are part of the general surroundings. Our immediate area still has a few small farms, several market gardeners grow food in our town for shipment to the city, and quite a few home gardeners struggle, as do we, with the stony subsoil that contributes more than a reasonable quantity of rocks to the thin layer of topsoil from which proceeds the food we eat. In this setting, the precious few inches of fertile topsoil, built up over stretches of time beyond our minds' imaginings, provide mute but eloquent testimony to the slow, steady, irresistible surge of life upward throughout our planet. In this setting, rhythmically attuned to seasonal shifts, there are moments for me when the sense of *khey ha-olamim,* the Life of the Universe, moves from the pages of the prayer book and almost palpably courses through the earth, making Itself felt here in this very place, the place where we live. It is not hard, at such times, to appreciate the khasidic saying cited by Buber:

> Everywhere
> God says to man as he said to Moses:
> "Put off thy shoes from off thy feet,
> for the place whereon thou standest
> is holy ground" (Exodus 3:5) . . .
> put off the habitual which encloses your foot
> and you will recognize that the place on which
> you happen to be standing at this moment is
> holy ground. For there is no rung of being on which
> we cannot find the holiness of God everywhere
> and at all times.

This is one "diaspora" Jewish experience that I have been granted.

Outside the house in which we now live is an old well, dug nearly fifty years ago by those who built the house. Fieldstone-lined, it was later filled with trash, dirt, and old shingling when town water was piped to this part of town. When I remove the cap to have a look, there is hardly an inch of water in sight, but old-timers tell me that when first dug and throughout its days of use, the well provided a steady supply of cool, clean water, thus vindicating the diviner whose rod suggested just this location for digging. It beckons, this well, and invites re-digging – reminiscent of Isaac's redigging of the stopped-up wells in his place and his time. Digging through the muck takes much of the summer and the bottom is finally reached the Friday afternoon before the Sabbath whose Biblical reading includes the ancient Israelite Song at the Well: "Spring up, O Well/ Greet it with song" (Numbers 21:17).

With the well now re-dug and cleaned, crystalline waters gush through the fissures of the bedrock eighteen feet below, by taste delicious, by test pure. The waters *do* well up, inviting song in *this* place at *this* time. And I find myself momentarily wondering: Is it "here" or "there," "now" or "then"? Or have time and place, no longer bounded, met and mingled across time and space?

The following morning, I attend Sabbath services at the Havurat Shalom community in Somerville, founded five years earlier by the gifted religious teacher and leader, Rabbi Arthur Green. Although it is mid-summer, at least forty persons are present, in age mostly from teens to early thirties. All are seated on cushions on the floor, and the service begins with Reb Avram offering some personal reflections on the well and water as symbols of religious inspiration. He then begins a *nigun*, and slowly we all join in, our bodies swaying, our voices rising and falling in unison. After some silence, parts of the morning service are recited, at times introduced by words that suggest the personal meaning of a particular phrase. How beautifully tradition and the moment blend.

The Torah reading that morning is characterized by lively and diverse discussion of the passages read, and a deeply moving moment comes when a member of the community who had narrowly escaped death in a boating accident is called to the Torah and recites the *gomel* prayer (a blessing traditionally recited by one who has survived a dangerous experience). Following the service there is a *kiddush,* and the *khallah* and shared wine seem especially precious. Symbols of life and joy, these are all the more appreciated as we realize the great blessing that is ours, the renewed life of one dear to all of us.

The morning has been rich indeed: a davening experience at once individual and communal, contemporary and traditional, and a sharing of excitement about Torah and concern for the life of a friend.

These are "diaspora" Jewish experiences, and they could be multiplied by countless other examples. The proliferation of Jewish scholarship and studies in academic departments of U.S. universities; the widespread development of extra-departmental "Free Jewish Universities" on campuses throughout the U.S.; the quest for more intimacy within established synagogue structures; interfamilial religious support and personal sharing of groups such as the Alternate Religious Community of Marblehead – each one of these could provide numerous additional instances of diaspora Jewish experiences.

"But are they typical?" one might ask. "Are they *representative* of diaspora experience?" Such questions as these are perfect examples of a tendency of thought, the urge to categorize and lump together discrete particulars of experience. Operating in many areas of human life, within Jewish life this century it has had free reign in attempted generalizations about "diaspora" Jewish experience. Yet when attention is paid to particulars, experience itself seems to resist such a lumping together.

Let me nonetheless face the question. Are the "nature" experiences "typical" or at least possible for "diaspora" experience? The answer clearly depends on the particular place, the particular persons, and the particular politics of the place. For a Jewish grape-grower in Chile or Argentina, given certain traditional grounding, certain personal sensibilities, and the continuation or restoration of political liberties in those places, such experiences are quite conceivable. On the other hand, for a Jewish apartment-dweller in the heart of Buenos Aires or Boston, such experiences are not very likely.

By the same token, the nature experiences cited might be available to some *moshav* or *kibbutz* residents, yet far removed from the apartment-dweller in Tel Aviv.

As for the inspired *tefila* of a Havurat Shalom, is that "typical" of diaspora services? Again the question is amiss in its categories. There are U.S. synagogues and temples in which little if anything of a warm or inspiring nature happens, and others in which worshippers come away feeling truly strengthened and inspirited. And is not the same true in Israel? Are there not places of worship there whose religious emptiness deadens the person, and others where life flows freely and vigorously?

And can one imagine the resentment if it were now to be asked, which is the "typical" or "representative" Israeli experience? "Are we specimens," Israelis rightly retort, a reply equally appropriate in the mouths of those of us who live elsewhere.

What is clear is this: The line of demarcation for the experiences cited does not correspond to the line that is often thought to be the most significant, that between diaspora and Israeli Jewish existence. The diaspora-Israel distinction is not significant in these cases.

"But how can you begin to compare Jewish religious experiences elsewhere with those that might take place in the Holy Land or at the site of the ancient Temple? Is all space the same?"

No, all space is not the same, but from this it does not follow that there is only one proper place for religious experience and worship. With respect to the Land of Israel, it is helpful to remember that Abraham was spoken to by God outside of as well as within the land. The Torah was given in the desert. Moses, our greatest leader, never entered the land. The most influential Talmud is the Babylonian, not the Palestinian.

As for the Temple site, however impressive the legends that regard the Temple as situated upon *even hash'tiya*, the Foundation Stone of the World, one who knew the Temple well proclaimed clearly: "the whole Earth is filled with His Glory" (Isaiah 6:3). Furthermore, Judaism had always acknowledged places other than the Temple site where worship was both efficacious and esteemed. Before the Temple was established, worship was widely diffused; even while it stood, worship took place throughout the land as well as abroad; before its destruction the second time, the prototype of the non-fixed place of worship, the synagogue, had seen its beginnings; and with the destruction of the Temple, the institution of the synagogue facilitated and validated the worship of the Divine in many places, not less in the diaspora than in Israel.

Clearly Jewish religious experiences never were limited to the land of Israel, and there is no reason to think that they are now. Traditionally and religiously speaking, whatever special atmosphere the land may contribute, that is an addition to, not a sine qua non of valid religious experience.

However, it has been primarily in the realm of political life that the full significance of the distinction between life in Israel and life in the diaspora has been most often asserted. Yet is this really so, either at the individual or at the group level? Upon consideration, I think not. Once again, specifics are revealing.

As an individual Jew, I should need to ask quite concretely how my effective political freedoms would differ were I living in Israel. Here, of course, answers will vary greatly as comparisons are made from political unit to political unit throughout the world. Replies from Chile at this point are surely different from those of last year, and sadly at variance with those from Great Britain or Canada. Brazil is not Mexico, and neither is the U.S. It must be strongly emphasized that here, too, the attempt to characterize the "diaspora" with a single description shows a disregard for the particularity of life in different places.

Once more let me be quite specific. Were I a woman, would my personal liberties in relation to marriage and divorce be enhanced by my living in Israel? Hardly, for the male dominance of Orthodox laws defining personal status, backed by State power, would reduce my liberties significantly as compared to life in most Western or even Soviet-bloc countries.

As a conscientious objector to war, unless I happened to be an Orthodox Jewish female, my situation would be far worse as an Israeli than as a citizen of Great Britain, the United States, the Scandinavian countries, and numerous other places in the world. Israel has no provisions for conscientious objection to war as we understand that right in Western democracies.

Were I an Israeli with concerns about life and politics in Israel extending to the situation of the Palestinians, and were I to undertake there direct action of the kind in which many of us here in the U.S. participated during the civil rights movement during the days of Dr. Martin Luther King, Jr., would I find the political atmosphere more respectful of civil disobedience than I did here? I think not.

Furthermore, from what I have read of the Emergency Defense Regulations instituted by the British and still invoked by Israeli authorities against the Arabs and in some cases of radical political dissent by Israeli Jews, it seems to me that, as a Jew concerned with issues of social justice, my freedom to participate in dissenting political activity is probably greater here in the U.S. than it would be in Israel. The same, I suspect, would be true for most Western European democracies compared with Israel.

On the other hand, the reverse judgment might obtain were I a Soviet Jew, or from numerous other places in the world where Jews do experience oppression and for whom Israel appears as a land promising greater freedom. (That the promise is not always experienced as fulfilled is given sober testimony by the figures of Russian-Jewish emigration from Israel.)

Once again, however, the central point should be reiterated: There is no uniform experience of being "a Jew in the diaspora" from which generalizations can be made. As for specific comparisons, they yield results that do not invariably support the vague impression that "of course it's better for a Jew to live in Israel."

"But what of Jews as members of a collectivity, as members of a people? Surely in that respect you must concede the superiority of Israel as a place for Jews to live? There is no anti-Semitism, no threat of expulsion, no marginality as in diaspora lands. Here, truly, a Jew can stand erect and assert him/herself as a Jew, a fully independent human being at last."

The above argument, or something like it, was the classical argument of political Zionism, and had this essay been written earlier, it might have required extensive counter-argument. At this point in time, however, the post-October 1973 era, the pathos of such expectations unfulfilled invites a sigh rather than an argument.

No threat of expulsion? No marginality for Jews? Viewed as an isolated entity, as a nation-state unto itself, such may be true of Israel. But of what value is any view that ignores the regional realities of the Middle East? Sovereignty is nowhere on this Earth what it once appeared to be, and even less so in the Middle East. The collective security of Jews in Israel is far from what Zionism had expected, and the precariousness of the Israeli position is widely felt among concerned Jews throughout the world.

Independence? Just after the October War, during a debate in the Knesset, Menachem Begin attacked the government for feeding the Egyptian Third Army, and referred to the embittered feelings of soldiers at the front concerning this act. Replying to this Likud attack, Minister of Defense Moshe Dayan said, according to the Boston *Jewish Advocate* (November 1, 1973): "'What the soldiers did not know, but what Mr. Begin did know, was that the shells they fired today were not in Israel one week ago.'" Referring to a U.S. resupply operation, Dayan noted that Israel did not feed the Third Army for humanitarian reasons "'but because we had no choice . . . Whoever suggests that we conduct a war while having a break with the United States suggests that we conduct a war without the capability to win . . .'"

Rabbi Arnold Jacob Wolf has expressed it most pointedly: "If Zionism means political self-determination of the Jewish people . . . concentrated in one center, we are no less vulnerable than were our pitiable ancestors in the diaspora . . . We are all *galut* Jews now, children of exile."

In a world unredeemed, could we have expected otherwise? By what misreading of secular, not to speak of sacred, history could we have imagined that "normalization" would yield anything other than the present fluctuations of Israeli fortunes marked by such dates as June, 1967 and October, 1973? Whatever the particular circumstances of its establishment may have contributed to Israel's present plight, such fluctuations have been, ever-repeated, precisely what we, as a diaspora people, have witnessed in the case of nation after nation engaged in power struggles throughout the centuries. The romanticization of nation status contributed to the success of the Zionist movement, and the success of that movement now begins to de-romanticize that status. Sought for and achieved, nation status, we now find, is less than we had previously hoped it would be.

So we may once again as a people come to appreciate the profound point of the Lurianic understanding of Exile: the essence of the human condition at this stage of history is *galut*, not less for Israeli Jews than for diaspora Jews, and not less for non-Jews than for Jews, if I am not mistaken. It would be helpful for this, the kernel of a theology of diaspora, to be restated and applied in quite specific terms to the situation in which we find ourselves today, and perhaps another occasion will invite such a restatement. From it might come both a deeper understanding of our common human condition and a more balanced relationship, critical as well as admiring, between diaspora and Israeli Jews. This will not happen easily. It will require both a renewal of diaspora self-esteem and an end to excessive Zionist claims. Meanwhile, my present sense of the interrelations between Judaism, diaspora, and Israel is probably best summarized in these words of Orthodox Rabbi Aaron Samuel Tamaret (Ahad Harabbanim Hamargishim), written in 1930 and still applicable:

> The one who travels to the land of Israel must go for his own sake, not for the purported sake of the Jewish people. Let him there build for himself a house, plant for himself a vineyard, take for himself a wife, sire unto himself children and grandchildren. But let him not build a "national home" for the Jewish people nor a "spiritual center" for Judaism.
>
> The Jew who immigrates to the land of Israel for self-fulfilment, and does so without any pretense of perfecting the Jewish people as a whole, does, in fact, yield satisfaction to that people; for it is a delight to the spirit of the people that its children are to be found living in the holy land of its longings and desires. Such immigrants are indeed precious to all the Jews of the diaspora.
>
> But he who enters the land of Israel with trumpets and shouting, who proclaims that he "goes up" for our sake, the community of the diaspora, that he goes to the "homeland" and the "national refuge" — such a one is, plainly put, a "troubler of Israel." For whoever builds a "national refuge" acts mistakenly, conceding thereby the Sodomite measure by which the dwellers of this planet are declared to be either "owners" or "intruders," with the former having the privilege of disposing of the latter as they see fit. Furthermore, such a one narrows the universal image of Judaism, demeans the image of diaspora Jews, and casts upon them shadows of despair.
>
> As for building a "spiritual center" for Judaism, such advocates reveal a failure to grasp the nature of Judaism. For Judaism at root is not some religious concentration that can be localized or situated in a single territory, with a "throne" for the sacred, anointed leader who draws the heavenly stream earthward through the doors of the heavens, which are opened directly opposite that "sacred place," he being intermediary between mortal men and God. Neither is Judaism a matter of "nationality" in the sense of modern nationalism, fit to be woven into the famous threefold mesh of "homeland, army, and heroic songs." No, Judaism is Torah, ethics, and exaltation of spirit.
>
> If Judaism is truly Torah, then it cannot be reduced to the confines of any

particular territory. For as Scripture said of Torah: "Its measure is greater than the Earth . . ." (Job 11:9).

And if Judaism is ethics and exaltation of spirit, then its task is not simply to perfect peoples, societies, or other such abstractions, neglecting on their behalf the particualr man. Rather is its task the perfection of the individual man, living and actual.

Hence the true locus and center of Judaism is within the heart, within the heart of every Jew whose heart is of flesh, not of stone. Wherever on all this earth such a Jew is found, there is the place of Judaism."

From *Israel and the Palestinians,* 1975

Ancient Visions, Future Hopes

Rabbi Aaron Samuel Tamaret's Objection to Zionism

Rabbi Aaron Samuel Tamaret (1869-1931), an Orthodox advocate of non-violence, has long been a compelling and inspiring figure for Rabbi Gendler, as revealed in this 2003 essay, which explores Tamaret's qualms about Zionist "normalization" of the Jews.

Thirty-six, 36, *lamed-vav*: In its classical source, Isaiah 30:15-18, the number is associated with righteousness, justice, and the hopeful certainty of Divine redemption through "turning and stillness, tranquility and trust." In later tradition, it alludes to the thirty-six righteous who, usually unrecognized, quietly sustain the world. Invariably poignant, the number this year – the thirty-sixth anniversary of the Six Day War – also stirs in me pain and distress.

Thirty-six years have passed since, to the "realists," the promise of peace seemed near at hand from the preponderance of Israeli power. In *realpolitik*, after all, are not power and peace coordinates?

Isaiah would have been profoundly skeptical. He long ago proclaimed that peace would be "the work of righteousness," and that the longed-for "tranquility and trust for ever" would also be "the result of righteousness" (32:15-18).

Why, then, despite the plaintive cries for "peace, peace," is there no peace? Is it entirely obduracy on the part of those who oppose a Jewish Israel? Without dismissing that as one factor contributing to the increasingly tragic impasse, this thirty-sixth anniversary should also invite a reexamination of possible elements of injustice, residues of unrighteousness, that were embedded in the very beginnings of the Zionist movement. These need full, yet sympathetic, acknowledgement if ever a peaceful future is to become a reality.

This is no easy task. Apart from unresolved general issues of social causality, there are also the passions of the moment. Who is to be trusted? To which voices shall we give ear? When are criticisms of Israel genuine, when do they mask other motives, provide expression for simple anti-Semitism? If only we could escape from the entrapment of our own times, hear a fresh voice that we could trust, know that its challenges and criticisms emerge from love of the Jewish people, not hatred, from fidelity to Jewish values, not their rejection!

There is, in fact, such a voice: Rabbi Aaron Samuel Tamaret's, in his final pained and impassioned critique of political Zionism, *Sh'losha Zivugim Bilti Hagunim*, "Three Unsuitable Unions," written in response to the Hebron riots of 1929. (Does nothing ever change in the Middle East?)

Born in 1869 and soon dubbed "the prodigy from Maltsh" in recognition of his prodigious Talmudic and Biblical learning, Tamaret served as rabbi of the village of Milejczyce, Poland from 1893 until his death in 1931. In contrast to most of his Orthodox colleagues, he early joined the political Zionist movement, and was a delegate to the Fourth Zionist Congress in London in 1900. That experience was profoundly disillusioning to him, however, and after a period of distressed silence, he began to denounce Zionism specifically and nationalism in general, a denunciation that became more intense with the passing years.

The true human costs of the Russian-Japanese War of 1905 were evident to him in the faces of bereaved villagers, and his penetrating analysis of World War I from a Torah perspective is astonishing for its passion, its eloquence, its tradition-based pacifism, and its political realism. His pen-name, Ahad Harabbanim Hamargishim, "One of the Passionately Concerned Rabbis," was entirely appropriate to his character, as summarized in the *Encyclopedia Judaica*: "an unusual figure in the rabbinical world: an Orthodox rabbi who fought against the fossilized halakhah in a completely original style and who attacked nationalism and political Zionism as anti-Jewish phenomena."

Can an outcry from seventy years ago contribute to a critical inquiry today? I believe it can, by affording us a fresh perspective on a number of recurrent basic issues, issues whose avoidance has impeded any genuine solution to the agony of the Middle East today.

In approaching any area of conflict, we tend to accept, as a given, the validity of boundaries and settlement lines established by the victorious powers after World War I, which shaped the geographic realities of today. Although many of these boundaries may not be sustainable (*e.g.,* Iraq, a volatile "union" of Sunni, Shiite, and Kurdish communities), they must serve as starting points.

The establishment of Israel as a modern nation-state was achieved by "joining the club," the system through which Europe reshaped the world after World War I (although the fruits of Zionism would not be harvested until after the slaughter of Jews during World War II). Appealing to the League of Nations to receive redistributed lands worried Tamaret, as it appeared to validate the bloodshed and destruction of the "Great War." He also found that the Zionist attachment to modern nationalism compromised both Jewish values and Jewish identity. Here are some of his words on this issue, in my translation from the Hebrew.

> The World War should have been truly assessed for what it was: an unmixed defeat for humanity. Any decent man should have scorned its outcome, never excusing its brutality and blood-letting by any purported future results. For nothing can compensate for millions of young lives lost, millions of parents deeply bereaved, and millions of joyless, suffering disabled. And what of the utter pollution of the spiritual atmosphere, which turned men into beasts of prey and ambush! . . . men have become wolves to one another, life has deteriorated seriously, and Jews, always the target, are more maligned than ever.
>
> . . . But our political Zionists have taken it upon themselves to praise and glorify this age of a new heaven and a new earth created by the war. Never do they cease from singing the praise of the spirit of "liberty" and "justice" which has awakened in the world as the result of nations girding themselves with swords and going forth to "free lands," or of the "righteousness" which has been awakened in the hearts of nations to correct the "historic burden" of Israel by returning it to its "birthplace.". . . "Not only in theory and words have our Balfourists shown solidarity with the rulers of the earth, but in practice as well. They founded the 'Jewish Legion' to fight with 'Nilolai Nikolovitz' – otherwise a persecutor of Jews – to 'liberate' Palestine from Turkey. Nor was this help insignificant.
>
> Physically, of course, the help of a few hundred Jewish soldiers was inconsequential compared with the millions of men fighting in the Allied cause. The ethical help, however, was substantial indeed, consisting, as it did, in the destruction of ethical feeling and the removal from men's hearts of any remains of religious reverence, prerequisites for enabling men to wage war and attack others whom they had not previously so much as seen or known. Such was the very considerable moral contribution of the 'Jewish Legion' to 'Nikolai Nikolovitz.'

Tamaret took seriously the idea that Jews have a Divinely directed, moral mission in the world, and while a fully observant halakhic Jew, he understood our purpose in universal ethical terms. Hence the pain and the passion of his recognition that if Jews were to adopt the time-dishonored, ethically tainted tactics of violent statecraft, a grievous moral injury would be inflicted on all of humankind:

> Small and humble is Jacob, and his ability to influence humanity for good is indeed limited. On the other hand, his ability to corrupt and pollute the moral atmosphere of the earth, should he pervert his way, is greater than anyone else's. For it unfortunately follows logically: if this frail and tender people, whose existence has always been secured by Moral Force, at last acknowledges the sword, how shall one answer those nations who have always lived by the Sword? . . .
>
> For Jews have suffered each time they saw, even from afar, the glittering helmets and flashing spears of a troop of soldiers approaching, and know well the terror which sends innocents running from shelter to shelter . . .
>
> But it is not only because of Israel's extraordinary suffering at the blade of the sword that Jacob, should he, too, now begin to lust after sword and ammunition, has this special capacity to befoul the ethical atmosphere more than any other nation; it is also because of his distinction as "the chosen people."
>
> How terrible is that corruption which would result from any evil example set by "Jacob, selected by God, Israel, His special treasure," were he, also, at last to adopt the faith of Esau. . . . One may be sure that when Jacob behaves deviously or dishonorably, the example will be duly noted along with his distinction, and suddenly he will become a valued authority who serves to sanction their own misdeeds. . . .
>
> The Junker philosopher, Nietzche, may have scorned the Jewish ethic of justice and dubbed it 'slave morality,' but the 'Jewish Legion' of Jabotinsky, however questionable its recruits, was welcomed with open arms and great rejoicing.

Might some of this moral dismay, vividly articulated by Tamaret, underlie the intense international focus on Israeli policies? Perhaps anti-Semitism plays some part, but Tamaret's eloquent description of such attention as reflecting world acknowledgement of the Jew as moral guide is not to be lightly dismissed. Even a cursory consideration of the current world interest in the Tibetan exile community, together with the adulation of the Dalai Lama for his nonviolent teachings, might suggest that Tamaret was an astute and realistic diagnostician of this deep human moral hunger. Am I the only one to whom it seems that, in recent decades, saffron robes have become the update of Jochanan ben Zakkai's *tallit*?

Another powerful source of our fear, distress, and despair is the widespread belief that the Palestinians and their Arab supporters refuse to acknowledge the legitimacy of a Jewish state in Israel-Palestine. It is not clear how true this belief is. What shall we make, for example, of the public proclamation last March, by all the Arab states, of readiness to recognize and establish relations with the state of Israel in exchange for full withdrawal from the territories occupied in the Six Day War? Regrettably, this offer was not, to my knowledge, ever explored.

"But look at the Palestinians' insistence on 'the right to return!'" is a frequent reply. "Doesn't this effectively deny the validity of the Jewish state?" In fact, I have heard from Palestinians proposals for their right of return that are willing to limit the annual numbers of those returnees to a percentage of Jewish immigration in that year. This surely bespeaks acquiescence to the Jewish need for self-determination, even if not conceding ultimate legitimacy to the Jewish state.

More to the point, however, is our unquestioning assumption of the self-evident justice of a Jewish state, as we have come to know it. It may well be that at this point in time, it is the least unjust, least injurious solution to an increasingly intractable human impasse; a viable-two-state "solution," one Jewish, one Palestinian, does seem to me the least worst next step. But this is far from claiming inherent justice for Jewish sovereignty, rooted in political power over a modern nation-state. Here again, Tamaret, a *rov* in a Polish *shtetl*, saw and articulated the profound ambiguity, from the very beginning, of settlement in a spirit of dominance rather than of sharing. Not for him the empty reassurance of "a land without a people for a people without a land;" such idle words did not set him at ease in Zion. Vividly, he portrays what we might, perhaps, designate, from his perspective, as the original sin of the political Zionist settlement.

> Travellers to Israel never entered as simple immigrants, merely desirous of a peaceful place in which to work and create a life for themselves, a place which would satisfy their romantic desire to hear echoes of the Biblical age still resounding on the mountains of Judah and which would, in due course, nourish their spirits with that revivifying air of the land of Israel.
>
> A modest arrival of this sort would not have frightened and aroused the Arabs, and so it would have been possible gradually to establish there, in the land of our ancestors, a Hebrew settlement to the satisfaction of Jews everywhere, even though this *yishuv* did not dream dreams of "statehood" and "sovereignty," nor presume to dominate Jews everywhere as "teacher of all Jews in the diaspora." It would have been possible to establish a simple Jewish settlement in the land of Israel like Jewish settlements

everywhere on this earth, that the land of our forefathers not be less than lands elsewhere. Thus Jews in the land of Israel would have joined Jews everywhere in waiting for the true coming of the Messiah, that ideal moral redemption which is anticipated in Scripture and Rabbinic Teachings. . . .

Armed with a piece of paper, the official permit obtained from Balfour, and with that pride which comes from having seen the face of the king, the Zionist leaders began to proclaim loudly and openly that they had come to establish a "Jewish State" and to become lords of the land. They further began to urge Jews to hasten from the four corners of the earth to the land of Israel, not because Jews personally needed to emigrate, but in order to achieve a Jewish "majority" and thereby become the "dominant people," outnumbering the original Arab inhabitants of the land, who would then become a "tolerated" minority. . . .

. . . [T[he Zionists hid their eyes from the fact that the actual place was not a newly-discovered, unsettled island located at the far ends of the earth, but was a place already inhabited by a people which was sure to feel the "nationalist" and "sovereign political" aims as a needle in its living flesh.

Thus the result resembles the tale told by Rabba bar bar Hana (Baba Batra 73b). A group of seafarers saw a slope which from afar resembled an island, and so they approached, left their boats, and spent several days resting on it. During this interval they wandered about, spread themselves out, and soon felt like absolute owners of the place. Finally they lit a fire with which to bake bread and roast meat, and at last discovered that, although it had appeared to their eyes as a lump of inert clay, this was not an island but rather a living whale. As soon as the fire was felt by the fish, he turned on his back, quaked, raged, and tossed them all into the sea. Had their boats not been near to rescue them, they might have drowned in the sea. The application is painfully evident.

The sharpness of Tamaret's analytical knife and the heat of his cauterization are enough to induce surgical shock; extraordinary, also, is his ability to describe the phenomenon of Jewish settlement as the Arabs then living in the land might have felt it. Would that current returnees from "solidarity missions" with Israel could offer us some comparably empathetic report on how Palestinians have experienced life under occupation since 1967. And what healing effects might we hope for from our serious self-scrutiny of felt injuries by the original Arab population, however unintentional on our part? Perhaps such a human perspective, gleaned from personal meetings, would enable us, as a community, to respond more adequately and more constructively to what is evidently deep despair and destructive hostility among the Palestinians. Might this be somewhat analogous to the moving efforts of the Christian church to look afresh at anti-Jewish elements in Christian tradition, even in the Gospels, and to try to respond to them? The healing effects of this *teshuvah*, this turning towards recognition of the deeper sources of pain and conflict, dare not be disregarded by a tradition such as ours, which occupies such a central place both in ethics and in theology.

Tamaret was entirely sympathetic to Jewish settlement in the holy land, but in a particular spirit.

> [O]ne who travels to the land of Israel must go for his own sake, not for the purported sake of the Jewish people. Let him there build for himself a house, plant for himself a vineyard, take for himself a wife, sire unto himself children and grandchildren. But let him not build a "national home" for the Jewish people nor a "spiritual center" for Judaism!
>
> The Jew who immigrates to the land of Israel for self-fulfillment, and does so without any pretense of perfecting the Jewish people as a whole does, in fact, yield satisfaction to that people; for it is a delight to the spirit of the people that its children are to be found living in the holy land of its longings and desires. Such immigrants are indeed precious to all the Jews of the diaspora.
>
> But one who enters the land of Israel with trumpets and shouting, who proclaims that he "goes up" for our sake, the community of the diaspora, that he goes to the "homeland" and the "national refuge" – such a one is, plainly put, a "troubler of Israel." For whoever builds a "national refuge" acts mistakenly, conceding thereby the Sodomite measure by which the dwellers of this planet are declared to be either "owners" or "intruders," with the former having the privilege of disposing of the latter as they see fit. Furthermore, such a one narrows the universal image of Judaism, demeans the image of diaspora Jews, and casts upon them shadows of despair.

How, then, does Tamaret view the proper relation of Israel and the diaspora? First of all, he is caustic in his rejection of Israel-centrism.

> [T]here is a strange capitulation of diaspora Jews . . . Periodicals show almost exclusive reliance on material from Israel or that having to do with Zionist politics. Jewish educators know only to teach the map of Israel, Zionist songs, significant Zionist anniversaries, love of "fatherland" and Sephardic pronunciation.
>
> It would appear to be widely accepted that the true task of diaspora Jews, including the intellectuals, is simply to do piecework at home for the chief culture factory in Israel. . . . It is a serious error for Jewish intellectuals to attach themselves as tail to the horse of political Zionism.

He further portrays the injury that "homeland-centered" Judaism inflicts on the Jewish people in these terms:

> Political Zionism, as developed thus far, clearly imperils the character of Judaism, which has survived so many centuries free from the defilements of "nationalism" and "homelandism."
>
> Additionally, the establishment of the desired political state with a Jewish majority would affect adversely Jews elsewhere, both physically and spiritually. Physically, this proclaimed preferable place for Jews gives implicit sanction to persecutors elsewhere who would like to oust "alien" Jews from other lands, for they can now say: Jews, what complaints have you against us? Why do you insist on residing here where, by your own Zionist admission, you are mere temporary aliens? Go on to your own country, Palestine, where you are now the dominant majority; and en route, be sure to thank us for our kindness in recognizing your "historic rights" to the land of Israel!
>
> As for the spiritual damage to Jews elsewhere, by exaggerating the delights and the incomparable dignity which Jews supposedly enjoy in the "fatherland," Jews elsewhere will come to despair of the quality of their lives as Jews.
>
> The Zionists, of course, insist that everywhere in the world Jews will point with pride to Israel and the people there, will come to subject themselves to the "fatherland," and will finally accept it as the source of a spiritual revolution. Yet I find these consolations offered the millions of Jews outside of Israel – namely, knowing that there, in the "homeland," a handful of Jews live a "life of honor" and "are equal to all men" – are even emptier than the promise of the Feast of Leviathan, which others offer to presently suffering Jews. For the latter at least promises a personal recompense in the future for the sufferings of the present, while the prophets of the idol called "homeland" offer merely generic consolations: that lowly Jews in the diaspora shall enjoy vicariously the lives of the proud Jews in Tel Aviv who dance the hora, and be satisfied that they are members of the same family. And even this only on condition that the Jews of the diaspora place themselves under the influence of the fortunate ones in Israel.
>
> Do you hear? We had always imagined that as a diaspora people, purified and cleansed of the pride of the sword, we should be able to share a goodly teaching with others. But now come the Balfourists and reveal to us the secret that we are lowly creatures who have no salvation except to listen to what proceeds from the mouths of our distinguished brothers in the "homeland," to make of their teachings a crown for our heads and whose words shall be our light.
>
> However, if it is simply by virtue of dwelling in a "homeland" or "fatherland" that our Balfourists have become superior men, sanctified already in the wombs of their mothers to be teachers and guides, providers of fare for

the souls of all the diaspora, then consider: Distinguished teachers such as these already abound for Jews in the diaspora! For in every single land where Jews dwell, there are many who try with all their might to stuff us with their own cultures, the culture of "by your sword shall you live." The Jews of the diaspora have no need whatsoever to bring from afar such false bread as this!

The final words of his essay restate the reasons for his principled religious rejection of the very notion of Israel as a "spiritual center." They also reveal clearly his understanding of traditional Judaism and its ultimate purpose:

As for building a "spiritual center" for Judaism, such advocates reveal a failure to grasp the nature of Judaism. For Judaism at root is not some religious concentration that can be localized or situated in a single territory. . . . Neither is Judaism a matter of "nationality" in the sense of modern nationalism, fit to be woven into the famous three-fold mesh of "homeland, army, and heroic songs." No, Judaism is Torah, ethics, and exaltation of spirit.

If Judaism is truly Torah, then it cannot be reduced to the confines of any particular territory. For as Scripture said of Torah: "Its measure is greater than the earth . . ." (Job 11:9).

Neither is Torah the monopoly of particular persons or particular places. Our Sages said of Torah (Yoma), and it is repeated by Maimonides (Laws of the Study of Torah): "The crown of Torah is prepared for all Israel." And in Abot our Sages said: "Prepare yourself to learn Torah, for it is not a biological inheritance." If Torah is not inherited from the womb, all the less is it the automatic inheritance of any "country."

If Judaism is ethics and exaltation of spirit, then its task is not simply to perfect peoples, societies, or other such abstractions, neglecting on their behalf the particular person. Rather is its task the perfection of the individual human being, living and actual. Hence the true locus and center of Judaism is within the heart, within the heart of every Jew whose heart is of flesh, not of stone. Wherever on all this earth such a Jew is found, there is the place of Judaism.

The preparation of this translation-summary has been a painful task; its reading will not be pleasant either.

No claim is made that Tamaret's analysis is complete, adequate, or without need of some qualification. Living before Hitler and the full Nazi expression of demonically destructive, racist nationalism directed against Jews, Tamaret does not, of course, address himself to that appalling phenomenon. Would it have affected his analysis, attitude, or response?

Might it have confirmed his worse fears about the ultimate distortions to which modern nationalism may be prone? Would it also have prompted a change of policy on his part, or would he have insisted that even then, *"en kategor naaseh sanegor,"* that extending the malady of modern nationalism was no way to cure the cancer itself? Would he have agreed that under the circumstances the Jewish people had to become "like all the nations" in order to save Jewish lives, or would he have rejected this as, finally, both a shortsighted, illusory solution and an ominous renunciation of the Jewish messianic function in world history? Who can say? The questions unfortunately must remain unanswered and unanswerable.

Notwithstanding, Tamaret's response to issues of hostile surroundings and persecution are important, for they strongly suggest that his stance would have been realistic if applied in the early stages of that period of horror, and that his position has relevance for us today. One example: Tamaret was, from the beginning of his rabbinate, concerned with societal problems; it was his activism that led to his early involvement with the Zionist movement. After breaking with political Zionism and directing his major attention to matters near at hand, as early as 1905 he advocated the formation of groups of Jews to monitor closely the relations between Jews and the people among whom they resided, urging timely responses to tensions that arose. These responses were to include, internally, the Jewish communal cultivation of the spirit of "living in peace and amity with all people, whether or not they be of the Jewish religion;" and externally, "whenever plans are afoot to stir up hatred among the common people by intrigues and agitators, to turn to the masses of the common people and, in their language, invite them to peace and brotherhood, at the same time showing them clearly the falseness of the accusations leveled against us . . . " Tamaret also discusses the advisability of "revealing before the masses the source of these accusations and the destructive interests of their creators, whose only intention is to distract the eyes of the people from their own interests . . ."

Meaning what in relation to Germany? First of all, even before the rise of the Nazi scourge, Tamaret would have been reaching out to his non-Jewish neighbors, trying to cultivate mutual understanding, establishing interreligious communities of support that could have been appealed to in resisting the Nazi program. Could such solidarity have made a difference in the face of the Nazi onslaught? Would resistance by fellow Aryans to the Nazi program have affected events? There are cases where it did, among them the ending of the early euthanasia policy. Even more astonishing is the case of the German wives of Jewish husbands, who banded together in 1943 and, by public demonstrations in front of Gestapo headquarters on Rosenstrasse, successfully saved their husbands from transfer to the death camps! (Nathan Stolzfus' *Resistance of the Heart* is a well-documented, probing study of this important episode.)

The cultivation and growth of intergroup sympathy, advocated by Tamaret as an important component of Jewish self-defense, was undeniably one significant factor in the rescue of the Danish Jews, and there are numerous other instances where it was a vital element in saving Jewish lives.

But what of his rejection of the nationalist doctrine of Jewish sovereignty over the Holy Land? Does this not represent the abdication of responsibility for providing a place of refuge for Jews in need of protection? In evaluating this claim, it is vital to remember that there were committed Zionists living in Palestine who, even in 1948, were vocal in proclaiming their opposition to the United Nations partition of Palestine and the establishment of two states. They included Judah Magnes, first president of the Hebrew University, Martin Buber, Ernst Simon, and, until her death, Henrietta Szold, founder of Hadassah. Residing in Palestine throughout those years, they can hardly be dismissed for lack of knowledge of the situation there. Neither dare one accuse them of lack of concern for the rescue of Jews in need.

A case can be made that a policy such as Tamaret's or, later, that of Brit Shalom, might have saved more Jewish lives during the Holocaust than the nationalist approach. How so? An analogy may be helpful. Compare William Penn's approach to the native inhabitants of Pennsylvania with the cowboys-versus-Indians approach all too common elsewhere. Was not the peaceable acceptance of Penn's newcomers testimony to the possibility of immigration and settlement in a spirit of mutual respect? Remember, also, stories of natives around Plymouth instructing the newcomers in helpful methods of agriculture in the new world.

Think now of a Jewish settlement process that had followed the spirit proposed by Tamaret, and which every step of the way took pains to establish relations of mutuality with those already living in the land, at no point threatening dominance. If such a basis for amicably sharing the land had been early established between Jews and Arabs, cannot one imagine that there might have been some Arab predisposition, or at least willingness, to offer refuge to other Jewish settlers in desperate flight from the Nazis? This is, of course, mere speculation after the devastating fact of the Holocaust. But don't we permit ourselves speculation about how a sovereign Jewish state would have altered the outcome of events of those years of horror? Indeed, it might have – but so might a process of settlement as advocated by Tamaret. Which might have offered the greater long-term security to Jews settling there? The question is again one which cannot be answered, but I would urge that we not unconsciously assume that the answer is obvious.

Two other elements in Tamaret's position especially invite further scrutiny and development beyond the space limitations of this article. Tamaret emphasized the importance of the diaspora Jewish moral renunciation of violence and statecraft, insisting that this does affect, at least to some limited degree, the ethical actions of power states in the world. Was this simply fantasy on his part? I think not. For evidence in support of his contention, look, for example, at the excerpt from Judah Magnes' *Journal* in which he reports on his interview with President Truman in May, 1948 (especially pp. 494-495 in *Dissenter in Zion*, edited by Arthur A. Goren, Harvard University Press). Magnes reports Truman's dream that "peoples whose life was based on the same moral code might get to understand one another." After referring to the common basis of Jewish, Christian, and Muslim moral codes, and his hope that this understanding "might help to lift the world from the materialism which was holding the world down to the ground and might destroy it," Truman laments: "But here it is – you Jews and you Arabs are spoiling things. You are not giving the Jews and the Christians and the Moslems of the rest of the world a chance to have confidence in one another. That is one of the reasons why I deplore so deeply this conflict in the Holy Land." However one may evaluate Truman's statement, it is clear testimony to the importance of the Jewish and monotheistic moral stance in affecting human affairs. In terms of today, I am confident that Tamaret would be among those asking about Jewish moral credibility and the policies of the Israeli government as permissive elements for U. S. foreign policy under the direction of President George W. Bush.

Finally, a brief word in support of the political realism, even today, of policies in the spirit of Tamaret, that is to say, policies that accord full, generous-hearted recognition to the valid human needs of "the other." In a remarkable "Letter from Porto Allegre: At a Leftist Summit, Cheers for a Separate Mideast Peace" *Forward*, February 7-14, 2003), Lucy Komisar reports that "20,000 participants in the stadium were crying and cheering as the peace statement was read with the sound system playing John Lennon's 'Imagine.'" Instead of an anticipated resolution condemning Israel and questioning its legitimacy, a statement emerged that, in Komisar's words, might cause even some "Jewish doves (to) flinch," as it was "a powerful pro-Israel statement" from the "point of view of many activists on the far left [who are] prone to rejecting the very legitimacy of the Jewish state." How did this "pro-Israel," pro-peace statement come about? There was serious dialogue and preparation before the forum by local Jewish and Palestinian communities in Porto Alegre; Brazilian Chief Rabbi Henry Sobel was involved; there was support from new President Lula da Silva's Workers Party; and personally present were Shulamit Aloni, Galia Golan, Ely Ben-Gal, Zyad Abu Zyad (a member of the Palestinian Parliament), Alam Jarar, and Lana Nusseibeh.

The statement affirmed "peace, justice, and sovereignty for our peoples, an end to Israeli occupation of the lands occupied in 1967, the creation of an independent Palestinian state by side by side with Israel along the lines of 4 June 1967 with Jerusalem as an open city, the capital of each of the two states, an agreed just and fair solution for the Palestinian refugee problem in accordance with UN Resolution 194," and an end to violence on both sides of the conflict. That such a statement could evoke cheers, tears, and tumultuous applause at an alternative global summit of nearly 100,000 people, and that it could be characterized as "the highlight of the conference," testifies, I submit, to the profound wisdom of Tamaret's insistence that conducted in the right spirit, Jewish settlement in Palestine could enjoy the support and esteem of all.

Rabbi Tamaret's outcry can, I believe, open our souls to fresh, creative responses to the tragic Middle Eastern tangle that is the focus of so much attention, concern, anguish, and longing on the part of all of us. Tamaret can also help us towards a much needed redefinition of the proper relation among Judaism, Diaspora, and Israel. For his courageous, unflinching statement, I am grateful.

Hebrew readers can now read Tamaret's autobiographical memoir, some scattered essays, and excerpts from four of his five published books – though none from his critique of Zionism – in the 1992 volume, edited by Ehud Luz, entitled *Pacificism and Torah: Works by Aaron Samuel Tamares* [sic], published by The Hebrew University and Hebrew Union College.

From *American Council of Judaism Issues*, Fall, 2003

A Year to Remember Gedaliah

Peacemaking in Ancient Times

The Fast of Gedaliah, marking the Babylonian conquest of Judea and the start of the Babylonian exile, is largely ignored by liberal Jews. This 2008 essay presents the figure of Gedaliah, who sought, as Babylon's appointed governor, to preserve the vitality of the Jewish commonwealth (and was assassinated as a collaborator for his efforts), as a figure relevant to Mideast peace efforts today.

*G*edaliah? Who's that? If such words express your first reaction to the title, you have plenty of company. Gedaliah is almost certainly the least known figure whose name designates a day in the Jewish calendar, and the Fast of Gedaliah (pronounced guh-dahl-yuh) itself has also been little noticed for many decades. Yes, it's still listed in traditional printings of Jewish calendars as 3 Tishre, the day following the second day of Rosh Hashanah (for those who observe two days), but even in these printings it receives only the un-informative description, "commemorates the climax of disasters that befell the Jewish Commonweath in 586 BCE." The calendars of the Union of Reform Judaism and the World Union of Reform Judaism take no notice of it, and neither Hayim Schauss in the 1938 UAHC volume, *The Jewish Festivals*, nor Theodor Gaster in his 1952 *Festivals of the Jewish Year* bothers to mention it. Quite likely, even many who use traditional calendars pay little attention to the day.

Why, then, propose that we remember Gedaliah? To answer the question, a few words about the historical period in which Gedaliah lived are necessary. During the turbulent times of 587/586 BCE, as the Babylonians advanced on Jerusalem to subdue the Judean kingdom, the Jews were sharply divided on the best response. One faction favored a political alliance with Egypt and its army to fight the Babylonian threat; another advocated a negotiated submission to the Babylonians to ensure the survival of a Jewish presence in Jerusalem and Jewish life and religious practices within the

Judean Kingdom. The prophet Jeremiah was a strong advocate of this neutralism, rejecting an alliance with Egyptian power as the safeguard against Babylonia. His words denouncing royal collaboration with the Egyptians angered pro-Egyptian Jewish princes and other prophets, and in a dramatic trial, Jeremiah was threatened with death (see Jeremiah 26 for the vivid account). In this situation, a member of a politically prominent family, Ahikam, son of Shaphan, used his high-level influence to save Jeremiah from falling into the hands of the people who wanted to execute him.

Following further periods of dramatic and dangerous prophetic activity (see Jeremiah 27-39 for the remarkably exciting details), with Babylonian advance units having already breached the walls of Jerusalem, Jeremiah again passionately urged accommodation with the Babylonians. This time, too, as popular feelings grew more heated, there were again arrests and threats to Jeremiah's life. This time it was Ahikam's son, Gedaliah, who, like his father, became Jeremiah's protector. Gedaliah used his political position and his personal power to ensure Jeremiah's survival. As events unfolded, Gedaliah became governor of those Jews who remained in Jerusalem and Judea, cooperating with the Babylonians while also securing concessions from the invaders to improve the lives of the conquered.

Was this treasonable collaboration or life-preserving accommodation? Just as our assessments might differ, Jews at the time also disagreed, some quite vehemently (for lively details, see Jeremiah 40-41). One faction, encouraged by the King of Ammon and led by Ishmael, son of Nethaniah, undertook a mission to assassinate Gedaliah. Advisors to Gedaliah warned him of the plot, but he refused to take seriously their reports, and was, indeed, slain, along with many of his advisors. According to tradition (the sources are not clear about the exact timing), this assassination occurred on the 3rd of Tishre, and to commemorate Gedaliah, the rabbinic sages enacted a fast day.

This enactment reflected the rabbinic judgment that there had been advantages for the Jews from the non-entanglement-with-big-powers policy that Jeremiah advocated and Gedaliah administered. Josephus (*Antiquities*, 10:9) gives details of an extensive resettlement policy. Jews who had fled the Babylonian invasion could return, reclaim land for cultivation, and live Jewish lives if they would accept Babylonian sovereignty. In the trenchant words of the eminent historian, David Biale (*Power and Powerlessness in Jewish History*): "The final destruction of any form of Jewish sovereignty in the Land of Israel came about not because of prior policies of Assyria and Babylonia, but because of the victory of the Jewish party of revolt over the party of accommodation." With this prophetic neutralism there is no rabbinic quarrel.

Yet the rabbis did not unequivocally approve of all Gedaliah's actions. There is explicit rabbinic condemnation (Talmud Niddah 61a) of Gedaliah's naiveté in dismissing the reports of Ishmael's assassination plans: "He should have taken note of the advice of Johanan the son of Kareah" [about the plot to kill him and his associates], and acted to thwart it. Because he failed to do this, one strain of rabbinic thought regards him as complicit in the slaying of his associates. One might say that the rabbis supported neutralism but not naiveté.

Reading this ancient, nearly forgotten history, we can understand why the Fast of Gedaliah became the most minor of the four minor fast days. But there is a coincidence of dates this year that suggest a fresh significance to Gedaliah, one that might stimulate us to take note of the day even if we don't choose to fast on it. This past October, 2008, in a resolution co-sponsored by 140 nations, the United Nations designated Gandhi's birthday, October 2nd, to be observed and celebrated each year as an International Day of Nonviolence. "Bearing in mind that nonviolence, tolerance, full respect for all human rights and and fundamental freedoms for all, democracy, development, mutual understanding and respect for diversity are interlinked and mutually reinforcing," the resolution asks that each year organizations and individuals focus attention on these interlinked basic human values. This year the International Day of Nonviolence, October 2nd, coincides with 3 Tishre, our traditional if mostly forgotten Fast of Gedaliah.

Is there any connection to be made? Viewed from our current perspec-tive, I see Gedaliah, the peace-seeking compromiser, as a forerunner of Anwar Sadat and Yitzhak Rabin. Both of these men were, like Gedaliah, killed by uncompromising nationalist zealots. While none of the three can be claimed as principled practitioners of nonviolence, all of them are certainly related in spirit to the two most effective nonviolent leaders of the past century, Gandhi and King, both of whom were also victims of fanaticism become violent.

How might this observance be given some acceptable ceremonial expression today? Reinstitute the fast? With the approach of Yom Kippur, forget fasting. More liturgical hymns, then, of Divine Sovereignty and poems of Self-Inspection? Immediately following Rosh Hashanah, too much already! However, to do some reading and to give some serious thought to neutralism, naiveté, nonviolence, their interrelations and their implications, could be a compelling contemporary way to observe this day commemorating Gedaliah. Is nonviolence practical? Isn't it a naïve approach to a tough world of power politics? But what is power? Obviously nonviolence has worked at some times in some places. Where? How has it operated? Can it become more pragmatic, more powerful? Reading for discussion of these issues at greater depth (see below) could be both a stimulating and an appropriate way to observe the Fast of Gedaliah this year as it coincides with the International Day of Nonviolence.

A group discussion or an individual study session could appropriately begin with the traditional blessing before studying Torah: *Barukh ata Ado-nai Elohenu melekh ha'olam asher kidshanu bmitzvo-ta v'tzivanu laasok b'divrey torah* – You abound in blessings, Eternal our God, Source of All Creation, making our lives holy through Your injunctions, and directing us to study Torah.

And the readings? For a beginning, I would propose some chapters from Jeremiah and two short pamphlets (both available from The Albert Einstein Institution, P.O. Box 455, East Boston, MA 02128), with a longer volume for further inquiry: Jeremiah 26-41; Gene Sharp's *From Dictatorship to Democracy* (a brief pamphlet that inspired, among others, the successful OTPOR student strategy that toppled Milosevich); Robert L. Helvey's *On Strategic Nonviolent Conflict: Thinking About the Fundamentals* (a compellingly non-naïve treatment of nonviolence by a retired U.S. Army colonel); and Gene Sharp's *Waging Nonviolent Struggle* (a 2005 summary and update of Sharp's classic 1973 work on the dynamics of nonviolent struggle, with numerous brief case studies of recent nonviolent actions around the world).

Are the secular readings listed above in any sense "Torah"? I would suggest that in truth they are. I see both Sharp and Helvey's work as "*Midrashim* of *Maaseh*," action-interpretation and applications of Isaiah's remarkable formulation of a nonviolent approach to power in 30:15: "In turning and tranquility shall you be saved in stillness and trust shall be your strength."

A fuller exploration of the meaning of each of the key Hebrew terms must await another occasion. But Sharp and Helvey provide numerous instances and analyses of how morality gains muscle, how spirit has sinews (my terms, not theirs). To do this reading and to give some serious thought to neutralism, naiveté, nonviolence, their interrelations and their implications, could be a powerful and significant contemporary way to observe the Fast of Gedaliah.

Finally, a personal note, or perhaps simply "full disclosure." Since our retirement from regular work commitments in 1995, my wife Mary and I have been helping the Tibetan exiles in India develop a community-wide educational program on Strategic Nonviolent Struggle for the Tibetan cause. With the approval of the Dalai Lama and under the guidance of the Tibetan Government in Exile, the project, after these twelve years of our intermittent, once-or-twice-a-year teaching tours, has now become a Tibetan-run, Tibetan-staffed Non-Governmental Agency, ANEC, the Active Nonviolence Education Center. And in a most auspicious coincidence of timing, its formal dedication will be (God willing) this year on the 2nd of October – Gandhi's birthday, the International Day of Nonviolence, and the Fast of Gedaliah. *"B'siman tov uv'mazal tov!"* May it, indeed, take place under these most favorable and fortunate of circumstances.

From *Tikkun*, September-October 2008

America and Israel

A History of the "Special Relationship"

This essay-review from 1984 explores the devolution of Zionism to "aggressive rather than humanitarian nationalism" and urges the U.S., and especially American Jews, to consider the historical American affinity for Israel from a moral as well as a strategic vantage point.

News headlines in recent weeks have testified to yet another reaffirmation of "the special relationship" between the U.S. and Israel. In this instance, the terms are, for the most part, military and strategic: coordination of U.S. Mideast policy with Israel, a resumed military-cooperation agreement, more grants of military aid to Israel, resumed shipment of U.S.-made cluster-bomb artillery shells, hope that Israel will serve to curb Soviet influence in the Mideast, etc. To many in the American Jewish community, such a reaffirmation must have seemed familiar; strategic considerations have increasingly come to characterize the U.S.-Israeli "special relationship."

It was not always so. There was a time when the understanding of this relationship was quite otherwise, and Peter Grose's *Israel in the Mind of America* (Alfred A. Knopf) is a rich and suggestive reminder of those earlier days. A long-time foreign correspondent and Moscow, Israel, and UN bureau chief for the *New York Times*, a former policy planner for the U.S. State Department, a knowledgeable researcher in Middle East and diplomatic matters, and an avid archivist who obviously delights in prowling through newly available documents, Grose writes crisp, clear, engaging prose.

Even before telling the tale of a major event of our century, the establishment of the State of Israel, he first presents an American preamble by skillfully interweaving policy issues and personality traits, public statements and back-channel gossip, departmental directives and public pressures. Grose's book might well be described in the terms he uses to characterize a Truman-Clifford-Lowenthal communications arrangement:

"all so much more human than the ponderous, shapeless bureaucratic documents that kept thudding upon the Chief Executive's desk" – or that often come thudding upon the concerned citizen's desk as she or he tries to look responsibly at important issues of the day.

Grose begins at the beginning, sketching very briefly "the awkward ambivalence" between the early American Christian and the early American Jew. Turning then to the evidence for the long-standing "special relationship" of Israel the people to the American psyche, Grose introduces a lengthy and colorful cast of characters. Of special interest are some non-Jews who long ago advocated "the restoration of the Jews" to their land and were religiously, rather than geo-politically, motivated.

One such figure was Pastor John McDonald of Albany, New York, who in 1814 delivered a widely disseminated sermon that interpreted Isaiah 18 as a call to "American ambassadors . . . to carry the tidings of joy and salvation to your Savior's kinsmen in disgrace!" and to work for the return of the Jews to the land of Zion.

Hezekiah Niles, Quaker editor of *Niles' Weekly Register*, regularly sounded a similar theme in less religious tones in that "most influential organ of political information and opinion in the United States" through the first half of the 19th century. Although Niles exhibited some negative attitudes towards Jews, his essential message was that "this singular and interesting people, scattered all over the world and everywhere despised and maltreated," ought to have a national home, their own country, where "the deserts of Palestine . . . may again blossom as the rose . . ."

William Eugene Blackstone, a financially independent, fundamentalist layman, often called "Reverend" by his large evangelical following, published in 1878 a work preoccupied with preparation for the Second Coming of Jesus that sold over a million copies. In its pages, he argued forcefully for giving back Palestine to the persecuted Russian Jews; by his wider political efforts, he recruited the signatures of over four hundred prominent Americans – among them John D. Rockefeller, Cyrus McCormick, J. Pierpont Morgan, and numerous high government officials – on behalf of his plan. In this Christian document, he proposed to settle Jews on public lands ceded by the Turkish state, with "no expulsion of the present inhabitants of the land . . ."

Even the State Department, whose later patrician, anti-Semitic tendencies are sharply sketched by Grose, manifested for more than half a century after the Damascus affair of 1840 "a constant element of concern for persecuted Jews." And if at crucial times nearer our own a Breckenridge

Long, a Wallace Murray, or a Loy Henderson cast a dark shadow over the practice of compassion, we are also reminded of the fair-mindedness of a Sumner Welles, the outspoken investigations of Treasury department representatives Randolph Paul and John Pehle on behalf of the persecuted Jews of Europe, and the basic human decency of an Earl Harrison.

Even more significant for a portrait of Israel in the mind of America, of course, and much more fully presented, is the variety of reactions by leading American Jews to the idea and reality of Israel. Here Grose treats us to brief but trenchant sketches of such early figures as Isaac Mayer Wise and Mordecai Emanuel Noah; fuller studies of well known personalities such as Brandeis, Wise and Silver; important information about significant though lesser-known figures such as Horace Kallen and David Niles; interesting details about Weizmann and Goldmann who, though not American, played an important role on the American scene; a sympathetic portrayal of the motives for the beginnings of "the Jewish lobby," its contributions to the establishment of Israel, and some of its negative effects; and along with all this, knowing nods in the direction of numerous others who played lesser roles in the drama.

Of further interest and importance is the wealth of detail about Roosevelt's and Truman's complex attitudes toward Israel. Grose makes use of previously unavailable archival material, and while his nuanced characterizations both tempt and resist summarization, even more do they invite a considered reading.

So engagingly and sympathetically does Grose tell the story of events and intrigues, currents and counter-currents surrounding and affecting U.S. policy at the time of the establishment of the State of Israel that there is a strong impulse to rest content with reminiscing and reliving the anxiety and the excitement of that period. Yet to reminisce without reflecting seriously would be to disregard half the author's motivation for writing this book.

One reason, as intimated before, was the irresistible appeal to a long-time newsman of searching through three just-unsealed official archival collections, American, British, and Israeli, surrounding "the drama of Israel's restoration," and making this "detailed and authoritative historical evidence" available to the public.

The other reason is more sobering: Grose's perception that the political leadership of the Jewish national movement has, through democratic elections in Israel, been replaced by a "militant minority faction with a vision of Israel quite different from that to which Americans – Jews and Christians alike – had grown accustomed." Such a change is clearly of concern to Grose, whose sympathies for the humanitarian dimension of the Zionist movement are evident throughout his presentation; it should be of concern to us Jews as well.

Evidence of these changes is not hard to find. It is reflected conveniently in three items which appeared in *The Boston Globe* in recent weeks. Each was authored by one or another of its quite responsible editorial writers, and as I relate each to relevant material from Grose, reasons for concern will become clear. In one case, a columnist devoted an entire article to an issue of Israeli territorial aspirations, answering in detail two printed letters that questioned an earlier assertion of his that since the "foundation of the Jewish state, Israel has longed for the territory of southern Lebanon as part of the completion of *Eretz Yisrael* and for the power and irrigation resources of the Litani River."

The Israeli consul's claimed that the sentence "lacks any foundation. Israel has neither longed for this territory in the past nor has it any designs on keeping parts of Lebanese territory, nor does anyone in Israel think that Southern Lebanon is part of the land of Israel." In response, the columnist cited documented material from Brandeis, Weizmann, Dayan, and others in support of his contention, and flatly stated that the Israeli consul's assertion "is so plainly contrary to the historical record and present fact as to amount, at best, to inadvertent disinformation."

In a second case, the author, just returned from a twelve-day American Jewish Committee-sponsored trip to Israel and Jordan, writes sensitively about Israel and the Palestinians. The headline reads: "In Israel, Lack of Urgency about Palestinians." The concluding sentences of the article read:

> U.S. strategic interests might ultimately convince me to support a continuation of the exceptional American support for Israel. However, a sustained business-as-usual occupation of the West Bank would tarnish, in my view, the specialness of that country and compel my reconsideration of the morality of the tilt in American policy toward Israel.

The third instance may be all-too-briefly presented. In a lengthy eye-witness report on a recent visit to South Africa, the author, discussing freedom of the Black press in Soweto, remarked, in passing: "The paper has a great deal more editorial license to criticize the government than, say, Arab papers on the occupied West Bank . . ."

On seeing such items, one's first reaction may be to dismiss them as misguided or superficial, hostile or influenced by Arab propaganda. That is too easy an out, however, for apart from the fact that this would be unfair to the three writers cited, in each instance precedents may be found in Grose's book that suggest that the issues were alive in the past and remain unresolved to the present time.

What about territorial aspirations? How shall one understand Golda Meir's reaction to the Peel Commission report of 1937, proposing the partition of Palestine into a Jewish and an Arab section? "Some day my son will ask me by what right I gave up most of the country and I won't know how to answer him." Or the remark of a pro-Zionist member of the House of Commons: "If partition is accepted and goes through, I hope that the Jews will treat it merely as a stepping-off ground for further advance."

Whatever ambiguity or overstating for bargaining purposes may be discerned in those remarks of earlier years, unambiguous was the meaning of Menachem Begin's reaction to the UN partition plan passed on November 29, 1947: "The Homeland has not been liberated, but mutilated . . . Eretz Israel will be restored to the people of Israel. All of it. And forever." Commenting on the remarks of an announcer for the Irgun underground radio at that time, who despairingly said, "A Jewish state without Jerusalem, without Hebron and Bethlehem, without the Gilead or the Bashan or the lands beyond the Jordan," Grose comments: "That, in the lifetime of Begin and his followers, would have to be corrected."

"Correcting" the UN partition plan is, of course, the policy that the Begin and Shamir government has proclaimed publicly and is pursuing openly, with some verbal objection but heavy financial support from the U.S. government. "Strategic" reasons may sustain this for a time, though strategic considerations are subject to quite sudden revisions as circumstances change, but the long-established ties of sympathy and respect for Israel in the mind of America are suffering severe fraying as the effects upon the Palestinians of these Israeli territorial policies become increasingly evident and more widely known. In this respect, Grose's sketch of the persistent tensions between political aims and philanthropic impulses in relation to the Zionist efforts is quite illuminating.

In 1936, Felix Warburg complained that the Zionists were interested in relief work only if "done through its political organization in Palestine." Another spokesman for the Joint Distribution Committee stated: "The principle that our help should follow the refugees wherever they may be brought is being twisted to mean that the only help and the only solution lies in Palestine."

Within the Zionist movement itself, there were significant differences between Stephen S. Wise and Abba Hillel Silver concerning the relative emphasis to be given "the 'immediate problem' of saving Jewish lives" versus establishing the Jewish homeland in Palestine. In words ascribed to Silver, "Zionism is not refugee-ism." Never really resolved, the issue was set to rest for a time during the early years of the state, when the humanitarian impulse expressed itself primarily in national-political terms through immigration to Israel. Now, however, as nationalist politics seeks goals which are no longer linked to the humanitarian, the tension re-emerges (as in the recent disputes concerning aid to Soviet Jewish emigrés who, in Vienna, elect not to proceed to Israel but prefer a different destination).

Within the non-Jewish American community, such tension was hardly discernible. From the evidence that Grose assembles, both Roosevelt and Truman, insofar as they attended to the matter, approached it in humanitarian terms. Roosevelt, whose flawed record in relation to the persecution of European Jews is freshly sketched by Grose, even preferred to think of the "refugee problem," not the "Jewish problem." For Truman, human compassion, a strong sense of fair play, and some identification with Cyrus' earlier restoration of the Jews to the ancestral home were the determining factors. It was only when the plight of the surviving Jews of Europe was combined with the political aspirations of Zionism that the latter received from Truman his crucial support – importantly mediated by Weizmann's personal appeal, not Silver's ideology and power plays, one must add.

What might this mean today? First of all, as Israeli policy toward the occupied territories is increasingly seen as primarily national-political in motivation, humanitarian support will steadily decrease. Secondly, as Palestinians are increasingly perceived as homeless and persecuted, the same American quality of compassion which directed itself to Jewish victims of persecution begins to extend to the Palestinians. Thirdly, if the most persuasive voices in the Jewish community were those linking the humanitarian impulse to the establishment of an independent Jewish nation-state, might not one reasonably expect that the same logic be increasingly persuasive when the question of Palestinian human needs is confronted? The sense of "fair play" can hardly be expected to deny to Palestinians the same rights of national self-determination in territory significant to them that Israeli Jews have won, whatever the practical complexities of achieving this may be.

One of Judah Magnes' statements from the 1940s is quoted by Grose: "The Jews have more than a claim upon the world for justice, but I am not ready to try to achieve justice to the Jew through injustice to the Arab." Increasingly, I think, that sentiment will gain adherents among Americans, both Jewish and non-Jewish, if I read aright Grose's portrayal of the major sources of sympathy for Israel in the mind of America.

Nor should this be deplored by American Jews. It would be a mistake to see this development as representing a shift of American sympathies away from Israel and toward the Palestinians. It may rather be seen as a *broadening* of those sympathies to include the Palestinians along with Israeli Jews as subjects of appropriate American concern for the ideal (however often violated in practice) of democratic self-determination for all peoples. If this be the case, one may hope that in this, as in other conflict situations, the more fully understood and the more justly addressed the diverse claims, the greater the likelihood of a resolution benefiting both the contesting parties.

Grose's Epilogue is less satisfying than the rest of the book, due mainly, I suspect, to the attempt to compress thirty-five years of complex history into seventeen pages! Yet even here, despite the surprising omission of any account of events immediately leading to the Six Day War, Grose continues to invite thoughtful reflection. His description of the contrasting fates of Jabneh and Masada is an example: "After 1967, when modern Israel astonished the world with its martial prowess, Jabneh was swallowed up in the industrial suburbs of Tel Aviv; Masada became a national shrine."

Is this symbolism an indicator of where Israel is heading? And is Grose correct in seeing the present Likud government as an aberration, a break with policies of the earlier Labor governments, or does he exaggerate the differences? Might Likud, in fact, be more accurately seen as the accentuation of a trend that could be earlier discerned as power shifted from Brandeis to Weizmann to Ben Gurion and finally to Begin? In this case, is modern Zionism the playing out of an aggressive rather than a humanitarian nationalism? Might we be passive witnesses or even active contributors to another Maccabeanization of a Jewish state (about whose earlier consequences one can read in Elias Bickerman's brief Schocken volume, *The Maccabees*)?

If one is willing to proceed to some further, somber soul-searching on this question, albeit not in these precise terms, one could hardly do better than to confront Noam Chomsky's important volume, *The Fateful Triangle: The United States, Israel and the Palestinians* (South End Press). Chomsky, unfairly maligned and dismissed in many sectors of the American Jewish community, provides impressive documentation from a remarkably broad range of respected Israeli, American, and international sources in support of his thesis that for some years now, probably dating from 1973, there has been an "international consensus – which has long included the major Arab states, the population of the occupied territories and the mainstream of the PLO – in support of a two-state political settlement that would include recognized borders, security guarantees, and reasonable prospects for a peaceful resolution of the conflict." Chomsky further argues that the Labor Party as well as the Likud coalition have, with the U.S. backing, practiced rejectionism rather than accommodation, with increasingly dangerous consequences for Israelis, Palestinians, and the entire world.

Chomsky's thesis, so baldly stated and without the nuances and substantiation that it receives in his full presentation, may, on first reading, seem so remote from received facts and common understanding that one is tempted to dismiss it without further thought. This, I think, would be a serious mistake, for it is clearly argued, carefully presented, and documented with a thoroughness that demands careful consideration. It is also, in important respects, supported by Seth P. Tillman's *The United States in the Middle East* (Indiana University Press), a knowledgeable analysis of "interests and obstacles," which, with a combination of breadth and detail, commands attention even as it provides illumination.

Neither in context nor in tone is the Chomsky book pleasant reading. Since his purpose is to focus on "what I think is and has been wrong and what should be changed, not on what I think has been right," the work is rather unrelievedly critical and often angry at what Chomsky sees as especially blatant examples of hypocrisy or double standards. One will read with some discomfort the details he assembles from reputable Israeli sources on post-1967 settlement policies of Labor as well as Likud; one will read with distress the testimony of Israeli soldiers about certain realities of Operation Peace for Galilee, corroborating as it does some of the world press reports so consistently denied by official voices in the Jewish community.

As with Chomsky's major thesis, the temptation may be strong to dismiss these matters as outright distortions or falsifications. Unhappily, these are not to be so easily dismissed, and the growing awareness in the mind of America of such Israeli attitudes and policies helps one understand the comments earlier cited from three responsible and decent newsmen in the *Boston Globe*.

Israel, in the minds and hearts of Americans, both Jewish and non-Jewish, has represented a humanitarian hope and a religious ideal. The reality, for all its flaws and imperfections, has received consistent honor and support from American diplomacy and the American people for the success of its primary aim of providing a home and a refuge for Jews in need. Such support remains unchanged to this day, yet both Grose and Chomsky, in quite different modes and moods, afford important insights to those of us concerned about maintaining such support for reasons of human sympathy and religious spirit rather than geo-political strategy.

From *The Jewish Spectator*, Spring, 1984

Immigration as Approval of Israeli Policy

Why Jews Stay Away

This brief 1972 essay challenges the term "aliyah" and argues that Jews are "voting with their feet" in protest of Israel's then only five-year-old occupation policy.

"Aliyah"? To use this term for immigration to Israel by Jews is already to weight a discussion. Bias is built into the term, for at root, "aliyah" means "ascent, going up." It is the term used for being "called up" to the Torah, hence has further overtones of religious duty, of merit, of goodness. In short, it is a heavy term, value-loaded; and as presently used, it implies that immigration to Israel by Jews is without question a meritorious act.

Since it is precisely this notion that I want to question, my substitution of "immigration to Israel by Jews" for "aliyah" is not a semantic quibble but an attempt to create room for genuine discussion.

And I think we do need discussion of this issue. To take for granted that immigration to Israel by Jews at the present time is a good thing is to avoid facing a number of realities in the situation today. Let me try to be specific and share some of the feelings that underlie my refusal to use the term "aliyah" and my personal inability even to consider immigrating to Israel.

The **Jerusalem Post** *of February 13, 1972 is quoted as reporting that* according to "authoritative opinion," in any future peace negotiations Israel will not return territory "in which civilian settlements have been established. . ." These include all the length of the Jordan rift, the Golan Heights, the southern flank of the Gaza Strip, as well as East Jerusalem and the approaches to Sharm-el-Sheikh. Defense Minister Moshe Dayan is quoted as having declared, "To me, the West Bank is part of the Jewish homeland. There is no difference between Tel Aviv, Hebron, and Jericho. Our soldiers should stay on the Jordan River" (*Jerusalem Post*, Feburary 16, 1972, cited in *The Middle East News Review*).

If one is comfortable with territorial policies that include such annexations, then fine, it is possible to immigrate to Israel now and help fill the expanded area, or release residents of the pre-June, 1967 borders to move into new areas that are *fait accompli.* But I am not comfortable with such policies, and it feels to me that were I to move to Israel at this point I would be, willingly or not, providing an additional Jewish presence that would help make such policies possible. Whatever my personal intentions might be, de facto that is how I would function in the power-political demographic game now being played.

Nor is it at all clear to me where and when the game will stop. What is the true extent of the "Jewish homeland"? What are the ultimate territorial aims of present Israeli policy? If Israel were really accepting of the pre-1967 borders, why have subsequent offers by Arab states to concede their validity been rejected out of hand? As I follow the course of negotiations, it is less and less convincing to assert that the sole purpose of the Six Day War was survival or even peace with security. There are territorial aims as well that have asserted themselves in distressing fashion, at least to me.

How is a new, "more secure" border not to become quickly enough yet a new line of contention? As Israeli borders move outward at staggering costs both to the Israelis and to the world Jewish community (24.7 percent of the Israeli Gross National Product in 1971-72 for defense versus 16.3 percent in '67-'68, including the Six Day War), doesn't the line of dispute move outward as well? Is it meritorious to provide the presence of one's person for the implementation of such policies? I have my doubts.

Even the question of Jerusalem seems to be me distorted by a rhetoric that avoids facing realities. It is not simply age-old anti-Semitism that has prompted UN condemnations of Israeli policies aimed at incorporating into an expanded Jewish Jerusalem as much area with as few Arabs as possible. Before settling in one of the new high-rise apartments, I'd need to give a lot of thought to the land expropriation policies that have made them possible. Were my need to flee desperate, I might not be able to afford such reflection – but leaving *this* land for Israel? How dare I not first think long and hard about such land and population policies?

Occupying occupied territories is not only a question of territory, but of persons. What about the displaced Arabs, the Palestinians? I'm not now referring only to those displaced in 1947 or 1948, but to the 140,000 who fled the occupied territories in 1967. Many of them had spent years in refugee camps, and now they have been displaced a second time. What about them? By what right shall I occupy their former lands in the post-1967 occupied territories to which no claims were previously laid?

If there are Jews (or others) in desperate need to leave lands of persecution, I can see a painful dilemma, though even in such cases I do not see how we can defend ousting some to make room for others. Besides, there is sufficient room in pre-1967 Israel, is there not? But again, in the case of those of us who live in comfortable circumstances, how can we possibly acquiesce in or benefit from such policies?

No, the U.S. is not perfection (neither is Israel). No, the U.S. is not Zion (neither is Israel, if one respects the full meaning of the term). Even so, my need at this time is indescribably less great than that of tens of thousands of former occupants of West Bank territory who are now doubly homeless. Given the present political policies of Israel, for me to immmigrate there at this time would contribute to making permanent this unjust situation.

There is another aspect of the population question that also contributes substantially to my inability to consider immigration to Israel at this point, and that is what seems to me the underside of the Law of Return. At the same time that any Jew anywhere is granted free entry to Israel, and citizenship, many Arabs face restrictions on becoming Israeli citizens, even if they were born in Israel proper. Only two categories of people receive automatic citizenship by law: all Jews, and those born to Israeli citizens. Those born in Israel to non-Jewish non-citizens (a category that includes thousands of Arabs, some of whom have lived in the land for generations but have not been granted citizenship for technical reasons) may apply for citizenship between the ages of 18 and 21, but the granting of this is at the discretion of the Ministry of the Interior, and citizenship is rarely granted to Arabs. Hence the status of non-citizenship is perpetuated from generation to generation, affecting tens of thousands of non-Jews living in Israel.

This does not affect Israeli voting rights, for in Israel one may vote simply by being a resident. It does, however, affect the granting of Israeli passports, and it makes travel possible only for one year with a special traveling card. Should the limit be passed, it is often impossible to regain admission to Israel, even when it is the land in which the traveler was born. There is nothing in Israeli law that corresponds to what we find in every other civilized country: the recognition of attachment of a person to a country simply by being born there, irrespective of any particular status definition.

Should those who, like myself, enjoy citizenship in situations of considerable freedom and opportunity accept the privilege of free immigration to and citizenship in another land when the exercise of that privilege is intimately connected to the denial to others of what, in most countries, is a basic human right, that of citizenship where one is born? Again, it seems to me that whatever personal meaning immigration to Israel might have for me, my moving there would contribute to a situation of grave injustice.

In all of the above instances, it seems to me that there is a basic religious and moral issue to be confronted: Can one person's true *aliyah* depend on another's *yeridah* (descent, misfortune, deprivation)? If, indeed, we all have One Father, this seems hardly possible. And when I apply this principle to the political and moral implications of my immigrating to Israel at this time under present political circumstances, I find my moving there contraindicated.

So at the personal level, which is what this discussion is all about, I am not open to considering immigration to Israel at this point, given the present laws and policies of Israel with respect to the occupied territories and Arab persons. Nor do such policies strike me as merely the aberration of a particular government. Unhappily, they seem to me inherent in political Zionism as it has developed, and I doubt that any change in such policies is likely under any imaginable Israeli government in the near future.

My reaction to the widespread use of the term *"aliyah"* is to wonder if we're not avoiding some harsh and painful realities by invoking this term of sanctification. Jeremiah called us on such tendencies long ago when he asked that we face the realities of our policies rather than soothing ourselves by such rhetoric as "the temple of the Lord" —

> Thus says the Lord of hosts, the God of Israel: "Amend your ways and your doings, that I may establish your home in this place. Trust not in deceptive words, such as 'the temple of the Lord, the temple of the Lord, the temple of the Lord is this!' For if you but amend your ways and your doings — if you practice strict justice toward one another, if you do not oppress the resident alien, the orphan, and the widow, nor shed innocent blood in this place, nor run after other gods to your own hurt — I will establish your home in this place, in the land which I gave to your fathers for all time."
>
> *Jeremiah 7:3-7*

Sad to say, if we substitute *"aliyah"* for "temple of the Lord, it seems to me that Jeremiah's message is still painfully to the point.

From Genesis 2, March, 1972

Martin Luther King, Jr. in the Holy Land

The Tragedy of His Absence[1]

Rabbi Gendler was personally acquainted with the Reverend Martin Luther King, Jr. during the civil rights struggle in the South and has been inspired throughout his life by Dr. King's philosophy of non-violent resistance to oppression. This 2013 essay considers how that philosophy, with all of its strategic considerations, might be applied effectively in the Israeli-Palestinian conflict.

> Today, we particularly need Hebrew prophets because they taught that to love God was to love justice; that each human being has an inescapable obligation to denounce evil where he sees it and to defy a ruler who commands him to break the covenant . . . The Hebrew prophets are needed today because decent people must be imbued with the courage to speak truth, to realize that silence may temporarily preserve status or security but that to live with a lie is a gross affront to God.
>
> Martin Luther King, Jr.[2]

Like Moses, his spiritual predecessor in the struggle on behalf of Divinely guided human liberation, Martin Luther King, Jr. was "a traveling man": many arduous routings, many challenging detours, many bruising

---

1. The choice of this title is not meant to suggest that Dr. King never visited the Holy Land. He and wife did indeed make a trip to that part of the world, and King's plan for another trip before his death was never fulfilled. However, King and his nonviolence, for whatever reasons, were never an active presence in resolving the conflicts in the Holy Land in his time, and this is indeed "tragic." See King's Easter Sunday sermon, "A Walk through the Holy Land," delivered at the Dexter Avenue Baptists Church, Montgomery, Alabama on March 29, 1959, in Clayborne Carson et al., eds., *The Papers of Martin Luther King, Jr.*, Vol. 5, *Threshold of a New Decade, January 1959–December 1960* (University of California Press, 2005), and Martin Luther King, Jr., *Strength to Love* (Fortress, 1981).

2. Martin Luther King, Jr., "My Jewish Brother," *Amsterdam News*, February 26, 1966; Martin Luther King, Jr., "An Address," delivered before the Synagogue Council of America, December 5, 1965; Israel Goldstein, "Martin Luther King's Jewish Association," *Jerusalem Post*, October 22, 1964.

encounters on the freedom trail. As with Moses, so with King: the Holy Land was an important point of reference in his religious life. In contrast to Moses, however, who could only climb the mountain to see the Promised Land from afar, King was able to visit part of the land in March, 1959. The occasion was returning home from his visit to India, where, with Coretta, he had visited significant sites in the life of Gandhi and deepened his understanding of nonviolence.

In the Holy Land, he was deeply moved as he followed the paths that Jesus had walked on the Mount of Olives and in the Garden of Gethsemane, as well as the burial places of Abraham, Isaac, Jacob, Sarah, and others. But as he pointedly remarked, he was at that time unable to experience the fullness of the land because of the separation barrier between Jordan and Israel. In the biblical narrative, God the Creator was first experienced as God the Liberating Redeemer in the exodus from Egypt, following which He directs His people toward the Promised Land. As I understand this narrative, the failure of Moses to set food in the land did not compromise its status as the final destination in this Liberation narrative, with all its later inspiring revolutionary effects throughout the history of the struggle for justice and human dignity. By contrast, the absence of King may have affected the destiny of this land in our age, diminishing its capacity to serve as a place where the liberating and healing power of the Divine was again made manifest. Regrettably, neither King nor Gandhi before him managed to bring to the Promised Land their charismatic embodiment of the efficacy and the power of nonviolence, thus depriving it of their desperately needed contributions to the reconciliation of contending claims and conflicting claimants.

Nonviolence in the Holy Land? On first hearing, the phrase does, indeed, sound like an oxymoron. Yet nonviolence has a lengthy, although largely fitful and frustrated, history in that strife-afflicted region. A brief review of a few incidents from the modern history of Israel/Palestine may be helpful in setting the context for what Martin Luther King, Jr. – had he indeed set foot in the land – might have contributed to the resolution of this seemingly intractable conflict. Since it was his regular practice to apply nonviolent principles to the particular conditions of a situation, we need at least some sense of the background of the present impasse in Israel-Palestine.

A word of explanation about the selection of these few background incidents may be helpful. For reasons of space, they must be few in number and abbreviated in their presentation. They are not intended as a full portrait of the issue in all its shadings; rather, they are strokes, integral to the texture of the situation, yet sometimes not noticed, whose appearance King surely would have discerned, filled out, and brought vividly to our attention. All are extracted from the overall canvas representing two deeply felt forces tragically colliding, both of which are too often oblivious to the similarities between them.

We are most accustomed to reading of conflicts and clashes, often violent, between Israeli Jews and Palestinian Arabs. The violent expressions of the profound differences between Jewish and Arab positions with respect to Israel/Palestine have especially gained attention from observers as well as participants in the conflict. Yet significant nonviolent elements and initiatives have been present from the beginning of the modern period of this ancient struggle. Some of the early Zionists, for example, were aware of the Palestinian presence in the land and hoped to overcome the possible resistance of the residents through an expansion of opportunities. Moses Hess, notes the *Encyclopedia Judaica* (1971), a full generation before Herzl, had in 1861 "imagined that a highly Westernized element such as the

Jews would be welcomed by the Arabs because of the leadership that Jews would provide in creating in the entire region an advanced economy and an advancing society." While this attempt to convert a zero-sum game to one of an expanding sum that could be shared was not universal among the early Zionist thinkers, others also sought to forge common purpose with the Arab residents.

Chaim Weizmann, central to the diplomacy that yielded the Balfour Declaration, corresponded directly with Emir Feisal Husseini, a prominent leader who was the Arab representative to the Paris Peace Conference of 1919, and the two signed an agreement. In a letter to Lord Herbert Samuel in 1919 that accorded recognition to the common interests of both peoples, Husseini said, "I personally deprecate any differences between the Arabs and the Jews who ought to unite their efforts in word and deed for promoting the development and happiness of our country." In addition, he signed an agreement accepting the immigration of Jews into the country and their development of it, subject to the protection of the rights of the Arab peasant and tenant farmers. Husseini, however, was a resident of Hejaz (Saudi Arabia) and was not able to represent accurately the far more negative feelings of many Arab residents of Palestine.

Despite little positive response from the Arab community, there continued to be Jewish Zionists and others associated with the B'rith Shalom (Covenant of Peace) movement who sought a more conciliatory path, among them Judah Magnes, Martin Buber, and Ernst Simon. Chaim Arlozoroff, a prominent early leader of the labor Zionist movement, also attempted to find ways for Arab-Jewish cooperation until his never-solved murder in June 1933, which deprived the Zionists of a figure central to the politics of the movement and keenly aware of the importance of achieving Arab-Jewish understanding.

Regrettably, attempts to cultivate a commonality with the Arabs of the region were compromised by other goals of early Zionism: the reassertion of the dignity of manual labor; the determined effort to expand Jewish occupations beyond the middleman-commercial role imposed by Russia's rulers; a quest for self-reliance that sought independence from outside forces, in this case the Arab inhabitants of the land. Each of these goals was understandable, even commendable, yet their combined effect was to marginalize and so exclude the Arabs from full participation in the expanding opportunities brought by the new settlers.

Adding to the difficulties of avoiding injuries to peasants while legally acquiring land was the opaque complexity of title procedures in the Ottoman Empire. For reasons clearly presented by William R. Polk (in *Backdrop to Tragedy: The Struggle for Palestine,* Beacon, 1957), a long history of subterfuge and misrepresentation had come to characterize the peasants' registration of land in the Ottoman Empire, thus making it especially difficult to determine ownership. To avoid the government's conscription of their sons as well as to protect their land rights more effectively, peasants often registered their land in the name of an important and influential man who could, through his influence, defend their traditional land rights. This resulted in a severe discrepancy between legal title to land and its actual possession and cultivation by peasants over many generations. Polk notes, for example, that when a Zionist purchasing group in 1921 openly and legally purchased an extensive plot of land in the Emeq (Hefet Valley) from the Beirut Christian family of Sursuk, some eight thousand peasants who were actually living on the land, many with little grasp of the technicalities of title deeds, were evicted to make way for the intended settlers. This tragic dispossession was entirely legal, yet it grievously violated the traditional peasant attachment to the land and the simple peasant sense that to live on the land and to cultivate it over generations constituted title to the land.

Polk contrasts peasant feelings about land with the Bedouin mentality, for whom there is no fixity in relation to the land: "For the settled peasant . . . land is one's own land, where ancestors were born, where they built, tilled, are buried, and where sons will be born. Land is a visible extension of man – as it were, the summary of life. In its terraces, holy places, and graveyards, the individual achieves a sort of immortality . . . It is perhaps the strongest emotional attachment known to peasants the world over."

Consequently, he continues, "land was the ultimate value to be saved at all sacrifice; in the peasant's mind it was saved so long as he worked it, buried his dead in it, and raised sons upon it. To him it was incomprehensible that through the edicts of a distant government, whose authority he had hardly ever felt, the land had ceased to be his." This legal situation compounded the difficulties of finding ways to minimize the destructive effects of Jewish settlement on the lives of those who had long lived on the land.

Harsh external circumstances also contributed to the lack of continuing attention to this vital element, which was destined to have so profound an effect on the continuing effort to increase Jewish settlement in the Holy Land. Twenty years after Hess's hope to create a common cause between the

Jews and the Arabs came the assassination of Czar Alexander II, followed by widespread pogroms against Jews throughout the Russian Empire and adjacent lands. Profoundly disheartening to Jews was the passivity of the Czarist government, which failed to defend them against the mob violence, and still more so the apparent acquiescence of even progressive elements in Russia in this brutal wave of bloodshed. Populist movements such as the Narodniks tended to view the uprisings as proto-revolutionary and showed little concern for the Jews who were being abused.

The Kishinev pogroms of 1903 further fueled the mass exodus of Jews from Russia and surrounding lands, with some 2,400,000 fleeing between 1881 and 1914. Most went to the United States, but there were some among them who, despite difficulties, emigrated to Palestine. Later, during the disturbances following World War I, over 100,000 Jews were slaughtered in Russia and Poland by Ukrainian and counter-revolutionary troops. Long before the unprecedented horrors inflicted by Adolf Hitler, such events contributed to a sense of urgency that trumped the search for conciliatory ways to resettle persecuted Jews in their ancestral homeland.

In resisting the perceived threat from Jewish immigration, Arabs in the beginning took largely nonviolent measures to protest. In her valuable comprehensive study of Palestinian nonviolence during the first *Intifada*, Mary Elizabeth King identifies antecedents in the widespread use of nonviolent methods, especially protest and persuasion, by Palestinians during the 1920s (*A Quiet Revolution: The First Palestinian Intifada and Nonviolent Resistance*, Nation Books, 2007): "formal statements, declarations, petitions, manifestos, assemblies, delegations, processions, marches, and motorcades." Because these methods failed to halt Jewish immigration to Palestine, many Arabs were discouraged from further using such tactics and turned increasingly to violent protest. What followed was a long, complex, painful, and all-too-familiar history of collision between Jewish determination to create again, this time in their historic land of origin, a refuge from their perpetual persecution, and an equally determined Arab resistance to a perceived threat to the longtime residents of the land.

The Balfour Declaration in 1917 explicitly affirmed that Great Britain favored and would facilitate "the establishment in Palestine of a National Home for the Jewish people." In the very same complex sentence, it explicitly affirmed that "in the achievement of this object . . . nothing shall be done which may prejudice the civil and religious rights of existing non-Jewish communities in Palestine." Details of how this was to be accomplished were lacking, and consequently it failed to gain the cooperation of the Arabs in this admittedly difficult endeavor.

Throughout the period of the British Mandate, a few voices were audible among both Jews and Arabs advocating a mutually rewarding solution. The members of B'rith Shalom, mentioned earlier, worked tirelessly for a binational state that would recognize and take account of the deep longings of both peoples for this land. Susan Lee Hattis notes (in *The Bi-National Idea in Palestine during Mandatory Times,* Shikmona, 1970) that in his moving testimony at the hearings of the United Nations Special Committee on Palestine (UNSCOP), Professor Ernst Simon reminded the Committee that "the members of the League (for Jewish Arab Rapprochement and Cooperation) still believe in man, in the brotherhood of nations, in the progress of mankind, and in the eventual triumph of the progressive forces . . ." There followed the more concrete statement of Aharon Cohen, also quoted by Hattis: "In our view, there is no conflict between the real interests and just aspirations of the two peoples. The Jews want freedom to develop unhindered their national home through immigration, settlement, and political independence. The Arabs seek progress, political independence, a rise in their standards of life, freedom from want and ignorance, freedom from economic backwardness and feudal domination." Although few Arab voices were heard in agreement with this position, at least one positively responding group, Falastin al-Jedida (The New Palestine), was formed in 1936 by Fauzi Darwish el-Husseini, a cousin of the Grand Mufti. The group had little growth during the following decade, but it did sign a document of understanding with the League on November 11, 1946, pledging to work together "to preserve the unity of the country and work for a solution of its political problems through an Arab-Jewish agreement on the basis of the [following] principles: full cooperation between the two nations in all fields; political equality between the two nations in Palestine as a means of obtaining the independence of the country; Jewish immigration according to the absorptive capacity of the country and the joining of the shared and independent Palestine in an alliance with the neighbouring countries in the future."

On November 23, 1946, Fauzi Darwish el-Husseini was murdered by unknown Arab nationalists. While speculating about whether Arab masses could ever be converted to this viewpoint, Hattis remarks: "The Arab masses had been told for thirty years that there was nothing to compromise about with the Zionists . . . To reverse this trend a man of extraordinary qualities and with an ability to command great authority was required." She leaves unanswered whether or not Darwish al-Husseini was such a figure.

Whatever hindsight one may direct at the situation through the first decades of the 20th century, a full violent collision between the two nationalist movements was not averted. The United Nations Special Committee on Palestine in 1947 proposed a partition of the land; the proposal was accepted by the Zionists, rejected by the Arabs, with the Arab-Israeli War of 1948 following immediately the end of the British Mandate in May 1948. The de facto partition of the land came about, followed by the armistice agreements of 1949 between the warring parties. Additional national armed clashes occurred in 1956, 1967, and 1973, with a major change in the territorial arrangement as a result of the 1967 Six-Day War, when Israel occupied the West Bank and Gaza, formerly held by Jordan.

Throughout the years following the 1949 truce, smaller-scale armed clashes and guerrilla actions continued, along with consistent Arab efforts to isolate, boycott, and refuse recognition of Israel. Following the Six-Day War, the Arab League adopted its widely known policy of three no's: no peace with Israel, no recognition of Israel, no negotiations with Israel. Within Israel itself, the Palestinian resistance was marked by the use of suicide bombers, whose attacks on civilians caused not only human casualties and material destruction but also a heightened sense of horror, anxiety, and insecurity among the Israelis. This regrettably reinforced the memories of recent mass extermination of six million Jews at the hands of the Nazis during World War II. The result was heavy military retaliation by the Israelis, along with hardened attitudes on both sides.

During this period, however, some resident Palestinian civic leaders and activist intellectuals began to explore nonviolent alternatives to the mutually injurious violent tactics then widespread among both Israelis and Palestinians. Mary Elizabeth King provides a lucid, detailed, thorough report of this important development in chapters 7 and 8 of *A Quiet Revolution*. She describes the Arab Thought Forum's three-day international conference in Amman in November, 1986, which included among its major presenters Dr. Gene Sharp, a pragmatic Western analyst and the author of *The Politics of Nonviolent Action*, and Narayan Desai, the principled Gandhian director of the Institute for Total Revolution. Some developments in Israel during those years are vividly and engagingly presented in Sari Nusseibeh's *Once Upon a Country* (Picador, 2007), which offers numerous instances of applied nonviolent resistance.

Illustrative is Military Order 854 and the Palestinian response. In 1981, the military government of the West Bank and Gaza ordered that "all foreign professors, whether Palestinian expatriates or internationals, apply again for work permits, and that they sign a loyalty pledge, specifically stating that they would not engage in opposition to the military government or have any dealings with a 'hostile' organization as defined by the Israelis, namely the PLO." The order was, according to Nusseibeh's analysis, calculated "to undermine our academic freedom and prevent a full-fledged civil society from taking root by threatening hundreds of professors . . . with deportation if they engaged actively in politics." Although the administration at Birzeit University, fearing the consequences of refusal, agreed to go along, the professors ignored the order. They publicized the issue in the Palestinian and Israeli communities and in the Israeli and foreign press, gaining widespread support. The president of the Israeli Academy of Sciences set up a committee of Israeli academics "to investigate the legality and morality" of the order; their findings supported resisting the order. A minor scuffle, during which an Israeli officer was pushed by a student and fell to the ground, resulted in the military government ordering a three-month shutdown of the university and deportation of seven professors. Still refusing to sign after the university was reopened, the professors received orders from the PLO's headquarters in Amman that they submit to the Israeli order. After consulting with representatives from all the West Bank and Gaza universities, the professors decided to resist the PLO as well, finding that it was "against the PLO's best interests" to submit to its order. With the support and urging of Abu Jihad, the PLO was ultimately persuaded to defer to the judgment of the local leadership.

Later the U.N. called for Israel to rescind Military Order 854, as did the International Commission of Jurists; the support of Israeli academics continued as well. In response, while refusing to rescind the order, the military government did suspend it for one year; at the end of the year, Nusseibeh notes, "they just chose not to enforce it."

From this episode, Nusseibeh gained the following crucial insight into Israeli psychology: "only after the first hint of violence" did they take action. Expanding on the importance of this moment of insight, he continues: "For thirty-five years every shot we took at the occupiers had ricocheted back at us tenfold: more land was seized, more people expelled, more of our future trampled upon. It was a losing battle, because they had a strategy, whereas we had only emotions. Now, for the first time, we were discovering our strength. The Israelis had nothing in their repertoire to defeat a dedicated nonviolent campaign of civil disobedience."

What an invaluable discovery! The further exploration, both in theory and in practice, of nonviolent strategies by the East Jerusalem Activist Intellectuals, as Mary Elizabeth King calls them, did indeed prepare the way for the unprecedented two-year *Intifada* that began in 1987, which involved general strikes, boycotts of Israeli civil administration institutions in the occupied lands, civil disobedience, widespread refusal to work in Israeli settlements, refusal to pay taxes, refusal to drive Palestinian cars with Israeli licenses, graffiti, and barricading, as well as stone-throwing and some use of Molotov cocktails.

Along with various nonviolent actions that challenged the consciences of Israel's occupying authorities, Nusseibeh recounts also the transformative experience of his encounters with what he describes as "two American Jewish visionaries," Professor Herbert Kelman and his wife Rose. On reflection, Nusseibeh found himself conceding the deep wisdom of the Kelmans' insistence that "Palestinians and Israelis would eventually have to sit down and negotiate a deal," and after much soul-searching, to his own surprise he reluctantly found himself ready to enter into negotiations with the Israelis on the basis of the pre-1967 borders. In effect, that meant recognition of the permanent presence of the State of Israel; by the same token, it also meant the implicit recognition by the Israelis of a Palestinian state.

Perhaps it comes as a surprise to many readers that the first Palestinian *Intifada* ("uprising," literally "shaking off"), from 1987 to 1989, was predominantly, though not entirely, nonviolent. Yet Mary Elizabeth King assembles massive, convincing evidence that this was the case. How do we explain the discrepancy between the actuality and the impression? How did it happen that the quantitatively minor amount of stone-throwing, mostly by Palestinian youths, so outweighed the vastly greater employment of pure nonviolence? The simplest, most compelling explanation is, I think, offered by Dr. Gene Sharp and Colonel (retired) Robert Helvey in their trenchant treatments of strategic nonviolent struggle.

Sharp, whose powerful theoretical work contributed directly to the 1995 success of Otpor! (Resistance!) students in Serbia and to the disciplined nonviolent movements in Tunisia and Egypt of the Arab Spring of 2011, has insisted throughout his writings that mixing even a little violence compromises and weakens any nonviolence movement by reducing outside sympathy and support, lessening the almost inevitable disaffection among opposing troops when facing resolute nonviolent resisters, and reducing the numbers of those attracted to the nonviolent movement (*Waging Nonviolent Struggle,* Porter Sargent, 2005). Helvey, his natural strategic gifts impressively honed by thirty years in the military, addresses the issue with characteristically illuminating directness in *On Strategic Nonviolent Conflict: Thinking About the Fundamentals* (Albert Einstein Institution, 2004). In his chapter, "Contaminants," he points out that contaminated fuel "can cause an engine to misfire and sputter . . . [or] stop the engine from running at all." On the basis of extensive personal experience and research, he says bluntly that a "single act of violence may provide the government with a convenient rationale for brutal retaliations . . ." Especially pertinent to our issue is this further assertion:

> Extreme examples of violence provoking violent retaliation were the Palestinian terrorist groups Hamas and Islamic Jihad and the suicide bombings against Israeli citizens during the second Intifada. Because the Palestinian Authority failed to aggressively disassociate itself from the these terrorist acts, Israeli public support for a negotiated homeland for Palestinians evaporated, and the international community began backing away from influencing restraint on Israeli settlement policies and Israel's violent occupation of the West Bank.

Although the above does not constitute a full analysis of the complex situation, its basic truth should not be overlooked: Positions again hardened on both sides.

Sadly, even the largely nonviolent first *Intifada* was not recognized as such. Part of this may indeed have been the result of the contamination from the widespread stone-throwing. However understandable as the spillover of almost unbearable frustration, and admittedly less lethal than bombs and bullets, it is nevertheless not a nonviolent tactic. In the words of the old, half-correct nursery rhyme, "Sticks and stones can break my bones, but words will never hurt me." Being the target of a hail of stones is both fear-inducing and anger-provoking; witnessing such events does not incline the viewers to trust the purely peaceable intentions of the stone-throwers. These physical threats to the soldiers almost totally nullified the usual disconcerting effects of courageous, restrained, determined nonviolent human confrontations on consciences, reducing seriously the effectiveness of the *Intifada.*

Another likely factor was the long-term conditioning of the Israelis to associate any Palestinian opposition with violence, blinding them to the differences of this first *Intifada*. Reuven Gal, a former chief psychologist for the Israeli Defense Forces, remarked (in Mary Elizabeth King's A *Quiet Revolution*) that Israeli officials regarded the *Intifada* in purely military terms: "The best proof is in the fact that Israel never handled the *Intifada* by police forces or semi-military forces, but . . . by brigades and divisions of the army – mobilizing full brigades, full divisions, not police, not riot control . . ."

In all likelihood, contributing further to this failure of recognition was the simple unfamiliarity of nonviolent protest to most people in the region. More than forty years had passed since Gandhi was alive, and more than twenty since Martin Luther King, Jr. had been alive and active in the United States. Even though "people power" had toppled Marcos in the Philippines the previous year, this was a period before the Velvet Revolution, the fall of the Berlin Wall, the liberation of Latvia, Lithuania, and Estonia, and the overthrow of Milosevic in Serbia, all largely by nonviolent methods. This unfamiliarity may also have contributed to the failure of the Israeli authorities to explore the potential contribution that a nonviolent movement offers for a mutually respectful resolution of the issues.

With the foregoing as an abbreviated background sketch, let us now try to imagine how Martin Luther King, Jr., had he lived to spend real time in the Holy Land, might have contributed to the resolution of this conflict. One suggestive hint comes from a preliminary plan, first sketched in the autumn of 1966, for a visit that was still being actively planned at the time of his murder. The Reverend Andrew Young, at the time King's primary coordinator, has related to me in telephone conversation that he and King, along with the Reverend Sandy Ray, the prominent pastor of a major black church in Harlem, and Governor Nelson Rockefeller of New York, formulated a tentative proposal for five thousand pilgrims to visit sacred sites in Israel and Jordan sometime in September, 1967.

At the time of preliminary planning, the sacred sites in East Jerusalem were under the rule of the Jordanians, those in West Jerusalem under the Israelis. Consequently, not coincidentally, this massive tourist influx, with its promise of a large infusion of highly desired foreign currencies to both economies, would require active coordination and cooperation from Jordan and Israel. When Jordanian officials raised questions about the feasibility of accommodations and facilities for such a large number of visitors, Dr.

King insisted that five thousand be the number; he wanted the nonviolent intervention to be of significant scale. Hotel reservations were made and deposits confirmed in December, 1966. The trip never materialized because of the Six-Day War of June 1967, and urgent events in the United States fully occupied Dr. King during the ensuing months.

In the spring of 1968, before there was a time to formulate fresh plans for a comparable trip under the changed circumstances, Dr. King was murdered in Memphis. Informed imagination, then, must provide the speculative sketch of what King might have contributed to the solution of the Israel-Palestine impasse. And rather than try to reconstruct that earlier period of time, it is more relevant to think in terms of the situation that Dr. King, were he alive, would confront today. He would surely have sensed a situation that on first sight defied satisfactory solution, for he was endowed with penetrating vision as well as elevating dreams. At the same time, he lived with the conviction, founded in faith, that God would not ultimately abandon God's beloved human creations to final frustration and futility. How, then, might we imagine him working toward a solution?

Key to King's approach was his commitment to a "a tough mind and a tender heart," which is, not by accident, I think, the title of the opening sermon in his *Strength to Love* (Harper & Row, 1963). By a tough mind, he meant "incisive thinking, realistic appraisal, and decisive judgment. This tough mind is sharp and penetrating, breaking through the crust of legends and myths and sifting the true from the false." The tough-minded individual, as a consequence, "has a strong, austere quality that makes for firmness of purpose and solidness of commitment." However, he continued, without an accompanying tender heart that provides "the capacity for genuine compassion," one will never be able to bridge the gap between oneself and the other. This deficiency leaves human beings isolated, passionless, denied the warmth and beauty of friendship and the capacity genuinely to relate to their fellow humans.

Also essential to King's approach was his commitment to finding a solution to the conflict that represented a recognition and response to the humanity of both parties. Unforgettable is this passage from his essay, "Loving Your Enemies," from the same book: "To our most bitter opponents we say: 'We shall match your capacity to inflict suffering by our capacity to endure suffering. We shall meet your physical force with soul force. Do to us what you will, and we shall continue to love you . . . One day we shall win freedom, but not only for ourselves. We shall so appeal to your heart and conscience that we shall win you in the process, and our victory will be a double victory.'"

Briefly summarized, King's commitment was to a method of nonviolent action that a) resisted evil; b) sought not to defeat or humiliate the opponent, but to win the opponent's friendship and understanding; c) directed its attack against structures of evil rather than against those persons doing the evil; d) maintained willingness to accept suffering without retaliation; e) attempted to avoid not only external physical violence but also internal violence of spirit; and f) was "based on the conviction that the universe is on the side of justice . . . [that] there is a creative force in this universe that works to bring the disconnected aspects of reality into a harmonious whole."

King did not view conflicts as zero-sum games. He practiced a Gandhian *satyagraha*, the aim of which, writes Robert J. Burrowes (in *The Strategy of Nonviolent Defense: A Gandhian Approach*, State University of New York Press, 1996), "is neither to harm the opponent nor to impose on them a solution against their will. The aim is to help both parties to achieve a more secure, creative, and truthful relationship . . . *Satyagraha*, then, involves consistent effort in the search for truth while converting the opponent into a friend as part of process. It is not used *against* someone; it is done *with* someone."

Since King took great care to begin the consideration of any intervention with a tough-minded "realistic appraisal" of the situation, what might the first outcome of such an appraisal have been? We had earlier characterized the Israeli-Palestinian impasse as the collision between two deeply felt, passionately asserted, elemental claims to a particular territory. Faced with this stark reality, I can imagine King immediately looking for alternatives to belligerent confrontation. Had there been any examples of land disputes in this area settled by means other than conflict?

Indeed, there were examples, among them the lengthy, impressively disciplined nonviolent resistance of the Druze inhabitants of the Golan Heights to the 1967 Israeli occupation – and the subsequent declaration of annexation and attempts to redefine the status of the Druze by imposing identity cards and citizenship. The specifics of the conflict are succinctly presented in R. Scott Kennedy's essay, "Noncooperation in the Golan Heights: A Case of Nonviolent Resistance" (in *Civilian Jihad: Nonviolent Struggle, Democratization, and Governance in the Middle East*, edited by Maria J. Stephan, Palgrave Macmillan, 2009): The Golani Druze, organized around "realistic objectives," were able to forge communal unity through compromise and "a consensus process," and related to the Israeli soldiers in quite striking ways. "Villagers defied a strict curfew confining them to their homes to place tea and cookies outside their doors for the Israeli soldiers. They engaged the soldiers in conversation and chose not to curse them."

What were some of the results? When soldiers were ordered to take repressive actions against the villagers, they "were really being torn apart, because they couldn't handle that type of nonviolence . . . [T]he morale and discipline of Israeli soldiers began to break down." A humanizing process had taken place that radically changed the terms of the confrontation. The villagers were somehow able to recognize that the perpetrators of the unjust policies were themselves human beings. Acting on this recognition, they reached toward the soldiers with one of the most basic of human gestures: food (tea and cookies, no less!). Could the toughest of combatants fail to turn? They were not threatened physically yet were deeply challenged emotionally, and could not continue to regard simply as "enemies" the human beings who had fed them as if they were their own children.

Principled nonviolent action, as practiced by Gandhi and King, applies political pressure while simultaneously releasing the transformative power of humanization of the enemy. In combination, these serve to establish a new basis upon which the opposing forces can reach an agreement. A striking illustration of this is Budrus, a Palestinian village whose residents discovered that the planned Separation Barrier would pass directly through their village. This projected path would destroy thousands of olive trees upon whose produce the livelihoods of some villagers entirely depended, skirt the village school, cut through the cemetery, and isolate Budrus from nearby Palestinian villages. A stirring documentary film, *Budrus*, written and directed by Julia Bacha, recorded some highlights of the ten-month nonviolent resistance campaign organized in the village under the leadership of Ayed Morrar – who explicitly recognizes the right of Israel to protect its citizens against terrorist attacks from the Occupied Territories, but insists that the barrier be erected along the Green Line, not on Palestinian land. His comprehension of what the Israelis have at stake, together with the disciplined nonviolent approach accepted by all factions in the village, attracted both international support as well as active participation from a number of Israeli Jews who saw and objected to the manifest injustice of the proposed path. Their presence was "like a dream" to the Palestinian organizers, and there are moving testimonies in the film to the humanizing effects of the Israeli presence: "Now I know that not all Israelis are bad and hate us," Morrar says. The demonstrations continue despite increasing injuries from the escalating severity of the Israeli soldiers' reactions and number of arrests. Finally, after more than fifty demonstrations, an alternative path was proposed by the Israeli authorities that saved 95 percent of the land and olive trees, avoided the cemetery, and was out of sight of the school.

Another issue that Dr. King would immediately have seen as a serious impediment to a satisfactory solution of the dispute is the rapid, continuing growth of Israeli settlements within the Occupied Territories. Now numbering more than three hundred thousand, the occupants of these settlements come for two major reasons. For the estimated two thirds or more majority, the cheaper housing subsidized by the state, along with convenient transportation networks established by the state to make commuting to work easy and safe, are attractions not to be resisted. For the rest, the sense of historic and religious rights and responsibilities for Jews to settle in particular sacred places is the primary motivation. To each of these, I can imagine King applying judiciously his cauterizing method that initiates the ultimate healing process.

Dr. King, like Gandhi, was realistic. He knew that appeals to conscience often need the heft of economic consequences in order to have full effect. Both in Montgomery and in Birmingham, the economic effects of boycotts and selective buying campaigns forced those in power to face the full human meaning of their segregation polices. By analogy, a carefully focused policy of economic penalties, imposed upon the State of Israel for its subsidized enabling of settlement activities, would almost certainly have immediate salutary consequences. The exemplary action of President George H.W. Bush is instructive in this respect: Confronted by Prime Minister Menachem Begin's policy of encouraging Israeli settlements in the West Bank, which was in direct contradiction to clearly enunciated U.S. and U.N. principles, President Bush simply stated that U.S. guarantees of Israeli loans would cease if these policies continued. Faced with the certain consequence of much higher interest rates that Israel would have to pay if the U.S. no longer guaranteed the loans, Begin immediately suspended the settlement activities.

Where are the economic leverage points today that could be used to end and reverse the current settlement policies? Widely acknowledged to be major obstacles to a peaceful resolution of the Israeli-Palestine conflict as well as a serious threat to a genuinely democratic Jewish state, these policies would, I imagine, receive immediate, careful scrutiny from King. Where do the funds come from that maintain settlement amenities and underwrite new activities? Are some charitable donations from abroad? Might governments that genuinely oppose the settlement policies respond by reducing their own foreign aid or trade concessions by commensurate amounts? In each case, the proposed actions would be narrowly focused on the grievance, avoiding any overall implication of rejection of the legitimacy of Israel's existence. King might in fact suggest, as he did in 1967,[3] that such an intervention, besides supporting valid demands of the Palestinians, will further affirm the legitimacy of Israel by securing for the Palestinians their rights to self-determination, thereby validating the full United Nations Special Committee on Palestine proposal that became the accepted resolution of the United Nations General Assembly in 1948.

The challenge of those settlers religiously motivated to reside in certain areas requires a different approach, again one for which King was ideally equipped. Here a direct confrontation with the meaning of the biblical promise is required. I can well imagine Dr. King's dear friend, fellow marcher, and spiritual brother, Rabbi Dr. Abraham Joshua Heschel, directing King to sources that would speak to the convictions of the religious settlers. One such source – dense, difficult, yet of great value for this task – is an astonishing article by Rabbi Dr. Andre Neher, "Rabbinic Adumbrations of Non-Violence: Israel and Canaan" (in *Studies in Rationalism, Judaism and Universalism: In Memory of Leon Roth*, edited by Raphael Loewe, Routledge & Kegan Paul, 1966), which introduces us to a significant strand

---

3. In 1967, King put out at least two statements affirming Israel's "right to exist in a state of security" and asserting the obligation of "the great powers" to "recognize that the Arab world is in a state of imposed poverty and backwardness that must threaten peace and harmony." King felt that peace "for Israel means security" and "territorial integrity," and that peace for the Middle East means "Arab development." He called for a Marshall Plan to deal with poverty and illiteracy in the Middle East, noting that "we must work passionately and unrelentingly through the United Nations to grapple with this years-old problem" in that part of the world. One finds here possible suggestions concerning how King might approach these issues today. See transcript of an interview with him on *Issues and Answers* (June 18, 1967) by Tom Jerriel, ABC Atlanta bureau chief, and John Casserly, ABC Washington correspondent (housed at the library and archives of the King Center, Atlanta, Georgia), as well as "Draft Statement Regarding SCLC's Participation at the National Conference on New Politics: Resolution on the Middle East," Chicago, Illinois (September, 1967, housed at the library and archives of the King Center, Atlanta, Georgia).

in classical Jewish tradition that is highly critical of Joshua for his methods of settling the land. Beyond the personal condemnation of Joshua implied in the sobriquets *"lista'a"*, robber baron, and pirate, the text insists that Joshua's true mission was to achieve "a peaceful coexistence of Hebrew and Canaanite in the Land of Canaan." The full implications of this critique for the dangerous dogmatism found among many settlers cry out for expanded interpretation and application.

I also imagine Heschel further coaching King in how to broaden the perspectives of dedicated religious settlers. Among these resources would surely be the stirring cry from Amos 9:7: "'Are you not like the Ethiopians to me, O people of Israel?' says the Lord. Did I not bring up Israel from the land of Egypt, and the Philistines from Caphtor and the Syrians from Kir?"

In *The Prophets,* Heschel also cites the startling passage from Isaiah (19:24-25) proclaiming the day when "Israeli shall be the third with Egypt and Assyria" and designating Egypt as "my people" and Assyria as "the work of my hands"!

What's that? God redeeming Philistines (might we read Palestinians)? Egypt as God's people? Assyria as the work of God's hands? The radical potential of such citations to loosen the shackles of the current terms of discussion, to provide a fresh view of the problem by this cleansing of the eyes of perception, hardly needs explanation.

Along with this economic-religious-spiritual approach of King to the perplexing problem of settlements, I imagine one additional element that must be mentioned even if space precludes any discussion. What shall happen to those displaced, perhaps, in this process? How are they to be resettled? With what resources? Or are they to remain where they are, with a mutually acceptable status defined in the details of an anticipated two-state solution? Or should there be a single, overarching state with safeguards for the rights of all to dignity, security, and self-determination? What is certain is that King's tender heart would not ignore this perplexing dimension in any settlement facilitated by the measured, effective intervention of his tough, realistic, strategic mind.

One overall element that affects every aspect of the confrontation must be mentioned in closing: the prevailing sense of trauma and victimhood that distorts each sides' perception of present realities. The late Anthony Shadid, until his untimely death as a seasoned and sensitive Middle East correspondent for the *New York Times,* wrote in a dispatch from Ramallah in the spring of 2002:

> The Israeli-Palestinian war is often seen through the lens of one side or the other. Israelis, in more numbers than ever before, see the conflict through the lens of terrorism. They feel a nation besieged by the lurking threat of suicide bombings that has disrupted lives . . . Palestinians see that same conflict through the lens of occupation. While Israelis may fear walking their streets, Palestinians point out that they cannot even enter theirs. The curfews, the checkpoints, the overwhelming superiority of arms Israel wields, have produced the humiliation of occupation that is stretching into a second generation . . . [N]either side comprehends the other's pain.

How else can one account for the disregard or belated recognition of important changes in the situation? Other than persisting Holocaust trauma reinforced by the counterproductive Palestinian strategy of terrorism, what can explain the failure to explore eagerly the startling Arab Peace Initiative of 2002? In contrast to the infamous "three no's" of 1967, this proposal, publicly offered by King Abdullah of Saudi Arabia, ratified by all members of the Arab League, and reendorsed in 2007, proposed normalizing relations between the entire Arab region and Israel, in exchange for a complete withdrawal from the Occupied Territories (including East Jerusalem) and a "just settlement" of the Palestinian refugee crisis based on U.N. Resolution 194 (which calls for a diplomatic resolution to the conflict and resolves that any refugees "wishing to return to their homes and live at peace with their neighbors" should be able to do so or, if they otherwise wish, to be provided with compensation). Notwithstanding the need for further clarification, this offer testifies that, contrary to popular rhetoric, there is indeed someone with whom to negotiate. To begin to understand this continuing, self-fulfilling, and self-defeating denial of evident reality, explorations such as Avraham' Burg's soul-searching *The Holocaust Is Over; We Must Rise from Its Ashes* (Palgrave Macmillan, 2008) seem essential.

For Palestinians, it would seem that the persistent pain of defeat and occupation – encapsulated in terms like *nakba*, "the catastrophe" – has impeded their recognizing such important resources as the human conscience for a just resolution of the conflict. We have already glimpsed, in the cases of Military Order 854, along with the Druze and Budrus, how effective this element can be – especially when coupled with traditional Jewish self-understanding.[4] (The frequent Israeli invocation of *tohar haneshek*, "purity

---

4. For example, the late distinguished scholar Nahum N. Glatzer cites this Talmudic characterization of the Jews from Yebamot 79a (in *Hammer on the Rock: A Short Midrash Reader*, Schocken, 1948): "This people is known by three signs: Being compassionate, shamefaced, and →

of arms," even if it has come to sound increasingly hollow in recent years, is but one testimony to this self-understanding.) Dr. King never lost sight of the vital importance of the human conscience as a resource that contributed to the resolution of conflicts in a manner affirming the basic human needs and dignity of all the contenders.

Martin Luther King, Jr. was an activist, a cauterizer, but above all a healer. When he would intone, "There is a balm in Gilead," his warm, resonant voice, coupled with the intensity of his conviction, seemed to bring to many of us a measure of healing at the mere hearing of those unforgettable words. This was never hollow rhetoric; it truly characterized the insistent yet loving quality of his interventions. If at times they hurt, the pain was always in the service of ultimate health, ever and again striving to bring what he called "the disconnected aspects of reality into a harmonious whole." How desperately the Holy Land needs King's Divinely inspired spirit of informed, incisive, loving intervention!

From *"In an Inescapable Network of Mutuality":*
Martin Luther King, Jr. and the Globalization of an Ethical Ideal, 2013

---

charitable. Everyone who has these three signs is worthy of cleaving to this people." For a powerful recent example of this continuing activity of the Jewish conscience in relation to the Israeli-Palestinian situation, see David N. Myers, *Between Jew and Arab: The Lost Voice of Simon Rawidowicz* (Brandeis University Press, 2008), with the full translation of Rawidowicz's startling essay.

Part Four

Between Us and Jewish Tradition

*Tradition is tending the flame,
it's not worshipping the ashes.*
—Gustav Mahler

The Return of the Goddess

A Revised Confessional

The transformation of progressive Judaism and the Jewish community itself through the infusion of feminist energies and Earth-based spirituality has been viewed as a blessing by Rabbi Gendler, who was himself an innovator in the havurah movement, in liturgical redesign, and in other refreshing influences. This 1971 essay is a cri de coeur that demanded and anticipated much of that innovation.

In the West, one part of the problem of our relationship with nature has to do with the suppression of the feminine. Note: "Feminine" and "female" or "woman" are not necessarily equivalent terms. "Feminine" is a quality found in females, but is found in males as well. We are all Yang and Yin, or, to cite a Jewish formulation: "When man is whole, both masculine and feminine are found in him" (Zohar 1, 34 b, my translation). The association of particular feminine traits and tasks with females is partly biological and partly sociocultural, but the ascription of feminine characteristics and functions exclusively to females is a culturally achieved distortion.

If J.J. Bachofen and Robert Briffault are correct,[1] there was an early stage in human culture of mother-dominance, the domain of the feminine/female. This was succeeded by father-dominance, and the shift was psychic, symbolic, and social, for all are interrelated.

Psychically, the shift was away from matter, instinct, and the unconscious and toward spirit, rationality, and the conscious. Symbolically, the shift was away from night and Moon and toward day and sun. Socially, the shift was away from property-in-common, inheritance through the mother, and agriculture, toward individual ownership, inheritance through the father,

---

1. See *Myth, Religion, and Mother Right: Selected Writings of Johann Jakob Bachofen,* translated by Ralph Manheim (Princeton University Press, 1967) and *The Mothers: A Study of the Origins of Sentiments and Institutions,* by Robert Briffault (Macmillan, 1927).

and city culture.

Crucial for our focus is the primordial association of the feminine with nature. Closely bound to soil and seedbed, the attack on the feminine (the goddesses) represented, psychically, an attack on the numinous quality of nature. The visible and the material were devaluated, and primarily the abstract and rational remained the locus of the sacred.

The Hebrew Bible comes on the scene at approximately the period of history when the struggle for masculine dominance has reached its peak. The Bible is, here and there, evidence of the struggle, but largely it is the justification of the shift to the new masculine-dominant order. This is part of the significance of the YHWH-only emphasis. A few feminine residues remain in scripture, but evidences of earlier practices are found mostly in denunciations of the fertility religions, closely bound to soil and vegetation.

At the same time, it must be noted that the Hebrew Bible does not succumb to that flesh-spirit, body-mind split, which has so devastated Western civilization. As Aubrey R. Johnson writes (in *The Vitality of the Individual in the Thought of Ancient Israel*, 1964), "in Israelite thought man is conceived not so much in dual fashion as 'body' and 'soul,' but synthetically as a unit of vital power or (in current terminology) a psycho-physical organism."

The Bible represented a strong thrust toward consciousness, out of what Erich Neumann describes as the "uroboric state."[2] This was a necessary stage in human development, psychically. However, long after the period in which the battle was won, there has continued to be an influence that has been largely negative toward nature as numinous and toward the unconscious as valuable. This is hardly the influence that we need today.

Our ecological plight, after all, is intimately related to our psychical plight. "[T][he abstract conceptuality of modern consciousness," writes Neumann, ". . . threaten[s] the existence of Western humankind . . . The one-sidedness of masculine development has led to a hypertrophy of consciousness at the expense of the whole human."

To redress the imbalance requires psychic, symbolic, and social redress. Consequently, we find renewed interest in re-claiming some (not all) of the subterranean, suppressed feminine elements in Western religion. Rabbinic Judaism does, in fact, preserve a few of these, and Kabbalah and Hasidism strongly emphasize them. But we need the Bible as well.

---

2. Erich Neumann, *The Great Mother*, translated by Ralph Manheim (Pantheon Books, 1955) and *The Origins and History of Consciousness*, translated by R.F. Hull (Princeton University Press, 1954).

For such purposes, it is helpful to read the Bible against the grain, as it were, and thereby reclaim, though obviously in a new context, those elements of the feminine that have persisted. In short, our motif at this stage of religion must be: No Spirit without Matter, and no gods/God without goddesses/the Goddess.

YHWH *is the tetragrammaton, the four-letter designation of the Divine* in Hebrew scripture. Consisting of four hardly audible Hebrew letters, its exact pronunciation was a secret once reserved to the High Priest, now lost. Yahweh and Jehovah are two common forms in English, the former preferred by scholars. (There is, needless to say, an entire literature on the subject.)

ADAMAH is the Hebrew word for "ground," and from it ADAM, "man," is clearly derived. In the Confessional that follows, ADAMAH is personified. This is as much or as little a play on persons as is YHWH. In short, a literal interpretation of the Confessional is neither necessary nor precluded. The issue is not the form of theological expression (personal or nonpersonal), but rather its fairness (masculine balanced by feminine).

The attack on the feminine took place both astrally, in the devaluation of the Moon, and terrestrially, in the devastation of the leafy groves. This is part of the meaning of the attack on idolatry. The centralization of worship prescribed in Deuteronomy is also an expression of this tendency, guarding against the reassertion of local cult practices, almost all of them rooted in the vegetation-fertility cycle.

My biblical allusions are numerous and must be left to the reader; hopefully most of them are evident. My few rabbinic allusions are, on the whole, either self-explanatory or not essential to an understanding of the piece. One, perhaps, should be spelled out: The "double endowment with urges" refers to a rabbinic doctrine concerning the ambivalent nature of human beings, and finds its scriptural support in the unusual spelling of "*va-yii-tzer,*" "and He formed/impulsed" man (Genesis 2:7).

Linguistically, "*d'khar v'nukvah*" is Aramaic for masculine and feminine. I use the Aramaic rather than the Hebrew (*"zakhar un'kevah"*) since the Zohar, the classic of Jewish mysticism, which explores rather brilliantly aspects of the masculine-feminine balance, is written in Aramaic. Yang/Yin, of course, are the classic Taoist terms for the same polarity.

CONFESSIONAL

Then the Lord [YHWH] God [ELOHIM] formed a man *[ha'adam]* from the dust of the ground *[ha'adamah]* . . .
Genesis 2:7 (N.E.B.)

. . . he came from the womb of mother earth . . .
Ecclesiastes 5:15 (N.E.B.)

ADAMAH, Earth Mother, Mother of Adam, Mother of Man, Mother of birds, of beasts, of herbs and trees, we have wandered far away from you.

Drawn from You while formed by Him, bodied from You while imaged by Him, we – *"d'khar v'nukvah,"* masculine-feminine, yang-yin – should have been that "one flesh" by which YHWH and ADAMAH, Heaven and Earth, Sun and Moon, Spirit and Flesh, Consciousness and the Unconscious, were forever joined. We, woman-man/man-woman, should have been that unbreakable link fused from the mating of YHWH and ADAMAH.

vaykhulu hashamayim v'haaretz . . .
And Heaven and Earth were wed . . .
Genesis 2:1[3]

Congelation of that conjoining, we, *"d'khar v'nukvah,"* were meant to maintain, in eternal renewal, that joyous and fruitful meeting.

But there was intrusion, and we erred; there was confusion, and we went astray. Where? How? Was it in eating from the fruit of the tree of distinctions? In redividing that which had been united? In splitting apart that which had been so joyously joined? in pitting Heaven versus Earth, Sun versus Moon, Spirit versus Flesh, Consciousness versus the Unconscious, Mind versus Instinct?

Why the urge to separate YHWH from connection with ADAMAH? Why the insistence to deny His existence in Earth-form, visible, material, and tangible? Why such severe condemnation of El, of Baal, of Tammuz, penultimate materializations of the Ultimately Immaterial?

Granted, there were abuses, mistakes, errors, even, let us admit, human indignities. Quite true, some of the rites of fertility were far from respectful

---

3. This fanciful play on the Hebrew word *vay'khulu* was suggested by Rabbi Arthur Green. Usually translated "finished," the Hebrew root is associated by Rabbi Green with the Hebrew word for "bride" (*kalah*), following a lead of Meir ibn Gabai, a 16th-century kabbalist who interprets *vay'khulu* as related to "intermingling."

of the full human being. Forgive us Mother; pardon us, Father. And yet . . .

Again we ask: Why the exile of YHWH in earthly form? Why needed we prohibit His dallying with, His delighting in His beauteous consort, ADAMAH? Was it jealousy on our part – a presumptuous, prideful pretense to possess Her as exclusively ours? Why this strange insistence that He abandon Her, abjure Her, write Her a bill of divorcement?

> The heavens are the heavens of the Lord,
> While the earth He has given to the children of men.
> Psalm 115:16 (my translation)

YHWH, all-too-indulgent Father, would that Your vaunted wrath had intervened at this stage of the drama, forbidding us any further influence over You in this marital matter. But no, You humored us, permitted us our distortions, to Your diminution and our own indescribable hurt.

For what followed? Suspicion of the beautiful, now enforced by the wrath born of Your bereavement, was loosed upon us. Oh so quickly the banishment of Her in Her various vestments, each winsome, each alluring, each enlivening. Asherah felled, Astarte dimmed, the Queen of the Heavens blotted out. Like Father like Son: dark bereavement.

> *Averah goreret averah.* Misdeed begets misdeed.
> Abot 4:2 (my translation)

With YHWH dematerialized, He grew more remote. With ADAMAH desacralized, She becomes more common in our eyes, and soon contemptible.

It begins in Heaven – or is it from Earth that it is cast upon Heaven? No matter. Whichever the direction, the Moon, "the purest of earthy bodies and the impurest of heavenly bodies,"[4] the heavenly earth, as it were, is soon reduced in dignity. Invidious distinctions are introduced, rank doing indeed!

> . . . God made the two great lights, the greater to govern the day and the lesser to govern the night . . .
> Genesis 1:16, NEB

What did such ranking mean for us?

> The "diurnal domain of the mind" is dominated by solar symbolism . . . a

---

4. J.J. Bachofen, *op cit.,* 45.

> symbolism . . . often the result of a chain of reasoning . . . The phases of the Moon showed man time in the concrete sense . . .[5]

Of course, the abstract over the concrete!

> The sun is always the same, always itself, never in any sense "becoming." The Moon, on the other hand, is a body which waxes, wanes, and disappears, a body whose existence is subject to the universal law of becoming, of birth and death . . . "Becoming" is the lunar order of things.[6]

Of course, inflexible Being over fluid Becoming!

> Man's integration into the cosmos can only take place if he can bring himself into harmony with the two astral rhythms, "unifying" the sun and Moon in his living body . . . religious experience is not a priori incompatible with the intelligible. What is later and quite artificial is the exclusive primacy of reason.[7]

Such, then, the outcome of the ranking: discord now rending what was formerly related in contrapuntal harmony.

But more was to follow. After depreciation came assault, denial, destruction: war on the Queen of Heaven, the Moon.

> These are the words of the LORD of Hosts the God of Israel. . . . "Do not do this abominable thing which I hate.". . . Then all the men . . . and the crowds of women . . . answered Jeremiah: ". . . we will burn sacrifices to the queen of heaven and pour drink-offerings to her . . . making crescent-cakes marked with her image and pouring drink offerings to her." When Jeremiah received this answer . . . he said: "The LORD did not forget those sacrifices . . . they mounted up in his mind until he could no longer tolerate them. . . . Your land became a desolate waste, an object of horror and ridicule, with no inhabitants. . . ."
>
> *Jeremiah 44:2, 5, 15-16, 19-23, N.E.B.*

Father, were You really so wroth? Did we hear You truly? Did we not tragically misunderstand?

> Nowhere in the history of religions do we find an adoration of any natural

---

5. Mircae Eliade, *Patterns in Comparative Religion,* translated by Rosemary Sheed (Sheed and Ward, 1958), pages 126, 154.

6. *Ibid.,* pages 154, 176.

7. *Ibid.,* pages 179, 126.

> object in itself. A sacred thing, whatever its form and substance, is sacred because it reveals or shares in ultimate reality. Every religious object is always an "incarnation" of something: of the sacred.[8]

Father, She being denied You, we also lost Her. You, perhaps, survived, depleted but not devastated. But we began to find ourselves cut off from that of our selves that abided in Her.

> It might be said that the Moon shows man his true human condition; that in a sense man looks at himself and finds himself anew in the life of the Moon.[9]

Wrath loosed in Heaven soon afflicted Earth, for are They not, in us, One?

> Adam encompasses above and below
> *Zohar 1, 34b (my translation)*

War on vegetation when it revealed too verdantly Your great, rhythmic renewals!

> You shall demolish all the sanctuaries where the nations whose place you are taking worship their gods, on mountain-tops and hills and under every spreading tree. You shall pull down their altars and break their sacred pillars, burn their sacred poles and hack down the idols of their gods and thus blot out the name of them from that place.
> *Deuteronomy 12:2-3, N.E.B.*

Mother, how we treated You!

All this was accompanied by cult centralization, the insistence that the great gifts of spirit, dematerialized, were the better to be found in Temple confines than on verdant heights.

> ... you shall resort to the place which the LORD your God will choose out of all your tribes to receive his Name that it may dwell there. There you shall come and bring your whole-offerings and sacrifices ... There you shall eat before the LORD your God ... you shall bring everything that I command you to the place which the LORD your God will choose as a dwelling place for his Name ... See that you do not offer your whole-offerings in any place at random, but offer them only at the place which

---

8. *Ibid.*, page 158.

9. *Ibid.*, page 184.

> the LORD will choose in one of your tribes.
> *Deuteronomy 12:4-6,7,11,13, N.E.B.*

No more the companionship of You, Mother, and Him, with sanctity widespread; no more those precious material gifts of spirit bestowed by You and Him together: the recurrent *miracle* of growth renewed.

And suspicion, consuming suspicion of the beauteous, culminating in Rabbi Akiba's dictum:

> Wherever you find a lofty mountain, a high hill,
> or a spreading tree, there you will find idolatry.
> *Abodah Zarah 3:5 (my translation)*

Desacralized and devaluated, how we treated her! Mother, cast off not in old age but while yet young and beautiful! Did we "cultivate and care for" You (Genesis 2:15)? Those were the words of our Father, were they not? But we chose instead to practice "dominate" and "subdue" (Genesis 1:26-28). Father, which was truly You speaking? Mother, how we betrayed You both!

Did we share Your bounty with our brothers and sisters, the beasts? The charnel stench of this planet's slaughter is answer enough. Birds, beasts, and fish; alien tribes, fellow men, and brothers: Who has escaped our minded murders? How quickly the earth was "corrupted and filled with violence" (Genesis 6:13). And how soon we rewrote Scripture to legitimate the slaughter (Genesis 9:2-3).

That, of course, is not the whole story. How could it be? Were we not doubly endowed with urges? There was, all along, a continuing impulse to consider You.

> When you enter the land which I give you, the land shall keep sabbaths to the LORD. For six years you may sow your fields and for six years prune your vineyards and gather the harvest, but in the seventh year the land shall keep a sabbath of sacred rest, a sabbath to the LORD.
> *Leviticus 25:2-4, N.E.B.*

That ADAMAH and YHWH share together the joys of the Sabbath!

The Moon, too, Your luminous counterpart, was ever respected by the folk. Monthly Her renewal was celebrated out of doors as the people exulted in the light of Her Presence. Even the Rabbinic tradition conceded the point.

> In the school of rabbi Ishmael it was taught: Had Israel merited no other privilege than greeting the Presence of their heavenly Father once a

month (by reciting the benediction of the renewed Moon), they would be contented!

Sanhedrin 42a (my translation)

There are many other elements as well, ADAMAH, which seek Your preservation and reflect concern for You. Yet basically, Mother, ADAMAH, in trying to steal You from YHWH, to seize and possess You, to lay exclusive incestuous claim to You, all we managed was to dispossess ourselves. For You were not destined to be possessed absolutely by man. "The land is mine," says YHWH (Leviticus 25:23, N.E.B.)

How presumptuous we were: reducing YHWH to entire rather than to Ultimate Invisibility! Denying the enlivening intermediate forms! With what results? YHWH reduced to ever-unseen deity, the *tzelem* (image of God) not taken seriously, and You, ADAMAH, dissected into chemical components: N, K, P!! Sentience, sensibility, and joy removed, cosmic harmonies drowned out by the roar of earthly machines, and our own connections with You severed.

Once upon a time, ADAMAH, we sensed the life coursing through You and related to You respectfully, lovingly, though not idolatrously.

> . . . earth itself is alive . . . The relation between the earth and its owner is not that the earth, like a dead mass, makes part of his psychic whole — an impossible thought. It is a covenant-relation, a psychic community, and the owner does not solely prevail in the relation. The earth has its nature, which makes itself felt, and demands respect. The important thing is to deal with it accordingly and not to ill-treat it . . . The task of the peasant is to deal kindly with the earth, to uphold its blessing, and then take what it yields on its own accord. If he exhausts it, then he attacks its soul and kills it; after that it will only bring forth thorns, thistles and whatever else pertains to the wilderness.[10]

Once upon a time, ADAMAH, we sensed the true ideal as well: every man under his own vine and fig tree:

> . . . they shall beat their swords into plowshares,
> and their spears into pruning-hooks;
> nation shall not lift up sword against nation,
> neither shall they learn war any more.
> . . . and each man shall dwell under his own vine,
> under his own fig tree, undisturbed.
> For the LORD of Hosts himself has spoken.
> *Micah 4:3-4, partially taken from A.S.V. and N.E.B.*

---

10. Johannes Pedersen, *Israel, Its Life and Culture,* Oxford University Press, 1955.

Idyllic and right, ideal and peaceful. How much might have been accomplished had we but maintained that intimacy with You, ADAMAH. The preparation of the soil, the planting of the seed, the protection of the tender shoot: caring and nurturing Your activities, Your image, our Yin, there for our acceptance. Defoliation might have come harder to us, mightn't it? The motherly in each of us might have been preserved.

> At the lowest, darkest stages of human existence the love between the mother and her offspring is the bright spot in life, the only light in the moral darkness, the only joy amid profound misery . . . The relationship which stands at the origin of all culture, of every virtue, of every nobler aspect of existence, is that between mother and child; it operates in a world of violence as the divine principle of love, of union, of peace. Raising her young, the woman learns earlier than the man to extend her loving care beyond the limits of the ego to another creature, and to direct whatever gift of invention she possesses to the preservation and improvement of this other's existence.[11]

Each man under his own vine and fig tree. And even the legislation to insure it, given by YHWH Himself, sentiment alone not being sufficient.

> You shall count seven sabbaths of years, that is seven times seven years, forty-nine years . . . and you shall send the ram's horn round. You shall send it through all your land to sound a blast, and so you shall hallow the fiftieth year and proclaim liberation in the land for all its inhabitants. You shall make this your year of jubilee. Every man of you shall return to his patrimony, every man to his family . . . When you sell or buy land amongst yourselves, neither party shall drive a hard bargain . . . No land shall be sold outright, because the land is mine and you are coming into it as aliens and settlers. Throughout the whole land of your patrimony, you shall allow land which has been sold to be redeemed.
> *Leviticus 25:8-11, 14-15, 23-24, N.E.B.*

So there it stands, ADAMAH, linked directly with Your Sabbaths! How much that might have done both for You and for us: fewer large landholdings, fewer dispossessed peasants, fewer exploited poor, fewer cruel accumulations of wealth; and fewer inhuman concentrations of humans cut off from You, fewer people removed from the magic of Your great cycle of birth-growth-ripeness-death-rebirth, fewer people totally passive and dependent on others in the getting of their basic nourishment, fewer human beings totally

---

11. J.J. Bachofen, *op. cit.,* page 79

surrounded by mechanisms rather than growing-fruiting-living beings.

Factory farming? Why? Monoculture? For what reason? Pesticides, lethal to insect and us alike? No need. Your preferred small holdings would have obviated these damaging developments. Pollution of our air by transports bringing our sorry foodstuffs from chemicaled countryside to choking cities? Unimaginable! Mother, to what orphaned state are we reduced?

Rabbi Ahai ben Josiah says:

> He who purchases grain in the market place,
> to what may he be likened?
> To an infant whose mother dies:
> although he is taken from door to door to other
> wet nurses, he is not satisfied . . .
> He who eats of his own is like an infant
> raised at its mother's breast.
> *Abot de Rabbi Nathan, Ch. 30 (translation by Judah Goldin)*

But finally, to what end this weeping? For could it have been otherwise? Without some break away from You, dark, encompassing Earth Mother, without some such thrust, would the Heaven in us have been felt at all? Might we not have spent our lives, generation after generation, in benighted bondage to You, anxious, fearful, unaware, infantile dependents? There is, after all, Your fearsome face as well as Your gracious one, Your devouring nature as well as Your sustaining one: drought and disease were not unknown to us. These, You realize, we had to contend with, that we might become Your mature collaborators rather than abject dependents. You are great, ADAMAH, but perhaps You, too, like Him, prefer us as partners, not subjects. And so we imagined, fantasized, rationalized, and reasoned our way to some measure of control over You, ADAMAH. Had we any choice?

Yet it is painfully clear now: The measure is too full, the break too complete, and we have strayed so far away from You that we now fear for our own lives, not to speak of Yours. As with our Zulu brothers, our being "far away" means: "There were someone cries out, 'O mother, I am lost.'"[12]

> O ADAMAH, Earth Mother,
> Mother of Adam, Mother of all men,
> Mother of birds, of beasts, of trees,
> we have wandered far away from You.

---

12. Cited in Martin Buber, *I and Thou*, translated by Ronald Gregor Smith, T. and T. CLark, 1952, page 18.

O Great One, from Whose womb we at first emerged,
O Mother of all living, whence we too came:
If we pare away pretense, pride, and presumption,
If we end exploitation and embrace appreciation,
if we weed out coercion and cultivate gentleness:
May we once again, yet as never before,
return to You, and with You to Him?
May we once again, yet as never before,
unite in ourselves
Spirit and Flesh,
Conscious and Unconscious,
Sun and Moon,
Heaven and Earth
d'khar v'nukvah,
yang and yin,
male and female?

If so, then again, yet as never before,
You and He shall unite once more;
and once again, yet as never before,
the morning stars will sing together
while all Your children shout for joy.

Discussion in Brief

Had we in the West managed, somehow, to take at full value, *"Av ha-rakhamim,"* one classical Rabbinic form of address to the Divine (or its equivalent), the foregoing remythicization might have been unthinkable. *Av ha'rakhamim* is usually translated, "Merciful Father," but etymologically the more literal and revealing translation is "Wombed Father." The phrase implies, in other words, a unification of the masculine and feminine elements in the Single Person. The value of this kind of monotheism for the full human being can hardly be overestimated, and it is toward this that we must work, it seems to me, both theologically and personally. However, in view of the fact that Western religion has tended to achieve "unification" of the masculine and feminine elements largely by simple masculine domination of the feminine, there may be some warrant for the foregoing confessional. At the very least, it makes the individual elements of *"d'khar v'nukvah"* available once again for a more satisfactory integration.

The direct ecological implications of this should not be underestimated:

> In a patriarchate . . . matter is regarded as something of small value in

> contrast to the ideal — which is assigned to the male-paternal side. . . .
> Unnatural symbols and hostility to the nature symbol . . . are characteristic
> of the patriarchal spirit. . . . The matriarchal spirit does not deny the native
> maternal soil from which it stems. It does not, like the Apollonian-solar-
> patriarchal spirit, present itself as "sheer being," as pure existence in
> absolute enternity, but . . . apprehending itself as historically generated,
> as a creature, it does not negate its bond with the Earth Mother.[13]

To reclaim the matriarchal spirit and our bond with the Earth Mother strikes me as necessary if we are to address at all successfully the ecological crisis confronting us. As we are now, split within, our world, too, is split. Distrustful of our bodies, Earth's body frightens us. Devaluing matter (however obscenely we accumulate), we maltreat our planet. Cut off from layers of our selves, we find that the world seems alien.

To heal the breach will require both religious reconsideration and a social policy concerning numbers and distribution of population that will permit all of us some significant relation to the soil.

One final note of clarification: None of the reopening of this religious question in any way denies the great advance that Hebrew prophecy brought to human beings. While dematerialization may have been, in the theological sphere, carried too far, the widespread tendency of ancient paganism to identify the king with the god was generally warrant for social oppression of a thoroughly distasteful kind, including the unconscionable accumulation of land. Furthermore, there was a tendency to determinism in ancient nature cults that also had to be confronted.

We must never forget that the emphasis on distributive justice and secure small holdings, so central to the biblical outlook as expressed in the Sabbatical and Jubilee legislation, in this respect relates the prophetic tradition most positively to both the ecological and the social issues of sour own age. ❧

From *ECOLOGY, Crisis and New Vision*, 1971

---

13. Erich Neumann, *The Great Mother*, pages 49, 50, 55

Identity, Invisible Religion, and Intermarriage

An Evolving, New, Social Form of Religion

This far-seeing essay from 1969 responds to incipient Jewish communal panic about interfaith marriage with a redefinition of "intermarriage."

> ... the possibility that a new religion is in the making.
>
> Thomas Luckmann

Conferences on religious identification and intermarriage continue; statistical studies multiply; the "problem" persists. Suggested analyses rarely seem adequate, proposed "solutions" rarely seem satisfactory. Might it be that our perception of the present is obscured by the past? That we are misled by analogies with former times?

These questions are prompted by a combination of certain of my rabbinical experiences and some studies that I have come across recently. The combination has, for me at least, sharply challenged some earlier assumptions about Jews and intermarriage, and led to some conclusions that are at variance with what I formerly thought. These conclusions have led to certain changes in my religious behavior, for they suggest that certain attitudes and stands I have previously taken as a rabbi are questionable, possibly inappropriate, probably harmful religiously.

To share the background of these conclusions requires references to several recent works dealing with religion. None of them is beyond challenge, and all are perhaps questionable in some respects. Their point will be further blunted by my extremely brief summaries of their arguments and considerations. Even so, they seem to me substantially correct in what they have to say, and they also seem to converge in what they may mean for the religious situation today.

Let me add immediately that the authors I cite are not to be held responsible for the conclusions I derive from their works. Perhaps they would find such conclusions warranted and appropriate, perhaps not. In any event, they and their works are cited with appreciation for the stimulation and illumination they have afforded me, but they are not necessarily to be associated with the argument as it unfolds.

I should also add that what I speak of here has reference primarily to the religious scene in the United States. Its applicability to other societies is an independent question. Furthermore, while the implications of these considerations are many, with application to other areas of religious concern and practice, for convenience I want to confine the consideration here to intermarriage.

My rabbinical involvement is quite clearly the stance from which I write, and this accounts for the specific focus of the last section on rabbinical participation in such "intermarriages." What this entire analysis implies for experimental and evolutionary religious communities is most appropriately addressed by the members of such communities themselves.

One last introductory word. I do not here present lengthy arguments on behalf of particular points. I prefer to think of this as an essay in shared recognitions: "This is how it seems to me; does it seem this way to you?"

The Definition of "Interfaith Marriage"

"A good Jew" means many things to many people. Even for those who might agree on the meaning, to describe any given person simply as a "good Jew" or "not a good Jew" would probably seem an oversimplification. Would not any person be "good" in some respects and "not good" in others? In practice, do we not, for meaningful and precise discourse, use "a good Jew" as a variable term rather than as a fixed attribute?

Similarly, suggests J. Milton Yinger (in *Journal for the Scientific Study of Religion,* Spring, 1968), there is a need to redefine "interfaith marriage as a variable, with possibilities of more or less." Urging that the definition of interfaith marriage not depend on "the single criterion of church membership or identification," Yinger suggests the value for research of transforming "a long-held dichotomy into a variable." He writes:

> If we begin to take account of the several dimensions of religion, we may discover that those who are intermarried when viewed in terms of one dimension may be *intramarried* when viewed in terms of another . . .
>
> Once we think of intermarriage as a variable, not an attribute, we can turn to the task of designing scales to measure it. Two scales, I think,

are needed. The first will measure the degree to which the couple is intramarried, considering the similarity on the many possible religious factors . . . The second scale will measure the extent to which a married couple is bound into an 'integrating' or 'separating' network of other persons and groups. If all the persons with whom they interact and all of their significant others are of the same faith, then they are strongly intramarried on this group dimension. If they interact with many other persons of a different faith, if some of their relatives are intermarried, then they are partially intermarried, even if they are members of the same church and hold the same beliefs.

Concluding these very suggestive remarks, Yinger adds: "The redefinition of intermarriage as a variable, with values produced by the interaction of two sets of forces, is already a drastic shift in our perspective. If we are to undertake more precise work on such problems as interfaith marriage, however, adequate to the task of multivariate analysis, we must demand of ourselves even more radical changes in our concepts."

If a change in the approach to intermarriage is a scholarly desideratum, might it not also be a practical religious desideratum? And might not the key definitional change be similar – from intermarriage as a simple dichotomy to intermarriage as a variable?

Obviously the recognition of this variable nature of intermarriage would manifest itself differently in the practical religious area. One need hardly subscribe to multivariate analysis, complete with statistics and ratings for each couple, to admit at least this much: For each, there are degrees, subtleties, and a variety of considerations that are not sufficiently accounted for in a final determination, on the basis of the traditional definition, that theirs is *either* an interfaith *or* an intrafaith marriage. Rather than continuing to accept such a dichotomy, at minimum we need to recognize the gradations in the different circumstances of different couples, and we need some variations of the traditional wedding ceremony so that it can be more exactly suited to individual situations.

The Nature of Friendship

Dr. J. Fentener van Vlissingen, a brother from the Taize community, a Protestant lay-monastery in France, recently completed an historical study of friendship (not yet translated into English). Very briefly, he suggests that three major stages of friendship may be distinguished in history, each with particular characteristics.

The first stage, the ethnological, finds friendship firmly set in the structure of society, sanctioned by values and symbols, specifically defined, and often contractual. Its main function is to mitigate tensions which arise from the social organism and family relations. Though the earliest historically, elements of this stage may persist even today in various societies.

The second stage is that which begins with Greek society, where friendship is defined in ethical terms and has as its purpose the ethical fulfillment of the participants. From Greek times to the 18th century there was a moral preoccupation with mutual perfection in friendship, which also implied a socially recognized value system that defined ethical perfection or offered models of it.

The third stage, the romantic, dates from the 19th century, and describes friendship that results from special feelings between people who, interacting, set their personal seals upon one another. Each in some measure determines the character of the other by the interaction. Here the psychological rather than the ethical is central, and the consequence is that personal-subjective rather societal-objective considerations are the primary determinants of the relationship.

For our purposes, one implication of this stage of friendship – certainly the predominant stage in our age – must be stated explicitly. In the case of a friendship between two persons of different religious traditions, not only is there some exchange of subjective characteristics but some exchange of those religious elements that constitute part of the persons. Thus the friendship serves as a bridge for the flow of symbolic meaning and feeling, and is the point of translation of symbols from one tradition to another.

The effects of this on religious configurations can hardly be over-estimated, especially over periods of time. In friendships of this kind, persons from different traditions discover that the human meaning of the particular symbols of each tradition can in significant ways be translated into symbols of the other tradition, and so an exchange of personal and religious feeling can and does occur at such points. The deeper the friendship, the greater the symbolic sharing, with each person participating in some measure in the appreciation or celebration of the symbols or rites of the other. Where, as in the United States today, interreligious friendships are numerous, each represents a point of significant religious interchange and an unspoken challenge to traditional claims of religious untranslatability and exclusiveness.

The religious effects of such friendships are reinforced by certain current symbolic and doctrinal developments.

The Symbolic Thaw

For a long time it had been assumed that the *meaning* of religious symbols was identical with their *explanation*. Explanations, of course, were formulated in the doctrinal terms of particular religious, theological or philosophical traditions. Even similar symbols (*e.g.,* candles, bread, wine) were regarded as having essentially different values or meanings in different traditions, and different symbols were taken as proof of insurmountable differences between traditions.

It is true, of course, that the doctrinal context does affect the meaning or value of a symbol to some extent, but it does not by any means determine its full meaning. As the late Erwin Goodenough brilliantly argued, the psychological or emotional impact that a symbol may have on human beings depends on much else than the formal interpretation of the symbol, and the evidence in his multi-volume *Jewish Symbols in the Greco-Roman Period* (1953-1968) constitutes an invaluable connecting link with the symbolic expressions of other religious traditions.

Meanwhile, the work of Carl Jung and his school has opened further vistas, and the emotional-psychological-spiritual meaning of symbols is no longer confined by the interpretations of particular traditions. Among especially illuminating treatments of religious symbols from this point of view, one might single out Mircea Eliade's *Patterns in Comparative Religion* (1958). The work of Erich Neumann has also been exceedingly valuable, and besides *The Origins and History of Consciousness* (1949), his "Note on Marc Chagall" (in *Art and the Creative Unconscious*) is a brilliant portrayal of deep currents moving today in the Jewish spirit.

At the same time, even particularistic symbols are beginning to be explicated in functional human terms, and so they too begin to have "non-sectarian" meaning for those "outside" the given tradition. A very moving recent example of this is James W. Douglass' *The Non-Violent Cross* (1968), with its beautiful and non-appropriative treatment of Ernie Levy, the Lamed-vav, the Ebed Yahweh, Gandhi, and others. By appreciating these figures in broad human terms rather than "claiming" them for particular "Christian" purposes, Douglas reveals rare religious sensitivity; yet relating them to the symbol of the cross in significant ways, he at the same time makes more widely available the non-doctrinal human meaning of the cross.

The release of symbols from institutional confinement is, I think, an increasing tendency, and the resultant fluidity of the situation will surely see new configurations take shape.

Doctrinal Developments

Writing in *The Christian Century*, Harvey Cox states: "We need as our theological starting point a Jesus who is neither the ecclesiastical nor the existentialist Jesus, but the Jewish Jesus . . . Our Christology must begin with the Jew who makes it possible for us to share the hope of Israel, the hope for a kingdom of Shalom."

In *The Center* magazine, September, 1968, Robert Gordis devotes an entire article to a survey of what he calls "Re-Judaizing Christianity." By this term Dr. Gordis means far more than the mere "Hebraization" of Christianity, as his summary makes clear:

> The demand for involvement in the world, the stress upon deed rather than upon creed, the sense of the dynamism of history, the ethics of self-fulfillment, the realistic yet positive evaluation of human nature, the recognition of sex as a divinely ordained attribute of man – and the willingness to draw the consequences in the arena of life – all these elements of Biblical and post-Biblical Judaism are in the direction in which contemporary Christian thinkers are moving. On the other hand, such Hellenistic elements as a static view of God and history, the conception of the dichotomy of body and soul, the doctrine of man's innate corruption, and the stress on dogma and war on heresy are playing an ever-diminishing role in the thinking of Christians today. It follows, therefore, that we may be entering upon a new era of ecumenism, on a far deeper level than the exchange of pleasantries or even the recognition of mutual rights in a pluralistic society.

The conclusion Dr. Gordis derives from this is modest: "Perhaps the day is dawning when Jews as well as Christians will recognize . . . that Judaism still has a vital contribution to make to the world today." Rather more to the point, it seems to me, are two final suggestions he makes: ". . . the concept of the Judeo-Christian tradition takes on genuine relevance in our day . . . each tradition can speak significantly, first to its own devotees and then to all . . ."

This does seem to me the case, but it is likely to carry us well beyond the "truly meaningful dialogue" between the traditions to which Dr. Gordis refers, if such "dialogue" presupposes that each participant emerges with a better "understanding" of the other but is to remain in precisely the same relation to his own and the other tradition as was the case before the dialogue. For in such exchanges, just as in friendship, is it highly likely that there will be a significant mutual determination of outlook with distinctly unique consequences.

Active Collaboration

Many clergymen have in recent years found themselves engaged in collaborative actions with those of other religious traditions. Usually they have acted together in areas of common concern, *e.g.,* the war in Vietnam; sometimes they have worshipped together. At times, as in Southern churches during the height of cooperation with the Southern Christian Leadership Conference, they discovered that the full meaning of worship and the Presence of the Spirit could be felt and shared by all those present, no matter what their denominational affiliations. At other times, in intimate discussions with other clergy, they have sensed that true colleagues are not confined within the boundaries of "their own" established religious institutions, but are often found beyond these boundaries. In calmer times as in crises, one's affective/effective religious community has been discovered to transcend the established boundaries of religious denominational groupings.

As with clergy, so with laymen. Powerful feelings of genuine religious fellowship, not conforming to established religious configurations, have developed among many citizens working jointly on projects of common communal concern.

This is especially the case on college campuses, to such a degree that one Jewish chaplain, responding at a conference to the suggestion of his Christian counterparts that there be active involvement by campus chaplains and their student constituencies in broadly ecumenical social action efforts on campus, replied by warning against any approaches "in which the ecumenical effort becomes a pitfall to the particular identity of the Jewish participants." Acknowledging that "Jews and Judaism have an essential stake in the social change," he insisted, according to the *Boston Jewish Advocate* (12/19/68), that "their contribution must be made not in universalistic terms but within the clearly defined context of the Jewish tradition." Since his own primary responsibility was "to keep Jewish students Jews," he emphasized that social action was to be understaken not "for its own sake" but rather as an expression of "Jewish tradition, history and experiences."

However one may react to this particular approach, there can be little doubt that "ecumenical effort" is indeed a "pitfall to the particular identity of the Jewish participants" – and, it is important to add, to the identities of the non-Jewish participants as well.

Identity and Invisible Religion

Considerations and developments of the kind cited above are, of course, matters of common knowledge. We have tended to deny their obvious implications, however, by assuming that despite these developments, religious outlook and religious identity are still functions of our established religious institutions. It is precisely this assumption that is learnedly and severely challenged by Thomas Luckmann in his brief, incisive work, *The Invisible Religion* (1967).

Challenging the uncritical tendency to identify religion with religious *institutions*, Luckmann instead begins with the question of the *function* of religion. Following the leads of Weber and Durkheim, he presupposes that "the problem of individual existence in society is a 'religious' problem . . . the values originally underlying church religion were not institutional norms but norms lending significance to individual life in its totality."

Luckmann substantiates this presupposition with a valuable discussion, inspired by George Herbert Mead, of how Selves develop: ". . . an organism becomes a Self by constructing, with others, an 'objective and moral universe of meaning.'. . . the organism transcends its biological nature by developing a Self."

And what has this to do with religion? "It is in keeping with an elementary sense of the concept of religion," Luckmann writes, "to call the transcendence of biological nature by the human organism a religious phenomenon." Insofar as this process of biological transcendence depends upon the development of symbolic "systems of meaning that refer, on the one hand, to the world of everyday life and point, on the other hand, to a world that is experienced as transcending everyday life . . . we may conclude . . . that the world view, as an 'objective' and historical social reality, performs an essentially religious function and define it as an *elementary social form of religion*. This social form is universal in human society."

This historical world view, Luckmann continues, which may assume different forms in different social conditions, and which usually includes rituals, images and language, also affects directly personal identity: "…the individuation of consciousness and conscience" involves the "internalization of an already constructed world view rather than in the original construction of world views," so that the personal identity of an individual is "the subjective expression of the objective significance of a world view. Earlier we defined the world view as a universal form of religion. Correspondingly, we may now define personal identity as a universal form of individual religiosity."

Luckmann is observing, in short, that there is a profound relationship between inherited world view and personal identity.

Whatever the case may be with simple societies, in our own, with what Luckmann describes as "increasing complexity of the division of labor, a large surplus over the subsistence minimum, and a correspondingly more differentiated pattern of social stratification," we also experience "increasing institutional specialization and rationalization, and the sharp segmentation of the several institutional domains that characterize modern industrial societies . . ." Among the institutions affected by this trend have been specialized religious institutions, for "institutional specialization of religion" has been, in fact, the form that religious world views have taken in our civilization.

Now, to speak in the plural of world views is already to reveal an important feature of a complex, differentiated society: that no religious institution can express "*the* hierarchy of meaning in *the* world view." This factor of pluralism we have, I think, faced squarely. What we have not faced squarely, however, is the full meaning of institutional specialization of religion in a context of general institutional specialization, segmentation, and rationalization. For not only do what were once "total life values" tend to become "part-time norms;" not only may any religion come to be "apprehended by the individual as the fulfillment of *particular* requirements" rather than as an overarching, integrating system of meaning that determines effectively the priorities by which people live; but even more important, "the primary public institutions no longer significantly contribute to the formation of individual consciousness and personality, despite the massive performance control exerted by their functionally rational 'mechanisms.'" As a result, "personal identity becomes, essentially, a private phenomenon."

Why is this? "Institutional segmentation of the social structure significantly modifies the relation of the individual to the social order as a whole. A person's 'social' existence comes to consist of a series of performances of highly anonymous specialized social roles . . . At the same time, the 'meaning' of performances in one institutional domain, determined by the autonomous norms of that domain, is segregated from the 'meaning' of performances in other domains and detached from the over-arching context of meaning of an individual biography." Thus the person experiences institutional demands of "conformity" at the same time that the institutions leave him, so far as personal identity or biography is concerned, very much subject to "individualism."

Should not the traditional religious institutions help coordinate the various institutional demands upon persons? Certainly "religion" should, but the nature of specialized religious institutions probably prevents their so functioning in our society. Luckmann's telling analysis – it repays very careful reading – can hardly be compressed further, but at least certain of the characteristics of institutional religion today should be mentioned in passing.

There is a growing incongruence between the "official" model of religion presented by the institutions and the actual systems of "ultimate" significance by which people do, in fact, order their lives. "Religious practices (such as service attendance) will be performed for a variety of 'nonreligious' motives," Luckmann writes, "and specifically religious beliefs will be compartmentalized into opinions (such as, God is almighty) which will have no direct relation to the individuals' effective priorities and everyday conduct." Rather than serving a truly integrating function in the lives of their participants, religious institutions frequently fragment them further with demands that can hardly be taken seriously. At most, specifically religious roles become "part-time" and partial rather than pervasive and unifying.

As for the effects on succeeding generations, this we know very well: "The everyday concerns of the fathers are no longer those of the sons and many of the concerns of the sons were unknown to the fathers." Even more serious, however, is this fact: "what the fathers preach but do not practice will be internalized by the sons as a system of rhetoric rather than as a system of 'Ultimate' significance."

It is thus extremely doubtful that the religious institutions we know are effectively performing the religious function of integrating the routines of everyday life and legitimating its crises. Yet no other primary public institution is performing this function either. "The effective social basis of modern sacred cosmos is to be found in neither the churches nor the state nor the economic system." Yet surely some norms do "determine the effective priorities in the everyday lives of typical members of modern industrial societies." What are these norms, and where are they expressed?

Luckmann responds to this question with the suggestion that we may, in fact, be witnessing a revolutionary change of profound social significance: "the replacement of the institutional specialization of religion by a new social form of religion" – "*assortments* of 'ultimate' meanings directly available to persons" who themselves "select certain religious themes from the available assortment and build them into a somewhat precarious private system of 'ultimate' significance." This individual religiosity tends to be supported by other persons who are of like inclination, and so one has partial sharings and even joint constructions of systems of ultimate significance, precarious though these may be. In the construction and sharing of such systems, the nuclear family is quite important and serves as the effective basis for such constructions. Yet in a profound sense, the new religion is "invisible" so far as its social institutional expression is concerned.

Among the major religious themes today, Luckmann discerns these: individual autonomy, self-expression, self-realization, familism, sexuality, and a mobility ethos. And where do the traditional religious institutions fit in this "emergence of a new social form of religion?" They may be seen, according to him, either as "a survival of a traditional social form of religion (that is, institutional specialization) on the periphery of modern industrial societies," or, more fruitfully as "one of the many manifestations of an emerging, institutionally nonspecialized social form of religion, the difference being that (they) still occupy a special place among the other manifestations because of (their) historical connections." In short, the traditional religious institutions now function largely as suppliers of certain religious themes, which, though of special importance due to historical associations, nonetheless are subject to the same individual preferences that finally determine the acceptance or rejection of other such themes.

As for the effects of this on personal identity, since individuals do, in fact, construct their own systems of "ultimate" significance, they in effect construct their own personal identities as well, since, as we noted before, "the personal identity of a historical individual is . . . the subjective expression of the objective significance of a world view." This personal identity is no longer merely a reflection of an inherited "official" model, however, but includes other elements from the "rich , heterogeneous assortment of possibilities" that are directly accessible to each person. In the deepest sense, personal identity, while relating to an inherited tradition, rarely if ever is wholly constituted by that world view alone. Each person today is rather a composite of many elements, and so the designation of him or her as Jew or Christian, etc. is less and less adequate to his or her actual religious identity.

Whatever questions one might raise about Luckmann's analysis, and whatever modifications one might suggest in applying it to the situation of Judaism today, it seems to me the single most adequate and illuminating treatment I have yet seen of the religious situation today in the United States, and its support of the other developments noted above is, I think, fairly obvious.

What does all this imply for our own attitudes and actions as concerned, radical Jews or as rabbis? In order to avoid speaking for others, and to assure that this remains an essay rather a treatise, I want to speak primarily as a rabbi and confine myself mainly to one particular issue: so-called interfaith marriages among so-called alienated college students (and in their first few years after leaving the campuses), especially those involved in social movements today.

These political and cultural activists are variously described by college chaplains as "alienated from adult social concepts and practices," "religiously motivated" and "the most spiritually sensitive generation that has appeared on the campus in a long, long time." They come together for various projects of genuine importance to themselves and their society. Their serious criticisms of the present order often stem from religious motivation, and in the projects, campaigns, and struggles they feel a profound personal involvement. They work with students of all religious backgrounds and affiliations, they are assisted by chaplains of various denominations, yet they experience a significant unity. Moments of intensity, "peak experiences," occur in these situations of natural involvement, which stem not from demands of the past but from urgencies of the present. In these crises, and in their group responses, they may feel "more of religion" than they have ever felt previously at church or synagogue. The power of passionate dedication, the need for clarity of goals, the sense of higher aims and purposes, the intuition of help beyond the limited ego-self – these profound experiences, which were our gift in Southern civil rights churches, may also be felt to some degree by the serious and involved students on campuses, whether in formal or informal religious situations. They also experience quite genuine encounters with one another, and associations that are not simply "social" but deeply personal, involving many levels of their being. Clearly, by any standard, these are experiences of religious significance.

These situations and experiences, the students notice, occur outside the established religious institutions – though at times they are related to them. Further, the situations and experiences are no respecters of established religious lines, and can be and are shared by persons from different traditions. In addition, students discover that if elements of various traditions are brought to bear on the situation confronting them, these elements tend to be more or less available to all, significant to all, and illuminating to all. Even if they stem from "someone else's" tradition, in such circumstances the human-functional meaning of these symbols, myths, or teachings, rather than their doctrinal uses, come to the fore and are thus widely shared.

The students, aware of the relevance and reality of religion in such situations, also retain some awareness of its too-frequent irrelevance and unreality in so many (not all) standard institutional religious settings. They are aware, also, that the "official" models presented them by parents and institutions are not really functioning models. They hardly need Luckmann to tell them that there is "a marked degree of incongruence between the 'official' model and the effectively prevalent individual systems of priorities." By the mere fact of having lived this many years, they will have noticed very well the effective priorities in their parents' lives, and the following will already be the case: "[W]hat the fathers preach but do not practice will be internalized by the sons as a system of rhetoric rather than a system of 'ultimate' significance."

When the time comes to consider marriage, the establishing of a home, and the continued sharing and transmission of the particular values which they have come to seek – and the aware students of today are far more sensitive to these issues than is sometimes realized – it is obvious to them that their own value systems relate to and draw from, but do not precisely correspond to, established classical models. On the one hand, they still relate in some fashion to the symbols, rituals, social ideals, and group feelings of their inherited traditions; they often want to retain some tie or connection. At the same time, they have established deep and meaningful religious connections with those of other inherited traditions; these can hardly be disregarded. In effect, a new, "invisible religion" has been formed in the intimacy of their relationship, and this, they would insist, must take precedence over the particular demands of their inherited traditions.

Hence they find illegitimate the demand of the established traditions that they conform their own lives to systems of ultimate values that are, even for those professing them, in practice and in priority systems of rhetoric in many respects. On the occasion of marriage as well as in their life together, people want to express those ties of feelings with their inherited traditions, but they are simply unable to subordinate their most profound intuitons and convictions to such demands as "conversion" or promises about the rearing of children. In all honesty, they insist that the rearing of children is a subtle task, and that in good conscience they must share with their children-to-come that combination of values that is the result of their relationship as it unfolds in mutual respect, with consideration for the values of each inherited tradition as well as for the other "assortments of 'ultimate' values" which are their inheritance as residents of this nation at this particular period of history.

As for the established tendency to characterize this as "intermarriage," even without reading the Yinger article they would know that the term is misapplied if simply confined to questions of institutional or group religious identification or affiliation.

The foregoing portrayal is admittedly sketchy and somewhat idealized. Even so, it has, I think considerable validity when applied to many of "the most spiritually sensitive generation that has appeared on the campus in a long, long time." It is also descriptive of many of the young persons whose commitment to *tikun ha-olam* continues past college, expressing itself in the dedication of their talents and efforts to work of obvious social importance.

From *Response*, Winter 1969/70

Ever Since Eden

Trees, Tradition, and Tu Bishevat

This 1999 essay seeks to place the Tu Bishevat (New Year of the Trees) seder closer to the center of Jewish environmental consciousness, despite "profound Biblical ambivalence" about the spiritual power of trees.

Ever since Eden, trees have played significant roles in the human drama, as portrayed Biblically and developed by later Jewish tradition. The enigmatic episode revolving around the Tree of the Knowledge of Good and Evil and the Tree of Life, with their simultaneous attraction and danger for humans, establishes early the intriguingly ambiguous character of trees in Jewish thought.

On the one hand, the tree as image often conveys a sense of approbation. Those who "delight in the law of the Lord" are

> like trees planted by streams of water,
> which yield their fruit in its season,
> and their leaves do not wither.
> *Psalm 1:3*

> The righteous flourish like the palm tree,
> and grow like a cedar in Lebanon.
> *Psalm 92:13*

These well-known honorific tree images from Psalms are also found in the Prophets:

> [Those] whose trust is the Lord . . . shall be like a tree planted by water,
> sending out its roots by the stream.
> it shall not fear when heat comes,
> and its leaves shall stay green;
> in the year of drought it is not anxious,
> and it does not cease to bear fruit.
> *Jeremiah 17:7-8*

Here the trees are similes for the faithful in God.

On the other hand, the tree as image can equally convey stir Divine disapproval:

> For the Lord of hosts has a day
> against all that is proud and lofty, . . .
> against all the oaks of Bashan.
> *Isaiah 2:12-13*

> Yet I destroyed the Amorite before them,
> whose height was like the height of cedars,
> and who was as strong as oaks.
> *Amos 2:9*

Along with these images of arrogance come associations with idolatry:

> For a spirit of whoredom has led them astray,
> and they have played the whore, forsaking their God.
> They sacrifice on the tops of the mountains,
> and make offerings upon the hills,
> under oak, poplar, and terebinth, because their shade is good.
> *Hosea 4:12-13*

> . . . on every high hill, on all the mountain tops, under
> every green tree, and under every leafy oak, wherever
> they offered pleasing odor to all their idols.
> *Ezekiel 6:13*

> On every high hill and under every green tree
> you sprawled and played the whore.
> *Jeremiah 2:20*

In light of this profound Biblical ambivalence towards the tree as a symbol, how could faithful Jews expand a rabbinic, agriculture-tithing calculatory device into a full, celebrative New Year of the Tree? Without necessarily subscribing to the exact terms put forward by Johannes Pedersen (in *Israel: Its Life and Culture*) – "the soul of the tree . . . the tree as a whole, but . . . also . . . the dominant will, or rather the upholder of, the psychic whole constituted by the life of the [tree] . . ." – it is hard to deny the ability of the tree to represent what he calls "the living cosmos, endlessly renewing itself." Mysteriously drawing moisture and nutrients from depths defying our observation, self-supporting in reaching heights at times almost beyond our measure, long-lived yet bountifully generous in their gifts to us, trees do seem numinous in essence. This quality may help account for both the initial attraction to the tree and its later abjuration within Jewish tradition, as one school of Yahweh purists came to construe this numinous quality as competition with, rather than a reflection of, the power of the Creator.

The initial attraction is well attested: "Abraham built three altars, one in Shekhem . . . one in Ai . . . and one in Hebron," says Midrash Hagadol. What the Midrash does not state, but the Biblical text substantiates, is that at each of these three places, stately terebinth or oak trees stood as the designating feature.

An oak or terebinth stood at Shekhem, the site of God's first promise of land to Abram just after he had left Ur of the Chaldees.

> Abram passed through the land to Shekhem, to the Terebinth of Moreh, the Oracle's Oak. At that time the Canaanites were in the land. And the Lord appeared to Abram and said, "To your offspring/seed I will give this land." So he built there an altar to the Lord, who had appeared to him.
> *Genesis 12:6-7*

An oak or terebinth stood at Bethel-Ai, the site of God's further specification of the promise:

> From there [Shekhem] he moved on to the hill country on the east of Bethel, and pitched his tent, with Bethel on the west and Ai on the east; and there he built an alter to the Lord and invoked the name of the Lord.
> *Genesis 12:8*

The further details of the promise are found in Genesis 13:14-15, 17. That a prominent oak did indeed stand at Bethel-Ai is attested in Genesis 35:8: "Deborah, Rebekah's nurse, died, and she was buried under the oak below Bethel, so it was named Allon-bacuth, the Oak of Weeping."

A grove of oak or terebinth trees stood at Mamre (Genesis 13:18, 18:1), where Abram settled after the promise at Bethel-Ai, and where he carried out the covenantal circumcision of himself, his son Ishmael, and all the males in his household (Genesis 17:23-18:1; cf. Rashi on 18:1, establishing that the circumcision did take place at the Oaks of Mamre). It was here, also, that Abraham first acquired land, publicly witnessed: the burial site of Sarah "in the cave of the field of Makhpelah facing Mamre (that is, Hebron)" (Genesis 23:19). With the exception of Rachel, the other matriarchs and patriarchs were also buried in that cave, before Mamre with its grove (Genesis 49:31, 50:13).

It is hardly an exaggeration to assert that at each of these defining occasions at the birth of the Jewish people, trees stood as stately, silent witnesses.

Throughout early Israelite life, the vibrant forces within notable trees drew into their locale important functions in the life of the people. Joshua chose Shekhem for the sacred compact with the people of Israel to "put away the foreign gods that are among you," and the rite included the following:

> So Joshua made a covenant with the people that day, and made statutes and ordinances for them at Shekhem. Joshua wrote these words in the book of the law of God; and he took a large stone, and set it up there under the oak in the sanctuary of the Lord.
> *Joshua 24:25-26*

The angel of the Lord who appeared to Gideon "came and sat under the oaks at Ophrah" (Judges 6:11). It is "by the oak of the pillar at Shekhem" that Abimelekh is made king of Shekhem (Judges 9:6). A Diviners' Oak *(elon me'onenim)* is a recognized landmark used to describe strategic movements in a battle (Judges 9:37). In her judging of Israel, "Deborah, a prophetess . . . used to sit under the palm of Deborah between Ramah and Bethel in the hill country of Ephraim; and the Israelites came up to her for judgment" (Judges 4:4-5).

Saul, in his search for his father's lost donkeys following his anointing by Samuel, is told by the latter that he will encounter "three men going to God at Bethel" at the Oak of Tabor (I Samuel 10:3) preceding his meeting with "a band of prophets" (I Samuel 10:5). At their death, Saul and his sons were buried "under the oak in Jabesh" (I Chronicles 10:12). "The man of God" who prophesies against Jeroboam was found "sitting under an oak tree" (I Kings 13:14). These and other examples make understandable why one philologist speculates (in *A Hebrew and English Lexicon of the Old Testament*, Oxford University Press, 1962) that the derivation of the Hebrew word for terebinth, *elah,* comes from *El,* divine. Some numinous connection with trees does seem evident in all of these instances.

This sensed association with the Divine receives interesting support in later Jewish tradition also. In a vastly learned, meticulously researched and carefully argued essay, the late Morton Smith makes a compelling case (in *Bulletin of the John Rylands Library,* March, 1958) that the menorah, a stylized tree, is a symbol of God for Jews during the Greco-Roman period, a symbol Biblically based and rabbinically sanctioned.

It seems fair to say that one source of Tu Bishevat flows from this sense of encounter with the numinous through the agency of the tree. Supportive of such an understanding is this citation from the Zohar, included in *Sefer Peri Eitz Hadar* ("The Fruit of the Majestic Tree"), a kabbalistic text about the Tu Bishevat seder: "By the word 'tree,' he also referred to the Holy One, who is the tree of life for all" (I, 102b).

Note also the remark of R. Shimon (Zohar II, 58b): "There is a mighty and wondrous tree in the celestial sphere which supplies nourishment to the beings above and below."

Even more striking is the bold reminder in *Peri Eitz Hadar* 3a that "the *gematria* [numerical equivalent] of *ilan* [tree] is YAHDWNHY" – the Hebrew spellings of the four-letter words for LORD and GOD in alternation, a favored devotional device in mystical prayer. The numbers, 91 in each case, are indeed equivalent. This is surely as bold an identification of the tree with the Divine as can be imagined.

It should not be surprising, then, given this assertion of the Divine nature of the tree, that it is seen as serving a divinatory function as well.

> Wherever Abraham took up his residence he used to plant a certain tree, but in no place did it flourish properly save in the land of Canaan. By means of this tree he was able to distinguish between the man who adhered to the Almighty and the man who worshipped idols. For the man who worshipped the true God, the tree spread out its branches and formed an agreeable shade over his head; whereas in the presence of one who clung to the side of idolatry the tree shrank within itself and its branches stood upright. Abraham thus recognized the erring man, admonished him, and did not desist until he had succeeded in making him embrace the true faith.
>
> *Zohar 102b*

The literal acceptance of this description may give us pause, but perhaps we should be equally hesitant to dismiss out of consideration the core assertion of the Zohar: by association with the tree, we are sometimes gifted with insights that might otherwise be beyond our ken. In Norse mythology, Odin wins the secret of the runic alphabet by virtue of Ygdrassil, the World Ash; in Buddish tradition, Gautama gains enlightenment beneath the bo tree; in Biblical tradition, as we have seen, patriarchs and prophetess, teachers and diviners, judges and angels regularly sit beneath oaks, palms, and terebinths. Is this legendary evidence to be entirely disregarded?

Contemporary testimony offers further support for the deep-rooted sense that something of insight/intuition/revelation is granted us through trees. This is the reflection of the photographer Cedric Wright (in *Words of the Earth,* Sierra Club, 1960):

Consider the life of trees.
Aside from the ax, what trees acquire from man is inconsiderable.
What man may acquire from trees is immeasurable.
From their mute forms there flows a poise, in silence, a lovely sound and motion in response to wind.
What peace comes to those aware of the voice and bearing of trees!
Trees do not scream for attention.
A tree, a rock, has no pretense, only a real growth out of itself, in close communion with the universal spirit.
A tree retains a deep serenity.
It establishes in the earth not only its root system but also those roots of its beauty and its unknown consciousness.
Sometimes one may sense a glisten of that consciousness, and with such perspective, feel that man is not necessarily the highest form of life.
Tree qualities, after long communion, come to reside in man.
As stillness enhances sound, so through little things the joy of living expands.
One is aware, lying under trees, of the roots and directions of one's whole being.
Perceptions drift in from earth and sky.
A vast healing begins.

This is the reverie of the Yiddish poet Yehoash (translated by Marie Syrkin in *A Treasury of Jewish Poetry,* Crown Publishers, 1957:

MYSTERY

I don't know how it was:
Upon the ground
I lay — warm summer-night
Wrapping me round.
I hear the boughs above,
The grass below,
Whisper and call
In speech I did not know.
Then someone out of me
Spoke answeringly.
Long, long I heard both voices blending, blending.
Uncomprehending.

It would seem that thoughtful moderns might well join traditional mystics in this meditative reflection from *Peri Eitz Hadar* 12a:

Maker, Shaper, Creator, and Emanator of Worlds above and below . . .
All in wisdom formed. . . .
diverse, yet destined to be One:

> You have caused trees and vegetation to spring forth from the earth, in stature and splendor,
> to provide humans with wisdom and understanding.

Knowing trees also characterized Solomon's wisdom:

> God gave Solomon great wisdom,
> discernment, and breadth of understanding
> as vast as the sand on the seashore . . .
> He would speak of trees,
> from the cedar that is in Lebanon
> to the hyssop that grows in the wall;
> he would speak of animals, and birds, and reptiles, and fish.
> *I Kings 5:9, 13*

Flora and fauna were so familiar to him that he could speak of them with authority. That such sensitivity to the qualities of each particular wood was not unknown is clear from other pages of the Bible. The differentiated use of acacia, cypress, cedar, and olive wood in the construction of the Tabernacle and Solomon's Temple is one example.

Impressive as was Solomon's knowledge of the great trees such as cedars, equally so was his acquaintanace with lowly shrubs such as hyssop, whose purifying use is well attested Biblically (cf. Exodus 12:22, Leviticus 14:4, 6, 49, 51-52, and more). It was a knowledgeable naturalist who occupied the seat of power at that time.

This tradition of respect for particularity and appreciation of each natural element in its individuality is reflected in the Tu Bishevat seder ritual. One notices the categorization of the fruits of trees according to the arrangement of their edible and inedible portions: an inedible shell outside but edible flesh within, the world of *Asiyah*; an edible outside but with an inedible pit inside, the world of *Yetzirah;* and edible both as outside flesh and inner pit, the world of *Beriyah*. Ten examples of each category are recommended for eating: grapes, figs, apples, etc. for the last; dates, olives, apricots, etc. for the middle; nuts, coconuts, pomegranates, etc. for the first. Also figuring in the ceremony are four cups of wine or grape juice, first white, the second white with some red added, the third with more red added, and the fourth mostly red with just a bit of white remaining. Thus is the ripening cycle mimed, from the wintry white of frost, snow, or ashen branches, through the blossoming of spring, to the fruiting of summer, and the full, red ripening of autumn. The eating and drinking, preceded and followed by blessings and readings, focuses awareness on both the wonder of the growth cycle and the tastes or textures of the various fruits and nuts.

Appreciation is enhanced by the deliberate and aware mode of eating. As we chew, we are asked to remember (in *Peri Eitz Hadar*) that "the thirty-two teeth correspond to the thirty-two times the name of God is mentioned in the story of Creation." Appreciation is also enjoined by the citation from the Jerusalem Talmud (Kiddushin 4:9): "Said Rabbi Ibun: A person is destined to give account for innocent delights which his/her eyes beheld but his/her mouth did not taste."

Encounter, Inspiration, Appreciation: All are occasions for receiving, the demand, if any, being that we accept the gifts, the bounty, the blessings. But there is reciprocity as well: A measure of response is asked, the acceptance of active responsibility for the preservation of the wonder. As the Talmud states (Berakhot 35a):

> One who enjoys the delights of this world without reciting a blessing is called a thief, for only by means of the blessing is the sustaining heavenly flow maintained, and the power of the guardian spirit of that fruit is renewed; so the fruit is nourished by this flow, and its power to grow renewed.

The blessing referred to here is simply the blessing traditionally recited before eating fruits of trees: *borei peri ha-eitz*. However one may assess the kabbalistic doctrine of the various trees having guardian spirits whose powers are released and recycled by humans reciting the prescribed blessing before eating, one fact is incontestable: Depending on our awareness of the vegetation cycle and our intervention in it, the fruitfulness of the Earth will be affected for good or ill. Healthy topsoil is alive, of course, teeming with microorganisms and earthworms that maintain its productivity. When nourished by organic matter and covered by plant life that protects it from erosion by wind and water, the soil is constantly renewed and remains fruitful over decades, centuries, even millennia. When subjected to thoughtless exploitation by humans – deforestation, overgrazing, overcropping, monoculture, herbicide, and pesticide overuse, etc. – then the land becomes inert, lifeless, and the flow of sustenance from and to the soil suffers fatal interruption.

Is not such injurious intervention, which interrupts the fructifying life flow, a case of global theft? Possibilities blighted and promises withered, our planet rotates less richly garbed, less fetchingly bedecked, by virtue of energy squandered, vitality stolen. Centuries before the development of the environmental language, the mystics intuitively grasped this cosmic truth and gave it ritual expression.

And today? At the confluence of the streams of mystical tradition, en-vironmental awareness, and Israel-focus, the current is strong and the water fresh. Millions of trees are planted in Israel on Tu Bishevat, while in Jewish communities throughout the world, financial support is offered for reforestation. The ritual eating of dried fruit in religious schools is often accompanied by rainforest charts and preservation projects, and may include one further innovation: The brittle *bokser* of earlier years (still a threat to the teeth), is often now accompanied by carob-covered peanuts and raisins, or carob chips, straight from the local health food store – sure signs of dietary change.

Tu Bishevat seders are more widely offered today, with several *haggadot* now available and more likely to appear, and a significant component of many is likely to be a focus on a current environmental issue. At the same time, some celebrants may emphasize the meditative possibilities provided by the categories of fruit, drawing analogies with personal defenses that may be summoned in various circumstances. At another seder the focus may be on the mystery of the seed, survivor of the death of one life cycle and bearer of life to the new. The spiritual diversity of this celebrative efflorescence will soon rival the vegetational diversity traditionally celebrated by Tu Bishevat.

The mystery of the seed and the image of the "mighty and wondrous tree in the celestial sphere which supplies nourishment to beings above and below" – how beautifully they are evoked, enacted, and joined on this New Year of the Tree. It is as if the third day of Creation were with us afresh and we were proclaiming anew the wonders of vegetation and plants, earth and trees, seeds and fruit (cf. Genesis 1:11-12, where these six terms occur nineteen times in two short verses).

The pull of Earth is strong, the rhythms of the year compelling. In the words of Edith Sitwell ("Harvest" and "Eurydice," in *The Collected Poems of Edith Sitwell*, The Vanguard Press, 1954):

> Gestation, generationa, and duration —
> The cycle of all lives upon the earth —
> Plants, beasts, and men, must follow those of heaven;
> The rhythms of our lives
> Are those of the ripening, dying of the seasons,
> Our sowing and reaping in the holy fields,
> Our love and giving birth — then growing old

And sinking into sleep in the maternal
Earth, mother of corn, the wrinkled darkness.
So we, ruled by those laws, see their fulfillment.

. . . Love is not changed by Death,
And nothing is lost and all in the end is harvest.

From *Trees, Earth, and Torah*, edited by Ari Elon, Naomi Mara Hyman, and Arthur Waskow, Jewish Publication Society, 1999

The Tree that Sustains All Life

Reviving the Tu Bishevat Seder

This 1980 essay celebrates and revitalizes the rituals of the often-neglected Tu Bishevat (New Year of the Trees) seder.

We prepare the soil, plant the seeds, tend the garden – then leave it. Each evening we leave – and it grows quite on its own. Each Shabbat we leave it – and it grows on its own. We take the children to camp – and it grows on its own. We go camping in Vermont – and it grows on its own. We visit Scott and Helen Nearing in Maine – and it grows on its own.

With each leaving, I experience a momentary pang, a start of anxiety, the agricultural analogue of "Who's minding the shop?" "Oy, who will tend the garden. Who will help it grow?"

Who indeed? For while it grows on its own, "its own" includes an incalculable number of helpers: microorganisms and earthworms among those inhabitants of the soil, numerous beyond all counting, who "seedtime and harvest, and cold and heat, and summer and winter, and day and night" tend the plants and help them grow. Any adequate notion of earth-covering herbiage and seed-yielding fruit trees must include this immense assemblage of living stuff, the true intermediaries of "The One Who brings forth sustenance from the soil." To recognize this reality is to begin to comprehend what food is and whence it comes.

Within Judaism there is a day devoted by the mystics to such a comprehension. Tu Bishevat, the New Year of the Tree, timed for the full moon of late winter when, in the Mediterranean basin, the sap in the trees begins to rise. Celebrative rather than cognitive in mode, its central ceremony is a seder with an ordered eating of a variety of fruits.

The ceremony derives its impetus from two propositions:

> Said Rabbi Ibun: A person is destined to give account for innocent

delights which his/her eye saw but his/her mouth did not taste.
Jerusalem Talmud Kiddushin 4:9

One who enjoys the delight of this world without reciting a blessing is called a thief, for by means of the blessing the sustaining heavenly flow is maintained, and the power of the guardian spirit of that fruit is renewed. . . . By reciting a blessing with *kavanah* (directed awareness), one avoids becoming a destructive agent who hoards and keeps to him/herself the sparks of vitality that were in the fruit. But by the blessing and the mastication with the 32 teeth, which correspond to the 32 uses of Elohim (God) in the Creation story, one both purifies and returns the sparks to the life-sustaining flow of Holiness.
Berakhot 35a

However one may assess this kabbalistic sense of guardian spirits of the various trees and their fruits, even the most naturalist-humanist construction of reality can, I think, identify with the importance of *being appreciative* of that which we eat and *being aware* of those forces that replenish it.

How did the kabbalists practice their Tu Bishevat seder? Recognizing that edible fruits may be divided into three categories – those with protective shells outside but edible inside, those edible inside but with an inedible pit, and those entirely edible – they sought ten examples of each category: grapes, figs, apples, etc. for the last; dates, olives, peaches, etc. for the second; nuts, coconuts, pomegranates, etc. for the first. Then, reading various passages from the Bible, Talmud, and Zohar relating to fruits and grees (and grains also), they would eat examples of the various categories.

Also figuring in the ceremony were four cups of wine, the first white, the second white with some red added, the third roughly half and half, and the fourth mostly red with just a bit of white. (Red and white Concord wine or grape juice work well for this, as do other compatible red and white wines.)

How might we put this into practice? Set a festive table with candles, plates of fruit, nuts, wine of two colors, and selections of songs and readings. A striking photo or drawing of a tree would also be appropriate, for according to kabbalistic thinking this is the Festival of *the* Tree, i.e., the Cosmic Tree that sustains all life.

Begin by lighting the candles, sing a song or two for Tu Bishevat, then the *brokhe* over the first cup of wine. One could then read Biblical selections dealing with vine and wine, sing another appropriate song, then prepare to eat from the first category of fruit. Start either with the "higher," that entirely edible, and "descend," or begin with the "lower," that inedible on the outside, and "ascend." Before eating the first category, read Biblical and other passages pertaining to that fruit or nut. Also, talk about how these characteristics of the various fruits may suggest analogies to us as persons, our behavior in situations that are threatening, our defenses, etc. After the *brokhe*, *"borey p'ri ha'etz"* (Creator of the fruit of trees), eat examples of that category.

Some more singing then on to the second cup of wine, mostly white with a touch of red, preceded by the *brokhe*. (A rather nice introduction to each cup of wine is the song *"V'hitifu,"* derived from Amos 9:13, which can serve to link musically the four cups of wine.) With each cup, think about the parallels between the deepening redness of the wine and the colors of nature as fructification proceeds.

More singing, some further readings (see below), then on to the middle category of fruit. Again, discussion, reflection, associations, etc. Next, the third cup of wine, this time half red and half white, then on to the last category of fruit and the final cup of wine. This last cup is almost all red but with some white to remind us of the essential imperfection and incompleteness of all that we know on this earth.

What about readings? Besides Biblical sources that can be found with the help of a concordance, and Talmudic passages that one can find with the help of M.D. Gross' *Otzar Ha-agadah* (check *ilanot*, trees, and *perot*, fruits, for a start), some possible passages from Zohar are these: I 33a; II 58b-59a; III 16a. 58a, 74a, 86a, 127a, 189b. All are in the Soncino English translation.

For other sources, Wendell Berry's *Farming: A Handbook* has some wonderful poetry. Tchernichovsky is another likely source (cf. the translation of one of his poems in *The New Jews,* p. 243). Modern Yiddish and Hebrew poetry are good bets also, as is the poetry of D.H. Lawrence and R.M. Rilke.

For suggestive readings about soil, the following may be rewarding: Helen and Scott Nearing, *Living the Good Life,* especially page 88 in the Schocken edition; Charles Darwin's *On Humus and the Earthworm;* Sir Albert Howard's *An Agricultural Testament,* Edward Hyams' *Soil and Civilization.*

From *Menorah*, January, 1980

Three Contributions to Prayer

In loving tribute to the memory of Abraham Joshua Heschel

In this 1982 recollection of Rabbi Abraham Joshua Heschel, Rabbi Gendler honors his teacher with both praise and interpretive support for his deep spirituality.

Crises of faith are not unknown among theological students, and as I look back on my own days at Seminary, it seems to me that there were times when I must have been a classic case. Painful questions about God and prayer weighed heavily upon me for what seemed like years on end, although by calendrical calculation the acute periods were most likely days or weeks.

Seeking anonymity at such times lest my lack of faith become visible to others, especially faculty, I would eat whenever possible away from the Seminary. But there were days when I had to eat lunch in the Seminary cafeteria, which was frequented by faculty also. On those occasions, I would slither into the cafeteria line, scurry through, gulp down the predictable fare, and make my escape, presumably unobserved by the Seeing Eyes of the faculty, earthly representatives of that menacing, All-Seeing Eye referred to in Avot. In this fashion I managed to add physical indigestion to my already acute spiritual heartburn.

For a time, this skulking about was an effective avoidance mechanism, but one day I was spotted by that astute reader not only of Hasidic texts but also of student spirits, Abraham Joshua Heschel, whose memory is indeed a blessing.

"Tell me, my dear Everett, is something the matter?" he asked in that special Heschelian tone, at once insinuating and inviting, an inflection reserved for those times when Sherlock Heschel, spiritual detective, was closing in upon a heretofore unapprehended spiritual suspect.

Oy! The evasion was at an end. I was both discovered and apprehended with a single question. So why pretend further? Back to his book-lined office we went, where with both reluctance and immense relief I poured out my troubles in a flow of words that somewhat resembled the sputtering of a faucet fitfully transmitting water drawn from a well nearly dry.

After hearing me out, Heschel smiled sympathetically and knowingly, went to a bookcase, and took down from his collection of prayer books a particular *siddur*. Showing it to me, he said, "My dear Everett, get yourself a copy of *Siddur Otzar Hatefilot* and read there the Introduction to *Siddur Avodat Ha-Lev*. It will help, I assure you."

The ordeal over and the verdict rendered, I skeptically set out to comply with the prescription. To my inexpressible surprise, it did help. The introduction to which Heschel referred me read as if written specifically to address my personal concerns. The author spoke in fresh ways about the place of petitionary prayer and the issue of the efficacy of prayer, precisely those problems that preoccupied me at that time of my life.

In succinct and scholarly fashion, the author rescued the root meaning of *t'fila*, prayer, from its identification with supplication or asking, and he did it by referring to compelling instances of its Biblical usage. He established that root meaning as a *clarifying* and *connecting*, a *judging* and *joining* of one's thoughts, impressions, and energies to Divine purpose as reflected in Scripture. He then assessed the significance of the fact that the Hebrew verb for praying occurs regularly in the *hitpael*, the reflexive form. Here he suggested that prayer works its effects first through affecting the pray-er, hence the reflexive voice. The process he describes is neither "auto-suggestion" nor "self-hypnosis"; his process is far more profound, with cosmic connections and ties to the very texture of Created reality and the Creator.

This preface to prayer helped me then as it has helped me ever since. Perhaps it will help others as well. In tribute to that beloved teacher and mystic, moralist and visionary, Abraham Joshua Heschel, I'd like to share in translation some excerpts from one part of that Introduction: "What Is Prayer?" from *A Prayer Book for the Service of the Heart,* by Aryeh Leib ben Shlomo Gordon, published in Jerusalem in 1915.

In Rabbinic tradition the word T'FI-LA, prayer, is sued as a synonym for T'CHI-NA, supplication, the asking of our needs from the Creator. Blessed be the Divine. But in Scripture we find it also used to denote the recital of praises of God.

And Hanna prayed, and said:

> My heart exulteth in the Lord,
> My horn is exalted in the Lord;
> My mouth is enlarged over mine enemies;
> Because I rejoice in Thy salvation.
> *I Samuel 2:1*

> And the Lord prepared a great fish to swallow up Jonah; and Jonah was in the belly of the fish three days and three nights. Then Jonah prayed unto the Lord his God out of the fish's belly. And he said:
>> I called out of mine affliction
>> Unto the Lord, and He answered me;
>> Out of the belly of the netherworld cried I,
>> And Thou heardest my voice.
>
> *Jonah 2:1-3*

> Now after I had delivered the dead of the purchases unto Baruch the son of Neriah, I prayed unto the Lord, saying: 'Ah Lord God! behold, Thou hast made the heaven and the earth by Thy great power and by Thy outstretched arm; there is nothing too hard for Thee . . .
> *Jeremiah 32:16-17*

. . . In all these instances there is only praise and adoration, and the rabbinic usage is in fact an extension of the basic meaning.

It appears to me that the root PLL in origin refer to the process of *sorting out* the confused mixture of thoughts and impressions that first present themselves to the mind. Appearing to the person in a confused state, they need to be sorted out and differentiated one from the other, sometimes by strict logic, sometimes by intuitive conjecture, the ones that more closely correspond to reality being thereby affirmed. For example:

> And Israel said unto Joseph: "I had not thought to see they face; and, lo, God hath let me see thy seed also."
> *Genesis 48:11*

Here LO PI-LAL-TI, "I had not thought," is used as a synonym for "I had not considered, I had not supposed." Had Israel used a more definitive term, such as "I had never imagined" or "I never occurred to me," I would have inferred that he had already despaired completely of ever seeing Joseph again, and so had erased that hope from his heart. But in truth, contrary expectations were constantly struggling within him, and he could not reach an unambiguous decision. Hence the word LO PI-LAL-TI. Another branch from the root PLL is PLH, to distinguish, to differentiate, used where an evident distinction is perceptible as well as conceptual. For example:

> "And the Lord shall make a division between the cattle of Israel and the cattle of Egypt; and there shall nothing die of all that belongeth to the children of Israel."
> *Exodus 9:4*

By contrast:

> Ye shall therefore separate between the clean beast and the unclean, and between the unclean fowl and the clean; and ye shall not make your souls detestable by beast, or by fowl, or by any thing where with the ground teemeth, which I have set apart for you to hold unclean. And ye shall be holy unto Me; for I the Lord am holy, and have set you apart from the peoples, that ye should be Mine.
> *Leviticus 20:25-26*

> And that time the Lord separated the tribe of Levi, to bear the ark of the covenant of the Lord, to stand before the Lord to minister unto Him, and to bless in His name, unto this day.
> *Deuteronomy 10:9*

In these cases, the word used is related to HAV-DIL, the distinction being less immediately obvious and less tangible.

Prayer, then, T'FI-LA, is the *clarification* or *judging* of the thoughts and impressions that fill the human heart, the distinguishing of the worthy from the unworthy, and the *connecting* or *joining* of them to the Divine. . . . For this reason, prayer is called "the service of the heart" (cf. Deuteronomy 11:13).

This is not an easy task for one not accustomed to it. Hence, "the early pietists spent one hour in silent waiting before they began their formal recitation of the prescribed service" (B'rakhot 30b).

The sequence of worship is this: The worshipper first clarifies and sorts out the mixture of thoughts, impressions, and impulses within; next externalizes them in the presence of the Creator; then recites songs and praises of the Creator; and lastly, *if* he or she so desires, may conclude with some petition.

Since the very definition of prayer, T'FI-LA, is the clarification and connection of one's thoughts with the Divine, central to prayer is the proclaiming of God's glory, with petition clearly secondary and optional.

From this it follows also that a central pillar of prayer is the devotional direction of the heart: prayer without KA-VA-NA, the intent of the heart, is not true prayer.

And why does the verb "to pray," L-HIT-PA-LEL, always come in the reflexive, the HIT-PA-El, denoting an activity of the agent that affects him/herself? Because prayer does not cause any change in the Will of the Creator . . . but rather works its effects within the worshipper as s/he offers heart and mind to the Creator. When the heart and mind of the worshipper change for the better through worship, by this change in the worshipper the worshipper's situation is also changed. . . .

For the Creator is ever-ready to provide benefits for all creatures who walk in the right paths; such is the nature of the world God created. But humans often, through misdeeds, erect a barrier between themselves and their Creator, and so the flow of goodness is blocked. But when they themselves remove this barrier through prayer, then of itself the flow resumes, and the worshipper experiences an elevation of spirit and becomes more receptive to the good.

In the words of Yehudah Halevi:

> The Divine power is like the rain which
> waters the earth if the earth be fit to
> receive it.
> *Kuzari* III, 19

And in the words of Joseph Albo:

> The mercies of God, Praised by the Name,
> are drawn by prayer unto the pray-er
> according to the ability of the pray-er to receive them.
> *Ikkarim* LV, 17

By now, our generation has seen quite a few "holy men," persons reputedly possessing special religious powers. Some are quite impressive and seem, indeed, charismatically endowed. Their personal presences are strongly felt, and one's attention is drawn to that endowment. For their gifts I am grateful, and may their numbers increase.

I have not, however, met many "holiness men," persons with a special capacity to direct one's attention to the dimension of the holy to be found throughout all of life. Heschel was one such, a "holiness man" par excellence, and for that I am especially grateful.

Not that he was without presence. Quite the contrary. As Dorothea Straus recalls, there was a "serenity in his dark eyes . . . his long white hair and a flowing beard . . . caused a participant at Selma to exclaim, 'Dere is de Lawd!'" (cf. "A Variety of Religious Experience" in *Showcases*).

Yet with Heschel such qualities were only momentarily the focus. He had a rare capacity to point with his very being toward that from which his own sense of *k'dusha* (holiness) flowed. I still remember vividly the experience, as a young seminary student, of taking an evening seminar with Heschel. Preparing as best I could the – for me – difficult text, I entered the seminar room on the sixth floor of the seminary expecting that we'd immediately begin with textual discussion. Instead, Heschel turned toward the window overlooking the seminary courtyard, looking outside at the darkening remnants of the light, turned toward us, and quietly announced, "Gentlemen, a great event happened a short while ago. The Sun set. Were you aware of that? Did you notice?" And only after that introduction did he design to direct our attention to the words before us.

Heschel's sense of the holy is, of course, superbly expressed in his writings. For me he stands in the company of Isaiah and William Blake. His reflections on the sublime, wonder, the mystery, awe and reverence, and the glory are classic, and offer new riches with each re-reading (cf. pp. 36-58 in *Between God and Man*, edited by Fritz Rothschild). Simply to read Heschel's words is to be stirred by the sense of *k'dusha*.

Yet to read about is still not to experience fully. It is by way of tribute to that special sensitivity that Heschel so freely and eagerly shared that I'd like to offer one possible *kavanah* (focus of attention) for the *k'dusha* of our own liturgy. To approach the *k'dusha*, centered about the words of Isaiah –

> Holy, holy, holy, is the Lord of hosts;
> The whole earth is full of His glory.
>
> *Isaiah 6:3*

– I'd like to proceed in three stages: a brief word of theory; an application of the theory via an image; and a brief presentation of some supporting material from traditional sources.

Israel Efros, in Ancient Jewish Philosophy, *suggests that kadosh, holy,* and *kavod,* glory, are two opposing concepts in a polar tension that has determined the course of Jewish philosophy *K'dush* is the dynamic version of what in static philosophic terms we call transcendence: "Holiness tries to lift the God-idea ever above the expanding corporeal universe," he writes. *Kavod* is the dynamic version of what in static philosophic terms we call immanence: "Glory tends to bring the Creator ever nearer to man." *K'dusha* is "unapproachable because of ontological and ethical excellence"; *kavod* is God's craving "for the nearness of man . . . for the concrete." *K'dusha* is the far off, *kavod* the near at hand; *k'dusha* is beyond our reach, *kavod* is within our grasp.

Since the *k'dusha* is recited only at morning and afternoon services (never at evening services), light naturally emanating from the Sun is regularly available during its recitation. This invites some simple exercises:

1. If possible, place yourself in the rays of the Sun. Feel the warmth.

2. Close your eyes lightly while facing the Sun, and notice the amount of light that penetrates the eyelids.

3. Close the eyes more tightly. Light still penetrates, though less than before. (To check this, now cover the eyes with hands and notice the difference.)

4. Think further on this "immanence," this *kavod,* as it were, of the Sun. Notice how light and warmth from this far-off source penetrate and suffuse the body. And are not all warmth, all light, and all life on our planet directly or indirectly derived from this inflowing energy from the Sun?

5. Consider, now, the Sun in its "transcendent" aspect, out of reach, utterly destructive were one to come too near it, yet responsible, by its immanence, for all life on this planet. Is this not a precise symbolic representation of *kadosh* and *kavod?*

6. Now think further, drawing on astronomical knowledge concerning the number of Suns in the number of planetary systems in our universe, etc. Think? Fantasy! Who can think of such immensities?

7. Finally, try to imagine/fantasize/think of God/YHWH/the Divine standing in relation to all those Suns as our Sun stands in relation to our planet Earth. Such is the beginning of a sense of *k'dusha,* holiness!

Are there traditional sources that would support such an interpretation? I believe there are. To cite but ten:

1. The association of *kadosh* with transcendence:

> *"Kadosh"* is repeated three times because of the Holy One, Blessed be He, is totally different (i.e., totally transcendent) from body, spirit, and even intelligence.
> *"EtzYosef," in Otzar Hat'filot, p. 325*

> Why is *"kadosh"* thrice repeated? To emphasize that YHWH is high and lifted up above this earthly world of activity, high and lifted up above the heavenly world of planets and constellations, high and lifted up above the world of pure intelligence.
> *"Iyun T'filah," in Otzar Hat'filot, p. 267*

> The first *kadosh* refers to *keter/khokhma/bina* (the upper three *sefirot*); the second *kadosh* refers to *hesed/g'vura/tiferet* (the intermediate three *sefirot*); the third *kadosh* refers to *netzakh/hod/y'sod* (the three *sefirot* just above our world of *malkhut*).
> *Siddur Bet Yaakov of R. Jacob Emden, p. 61a*

2. The association of *kavod* with immanence:

> "The whole earth is full of His Glory," as in "and the earth did shine with His glory" (Ezekiel 43:2).
> *"Etz Yosef," in Otzar Hat'filot, p. 267*

> Afterward he brought me to the gate, even the gate that looketh toward the east; and, behold, the glory of the God of Israel came from the way of the east; and His voice was like the sound of many waters; and the earth did shine with His glory.
> *Ezekiel 43:1-2*

> "The whole earth is full of His glory": this is *Malkhut* (the *sefira* of our world).
> *Siddur Bet Yaakov, ibid.*

The Talmud's Kiddushin 31a and Berakhot 43b cite "The whole earth is full of His glory" in support of the rabbinic teaching that one must not walk "with stiff bearing or haughty mien" for even four cubits lest he "push against the heels or feet of the Divine Presence," the latter being identified with *kavod* or immanence.

3. The association of *kavod* with light and sustenance:

> As the appearance of the bow that is in the cloud in the day of rain, so was the appearance of the brightness round about. This was the appearance of the likeness of the glory of the Lord. And when I saw it, I fell upon my face, and I heard a voice of one that spoke.
>
> *Ezekiel 1:28*

> And the appearance of the glory of the Lord was like devouring fire on the top of the mount in the eyes of the children of Israel.
>
> *Exodus 24:17*

> And in the morning, then ye shall see the glory of the Lord; for that He hath heard your murmurings against the Lord; and what are we, that ye murmur against us?
>
> *Exodus 16:7 (referring to the mannah)*

> For the Leader. A Psalm of David.
> The heavens declare the glory of God.
> And the firmament showeth His handiwork.
>
> *Psalm 19: 1*

Here in Psalm 19 the association of *kavod,* glory, with the light is made explicit in verse 4, where reference is made to the Sun:

> There is no speech, there are no words,
> Neither is their voice heard.
> Their line is gone out through all the earth
> And their words to the end of the world.
> In them hath He set a tent for the Sun,
> Which is as a bridegroom coming out of his chamber,
> And rejoiceth as a strong man to run his course.

Heschel refers to this passage in his remarks on "The Glory."

At the same time, we must not *reduce* glory to this numinous experience from the realm of nature. Equally a part of Biblical *kavod* is justice in the human realm. Efros cites passages that illustrate such a connection, for example, Exodus 33:18-19 and 34:6-7, and Numbers 14:19-21, where *kavod* is associated with God's Thirteen Attributes and the compassionate involvement of the Divine in human history.

Holiness also at times has such a connotation. One of Heschel's favorite verses was "But the Lord of hosts is exalted through justice,/And God the

Holy One is sanctified through righteousness" (Isaiah 5:16). There is clearly a connection among holiness, glory, and social justice.

Heschel lived this dimension, too. He was often seen marching on behalf of racial justice with his dear friend and colleague Dr. Martin Luther King, Jr., and just as often on behalf of the Vietnamese victims of destruction with his friend and colleague Father Daniel Berrigan. Heschel's was no limited aesthetic sense of *kavod*, the numinous glory; it penetrated the texture of the daily life of our society as well, demanding that all of life show recognition of the inexpressible preciousness of God's creation.

With the important qualification, then, that the preceding "Sun *Kavannah*" be seen as but one facet of *kadosh-kavod*, not its entirety, I have offered it for consideration. Perhaps awareness of the Sun may give fuller life to Efros's exclamation: "And when Isaiah's Seraphim sing 'holy, holy, holy' and add 'the whole earth is full of His glory,' we hear the whole song of Israel containing both transcendence and immanence."

Has it any validity? The final test, surely, is neither theory nor proof texts but rather the experience of the worshipper in prayer. Perhaps in some small measure this *kavannah* will help increase our sense of *k'dusha* and *kavod*, of holy and glorious wonder, of "the miracles that are daily with us."

Toward such an end, in loving memory of Dr. Heschel, it is intended.

A *Niggun*

For some years, now, I have been off and on fascinated by one particular hymn from the Shabbat morning service, KHEY OLAMIM, found in Sephardic and Hasidic prayer books. One of the hymns from "The Greater Hekhalot," it is a powerful heaping of praises, alphabetically arranged, upon "The One Who Lives Forever."

Gershom Scholem talks about this Merkabah hymn and gives some backround in *Major Trends in Jewish Mysticism* (second lecture, section 5). Needless to say, there is much to discuss, especially regarding its nonrational, numinous characteristics. This, however tempting it may be, is not what I want to deal with here.

Instead, I'd like to share a *niggun*, a melody that I find helps the words of the hymn gain more effective expression. The *niggun* presented itself as suitable for these words, and I have found it to be so. (The only problem is one of mil-el/mil-ra, ultimate/penultimate stress, but that strikes me as not major and can be corrected if one so wishes.)

Once again, though this time indirectly, the spirit of Heschel hovers, for he loved a *niggun*, appreciated a melody. To him, singing was not incidental to the life of the spirit, it was essential. "We are losing the power of appreciation;" he wrote, "we are losing the ability to sing." By singing, he did not mean simply vocalizing or the production of sound, however beautiful. Though he had a keen musical appreciation of the vocal art, he was more concerned with singing as the expression of spirits lifted high by the awareness and celebration of existence: "The meaning of existence is experienced/by moments of exaltation."

For Heschel, both a reward and a responsibility of being human was "quiet exaltation, capability for celebration," and he found this expressed in a phrase that Rabbi Akiba offered to his disciples (cf. Sanhedrin 99b): "A song every day, a song every day." *Ze-mer b'khol yom, ze-mer b'khol yom.*

It is in this spirit that the following niggun is offered, together with a transliteration of the Hebrew:

From *Response*, Fall-Winter, 1982

The Process of Becoming

A Verse of Scripture, Framed by Memories

This 2015 essay-review explores process theology as practiced in Charles Hortshorne's Omnipotence and Other Theological Mistakes.

Ever since my first reading of Exodus in Hebrew school so very many years ago, I have been intrigued by the episode in which Moses asks God for the Divine Name by which S/He shall be made known to the people. Ehyeh is the terse reply: Ehyeh Asher Ehyeh.

Even then, the usual translations were feeble and unconvincing. "I am that I am?" Hey, give me a break. Even this beginning Hebrew student knew that *ehyeh* points to the future; it is not just a static term about the present. There began my decades-long search for an English rendering that would somehow convey the dynamism of that Name, with its intimations of impossible-to-imagine, novel events to come.

Reflecting on some personal events during 1962 to 1963, I can easily understand why Ehyeh exerted such a powerful pull on me as the Torah cycle came around to that verse in *parshat vayera*. I had just begun a six-year tenure at Princeton, New Jersey, my first U.S. congregation, in August. That same month I was jailed with Dr. King and other clergy colleagues in Albany, Georgia. Events during the following months were comparably startling. In Rodgers and Hammerstein terms, Ehyeh was bustin' out all over.

Especially memorable was my participation in a rabbinical delegation to Birmingham, Alabama in May, 1963, to lend support to the black community as it was assaulted with police dogs and fire-hoses in a manner that shocked our consciences and mobilized people to action throughout the nation. Follow-up talks for the NAACP in Oklahoma City and at a temple in Kansas City were the backdrop to my meeting Mary Loeb, my wife-to-be. What rendering of Ehyeh could possibly be dynamic enough to capture such a dramatic sequence of events? What wording could encapsulate the sense of limitless, undiscerned potential that might lurk in any given moment?

As *parshat vayera* came around, I tried several versions: I am in the process of becoming that which I am in the process of becoming; I Am Becoming that which I Am Becoming; I am the Process of Becoming that which I am Becoming; etc. The permutations and combinations were obvious attempts to link this enigmatic report of a Divine revelation to Moses with the process philosophy of Alfred North Whitehead, as given the fullest and most opaque expression in his *Process and Reality*. That daunting volume, based on the Gifford Lectures of 1927-28, represents a millennial advance in philosophical-theological thinking with its systematic, convincing substitution of Becoming for Being as the most basic term for understanding reality and expressing it as a whole.

The significance of this monumental reformulation for both theological consistency and people's day-to-day belief is the central theme of Charles Hartshorne's valuable volume, *Omnipotence and Other Theological Mistakes* (1984, SUNY Press).

Although carefully formulated and meticulously argued, the book is not a technical philosophical work (as are most of Hartshorne's other publications). It benefits, in fact, from the *al regel akhat* (off-the-cuff) circumstances of its composition. Quite analogously to Hillel's rising to the challenge of summarizing Torah while standing on one foot, Hartshorne feels moved to summarize and apply the significance of Becoming to some common problems of popular belief. The occasion? Two successive conversations with intelligent, educated women who were troubled "by what they felt were absurdities in the idea of God" familiar to them. In response, Hartshorne spends five weeks trying to explain, with precision but in accessible terms, "process theology," in the belief that "lives can be changed by showing that some of the traditional problems of belief – for instance how to reconcile the power and goodness of God with the evils we encounter in life – are genuinely solved, or at least greatly alleviated, by the view presented in this book."

Does this not describe countless rabbinical conversations with congregants? (Obviously Hartshorne's volume was not available to me in Princeton in 1962, although both I and my rabbinate did benefit enormously from my earlier studies with Hartshorne at the University of Chicago.) In fact, *Omnipotence and Other Theological Mistakes* is both convincing and helpful in resolving some profound yet common issues of faith that rabbis and their congregants confront daily.

It is also exemplary in demonstrating the practical importance of what might at first seem a remote theoretical matter. Becoming rather than Being as the foundation of a worldview? The practical consequences of this momentous shift for our human morale, for our trust in the world and our confidence in the value of human effort, are evident throughout the book.

Straight to the point, he begins by listing and explaining briefly six common mistakes about God, among them that God is perfect and unchanging. This is usually understood to mean that God is not affected by the world since He (the pronoun is reflective of a male bias that Hartshorne challenges), being perfect and infinite, can receive nothing from the world. But wait, Hartshorne asks, "Do or do not finite things contribute something to the greatness of God? . . . If you reply that the world contributes nothing to the greatness of God, then I ask, What are we all doing, and why talk about 'serving God,' Who, you say, gains nothing whatever from our existence?"

The obvious conclusion is that "the traditional idea of divine perfection or infinity is unclear or ambiguous." Further, it denies our dedication, our efforts, our lives any significance, so that "persisting in that tradition is bound to cause increasing skepticism, confusion, and human suffering. It has long bred, and must evermore breed, atheism as a natural reaction."

In like manner, he lists, analyzes, and clarifies other traditional characteristics of God that he finds unclear, ambiguous, or in error, among them the crucial notion of omnipotence. The usual rendering, God as allpowerful, is taken to mean that God is the possessor of the power to "strictly determine, decide . . . every detail" of happenings in the world. This invites immediate objections: What, then, of human freedom and responsibility? What, then, of the horrors of history? Hartshorne clarifies and refines the traditional idea of omnipotence, contrasts despotic and parental modes of power, scrutinizes the idea of determinism with full attention to modern physics, discerns "the significance of freedom . . . in the causal structure of the world," and concludes: "The only livable doctrine of divine power is that it *influences all* that happens but *determines nothing* in its concrete particularity" (italics added).

After a brief chapter on the physical and the spiritual that I found only moderately interesting, Hartshorne turns to the still-burning issue of evolution and creation. "Creation through Evolution" ranges widely and probes deeply. Among the topics briefly but insightfully addressed are evolution and belief in God; evolution, chance, and natural law; Darwin's mistake (Darwin, writes Hartshorne, failed to recognize that "God takes chances with free creatures" and instead saw – and feared, one might add – chance as an atheistic concept); chance, freedom, and the tyrant idea of God; the religious opposition to evolution; how God "makes things make themselves"; and creation neither out of nothing nor out of matter. In this latter section, he introduces the vital distinction between consciousness and sentience, and explains how this affects our entire understanding of the world and its development. Involved in this, it turns out, is our relationship to God and God's very nature!

> In the Bible, God is not just an unmoved "pure actuality," in purely eternal fashion planning the very details of worldly existence. According to Genesis, the initial creative action took time . . . At each stage God received new impressions of the goodness of the result. And then, as human beings came on the scene, God saw something not entirely good in the result and acted accordingly . . . there was action and reaction between Creator and creatures. There was the Covenant between God and Israel. The whole thing was a social transformation. Even the relations of God to "inanimate nature" seemed to take this form.

Earlier in the book, Hartshorne cites Harry Wolfson's definitive judgment that "the scholastic theology utterly failed to express the Biblical idea of God." In contrast, Hartshorne notes, with process philosophy and its portrayal of the universe in terms of organism, "we now have a philosophy in which the social structure, fully generalized, is the structure of reality." Both science and philosophy, so understood, view Creative Becoming as "much more pervasive and more nearly ultimate" than the static Being of medieval thought. Along with this monumental change come numerous implications, almost all for the better, in relation both to our Biblical understanding and our contemporary theologies. Hillel-like, at one point Hartshorne asserts in italics: "*Value and Sympathy as the Keys to Power: The Final Mystery.*" That, in like manner, carries with it the clear mandate to go forth and learn further!

For our everyday understanding of the universe in which we live, it is important that there be a primitive form of sentience included within the primal matter of creation. This paradigm shift from materialistic-mechanistic to organic-intentional clarifies many of the questions we confront, such as where/how did consciousness emerge if brute matter had no mental component, however tiny or alien. (A clear, understandable explanation of both the scientific and the religious meaning is provided by my colleague William Kaufman in *The Case for God,* Chapter 5, "Creativity and the Cosmic Adventure," 1991, Chalice Press.)

I'm tempted to linger further on Hartshorne and evolution, especially since, as the *Stanford Encyclopedia of Philosophy* reminds us, he is the first philosopher since Aristotle who is also a recognized ornithologist. Indeed, Hartshorne makes brief reference to his own work, *Born to Sing: An Interpretation and World Survey of Bird Song* to provide "quantitative observational evidence . . . for the hypothesis that singing birds have a primitive form of what in us we call an aesthetic sense of musical feeling." The volume, published in the gold-standard ornithological series by Indiana University Press, thus provides a significant natural phenomenon that is scientifically supportive of the view that the more logically coherent interpretation of reality is the organic-intentional, not the materialistic.

Early in *Omnipotence,* Hartshone remarks that "God, I hold, is no mere abstraction." The tone of engagement throughout the book becomes even more intense in the final chapter, "Equal Love for Self and Other, All-Love for the All-Loving." After some trenchant remarks about heaven and hell as well as an illuminating analysis of the question of personhood and abortion, he turns to "the two great commandments (as designated by Jesus): 'love God with all your being (heart, mind, strength) and your neighbor as yourself.'" Since these are the opening lines of *v'ahavta* (Deuteronomy 6:9) and the *khay* verse of Leviticus 19, his interpretations are at least of midrashic interest. They provide the context for a number of comments about aspects of God that have not been earlier addressed, and they prompt the evolutionary reminder that "God does not simply and completely make things, but brings it about that they partly make themselves and one another." He also quotes "from a Jewish ritual, God 'gives to our fleeting days abiding significance.'"

The quest for Jewish spirituality must ultimately involve us in questions of theology. Twenty-first-century responses to questions about God need both grounding in past efforts as well as awareness of contemporary advances in thinking about God. Not only rabbis, but increasing numbers of congregants, are seeking such exploration and clarification. Never has the need been more urgent, and not since Maimonides, I suggest, have we had such excellent theological resources at hand to address the need.

From *CCAR Journal: The Reform Jewish Quarterly,* Spring, 2015

Turn, Turn, Turn

Prayer Wheels and Judaism

This Buddhist Prayer Wheel and the Blessing of the Sun ceremony are given a place in Jewish worship in this 1982 essay.

So here it is, early spring. I'm fantasizing about the *Birkhat Hakhamah* (Blessing of the Sun) ceremony soon to be celebrated, and these words and the popular tune (by Pete Seeger) that accompanies them keep sounding in my mind's ear: *To everything (turn, turn, turn) there is a season (turn, turn, turn . . .)*

But wait a minute, these are out-of-season! Verses from Ecclesiastes? They're part of autumn's ritual, not spring's.

Though out of season, they persist, and no attempt on my part to think them away has any effect. So I 'enter' those words, turn with them, and then realized that the forthcoming Blessing of the Sun ceremony indeed needs something 'turning' as well. What might that be?

Why not a round disc rather like the sun, whose rotation and completion of a great circle we were soon to celebrate? Hmm, interesting.

But what should it look like? Clearly it should be round, and large, and able to rotate. It should also carry on it words from the tradition that accurately expressed what this special celebration is about. But which words?

Well, why not the fine acrostic *"El Adon al kol hamaasim"* from the Shabbat morning service? It celebrates God as Creator of the Luminaries and is, in fact, traditionally associated with this once-every-twenty-eight-year ceremony. Yet beautiful though it is, it is also somewhat too long and wordy for this particular purpose.

But it has an abbreviated counterpart in the daily morning service, also alphabetical, celebrating God as Creator of the Luminaries, powerfully rhythmic, and terse – only one word for each letter of the *aleph-bet*:

El barukh g'dol dea,

hekhin ufa'al zohore khama
tov yatzar kavod lishmo
M'orot natan s'vivot uzo
Pinot tz'vaav kedoshim, romeme shadai,
Tamid m'saprim d'vod el ukedushato.

The Blessed God, great in knowledge
designed and shaped the brilliant sun.
The Beneficent One thereby glorified the Name,
The Ever-Caring One placed luminaries round the Cosmic Majesty.
The chief hosts are holy beings that extol the Almighty.
They constantly recount God's glory and holiness.

Not only does it stand on its own merits, but a most intriguing legend of origins accompanies it (as told in *Sidur Otzar Hatefilot,* commentary of "Etz Yosef"):

> When R. Eleazar Kallir wanted to write *piyuttim*, he ascended to heaven by means of the Divine Name, there to ask [the Archangel] Michael in what manner the angels sang God's praises and what shape their songs assumed. And Michael replied, "They sing in order of aleph-bet." And so R. Eleazar Kallir also wrote acrostics in praise of God. Thus here (in El Barukh) one finds both the acrostic form and, where the acrostic ends, M'saprIm K'vod EL, MIKaEL, alluding to Michael.

An Eleazar Kallir acrostic celebrating God as Light-Giver, written under the influence of a heavenly consultation with the Archangel Michael; could there be a more fitting inscription for an authentic Hebrew Sun Wheel?

Between inspiration and execution there is sometimes a chasm. Fortunately, an exceptionally gifted liturgical artist, Karen Frostig, picked up the cues and designed a perfectly stunning Sun Wheel. The disc itself, four feet in diameter, I had cut at a precision machine shop from white birch plywood. The edges are just enough larger than the closet pole that I purchased so that, after carefully sanding, waxing, and polishing the pole, the disc would just slip on and rotate smoothly. Two doughnut-shaped small pieces of plywood slipped on at either end of the

pole helped keep the disc upright for its numerous spinnings during the ceremony. As for the design itself, Karen wrote this:

> On the Fourth Day
> Sun
> Sun Wheel
> Round Center
> Center of the Universe
> Center of the Spirit Self
> Infinite Home.
> Watersrushing Landbeing
>   Airknowing Firespeaking;
> Sun
> Sun Wheel
> Round Round Center.

Needless to say, the Sun Wheel was a wonderful energy focus at the sunrise ceremony we held on the beach. Its gold-green-yellow-orange-red-blue-purple-white colors shimmered undulatingly before the eyes. During singing and dancing, chanting and movement, how it turned, how it spun, how it glistened in the sun! Besides the sheer aesthetic enjoyment, its energy reflected and augmented our own.

Small wonder that the prayer wheel is highly esteemed in some cultures. Might there not be a place for authentic Hebraic designs on such wheels as part of our own traditional celebrations today? Wheels, after all, have an honorable history in Jewish religious life through the ages, and are intimately associated with the numinous experience. From Elijah's chariot through Ezekiel, and from the circular sun-centered Zodiac mosaic of Bet Alpha through the circular signs of the Zodiac in Polish wooden synagogues, such wheels function as powerfully evocative symbols of the nonrational. My own experience leads me to believe that the time is ripe and the spirit ready for a reinitiation of such aids to *kavanah* at our services, especially as we seek fuller expression in prayer for the numinous-seeking parts of ourselves.

Now that the *Birkhat Hakhamah* is over for another twenty-eight years, what happens to this Sun Wheel? Since at Temple Emanuel we celebrate each change of season with some special addition to the service, four times each year the Sun Wheel will spin again, God willing, on the *bimah* of our temple, in celebration of the never-ceasing cycle of "seedtime and harvest, and cold and heat, and summer and winter, and day and night," so long as our earth exists.

From *Response*, Numbers 41-42, 1981

From Chore to Ceremony

Reconnecting Work with Worship

This 2009 essay tells a story of personal transformation of the chores of living into moments of worship.

Work and worship: what is their connection? Since the Hebrew word *"avodah"* can refer to either or to both, presumably they are linked in some way. But how? The same might be asked about "karma," the well-known Hindu term that refers both to simply doing something, engaging in action, and to devotion through doing, worship by performing certain actions with distinct intentions.

The question is intriguing, and I used to struggle for a convincing answer. Looking back, I'm embarrassed to think about all the comments I inflicted on congregants as I was trying to clarify these ancient equivalencies. I would lament how weakened their connection had become in our contemporary, advanced but perhaps not advantaged ways of living. When I would talk about this attenuation between the daily and the devotional, I'd often detect an undertone of longing in my voice, wishing that our lives were not so spiritually zoned, the sacred so safely separated from the secular.

On several occasions over the years, I tried to explore possible ways of strengthening the connections between the world of work and the world of worship, but rather than finding present-day examples, I ended up mostly with words, not deeds. I continued to find the idea appealing, but the secret of how to give it lived expression, not simply verbalization, remained hidden from me.

Now, in that state of idleness/puttering/reverie/contemplation to which a passport stamped "retirement" gains one entrance, a few parts of the secret have at last come my way. The discoveries are quite a delight, and I'd like to share them briefly. But first, to reassure skeptics, a word of clarification. To assert that some routine tasks can be ritualized, thereby conveying a sense of the broader context within which we live, is not to claim that all drudgery can be redeemed from its enervating effects. There is, after all, along with the classical work-worship equivalence, also the category of *m'lekhet avodah*, servile work that resists spiritual rescue! Post-Eden, at least some drudgery has been a constant in human experience.

Let me now share, step by step, the stages through which my discovery moved.

Once, near the time of summer solstice, I was changing the filter on the water system for our house in the Berkshires. Because municipal water lines do not reach our part of town, our water comes from a drilled well near the house, and the system requires some personal maintenance. For reasons that not even the well-driller can figure out, the water from this artesian well, although of generally fine quality, still contains some very fine sediment eight years after the drilling was completed, so a fine-sediment filter is essential, and it needs to be changed every three months or so.

Certain flow and shut-off valves need to be turned; the canister containing the filter needs to be loosened, the old filter removed, the canister cleaned, the new filter inserted, petroleum jelly applied as a sealant at the top, the canister tightened, and the valves again turned. Nothing elaborate, a simple task.

Near this particular solstice, I was thinking that the water filter would soon need changing, and I was also rereading the section on Season (*t'kufah*) from J.D. Eisenstein's *Otzar Dinim Uminhagim* ("A Digest of Jewish Laws and Customs," Hebrew Publishing Company, 1917). As I read it this time, the familiar section, before only theoretical, now seemed to relate directly and practically to the task at hand: "It is customary to take care to avoid drinking water at the precise time of the turning of the seasons." Hmm: an association of water and seasons. What is this about? Eisenstein then quotes a fascinating explanation by David Abudirham, the 14th-century Spanish commentator from Seville who often includes folk customs and mythic material in his commentary (my translation):

> I have found written that one should take care, at each of the four seasons, not to drink water at the hour of equinox or solstice, for at such times there is danger of swelling and illness from drinking the water.
>
> For it was at Vernal Equinox that the waters of Egypt were turned to blood (Exodus 7:19-25). It was at Summer Solstice that Moses and Aaron struck rather than spoke to the rock, and blood gushed forth (cf. Numbers 20:8). It was at Autumnal Equinox that Abraham, binding his son Isaac upon

the altar (Genesis 22), shed some drops of Isaac's blood, which spread through all the waters. It was at Winter Solstice that Jephtha's daughter was sacrificed (Judges 11:29-40), and all the world's waters were turned to blood. And so annually, at each turning of the seasons, the ancient contaminations may recur.

Abudirham is aware of skepticism and a division of opinion within the community. Not having Sir James Frazer's *The Golden Bough* at hand, he responds (in *Shaar Hatekufot,* as cited in Rabbi Abraham Isaac Sperling's *Taamei Haminhagim,* 1890):

> Some call these divinations or old wives' tales. But others say that for each season a guardian is appointed over the waters. Along with each change of seasons comes a changing of the guards, and at the precise moment of the exchange, the waters are without protection.

One need not be persuaded by the explanation of the changing of the guardians to wonder: Might this myth represent an unconscious memory of seasonal sacrifices offered in the dim past of human nistory? Were there such ceremonies? Scholarly opinions vary. I find that Sir James Frazer, Theodor Gaster, and Mircea Eliade always provide stimulating reading; the fascinating details of various seasonal practices that they amass are quite compelling, and some do involve the shedding of blood.

However, for this practice-oriented discovery, let me remain focused on how to convert chore to ceremony. I simply note that some association of blood with the succession of the seasons clearly persisted in the 14th-century Judeo-Spanish community, and it provided a rationale for two specific religious practices that Abudirham now describes:

> At these times [of seasonal changes] some place a piece of iron (*barzel*) upon well covers, storage tanks, and water containers, confident that the Merits of the Mothers Bilhah, Rachel, Zilpah, and Leah (BRZL) will protect us all from harm.
>
> Still others, avoiding drinking water at those times of turning, eat sweets instead, that the coming season be a sweet one.

Lest there be misunderstanding or suspicion of reliance on other deities, Abudirham adds these words to his description of this latter custom: "But I say that for the person who worships the One God, trusting in Him alone, each season will be sweet in its turn."

How might this myth and these folk practices serve us today? I have begun to experiment with a number of different ways to incorporate this mythic-ceremonial material into the chore of changing the water filter. So far I've not come up with an appealing way to adopt the iron bar, but let me share some of the other customs.

First of all, I try to change the water filter on or very near the seasonal solstice or equinox. If that coincides with Shabbat, then either the day before or the day after is the time I select for changing the filter.

Next, I reread the material from Abudirham, and recite this *b'rakha* (devised for another seasonal ritual by my colleague Rabbi Neil Kominsky):

> Barukh atah Adonai, Eloheinu Melekh ha'olam,
> Hamakhalif et haz'manim.
>
> You overflow with blessings, Eternal our God, Sovereign of All Creation, impelling the succession of the seasons.

I then turn off the flow valves, change the filter, clean the canister, and replace the filter. After turning back on the flow valves, I read Genesis 8:22 in Hebrew and English:

> While the earth remaineth,
> seedtime and harvest,
> and cold and heat,
> and summer and winter,
> and day and night
> shall not cease.

Following that, I read the appropriate poem for the season from William Blake's *Poetical Sketches*. For this approaching autumnal equinox:

> To Autumn
>
> O Autumn, laden with fruit, and stain'd
> With the blood of the grape, pass not, but sit
> Beneath my shady roof; there thou may'st rest,
> And tune thy jolly voice to my fresh pipe,
> And all the daughters of the year shall dance!
> Sing now the lusty song of fruits and flowers.
>
> "The narrow bud opens her beauties to
> The sun, and love runs in her thrilling veins;
> Blossoms hang round the brows of Morning, and
> Flourish down the bright cheek of modest Eve,
> Till clust'ring Summer breaks forth into singing,

And feather'd clouds strew flowers round her head.

"The spirits of the air live in the smells
Of fruit; and Joy, with pinions light, roves round
The gardens, or sits singing in the trees."
Thus sang the jolly Autumn as he sat,
Then rose, girded himself, and o'er the bleak
Hills fled from our sight; but left his golden load.

The foregoing is the kernel of the ceremony, the *matbea*, as it were, of the ritual. What comes next depends entirely upon circumstances. If it is a leisurely day, I might listen to the appropriate instrumental selection from Vivaldi's "The Four Seasons," or if in a vocal-choral mood, the parallel section from Haydn's "The Seasons."

Of course, there is a much other classical music that for me also feels naturally associated with given seasons. A few examples: For spring, Stravinsky's "Rite of Spring" and Parts 3 and 4 of Mahler's *"Das Lied von der Erde."* For summer, Berlioz's *"Les Nuits d'Ete"* and Bernstein's "Jeremiah" Symphony. For autumn, Brahm's Horn Trio Opus 40 and Parts 1 and 2 of Mahler's *"Das Lied von der Erde."* For winter, two of Handel's Oratorios, "Jephtha" and "The Messiah."

Those with different musical predilections could certainly compile comparable lists. "Turn! Turn! Turn!" and Carole King's "You've Got a Friend" come immediately to mind, and there are surely many more from which to choose. Poetry? Or course. Add your own favored poems of the season.

Meditation/reflection almost always adds a dimension to any worship experience, inviting both inward exploration and outward expansion. Since our focus here has been water, consider the familiar verse from Isaiah (12:3) that we often sing: *ush'avtem mayim b'sason*, "And you will draw water joyfully from the wells of salvation."

Inwardly, we might consider: What are for us "wells of salvation"? What are the spirit-sustaining, life-enhancing sources of inspiration for each of us? Which are traditionally Jewish? Have we additional wells that inspire us? Perhaps special teachings or practices from other religious traditions that deepen our own Jewish practices? Perhaps cherished teachings from philosophical traditions that we find especially uplifting? How do we "draw" from these wells? Are there problems with the waters mingling and mixing? How do we integrate these elements so that our lives, fed from many streams, become truly *mei m'nuchot*, "still waters," not whirlpools? Exploring these questions can be a personally refreshing experience.

And if, however unlikely, you also have a well, then outwardly speaking, you might find it interesting to ask: What kind of well is it? A shallow-dug, a deep-drilled, or an artesian? What is the water quality? Is there sediment in the water? What does this reveal about the course of the water and the effects of digging or drilling? Further, how is it that water in direct surface contact with dirt is contaminated, whereas water that seeps through twenty feet of dirt is purified? Ashes of the red heifer quickly come to mind, don't they, with their purifying and polluting capacities? At this material level there is, indeed, material for meditation.

Sweets? Why not follow the Judeo-Spanish custom to which Abudirham refers and eat sweets that the season to come be a sweet one? Begin with the blessing, *shehakol nihyeh bid'varo*, "by Whose word all came into being," followed by a *shehekheyanu*, and then munch on some *turron*/Spanish nougat, sesame candies, heart-healthy dark chocolate, *rugelakh, teyglakh*, marzipan, who knows? Perhaps a small selection of sweets, to be washed down by a cup of the now freshly filtered water? The possibilities are endless and not to be resisted.

This detailed description of a simple chore that invited cermonialization will, I hope, stimulate others' discovering other examples that could sustain similar ritualization. We must be wary of contrivance, of trying too hard to construct connections that aren't anchored in the reality of the task itself. If we are alert to this possible way of reconnecting work with worship, however, it is my sense that with time we shall discover many more such connections than we can now imagine. Those discoveries might be the links that can once again, on occasion, bind work and worship for our own lives today, and so reclaim the full meaning of *avodah*.

From *The CCAR Journal: The Reform Jewish Quarterly,* Summer, 2009

The Parsley versus the Potato

A Passover Remembrance

For Rabbi Gendler, a childhood in the agricultural state of Iowa was marked by a potato on the seder plate.

Potato *versus* parsley? Surely a misprint, a reader might think, familiar with that old American standby, parsleyed potatoes. Yet however harmonious their culinary relations, their ritual rivalry was quite another matter in the days of my childhood.

Each year our Passover plate had on it *kharoset*, horseradish, an egg, a shankbone, a potato, and the bowl of salt water. Thus was the mandate from Sinai, rabbinically interpreted, played out at the Gendlers' table in Chariton, Iowa, the farmtown of 5,000 where I spent my first eleven years. The familiarity of the plate was reassuring, and the potato dipped in salt water, eaten so soon after the sweet *kiddush* wine, was just the carbohydrate fix that a small child needed to sit through those seemingly endless pages of prayers.

All was coherent, even unto the blessing, *bo-re p'ri ha-a-da-mah,* Who createth the fruit of the ground – for the potato, like all vegetables, was not only appropriately designated fruit of the earth, but could even lay claim to a special connection with soil. Most vegetables, after all, grow above ground, while the potato tuber, the edible part, develops totally within the earth's protective soil. If ever there were a proper candidate for the blessing, *p'ri ha-a-da-mah,* the potato had strong claim to the honor. From one Passover unto the next, the potato annually occupied the place of honor as the first item eaten from the seder plate.

Let it be admitted that even amidst this wholeness and harmony there was one discordant note: When I learned to read and looked myself into the *Maxwell House Haggadah,* something seemed amiss; their instructions made mention of lettuce or parsley, not potatoes. Concerned inquiries directed to my parents yielded no answer but the mere reassertion that, whatever that *goyishe* book might think, of course the potato was the proper vegetable for the seder plate. So it had been with their ancestors in the Ukraine, and so it was to be here in Iowa as well. There the matter rested.

Until we moved to Des Moines. There in the big city, our traditional country ways were once more seriously challenged. There, too, the *haggadot* seemed to favor parsley or lettuce or even celery! Worse yet, from informal discussions with my Hebrew school classmates it became obvious that ours was a backward home, out of step with the sophisticated Jewish world of seder plates graced with delicate, lacy greens, not lumpy boiled potatoes.

Throughout the years of my adolescence, as time to prepare the seder plate approached, the issue would erupt anew. Eventually, nearly as I can recall, parsley also occupied the seder plate, but boiled potatoes were also present, dominated but not wholly dispossessed. The parsley would be dipped first, but the potato followed immediately. Even I, the advocate of the big city assimilationist intrusions on our traditional seder plate, even I had to admit to myself (though never to my parents) that the potato was, indeed, both more tasty and more filling than the parsley newcomer.

Looking back, to me now, the reason for this variation of custom is obvious. It was a climatic variation determined by environmental conditions. Long ago in the Ukraine, where winter lingered late, where Bio-Snacky seed sprouters were unknown and fresh greens from California or Florida were beyond anyone's ken, what else could serve for the blessing over the fruit of the ground but some remainder of a root crop from the previous growing season?

Today on our family seder plate, parsley and potato peacefully coexist, their sharing yet another sign of the marvelous adaptability of Jewish ritual tradition. But in these days of increasing environmental awareness, they serve, also, as reminders of the wondrous variety of climates and circumstances in which our people have lived through the ages. May both the awareness and the variety long continue!

From *Ecology and the Jewish Spirit:
Where Nature and the Sacred Meet,* Ellen Bernstein, editor, 1998

Lag B'Omer and May Day

Counting the Omer with Actual Plantings

This brief, practical 1985 essay describes Lag B'Omer as the Jewish May Day and prescribes some joyous ways to celebrate.

It was Theodor Gaster who pointed out (in *Festivals of the Jewish Year*), with substantial supportive evidence, that Lag B'Omer, the thirty-third day of the Counting of the Omer, is our Jewish equivalent of May Day. If not equivalent, they are surely related – in both instances, anxiety over whether things will grow on schedule is expressed in symbolic actions that break up the tension – and they syncretize most harmoniously.

For many, many years, our family has held an annual May Day-Lag B'Omer celebration in our small hay-field. Selecting a Sunday more or less near both dates – with allowance, of course, for New England's unpredictable spring weather – we've invited friends and neighbors to join us for a variety of outdoor activities. Most distinctive is a ritual procession around the periphery of the field, each person carrying some freshly cut winter rye, while at the head of the procession is a recently cut, eighteen-foot-high tree with eighteen ribbons stapled to it near the top (the *khay* motif). Also at the head of the procession is carried a *keter,* a crown for the May/Omer Pole, constructed earlier in the week from freshly cut branches. Attached to it are brightly colored pieces of fabric inscribed with appropriate verses from Torah, from Chaucer, or from e.e. cummings, or whatever choice our fantasy may dictate that particular year.

After marching around the edges of the field, we head for the center, place the crown atop the pole, then erect and plant the May/Omer Pole securely. At this point, everyone joins in dance to do the traditional weaving of the ribbons around the pole.

Further possibilities exist for giving substance to the otherwise abstract ceremony of numbering the seven weeks between Passover and Shavuot. For some years now, both at home in the garden and at synagogue with students, I've planted winter rye during Sukkot. The rye generally germinates within ten days, grows a bit, then braces itself for winter. In early spring, well before the ground can be worked, the rye resumes its growth. Depending on seasonal conditions and how early or late Pesakh arrives, by the time the omer counting begins, one can cut each night (or prior to Shabbat) a good handful of rye for the numbering. As the counting continues, the rye grows steadily taller, and usually begin to head out before Shavuot, forming spikelets and revealing the grains-in-formation.

Not only is the steady development of the grain exciting to watch, one can make use of the lengthening stalks, bound into sheaves, to perform the beautiful acts of "waving" prescribed in Leviticus 23:15-16, 20.

In these ways, one can achieve a renewed sense of the wondrous and life-sustaining power of the grain cycle, a central seasonal theme of the Passover to Shavuot passage.

Other rhythmic, seasonal resources that invite adoption include Summer Solstice readings and ceremonies, Winter Solstice readings and ceremonies, and a Lunar Torch for use at New Moons and Full Moons. Suggestive starter details of these possibilities are available from me – just ask!

> Adapted from *The Jewish Holidays: a Guide and Commentary*
> by Michael Strassfeld, 1985, Harper Row

Post-Biblical Paganism

The Case for *Tammuz*

The summer month of Tammuz, according to this essay, is marked on the Jewish calendar as a reminder of the ancient pagan appreciation of the power of nature.

Hebrew-speaking Jews, like plain-speaking Quakers, designate the days of the week ordinally: first day, second day, etc. Except for the Sabbath (and perhaps the echoes of the Creation epic in Genesis, which so designates the days), among Jews no day of the week carries with it any hint of the religio-cultural background from which it emerged. This stands in rather sharp contrast to the common designation of the days of the week in English, each of which draws attention to some heavenly body or mythical figure after which it was named: Sun, Moon, Mars, etc.

Hebrew months, unlike the days, however, are not designated ordinally. Each has a name, and some of the names are directly suggestive of their origins. An example is the Hebrew month of *Tammuz*. Corresponding to June-July in the secular ordering of months, this denizen of summer is well known to antiquity. Called Adonis by the Greeks, for the Mesopotamians he represented "the divine power to new life" in four different aspects: "1) a power in the sap that rises in trees and plants, *Damu;* 2) a power in the date palm and its fruits, *Dumuzi Ama-ushumgal-anna;* 3) a power in grain and beer, *Dumuzi* of the Grain; and 4) a power in milk, *Dumuzi* the Shepherd" (Thorkild Jacobson, *Toward the Image of Tammuz*, Harvard University Press, 1971).

So it happens that annually, as the Blessing of the New Moon is recited during the Sabbath morning service preceding that month, synagogues throughout the world echo the proclamation of the name of *Tammuz*. Thus it is the Hebrew calendar, our catechism, that reminds us of an ancient appreciation of a power in nature symbolized by *Tammuz*. The pagan, *i.e.*, rural, residue persists even to this day.

How shall we regard this residue? Shall we ignore its existence, deny its significance, or enjoy its presence? There was, I believe, a period in the history of human consciousness when the first two responses were appropriate. The multiplicity of god and goddess figures was still too powerful psychically to be tolerated by the slowly-emerging slip of consciousness, and so the representations and projections of elemental or unconscious forces had to be held firmly in check.

In our own time, however, that seems to me to be no longer the case. It is now appropriate to welcome *Tammuz*, not as Deity, but rather as an imaginative, evocative figure symbolizing a power in nature to which we can all relate appreciatively. Subordinate to our sense of the Divine, *Tammuz* may well have a place in our contemporary worship which, at its best, seeks to re-awaken our awareness of that wider sphere of nature within which our life on this earth is lived.

Thus a service at the beginning of the month of Tammuz might include some special nature poetry, Tchernichowsky's "Lament on the Death of *Tammuz*," and excerpts from the interesting Jacobsen essay cited earlier. *Ama-ushumgal-anna,* "the power in and behind the date palm," might be chanted, accompanied by the sounds of tambourines, as dates are distributed for eating with special *kavanah*.

No longer in competition with *Kudshah Brikh Hu* (The Holy One, Blessed is He), now clearly but a partial manifestation of the Life Stream, Tammuz can serve to increase our appreciation both of this earth and of the Great, Unseen Giver of All Life, YHWH.

Inheritors of the Biblical process of pagan purification, this seems to me one instance where we might feel free to reclaim elements which are consonant with our general religious outlook, and so enliven both our worship and ourselves.

1974

Illumination and Renewal

The Markers of Rosh Hashanah

How do we strive for renewal rather than repetition during the familiar rituals of the Jewish New Year? How do we cope with the anxiety of self-transformation? This brief essay from 1984 offers some clues.

I have always found that the onset of a new year provokes in me both hope and fear. I hope, of course, that the new year will be new not only calendrically but personally. Along with the fresh pages of the calendar, I'd like some fresh insights, and fetching new pictures should ideally hint at fetching new experiences waiting to surprise and delight me.

But I'm also fearful. What if the new year ahead is mainly a re-run of the one I've just survived? What if the odds point to enervating repetition rather than exhilarating renewal as the likely experience of the year to come? After all, the same old job or same old school, same old professors or same old people are what most of us see as we glance at the year ahead. Stability and continuity may be the benefits of such repetition, but boredom may be the price, and who wants to pay it? Altogether it's an irksome dilemma, and there's no easy way out.

Sorry to say, I don't know any magical formula to resolve it, and so I face it annually along with most other mortals. I am also aware, however, that in subtle but significant ways my own experience is, on the whole, one of a reassuring amount of novelty and renewal within the established patterns of my life and work.

How does this happen? One part is plain old *mazal*: the good fortune of having intrinsically interesting work in congenial and supportive settings, together with loving family relationships and ongoing friendships which continually grow and develop. For these I'm grateful – when I don't take them simply for granted, or, worse yet, fail to notice them.

But *mazal* alone is not enough. We're all prone to fall prey to routinization of the everyday, even when it's filled with possibility, simply because of the unavoidable repetitiveness. How to deal with this danger? Personally, I am helped immeasurably by my acquaintance with some valuable teachings from Jewish tradition about ways of renewing our life experiences so that they retain (or regain) their freshness, even after long familiarity. One of my favorite teachers of such wisdom is Reb Judah Aryeh Leib of Gur (1847-1905), head of the Gerer dynasty from 1870-1905, whose teachings of Torah and holidays were recorded by his students in the work *S'fat Emet*.

Some of Reb Judah's comments on Rosh Hashanah and its symbols are revealing of ways of renewal, and I'd like to share, in interpreted translation, a few of his words about the Rosh Hashanah verse from Psalm 81: "Sound the shofar at the New Moon,/ When the hidden marks our feast-day."

Along with these, I'll add some suggestions for their application.

"Rosh Hashanah refers to a time before the Flow of Divine Vitality suf-fered differentiation," says *S'fat Emet*. "When the Divine emanation entered this natural world of time and space, the formless spiritual became material form. Rosh Hashanah takes us to the Primordial Fount of Being, a Source whose origin precedes any material form. . . [T]he sound of the *shofar* is a voice without words, reminiscent of the Divine voice at creation which, prior to its becoming words and meanings, was single, undifferentiated, and attached to its Source. On Rosh Hashanah, the Creative Vitality is once again attached to its Source, as in primordial, undifferentiated time."

Those of scholarly bent might recognize (perhaps with some surprise) the above as a succinct, classic portrayal in some respects of *ila tempore,* the mythic state preceding time so well described by Mircea Eliade.

Those of reflective bent, seeking to put the rebbe's words to personal use, might try some imaginative exercises. Let me suggest one:

Focus on your job/profession/calling/vocation. Summon in detail the requirements and restrictions it places upon you, and recall the specific acts you regularly perform in conformity with those requirements and restraints.

Next, formulate very precisely the central aim or chief purpose of your calling. Holding onto that basic sense of purpose, try to dissolve the forms and conventions, rules and regulations that presently govern your actions in this field.

Finally, fantasize some new ways of acting to serve that purpose, new ways of doing to reach that goal, new ways of thinking to achieve that end.

Find some new ways? Great: That's a start toward more novelty amidst the routine. End up with the old ones again? Fine: Appreciate anew their value in realizing (making real) that goal, and enjoy them afresh for their contribution to that purpose. Either way, you're a winner and life's the fresher.

Returning, now, to the Gerer Rebbe: "Even though Rosh Hashanah is a Day of Judgment, on it, as on every other Jewish festival, there is augmented light for every Jew. Hence the designation *yom tov* (literally, a good day), by virtue of the hidden light which shines forth on each such holiday. For every Jew on such occasions there is illumination by the hidden light of goodness, that 'light sown for the righteous' which lies hidden within.

"Though of necessity concealed from worldly view, within the heart of each Jew there exists a point directly connected with the Divine . . . It is important for a person to know inwardly that of the Divine within the self . . . for the greater a person's awareness of this hidden Divine Within, the stronger the person's connection with the Divine. Hence, 'when the hidden marks our feast day.'"

A dangerous but redemptive teaching, this one! The dangers? Self-inflation and smugness, self-righteousness and superiority. On the other hand, given the diminishing self-respect we seem able to extend to humankind at this point in history, a sense of the Divine Within may be essential to your salvation. Unrealistic illusions about how good we are may damage us; erroneous convictions about how bad we are will destroy us. Not from despair but from chastened hope may redemption come.

Understandable, then, the Jewish emphasis on the *tzelem elohim* (Divine image) of Genesis, the Quaker affirmation of "that of God in every person," the Hindu identification of Atman with Brahman, the Buddhist proclamation of the Buddha-nature, the Taoist discernment of the uncarved block, etc.

So where does this leave us at Rosh Hashanah? Invited to discover new aspects of ourselves, qualities hitherto unknown or unappreciated but perhaps of unanticipated value to others and to ourselves. Isaiah's "treasures of darkness, and hidden riches of secret places" may well be the rewards of some careful attention to these less known, sometimes deliberately voided, qualities within.

Let, then, the light of Rosh Hashanah shine brightly and penetrate the self, that new discoveries of the Divine Within truly renew the year to come.

L'shana tova tikatevu.

From *Genesis 2,* September-October 1984

On Illuminating the Sukkah

The Yaakov (Jacob) Lantern to the Rescue

This 1985 essay suggests importing the Halloween Jack-o'-Lantern into the Sukkah to extend our time there and renew our sense of Sukkot as an agricultural festival.

Since eating in a *sukkah* is part of the point of building one, the more meals eaten in it, the better. At night, despite the brilliance of the full moon, additional illumination is almost always needed, especially later in the holiday when moonrise is much later than the usual dinner hour. What are the possibilities?

Some use electric lights or lamps, adequate for illumination but not authentic reminders of desert wanderings or ancient harvest booths. Covered with Japanese lantern shades, they're better, but still not quite right. Kerosene lamps look good, give off adequate light, but their petroleum fuel and their fumes might give one pause. Propane lamps hiss excessively and also emit fumes. Candles are nice, yet can hardly be kept lighted in the wind without protective covering of some sort. Glass hurricane lamps? Not bad, but rather breakable for outdoor table use, so still not it.

We've used for many years a different source of illumination, which we highly recommend: the Yaakov (Jacob) Lantern, a recently discovered Jewish offshoot of the primordial autumnal pumpkin whose more widely known descendant is the Jack-o'-Lantern.

The Yaakov Lantern, a pumpkin carved with the *magen David*/Star of David, can nicely accommodate a thick candle. The bright orange shell protects the flame from the wind and brightens the *sukkah* with its color, while the *magen David* openings permit maximum light of significantly appropriate shape to emanate from the candle. Alternately, one side can be carved with the *magen David* while the other side can have a traditional Jack-o'lantern face with small stars of David for eyes and an elongated star of David for the nose.

The advantages are several. Here in the U. S., the lantern has a real seasonal feel and, pumpkins being easy to grow in any home garden, can connect the *sukkah* more closely with its agricultural origins. Having further associations with the return of ancestral spirits (as on Halloween), the lantern is appropriate for the summoning of the *ushpizin*, the faithful ancestral visitors, into the *sukkah*. Finally, being a relative of the gourd, the pumpkin might even remind you of the *kikayon*, the gourd in Jonah, thus connecting the Feast of Sukkot with the immediately preceding Fast of Yom Kippur.

This new *minhag* (custom) clearly has much to recommend it. ❧

From *The Jewish Holidays*, edited by Michael Strassfeld, 1985

Cupid Comes to *Shul*

For Valentine's Day

The cherub is not exclusively a pagan symbol, according to this 2013 essay, and deserves its place in Jewish settings as a reminder of both Divine and human love.

Cupid in *shul?* Valentine's Day? Is this a *Jewish* essay?

The story begins in 1969, when Pope Paul VI declared Valentine's Day no longer a day for universal liturgical veneration in the Church calendar. This released the day from the Church's possession and restored it to its former state as a traditional mating day of birds (and humans too) in the English folk calendar, as described in *Midsummer Night's Dream*: " . . . St. Valentine is past; Begin these wood-birds but to couple now?"

Romantics and lovers of chocolate immediately took advantage of the opportunity to reclaim a Cupid liberated from religious baggage. As for Jews, at least some of us welcomed this timely opportunity to assert a simple but not widely known fact: Cupid is not exclusively a pagan symbol! Without trying to sort out the connections between the classical figure of erotic power and the Biblical cherubs prescribed for the sacred Ark, we rested our case on interesting archeological evidence: Cupid appears on Jewish sarcophagi in Rome, on paintings in Jewish catacombs in Rome, and most significantly, above the door of the synagogue at Capernaum — six of them over the main entrance! Clearly, if Palestinian Jews of the 1st century found it fitting to go to a *shul* where they were greeted each time by Cupid's form, the winged one is not to be entirely dismissed from Jewish religious consideration.

What, then, is the significance of this figure in Greco-Roman times? What might he be saying as he stands there, vivid in bas relief, above the entranceway? The late Professor Erwin Goodenough's fine and suggestive treatment of this figure (in his *Jewish Symbols in the Greco-Roman Period, Volume 8*) is most helpful in our comprehending Cupid's message — and an interesting message it is:

1) Love intoxicates: Cupids are often represented holding cups and are often associated with Dionysus, suggesting at one level that love intoxicates. True, no? Giddiness, faintness, a sense of bedazzlement, a veritable drunkenness, are widely attested in literature. "I am faint with love," says the Song of Songs. "...Turn your eyes away from me, for they undo me... You have ravished my heart... Eat, friends, drink, and be drunk with love."

Categories disappear, for "love's function is to fabricate unknownness," in the words of e.e. cummings.

This may sound like simply a personal luxury, an indulgence, nothing more. Love is, however, more profoundly, a personal necessity, not a frill.

2) Love releases from the hell of isolation: "Initiates of Eros have a better fate in Hades," writes Goodenough, quoting Plutarach. "[T]here is for lovers a way up out of Hades into the light."

This notion is obviously not only Greek. Long-established in the rabbinic tradition is the inappropriateness of isolation. "It is not good for a man to be alone," says Genesis. To live in isolation, says the Talmud, is to live "without joy, without blessing, without happiness" (Yebamot 62b). There is even a rabbinic legend (Bereshit Rabbah 8:1) similar to the Greek one reported in Plato: "Said Rabbi Shimon ben Gamliel: At the time when the Holy One, Blessed be He, created the Primordial Person, that Person was created with two faces (one male, one female). That Person was then cut in two, and separated."

And could it be better said than by cummings?

```
one's not half two. It's two are halves of one:
which halves reintegrating,shall occur
no death and any quantity . . .
```

This re-uniting is not only right but wondrous:

```
what's wholly
marvellous my

Darling

is that you &
i are more than you

& i(be

ca
us
e It's we)
```

But the effects of love, thought the ancients, were not simply personal, they were social as well.

3) Love fills mean souls with grace: "The saving effect of love," writes Goodenough, "is not only that it makes men pleasant who were far from affable, but that it makes a 'soul that is narrow, debased, and misbegotten to be suddenly filled with understanding, a sense of humor, grace, and liberality.' When we recognize the change, which is like putting a light into a house at night, we should exclaim with Telemachus, 'Surely, some god is within.'"

The persons who will save us, who will usher in the new society, can hardly be the narrow, constricted, often hate-filled reverse copies of today's destroying spirits. Love may not be all we need, but neither is it entirely beside the point.

It seems appropriate to recall that the great lover of the Middle Ages, Peter Abelard, was, according to Malcolm Hay (in *Europe and the Jews*), "the only leader in the Middle Ages who ventured to attack, openly, the anti-Jewish tradition of Christendom. He attacked the tradition at its root. He said the Jewish people were not responsible for the death of Christ . . ." For this he was bitterly criticized by other churchmen, including the Benedictine author of *A Literary History of France* (1789), who opined: "Abelard was led astray by his tender heart and inquisitive mind . . ."

It is reassuring to think that the love of Heloise and Abelard may have had some political as well as personal effects on our world, and that may well be so. Would that more in positions of authority might be "led astray by tender hearts and inquisitive minds"!

Finally, in Goodenough's summary,

4) Love makes the world go 'round: It is is "love which makes the world go round. Love is the meaning of work and play alike, the source and center of its beauty. Love is capricious, often naughty and troublemaking, the pictures tell us, but still the one meaningful element in all activity."

In the words of Rabbi Shmuel bar Nahman: "Were it not for the libido (*yetzer hara*), no one would build a house, wed, conceive and bear children, engage in trade," and so on (Bereshit Rabbah 9:7). It is, I think, fair here to construe *"yetzer hara"* as referring to the erotic or libidinal. This is supported by the rabbinic legend that when Eros the Tempter stopped functioning, hens stopped laying, cocks ceased crowing, and the world nearly came to a halt.

Small wonder, then, that a force which intoxicated, which rescued from the hell of personal isolation, which filled mean souls with grace and so affected the social order, and which made the world go round, was seen as a fitting representation to place above the main entrance of the synagogue at Capernaum. For love was regarded by Philo as the "saving force . . . or what releases the saving force of God's nature."

And considering the association of the Cupid figures with the themes of immortality and eternity through the sarcophagi, some Jews of that time might even have concurred with e.e. cummings' proclamation that

> love is the every only god
> who spoke this earth so glad and big . . .
> so truly perfectly the skies
> by merciful love whispered were . . .

Using *gematria*, we find that *ekhad*/One=*ahavah*/Love. Let us, then, once each year, with the presence of Cupid warmly welcomed, and with a nod in the direction of romantics and chocolate lovers, dare to translate the *Shema* in these words: "Hear O Israel, the Eternal our God, the Eternal is Love!"

From *Berkshire Jewish Voice,* January-March, 2013

Part Five

Between Mind and Heart: Personal Reflections

It's good . . . to have come upon the soul
With tiny strokes of the oars,
For it is scared away
By a brusque approach.
—Jules Supervielle,
translated by Kenneth Rexroth

Darkness and Light

Rabbi Gendler's Senior Sermon, 1957

"I am amazed," says Rabbi Gendler about this senior sermon from rabbinical school (Jewish Theological Seminary), "by the consistency of my political optimism over the years, and its rootedness in Judaism."

Even we city-dwellers, who have so little contact with the world of nature, are aware, at least by report, that there are natural phenomena with the capacity to impress, to frighten, even to terrify human beings. The periodic mass invasions of Eastern lands by swarms of locusts, which denude the countryside of all growth and lay utterly bare the face of the ground; the earthquake that grinds the ground beneath our feet – such occurrences as these are surely terrifying to those who experience them. Even we who live sheltered by our own constructions have occasion to experience some of nature's impressiveness first-hand, when an electrical storm comes our way, or when a gale or blizzard or hurricane accosts us. I take it, then, as well established that such unexpected and forceful natural events do make an impression upon people by virtue of their might and their unexpectedness.

There is, however, within the regular, recurrent order of nature one phenomenon which also has this capacity to sober, perhaps even frighten human beings, and which does so not by might or power but rather in softness, gently. I refer to the event of nightfall, that descent of darkness that we experience so regularly as a part of our lives. Now, I do not mean to exaggerate its effect upon us. I doubt that any of us reacts to the night as did the author of the ancient Egyptian Hymn to the Aton, the sun disc:

> When thou settest in the western horizon,
> The land is in darkness, in the manner of death.
> They sleep in a room, with heads wrapped up,
> Nor sees one eye the other . . .
> Darkness is a shroud, and the earth is in stillness.

Such foreboding gloom is not precisely expressive either of the traditional Jewish or the modern secular reaction to darkness. Yet we must, I think, admit that some element of truth remains in the description. Darkness does conceal, hide, shroud, as it were, the reality that we know with our senses. Darkness does obliterate the surroundings, does create a sense of isolation, which is not merely superstition but perceptible fact. Perhaps no other event of nature, no matter how forceful or mighty it may be, can so seriously challenge our sense of existence.

Small wonder, then, that darkness can arrest our attention, and that that people throughout the ages have been fascinated by it. Small wonder that, in this week's *sidrah*, our own attention might have been strongly drawn to that very brief passage of only three verses that describes the ninth plague of the traditional ten visited upon Egypt: the plague of darkness. In quantity the description of this plague is not impressive. Unlike the other plagues, it has no introduction of any kind: no discussion between the Lord and Moses, no communication or warning to Pharaoh by Moses. It is commanded, realized, and its impact recorded in the space of three verses (Exodus 10:21-23), the least space accorded any one of the ten plagues.

> And the Lord said unto Moses: "Stretch out thy hand toward heaven, that there may be darkness over the land of Egypt, even darkness which may be felt." And Moses stretched forth his hand toward heaven; and there was a thick darkness in all the land of Egypt three days. They saw not one man his brother, neither rose any from his place for three days; but all the children of Israel had light in their dwellings.

That is the description in its entirety. No more space is required. Sufficient unto it is the darkness thereof. The resonance within each of us can be depended upon to complete in its fullness the message of the text.

Yet certain other elements come to our attention, for the text contains not only darkness but light: "but all the children of Israel had light in their dwellings."

Light we have, but hardly clarity. The rabbis noticed something puzzling about this description (Midrash Rabbah, Shemot 14:3): The darkness and the light are not separated geographically. Unlike the other plagues, the line of division is not between Egypt and the Land of Goshen, the residence of the Jews. "It does not say," the rabbis observed, 'in the land of Goshen' but 'in their dwellings,' to show that wherever a Jew went, light accompanied him . . ."

Suddenly the focus is shifted. It is no longer possible to construe this passage as describing only the sunlight and shadows of the external world, for in that dimension of existence it is not possible for two men to stand next to one another, the one bathed in light, the other shrouded in darkness. Clearly something other and deeper is suggested, and the rabbis, with their genius for using events of nature to illuminate the inner life of man, guide us in perceiving what this deeper significance is.

"Darkness – that their eyes and their hearts were overcome by darkness," the rabbis write. Not only darkness of the eyes but darkness of the heart; a lack of vision at the deepest human level; the failure of the heart, the true organ of vision, to see – this is the only possible explanation of the uncanny spectacle of two men standing beside one another, the one knowing light, the other cast in darkness.

Intriguing, and yet unsatisfying: intriguing in that all of us surely have known, and very likely do know, some measure of inner darkness; unsatisfying in that the nature of this inner darkness and inner light is as yet unclear. So we must ask further, what is the cause of the darkness and the source of light? To these questions, too, the rabbis addressed themselves.

The cause of darkness? "Note well: The Holy One, Blessed be He, does not exact payment from the wicked except by darkness. The path of the righteous is illumined by light, the way of the wicked is deep darkness."

Which is to say, I believe, that the cause of inner darkness is that way of life, that outlook which cuts one off from the sense of the Divine in the universe. And this assertion is not merely a shallow moralizing about wickedness or badness in any conventional sense. Rather, it is a realization that in the very nature of things there are attitudes and ways of living which do cut off the individual from any awareness of God at work in the world. That, in the eyes of the rabbis, is the true cause of darkness, the absence of any intimation of the Divine.

"Perhaps," they continue, "the darkness of Egypt was that very darkness which is described in the Psalm: 'He has made darkness His hiding place.'"

Having followed the rabbinic analysis this far, I suspect that we can, on our own and without further assistance, answer the remaining question concerning the source of light. For if the cause of darkness be the hiddenness of God, surely the source of light will be the Presence of God through Torah. And indeed the rabbis are quite explicit about this: "but all the children of Israel had light in their dwellings 'in that they were occupied with matters of Torah, as it is written: 'For Torah is light.'"

So concludes the rabbinic exegesis of that brief passage in Scripture, and a beautiful exegesis it is. Beautiful, yet somehow not fully satisfying, for it speaks of light, but provides us none for ourselves; it speaks of illumination, but seems to leave us as much in the dark as ever. And this is not enough, for it was not only that generation in Egypt which knew darkness. Every age has its darkness, as does every human being. Every group and every person knows a substantial measure of trouble, confusion, and fear – and for living it is not sufficient to be told that previous ages received from one source or another illumination and guidance. We ourselves want illumination for our own lives.

It remains, then, for us to see how, more concretely and specifically, Torah may grant us that light by which to see even in this day and age. And since our *sidrah* this week is primarily concerned with a series of events largely societal in nature – a people on the move, social upheaval, the tottering of an empire, unrest, confusion, fear – we, too, might well turn our attention to this aspect of our lives today, the societal in the largest sense. It is not the only source of the darkness that we experience, but it surely does account for some of our fears and for some of our uncertainties.

Well it might. Our age, as we well know, is itself a time of tremendous upheavals, crises, and confusions; in our own time we have seen a nearly complete overturning of the political order which once seemed so firmly established. The Earth has shifted on its axis, eastward, toward Africa and Asia. It has shifted from the abode of millions to the abode of the billions in startling fashion, and I think all of us at some level are aware of this and troubled by it.

The signs are not far to seek. A conference at some obscure island town of Colombo suddenly equals, and probably surpasses in importance, a national political convention in this great country. A meeting of NATO powers, the pride of Western statesmanship, can no longer take for granted an automatic majority; subject peoples vote against their erstwhile masters and carry the day! Almost daily, these amazing facts force themselves upon us.

And consider for a moment the individual leaders of these nations. Without exaggeration we can say that most of them were previously agitators against our closest allies, the Western powers that then controlled them, and that many of them have spent substantial portions of their lives in jails. Need one name more than Sukarno of Indonesia or Nehru of India to make the point? Suddenly these men, former prisoners, ex-convicts as it were, are world leaders, figures to be reckoned with; and one of them is almost certainly more influential than any single Western statesmen, not excluding our own president.

These are but instances of what is happening in our world today, of the situation we face. And the great shift has hardly begun. Asia, after all, is a mere child, hardly ten years upon the world scene, and with much growth ahead. Africa is really not yet born, though it can be distinctly felt thrashing in the womb. In even so brief and sketchy a chronicle as this, Latin America should not be omitted, for though barely conceived, its time too will come, and is not far off as we in the colossus of the north like to think.

It is an amazing period of history in which we live: unsettled, in turmoil, and understandably frightening. To some, it seems dark indeed. A prominent French official voices serious misgivings about the future of the United Nations if "certain power blocs" can wield so much influence, which is, perhaps, a polite way of saying that democracy isn't so much fun as it used to be, now that the West is outvoted from time to time. Another important French official, less polite, states that his country's policy will not be determined by people who have "only recently achieved the cultural status of barbarians." An extremely important figure in our own country responds to a question about the split in the Western alliance in these terms: "the white race" undoubtedly is going to "hang together" in world affairs. These, I think, are not untypical voices, and they do very likely express some part of what we feel. But we must also note that they are voices that speak from seeing the world as essentially in conflict, which see our own interests threatened by this upsurge of formerly subjugated peoples. In short, they are voices that speak out of darkness, seeing chaos, danger, and destruction, and responding accordingly.

Not for a moment would I suggest that there is not much confronting us about which we might well be apprehensive; neither would I deny that there is a component of darkness in our situation. But I would assert that in the world today there in infinitely more light than darkness, far more cause for rejoicing than for despair, and that it is precisely the light of Torah which can reveal this to us. For in our *sidrah* for the week, Torah is explicitly defined in one aspect: "that the Torah of the Lord may be in thy mouth: that with a strong hand hath the Lord brought thee our of Egypt" (Exodus 13:9).

Is it not this, after all, what is truly afoot in the world today? Those of us endowed with the tradition of Torah, which constantly reminds us of our own redemption from bondage, must surely recognize in all these seeming cataclysms that very Spirit of Redemption at work in the world. Is the emergence of Asia simply a threat to Western civilization? Perhaps, although surely it need not be. Is it not far more profoundly another group of people experiencing the beginnings of their liberation after centuries of servitude? Is it not in reality the manifestation of the Lord of History extending His domain actively to the far corners of the earth? The frail man in the loin cloth who without hatred or violence led his people to freedom; his fellow prisoner and successor who now leads a great nation – have we a more striking example in our day of "the Lord looseth the prisoners, the Lord raiseth up them that are bowed down"? (Which is not to suggest that these men are necessarily perfect or saints, for where do we read that the Lord's concern extends only to the perfect?)

This spirit is not confined only to politicos and famous figures. One need only speak to students from recently liberated lands such as India, or even those not yet independent, such as Kenya and South-West Africa, to detect this same spirit. It is a dedication to achieving the growth skills necessary for taking control of their own destinies, a determination to have no more Western domination – and they will tell us to our faces that this is their intention. Shall we then see it as an expression of darkness? Is it not, rather, another inspiring example of the beginning of self-assertion toward full human dignity? Is it not another instance of the Spirit of Redemption abroad upon the earth?

Actually, we need not look outside our own borders to see this Spirit at work – for what in American politics or religious history can compare with the phenomenon of Montgomery, Alabama, where the downtrodden and the oppressed, with great dignity and without malice, achieved new rights for themselves through action rooted in their knowledge that their Redeemer liveth?

If we can but realize how much of this is happening in the world today, perhaps we shall have somewhat more light.

Having said all this, I would not like to pretend that things will necessarily be as comfortable for us as they have been up to now. Our Creator has richly endowed this planet on which we live, yet two-thirds of the people on the face of this Earth go to bed hungry each night and know poverty as their constant condition. I am not at all sure that, as they grow stronger, they will remain content to see valuable and badly needed resources channeled toward providing Americans with a new yearly indulgence in the shape of an automobile two inches longer, shorter, taller, or smaller. The trend, in fact, is quite the other way, and once again examples are not far to seek. It really is too bad that it was Nasser who nationalized Suez, what with his deplorable policies of squandering funds on arms, refusing Israeli ships equal access to the canal, inciting to violence, etc. These issues have blinded us to the fact that Nasser does express, in however distorted manner, the legitimate strivings of his people for greater benefits from their resource and greater independence from foreign domination; and in this respect he enjoys the support of billions of people in the world. If we fail to recognize clearly and respond to these urges of the peoples of the world, then we only insure that these legitimate and even Godly strivings will be misused by those who at least recognize and take seriously their existence.

It is such hard facts as these that we must recognize if we are to have not only clarity but the ability to respond constructively to the challenges we face. Referring for the final time to this week's *sidrah*, I call to your attention a comment by Rabbi Isaac Meir of Ger. Commenting on the passage in this that reads: "they saw no one man his brother, neither rose any from his place," Rabbi Isaac Meir remarked: "He who will not look at his brother will soon come to this: He will cleave to his place and not be able to move from it."

That is the final and the great truth. If we can but see one another, we shall know now to respond to the crisis that confronts us today; if not, we shall remain selfish, immobilized, and shall surely perish. To look at and know our fellow human beings – that is the one indispensable thing. But not to know them simply as people grabbing things we want or have; not to know them simply as primitive people who haven't the capacity to appreciate the finer accomplishments of Western civilization; not even to know the most aggressive of them as simply evil aggressors, the position we all-too-often take. Rather, to know them as children of God, as creatures who, like ourselves, embody the Divine image; to see in their struggles and strivings, even those directed against us, the expression of that Divine urge toward redemption which is the heart of history: that is the path and that is the way which yields light.

We above all peoples are blessed in inheriting a tradition of Torah which has as its central awareness God the Redeemer manifesting Himself in history. Curiously enough, in this age as in former ages it proves to be our most valuable possession, for by this insight and by this light we can look at the world searchingly and truly and yet see light, and with this we can penetrate the darkness and live. In the words of the Psalmist: "For with Thee is the source of life, And it is by Thy light that we do see light."

Not Tired, Merely Retired

Loosening the Daily Ties

This 1997 reflection was written two years into a retirement that has now been keeping Rabbi Gendler busy for eighteen.

Aging first directly confronted me when I was 62½. Its agent was a computer printout at the private school where I taught, informing me that the normal but not mandatory retirement age where I worked would come in two and a half years, the summer I turned 65. I still remember my reaction of outrage and hurt: "Hey, I'm too young to be 62½. There must be a mistake somewhere!"

Chronologically, of course, there was no mistake. Birth certificate and family photos confirmed the calculation. Yet in terms of health, energy, and engagement with my work, retiring at 65 seemed premature. Happily, it also seemed premature to colleagues, students, and congregants at both the school and the temple where I was a rabbi. Turning 65 became a signpost, not a stop sign.

The question, however, was merely postponed. At what point should I seek release from the still-satisfying, still-stimulating, yet confining daily commitments at school and temple and redirect my energy more freely? It was in these terms that I considered retirement. In attempting to answer this question, I felt that societal as well as personal considerations were appropriate.

Although early retirement lets the next generation advance more quickly to more challenging work, it may also, over time, impose greater financial burdens upon the young through lengthier Social Security and pension payments to retirees. After learning that the standard Social Security retirement age would be raised to 67 in 2009, I decided to take this age as my guideline.

Yet continuing satisfactions from my work made retirement seem, at times, unreal. So much intimacy, spirituality, and celebration at our temple Shabbat evening services; such exhilaration from ecumenical and ceremonial occasions at school; such joys from teaching. Why even think of retirement? Amid these daily and weekly delights, however, some slight yet significant internal shifts signaled gentle warnings and offered subtle guidance. For example, while I still enjoyed waking up for an 8:00 a.m. class four mornings a week, reaping pleasure from the discussion and the student papers, every now and then, while encouraging and focusing student discussion, I would recognize a slight urge to speak myself, at greater length and complexity – and while writing comments on student papers, I occasionally felt just a slight twitch of the pen wanting to write my own essays rather commenting on theirs.

Tutoring bar/bat mitzvah candidates at our temple, as I had done for more than twenty years, continued to be a lively and dynamic process, culminating in a celebrative service that represented a religious commitment, a rite of passage, and a communally recognized personal achievement. Yet every now and then during the tutoring, I, the *melamed*, the teacher, would detect an internal desire to delve more deeply into Abulafia's mystical vowel combinations rather than help a student distinguish between long and short vowel sounds.

Such stirrings, although slight, seemed to me likely to grow, perhaps gradually at first but almost surely with increasing insistence as time passed. With such growth, wouldn't the blessed preponderance of satisfaction to dissatisfaction in my work decline proportionately? Needless to say, such clarity is an after-the-fact formulation, not a during-the-process description. But it was some such intuition, however dim, that inclined me toward retirement during the summer that I would turn 67.

One other personal consideration also nudged me toward this timing. If, indeed, I wanted retirement to represent a redirection of energy rather than the recognition of its demise, I would do well to retire while there was still energy to redirect, and while the question on people's lips would be "Retiring already?" rather than "Not yet retired?"

Curiously, classical Judaic texts and teachings played a lesser role in this process of deciding when to retire. I say "curiously" because most areas of my life are significantly shaped by rabbinic tradition. Why not in this case? Partly, I suspect, because the practice of retirement as we have come to know it is not part of rabbinic or later Jewish tradition. Even a brief glance at an

English-Hebrew dictionary makes clear that the words for retirement are not words from classical Hebraic tradition. Differences in life expectancy are probably one factor, the absence of surplus resources to sustain a public social security system another. Further, the association of age with wisdom would probably have made retirement as we know it seem an unacceptable social waste. Besides, is one ever free from the Divine demands of Torah and *mitzvot*? If not, and if one's work is so blessed as to involve them daily, why would one want to retire? For all these reasons (and surely others as well), Jewish texts and traditions offered guidance only in the most general sense of articulating basic truths about life, the universe, and our place in it.

Societal and personal considerations, coinciding with the institutional, made the decision to retire easier for me – though obviously not all that easy! Of invaluable assistance and profoundly affirming were the deeply moving farewell gatherings held for me at both school and temple. Each was a regretful yet joyous review in words and music, reflection, and revelry of many wonderful experiences through all those years. This rich harvest of memory, so abundantly gathered and generously given to me by students, colleagues, and congregants, has provided true sustenance for my spirit. I'm sure it will continue to nourish me for years to come.

Although retirement is still quite fresh and I continue to enjoy that generous gift of memory, I can report an intermittent anxiety: the fear that loosening the daily ties to the life of the temple and academy may sever completely my connections with the future. What can possibly substitute for the daily joys I have just relinquished? In the absence of such life-filled bonds, how – if at all – can I remain connected with life as it surges toward the future? These questions have haunted me most consistently while I was deciding when to retire and since retirement.

The answer? Again, it is tentative and highly speculative, since my new status is so recent, and the full force of the question is temporarily blunted by the current adventure of traveling in Asia during these first months of transition. Only when I return home will a realistic answer emerge. Meanwhile, even here, experiences and imaginings offer some clues to the challenge of a retirement not dictated by weariness, exhaustion, or boredom.

I am often convinced that human life is greatly assisted by well-intentioned, well-designed, well-functioning institutions. As a consequence, I invested much of my professional attention and energy in two institutions: the synagogue and the academy. Now, I need to remind myself of the obvious but sometimes forgotten truth that valuable though such channels may be, they are not the only conduits through which life flows. As we travel we meet many people, some of whom are kindred spirits. Such encounters affirm our life-spirit and our values.

One immediate example: Presently, we are in Dharamsala, India, a community of Tibetans in exile whose main temple in Lhasa has be profaned by the Chinese occupiers just as ours had been by the Greco-Syrians some 2,150 years earlier. What better place to light Chanukah candles than in the courtyard of the Namgyal Monastery, the Dalai Lama's "shul," the Tibetans' primary exilic temple surrogate and the usual site for public gatherings? So we went there each night to light our candles, to sing, and to enjoy lovely interchanges with Tibetans reciting their prayers, carrying their candles, and lighting their butter lamps. We shared songs, melodies, snacks, and stories. While not an institution, our gathering was surely a blessed vessel for light – both external and internal. It was obvious, of course, that I could enjoy a challenging spiritual and intellectual life outside of the institutions that had nourished me for so many years, but at this time of disengagement from familiar institutional links, I do need reminders of this truth.

As for imaginings, let me share one image from my life that helped me make the step toward retirement. The constancy in our personal life enabled us to rear two daughters as well as raise organically grown crops on our small acreage in Andover, Massachusetts. At the same time, we enjoyed such fresh experiences as camping, travel, and extrainstitutional involvements. Some seeds from this life have borne fruit worth harvesting.

Among the courses that I taught at Phillips Academy was "Nonviolence in Theory and Practice," which focused on the work of Mahatma Gandhi and Martin Luther King, Jr. The class, which was one way to continue my earlier participation in the nonviolent movement for social change, explored both the dynamics and the philosophical and religious implications of spirit flexing its muscles. Although I no longer teach, new opportunities are already opening for me to express my long-standing beliefs as I help Tibetans apply nonviolent strategies in their political struggles.

My temple has experimented over the decades with reincorporating into its regular worship elements of nature in Judaism that were ancient, authentic, but often overlooked. Among the widely satisfying results were fresh ways to celebrate the cycles of the sun, the phases of the moon, the succession of the seasons, and the times for planting and harvesting. These fruits of our liturgical life contain, as do all fruits, seeds for further planting;

in this way, life renews itself again and again. The seed is simultaneously the end of one life cycle and the beginning of the next. It symbolizes the constant renewal of life, the annual proclamation that death is indeed followed by resurrection.

If God grants me additional years of life and vigor, I imagine that I will share even more widely the seeds of this harvest through writing and occasional weekends with receptive congregations. The joyous, invigorating task of gathering these seeds, preserving them, and transmitting them to others for future plantings will connect me with life in its fullness. Harvesting will be the reassuring response to my fear of finding myself prematurely disconnected from vital life in its forward motion.

I can conceive, though not actively imagine, that further along life's path I will experience more of the decline of powers portrayed by Ecclesiastes and Shakespeare. For now, however, not tired but merely retired, I am delighted to discover that there are ways in which I can still be bound up in the bonds of life. *Ken y'hi ra'tzon.* May this be God's will. Amen.

From *A Heart of Wisdom*, edited by Susan Berrin, 1997

Fifty Years in the Rabbinate

Delighted Amazement

This reflection on half a century as a teacher in the Jewish community offers a tidy summation of Rabbi Gendler's career.

To adapt and adopt from our beloved Heschel, I'd characterize my rabbinical years overall as "delighted amazement."

How was it that a kid who was born and spent his first eleven years in the small farm town of Chariton, Iowa, ended up a rabbi? Probability tables don't easily answer that question.

How was it that some of my early rabbinical posts seemed to illustrate a poster reading, "Join the rabbinate and see the world?" Between 1957 and '61, two years of alternative service to the military chaplaincy serving a small English-speaking congregation in Mexico City, Mexico; then half a year as associate rabbi at the liberal synagogue in Rio de Janeiro, Brazil. In 1968-69, a month at *Yamim Noraim* and a month at *Pesakh* in Havana and throughout Cuba.

Post-"retirement" in 1995, how is it that my wife, Mary, and I have made eleven trips to India, helping the Tibetan exile community develop a popular education program on strategic nonviolent struggle — a pragmatic Western complement to the Dalai Lama's principled teachings?

Not that adventure was lacking at The Jewish Center of Princeton, 1962-68. Less than ten days after beginning my tenure, I was jailed with Dr. King and other clergy in Albany, Georgia; in May of 1963, I was privileged to lead nineteen of us from the Rabbinical Assembly Convention in the Catskills to Birmingham, Alabama; in '65, Mary and I marched in Selma, Alabama. Plus anti-Vietnam War demonstrations with Dr. King, Dr. Heschel, and other clergy at the Arlington National Cemetery; collecting draft cards in Palmer Square; etc. The legendary 1960s were real for this rabbi.

As for a few of ever so many delights:

In Princeton, when weather permitted, we held summer services out-of-doors, reclaiming some of the connections of Jewish worship with nature; *l'shem Yikhud*, I also began including in services readings from (Reb Hayim David) Thoreau, (Reb Meir) Rilke, etc. During almost twenty-five years as rabbi at the liberal Temple Emanuel in Lowell, similar experiments and innovations continued: major Tu B'Shevat seders; the conversion of the temple Eternal Light to solar power in 1978; celebrating the succession of each season with a 48"-diameter sun-wheel that incorporated *El Barukh G'dol Deah*; planting winter rye at Sukkot for cutting at Omer time, thus palpably connecting the three *r'galim*; a "sleep service" at the dark of the year; a Rosh Hodesh/Mozart 200th Yortsayt evening; etc.

As for the stimulation and satisfactions of nearly twenty years teaching and being part of the first ecumenical chaplaincy at a New England boarding school, Phillips Academy, Andover, another lengthy reverie of delights: annually building a Sukkah in the middle of campus; serving as adviser to both the Jewish and the Muslim Student Unions; reciting in Hebrew the invocations and benedictions that my fellow chaplains and I offered at convocations, commencements; etc.

The disappointments? Amazingly few!

On reflection, besides *she-he-khe-ya-nu*, I feel moved to affirm my delighted amazement with two additional blessings: *hagomel l-khayavim tovot,* and *hatov v'hametiv*. For fifty blessed years this *khut ham'shulash* has not been sundered. ❧

Delivered in 2007 to the Rabbinical Assembly Convention, Boston

Woodchucks in the Garden, Beavers in the Stream

And Messiah Nowhere in Sight

This storytelling essay describes a war with four-legged, flat-tailed neighbors that revealed the limits on romanticizing nature, even for the "zeyde of Jewish environmentalism."

In anticipation, the summer looked idyllic. An unprecedented New England spring, with day after day of bright sunshine, low humnidity, and moderate temperatures, had not only lifted our spirits but encouraged our home garden to produce in abundance. The spinach was deep green and flavorful, the strawberries bright and plentiful, the tall peas as sweet as one could imagine. Amidst this abundance, the thought of heading 140 miles west to our campsite in the Berkshires felt just a little like leaving Eden.

Just as plausibly, however, it could have been descriabed as leaven Eden for Paradise. The Berkshires themselves are softly rounded, invitingly green, gently restful, and filled with the cultural equivalent of זיו השכינה, the Splendor of the Divine Presence. Fifteen minutes from the land where we camp, the Boston Symphony Orchestra performs heavenly music in gorgeous natural surroundings; equally near our campsite is the Edith Wharton Estate, where Shakespeare and Company takes full advantage of the outdoor setting for rich and stimulating dramatic offerings.

Yet without any of the foregoing, our campsite itself is surely a bit of Paradise: a meadow one-quarter of a mile from the road, at least that distance from any other dwellings, facing a graceful and thickly forested slope of Beartown State Forest, with a small stream for bathing perhaps 150 yards away. Even with Mary (my wife) having to work some days each week at the social service agency she co-directs, the anticipated alternation between Andover and the Berkshires seemed in prospect like gently swinging from Eden to Paradise and back again.

And so, perhaps, it might have been. But in reality, as the learned sages would have foreseen, this foretaste of the world to come was to be only a *nosh*, an hors d'oeuvre rather than a full-course meal. For during the days that we were mulching the garden, setting the house in order, and assembling supplies for the shift to Paradise, there was unmistakable circumstantial evidence of woodchucks in the garden! Carrot tops were nipped, squash vines nibbled, broccoli and kale gnawed to near extinction. As any gardener knows when fully in touch with the terror of such a discovery, the return of the serpent might well be preferred, for after all, whatever the long-term consquences of its reappearance, at least the plants are spared immediate devastation.

But all was not lost, at least not for now. A live animal trap baited with peanut butter and honey on whole-grain bread lured two woodchucks in three days – unprecedented luck, and not even an unwelcome skunk in the trap to slow down the population transfer. With two woodchucks duly transported to a nearby unpopulated area – plenty of woods, two ponds, grass, and all the amenities – the possible third might be caught by a helpful neighbor and taken to join the others. So we left with minds fairly at ease.

The arrival at our campsite, nestled against a small hill the second ridge down from the road, was uneventful. There was still plenty of time to set up before dark, and so we headed down for a look at the stream. Even from a distance we could see that the water level looked surprisingly high for such a sunny, dry spring; as we approached our bathing area, we were puzzled by the marshiness of the ground; and as we finally made our way to the bridge and logging road, the mystery was solved: Next to the bridge, and has high as its floor, was a sizable, sturdy, and appallingly effective beaver dam! The spare trickle of water that washed over its top did little to reduce the flooding of the nearby fields or lower the eighteen inches of water inundating the old logging road that gives our neighbor access to his back acres and us to ours.

Shocked by this unforseen development, we inflated our air mattresses and paddled upstream for a further look. The previous autumn, the current had been steady, the water clear, the stream bed clean; now the water barely moved, the stream bed was rampant with stream grass and weeds, and the leech population had multiplied distressingly. The banks, so trim from years of tending, were a soggy mess, and ten years of accumulated piles of brush, painstakingly cut and dredged from the channels, were beginning to wash back into the swollen, stagnant stream. How unfair! A campsite with no plumbing, yet our "bathtub" is stopped up; and what plumber will respond to our call?

From woodchucks in the garden to beavers in the stream! Not an encouraging progression. Woodchucks may damage some crops for a season, but with persistence and luck can be caught in live animal traps and relocated in congenial areas far from any garden. Beavers, however, flood entire areas, with effects that may last for decades. The prospect of our neighbor losing access to his back ten acres, us losing access to our back 155 acres, and all of us losing the beauty and freshness of the stream was quite unthinkable. What should we do? The question proved far more difficult, both practically and morally, than we could have imagined.

We first took advantage of a power shovel that we had earlier engaged to do some erosion repair work further up the logging road. As the machine was exiting, the skillful operator maneuvered a log with the claw of the shovel and opened the dam in forceful fashion. The waters burst through, debris flowed a short distance downstream, and the waters began to recede from the logging road, the soggy stream banks, and the flooded fields. We could have cheered, but the cheer would have had to be muted.

First of all, we were technically in violation of the wetlands laws, which prohibit the demolition of beaver dams. Here we were, long-time card-carrying members of The Wilderness Society, The Sierra Club, The Audubon Society, etc., generally law-abiding citizens, violating the laws of the land, which had probably made their way onto the books with the help of our organizations. It was not morally pleasing! We could support and would obey a law preserving the status of land, wet land to remain wet and dry land to remain dry. But legislation that gives beavers free reign to change the status and prohibits humans from preserving it? This, too, is speciesism, quite unacceptable but all too generally unacknowledged!

Secondly, those knowledgeable in matters of beavers assured us that the struggle had barely begun. How right they were! The next morning there appeared a new layer of freshly cut branches and some old logs, the sharp ends sturdily set downstream into the silt of the stream bed, the leaves and foliage wattled upstream. It took the two of us over forty-five minutes working carefully with the tao of water – wiggling and jiggling the sticks and mud – to disentangle and dig out that one night's energetic accomplishment. The unavoidable cuts and splinters, we soon discovered, quickly became infected because of the stagnant water, reducing our efficiency and our eagerness.

For some days the struggle continued in that manner: nightly the beavers returned and rebuilt; daily we demolished and carted away the twigs, branches, logs, saplings, and wattle. The brush pile, a good ten to twelve feet in width, grew higher along the logging road, and at five feet high we had to begin a second. The beavers, we hoped, had further to go in their search for building materials.

Other factors intervened. A cool spell chilled the water; we saw no evidence that the beavers even noticed, but often we found it unpleasant to enter the stream and work away. Especially chilling were our additional daily efforts to speed the current by weeding, for pulling the grass and weeds by their roots from the stream bed meant almost total immersion, not to mention the feast we provided the leeches.

Curious to see our tormentors at work in the early days of the struggle, we often went down to the bridge at dusk. We were fascinated by the agility of these fearless workers, who hardly paid heed to our presence on the bridge. The three, one a huge hulk, a second quite large, the third moderate in size, simply continued to push the floating branches with their noses, nudged them into place, then put mud on the exposed leaves to secure the dam.

This early period of nightly construction, daily demolition, and curiously disengaged encounter, was not destined to last for long. Soon we'd have to return home for Mary's work, and what the beavers would do in our absence was not pleasant to contemplate. We had just spent more than we would have wished paying for two loads of fill to repair the washaway from the earlier flooding, and we doubted that the beavers would be moved to observe a truce in our absence. And so began a series of anxious consultations with those wiser and more experienced than we in matters of beavers and their industrious habits.

We launched a lengthy series of calls from the phone booths in a shopping mall in Great Barrington – the public phones nearest our campsite. The irony of discussing beavers-in-the-wild from our asphalt and concrete setting in front of K-Mart and Price Chopper did not escape us; a solution to our problem did.

We had noticed that the Massachusetts Audubon Sanctuary in Lenox listed a weekly program called "An Evening at Beaver Pond." Envious of those whose encounters with beavers could be limited to a single evening, yet hopeful that the purveyors of such a program would be wise to the ways of beavers, we dialed a succession of numbers as the humid heat of July poured over us in the parking lot. The Pleasant Valley Sanctuary referred us to the Audubon Hot Line; the Hotline folks were more attuned to hazardous waste spills han beaver spillways. Their opinion was unanimous and superfluous: unwelcome beavers were, indeed, a problem. Beyond some commiseration with our plight, no further help was available from that source.

Where to turn? Talking with a neighbor who owns land in a nearby rural community, we were interested to learn that he *wanted* beavbers in his stream to expand the wetlands in his area. An obvious solution to the problem: transport the beavers to where they'll be welcomed! However easy the concept, the execution was quite otherwise. The wisdom of the ancient Talmud dictum was suddenly obvious: "cows by pulling, persons by persuasion." How to pull or persuade the beavers elsewhere? Lacking the power of words, we needed to find a trap. Asking around, we were told that the Fish and Wildlife Division of the U.S. Department of Agriculture had personnel with traps who, when warranted, would trap out the beavers. And such seems to have been the case in the days before budget reduction and conservation legislation, but at present, we were informed, there wasn't enough staff to offer the service.

"Then might we borrow a trap and set it ourselves?"

"Not possible. It's now against the law to trap and relocate wild animals."

"Why is that?"

"They might damage other property, and it is traumatic to the animals to be relocated."

"But what if they're doing serious damage to our land?"

"Then we can issue you a permit to shoot them."

"But isn't shooting them a lot more traumatic than trapping and moving them?"

"That's the law."

Shooting the beavers had just come up in a discussion with another neighbor, a person very much at home in the woods and, in season, a thoughtful and considerate hunter, quite skilled with bow and arrow as well as rifle. When first informed of our problem, he generously offered to shoot and remove them. But we, vegetarians for more than twenty-five years, have moral qualms about killing animals and were understandably hesitant to sanction immediately such a drastic and irreversible response to the problem.

At an impasse, we returned to Andover and Mary worked her work. As we anticipated returning to the Berkshires this time, it was as much with dread as with eagerness. Nor was the anxiety unwarranted. In our absnece, the beavers had rebuilt the dam to impressive heights and raised the water level to the very edge of the road. At least it wasn't over the edge! Several hours sufficed to reduce the dam to a reasonable height as we started yet another brush pile some yards further up the logging road. Meanwhile, two or three hours of weeding each day began to freshen the stream as the water flowed more freely. Nor did the irony of our situation in "Paradise" escape us: With the garden well-mulched at home to avoid having to spend the summer weeding, here we were spending more hours weeding the stream than ever we had spent in our sizable home garden. As for mulching the stream, ha! If we could do that, the stream would be dead.

There was one brief period of tempered elation during these weeks. It followed a remarkable encounter late one night between the beavers and us. We had attended an exquisite recital at Tanglewood by Frederica von Stade, had an ice cream afterwards, and returned to our campsite. Down to the bridge with our flashlights we went, where the beavers were working with even greater energy than usual. But fueled by the music and late evening dessert, our own energy levels were up also. Was it that delectable combination of music and ice cream that suddenly propelled me down the bank beside the bridge and impelled me to begin, with the help of a long pole, to pull to the side and up the bank every branch, stick, and sapling that I could reach without falling into the stream?

While Mary held the flashlight to illuminate this midnight raid, I continued the work until the beavers returned. For the first time this summer they appeared bewildered. Two of them swam rather aimlessly, circling about and finally letting the sticks float up against others rather than fixing them in place.

Yet more remarkable was a subsequent reaction. As the two near the bridge turned back upstream, their latest intention at least temporarily foiled, we heard an unprecedented sound directed toward the third, which was just now approaching. Instead of the usual warning slap of the tail against the water, they uttered sounds from their throats: a brief explosion of high-pitched chatter! What were they saying? What were their thoughts and feelings at this moment? We were no more privy to their thoughts than to their words, both of which remain cloaked in that mist of unknowing that is the human condition in relation to so many of our fellow creatures on this planet.

One official guide to self-defense against beavers assures the reader that contrary to popular opinion, the regular removal of their damming does not deter their efforts. We must report, however, that for a period of almost two weeks, no further beaver activity was visible anywhere nearby! Where did they go? Why? We had no answers but felt grateful for the surcease.

But a truce, alas, is not a peace, nor was it in the form of any mutual agreement. We were not surprised, then, when the beginnings of a dam reappeared at the bridge, and with it, perhaps twenty yards further downstream, a second ridge utilizing some of the debris from the original dam. Once more we demolished, and no less persistently the beavers built. They were more circumspect now than earlier in the summer. No longer did they begin at dusk, swimming so near to us that we could almost touch them, nor late at night did they linger as they placed the wattle on the leaves of the branches; they seemed more cautious of our presence. Cautious but not deterrred: Their activity did continue, though less forcefully, it seemed to us, and less effectively than earlier in the summer. Yet our brush piles did grow as we completed the second, went on to a third, and finally topped off a fourth.

Meanwhile, our original dilemma confronted us with growing intensity. At summer's end we would be leaving, while the beavers, year-around residents of the area, would remain. Left unchallenged, they would soon flood the road again and perhaps, were there to be heavy snows this winter, cause the destruction of the bridge itself. The damage to both our neighbor's land and our own was finally not acceptable, yet the killing of the beavers, though legal, was a painful, chastening alternative.

One final, fleeting glimmer of hope appeared. Perhaps the beavers could be stunned by a sedative dart, captured, and moved to the new site? A consultation with a veterinarian and the Wildlife Care Center of Tufts School of Veterinary Medicine soon banished this notion. Quite apart from the difficulty of obtaining the needed medicine and delivery apparatus, suppose one did, indeed, manage to inject the sedative by a well-aimed shot. By the time the potion took effect, the beaver would almost certainly have swum some distance away; hence drowning rather than relocation would be the most likely outcome of this procedure.

How I longed at that moment for the legendary learning of Solomon, who, the Book of Kings tells us (as recounted in Louis Ginzberg's *Legends of the Jews*, Vol IV),

knew the languages of the beasts of the field,
the birds of the air, the creeping reptiles,
Demons, spirits, shades, ghosts,
And the specters of the night.
He knew the languages of all of them
And they understood his tongue.

How happily we would have settled for just one language, that of the beavers. To have been able to communicate with them, to let them know that we bore them no ill will, that they were wanted elsewhere; what a difference it might have made.

Or were the Messiah on the scene, or at least soon to arrive, we could, of course, wait. If, as Isaiah envisioned, wolf and lamb shall live togehter, and leopard and kid, calf and lion, cow and bear manage amicably, then a territorial settlement with the beavers would be a breeze. Isaiah may indeed, have been of the city, as traditional opinion believes, but he nonetheless knew well something of life in the countryside with its profound harmonhies and equally profound conflicts. How his vision of creaturely reconciliation touched our hearts at this point in the summer!

Or, lacking the Messiah, at least *teku*, תיקו. Let the Tishbite, Elijah, the Messianic precursor, resolve this impasse!

Sadly, however, with woodchucks in the garden, beavers in the stream, and Messiah nowhere in sight, the painful irreconcilability of these conflicting creaturely claims – ours and the beavers', ours and the woodchucks' – was forcefully thrust upon us; a sense of defeated aspirations dimmed the lustre of our few remaining days at the campsite. Reluctantly yet appreciatively, we would accept the offer of one neighbor to trap and remove the beavers later this autumn. Perhaps our other neighbor would manage to relocate them before this final fate, but אין סומכין על הנס – one must not rely on miracles. With patience and luck, we could humanely relocate the woodchucks; with the beavers, however, the unredeemed state of our world and the deep ambiguities of our own existence on this Earth became unavoidably evident.

Our garden at home, though injured, remains productive; the Berkshires are still as beautiful as any imagining. Yet how poignantly clear, at the end of this summer, that the one is not Eden nor the other Paradise. ❧

From *The Melton Journal,* Spring, 1992

A Conversation with Rabbi Everett Gendler

May Day, 2015

This interview was conducted by Lawrence Bush, editor of Jewish Currents *magazine, at the home of Everett and Mary Gendler in Great Barrington, Massachusetts.*

Lawrence Bush: Given the title of your book, *Judaism for Universalists*, I thought I'd first ask you a very particularist question: What do you see as the particular strengths of Judaism?

Everett Gendler: Judaism gives a ready-made connection to the rhythms and dynamics of the universe. The Sabbath, with its dual emphasis on Creation and Liberation, is for me a formula for participating in everything that is vibrant and rewarding on this Earth.

Judaism affirms Creation, and it is happy to accommodate Darwin and the marvels of how this all came about. It does so with the sense that there was intentionality, a purpose unfolding. So many of the seasonal rituals, as well as the Sabbath, invite contemplation of this, integration with this.

The other aspect, Liberation, is what history testifies to as the striving of humankind – fitfully achieved and often reversed, but that liberation from Egypt has been the paradigm.

It is a great treasure to preserve a tradition, with its observances and its communality, that aligns me and integrates me rhythmically with these aspects of reality.

LB: Many universalists, perhaps especially Jewish universalists, will emphasize that "all religions are the same." Is there something in Judaism that you're willing to say is unique, maybe to invite universalists to check it out?

EG: I'm really fond of many religious traditions. In Mary's and my travels, whenever there was another tradition celebrating at the new Moon or the full Moon, as was usually the case, I would take my prayershawl, my prayerbook, my *kippah*, and I would go to their '*shul*,' and it would feel very compatible. Judaism is one among many. I think it has a very elevated and sustaining message, but when I recite the *kiddush*, I like to say, instead of "And You sanctified us out of all the nations," I always say "And You sanctified us *with* all the nations."

Still, while all these traditions do have particular insights, I have only one pair of eyes, and I need to focus them.

Judaism, I have found, is a wonderful base for *inclusiveness*.

LB: And who are the Jews, to your mind? Who are the Jews of the Bible, of history, of today? When I say, "I am a Jew," what would you like me to mean?

EG: Let's begin with an obvious fact: To say, "I am a Jew," establishes me in some relation to a religious tradition, but it doesn't necessarily imply that I am an active participant, or even an affirmer of that tradition. So on one level, to say "I am a Jew" is simply to identify with a body of people so identified, by the world, by themselves, by some combination.

But I would like, when anyone of us says, "I am a Jew," for that also to have a certain value overtone. I would like it to mean that I am someone who is committed to, and appreciative of, and active in, the preservation of the rich gift of Creation, of beauty, of the wondrous deliverances of the human spirit. I would like it to imply the appreciation of sustenance, and support for the liberation of individuals and of peoples from unnecessary constraints. There are necessary constraints, of course: The loss of all boundaries is terrifying, not liberating. But the expansion of freedom, that's what I would like being Jewish to mean.

To say "I am a Jew" means I am associated with a group of people whose basic dedication is to these goals. Some of them will do it in our traditional ceremonies, others will do it in less distinctive, more general fashion – but we all have a feeling of relationship to one another.

LB: To what extent do you personally find, and as a rabbi find for others, that the existing Jewish liturgy and ceremonials fulfill the power of Judaism?

EG: The liturgy is both an enabler and a disabler, I find. Some of the portrayals of the Divinity are a little too pat. And while none of it predates tragedy in the world, *all* of it predates the immensity of the Holocaust and other elements of human destruction in our age. So there is, operating within the liturgy, an affirmation that God is both benevolent and omnipotent, both all-good and all-powerful, and those are simply in logical and emotional contradiction. One of my teachers at the University of Chicago, Charles Hartshone, a follower of Whitehead and process theology, made clear that you cannot sustain both of these beliefs meaningfully. I think we need to look at the prayers again and see what to do so that the worshipper is not caught in this feeling of contradiction. We've got to qualify our sense that God is determinative of all.

In my own religious practice over the course of decades, I've also found that the sources of my illumination and inspiration are numerous, they're not confined to the Jewish texts. I mean, hurrah for Gutenberg! Maybe he's now, finally, becoming outdated, but the broad availability of sacred and philosophical texts is wondrous. If worship is to be a unifying experience that gives me both a sense of more connectedness to God, the Divinity, the Supreme Power, and at the same time to myself and my interests and impulses and feelings, it needs, for me, to draw from a broad pool of these materials.

I used to refer to R.M. Rilke as "Reb Meir Rilke." Some of his poetry is simply that illuminating!

LB: You're often referred to as the father, or now the grandfather, of Jewish environmentalism, and your book is filled with essays that display your environmental consciousness, both politically and spiritually. You're also a longtime advocate of non-violence as a path of social change. One of your essays, though, tells about your battle with local beavers, a battle to preserve your property as you wanted it to be. Sometimes, living in the world – that is, living the way we want to live in the world – involves the exercise of power, even violence. Even gardening involves a fair amount of violence towards weeds and bugs and things we don't want to be with us. How do you reckon with those aspects of life in this very beautiful valley?

EG: Not long ago, coyotes got our cat, Muffin. It was awful. Nature is not sentimental, and the possibility of life far exceeds nature's carrying capacity. We have to make choices. Gardening certainly teaches us that. We have guidelines: consideration for other creatures, yes, but not surrender to them. There is a combative side to our relationships with them, and the messianic vision of our lying down harmoniously together is far off.

I've always had some difficulty with the 'deep ecologists,' and I've found some of the easy talk about 'speciesism' to be misguided. But I don't think the Book of Genesis is a guideline for human exploitation of everything that surrounds us. I am of the stewardship school of environmentalism. I think we have both the mandate and the privilege of expressing ourselves, exploring, and transforming, but always with consideration for the life and well-being of other creatures, other species, other life forms.

What I find quite unacceptable is factory farming, the ways in which animals are kept in the mechanics of life but without any pleasure. And I support doing a maximum of medical experimentation and testing *in vitro*, not on more sentient creatures. I am very ambivalent about advances in human medicine at the cost of creatures; at the very least, I want it to be strictly regulated to minimize suffering.

LB: I'm consistently disturbed by how much we underestimate the capacities of other creatures. The varieties and depths of animal communication, of parental and communal feelings among them, of their navigational abilities, their intelligence, and so on – by the time our scientists and naturalists find out about it, by the time *National Geographic* writes about it, we've usually gone quite far in exterminating them.

EG: And to the extent that the deep ecologists and other parts of the environmental movement have emphasized our connectedness with other creatures, I say hurrah! But I cannot entirely surrender the privileging of the human. I think the Jewish tradition challenges us to recognize our intimacy with other creatures, yet it also suggests that we have moved beyond them in terms of our sentience and certainly our responsibility.

LB: I see at least four themes in your book: awakening to environmentalism in a Jewish context; instilling, or perhaps reinstilling, the feminine principle into Judaism; nonviolence, and your relationship to Buddhism; and universalism, specifically, non-Zionism. This last one is particularly unusual for a contemporary Jewish book.

EG: Yes, and it's the one that Jews seem most concerned about: Israel. So let me say that I am overwhelmed and delighted by the outpouring of scholarship and culture and the sheer fruitfulness of Jews living together and sustaining institutions in that land, but I have personally not found visiting Israel to be a positive experience. I've been there only twice: in 1959 and in

1988. I have not experienced the thrill that many seem to experience. My painful feeling has been that Israel has become a too-available substitute for Deity or even values in defining Jews and Judaism. Israel-centrism is a great danger for Jewish identity, and the behavior of what I have since the 1967 war called "imperial Israel" is a great danger to Jewish values.

LB: If Israel had been founded alongside a successful state of Palestine in 1948, or if there were at last a two-state solution, would you feel less apprehensive about the dangers of Israel-centrism?

EG: Much less, yes. I could feel much more comfortable participating in the reality of Israel because it would not involve the repression of another people.

You know, the number of non-Zionist Jews in the American Jewish community is quite sizable. And in my congregations, people who shared my discomfort with Israel, especially with its displacement of the Palestinians, had a place to come. In Princeton, after the Six-Day War, my sermon on Yom Kippur was on "Like All the Nations? Jews, Judaism, and Zionism," in which I really raised the issue of "imperial Israel" threatening Jewish values and Jewish survival. There was great consternation in the congregation, just as there was great consternation about my outspoken opposition to the war in Vietnam. There were people in that congregation, after all, who were consultants to the Pentagon. Yet when, at the end of six years, I offered my resignation – we wanted to go to Mexico – the board asked me to take a sabbatical instead. I was deeply moved by that.

I would say that my non-Zionism probably accounts for the fact that I have received very few invitations from the major Jewish organizations to speak, to teach, and so forth. But in the congregations I have served, it was never a predominant issue.

LB: How do you now, in retrospect, measure your impact on Jewish life? You're among a small group of Jewish leaders associated with Jewish environmentalism, feminism, the *havurah* movement, breaking open Judaism to find its spirituality, and more. How do you feel, in general, about the legacy you're leaving?

EG: My experience is that Jewish life, at least in the synagogue communities where I've attended, is remarkably vital and alive, with a lot of experimentation and energy. If I've made a contribution to that, I'm very gratified.

But one of the dangers I see is lack of depth: The tradition of Jewish learn-ing, especially, seems to me somewhat compromised. At one time, in order to initiate change or to innovate, it was assumed that there was a depth of knowledge, but I don't sense that so much any more. Instead, there is a slight danger of merely imitating what has become the new, innovative norm; it feels imitative instead of innovative.

LB: Spoken like a rabbi!

EG: A retired rabbi, yes. You see, at one time, my worry about congregations was about the cost, the buildings, the clergy – can we afford them, can't we just do it ourselves? What I didn't give full weight to was the fact that in supporting clergy we are supporting Jewish learning. It's like supporting scientific research, basic research, not just engineering innovation. If you don't sustain basic scientific pursuit, without immediate payoff, you're going to end up losing the utilitarian race. I fear that this is happening because of the independent spirit that I helped to engender.

LB: Are you nervous that liberal Jews are more and more drifting away from taking Jewish identity seriously? This seems especially true of unaffiliated Jews: they like jazz, they like fiction, they like farm-to-table food, they like 'Jewish.' It's a product, not a profound part of identity. This trend seems to have accelerated despite the opening up of Judaism that pioneers like you have wrought, away from the boring, rote worship of the 1950s to something far more exciting and accessible today.

EG: When I was serving the congregation in Lowell, I found that a lot of unaffiliated people in the Boston area would actually come and participate and enjoy our temple. That encouraged me to think that if it's really vital enough, if we really manage to make this available as a path for people to really *connect*, they will become truly involved and the tepid, shop-around attitude that you're describing will shift. They'll even develop a sense of community, because we're walking this path together and sharing some of these instruments for relating to the world around us. But I do share your concern. It's a concern about commitment. This is a general societal problem today.

LB: The sense of communal primacy that is such a part of Jewish tradition is quite vanished in American culture. We're a society of individuals in voluntary association. There's liberation in that – we're not caught up in *involuntary* community, as people have been for so many centuries in so many parts of the world – but a sense of true belonging is now very hard to achieve.

EG: Even for Jews, yes. Those habits of the heart that held Jews together are no longer habitual. They have to be cultivated.

I think some of the strength of today's conservative movement, which worries us so much, lies in the fact that they speak to that concern, they address the issues of caring for one another, of community, of responsibility.

I think I understand issues of community and lack of it. My own marginality was established at birth: Until I was 11, we lived as Jews in a small farm town in Iowa. My mother, who kept a kosher home, had been born in Iowa; my father came there at 7 from the Ukraine. I was a block and a half from hundreds of miles of cornfields. Once a year we would go to Albia, where my father's parents lived, and attend services in a rented American Legion hall. Then we moved to Des Moines, where the congregation was active and terrific, the rabbi was lively, it was really quite wonderful – but there was a great deal of social conformity, which I found irritating. By the time I went away to the University of Chicago, in 1946, my dissatisfaction with the idea that you just do it because that's how it's done was very strong.

On the other hand – talk about marginality! – the University of Chicago was a *terrifying* place for me. All of these World War II veterans, all of these sophisticated people from big cities, especially New York, they seemed to be from another world!

LB: Were you already committed to the path of nonviolence during World War II, in your teen years?

EG: Well, I was certainly rooting for the Allies, but I was just appalled by the destruction, and I found it difficult to reconcile "Thou shalt not kill" with what was going on. It was at this point, whether by accident or Divine guidance, that I became involved with the American Friends Service Committee, which had a regional office in Des Moines. So I received support for the feeling that one cannot live in peace with such destruction – but I certainly had no alternative to offer. But I remained involved with the Quakers, even while I was in seminary.

I have three striking memories of my synagogue in Des Moines, where

I was quite active as a young man. One is that the destruction of European Jewry seemed to have no place in our discussion. I cannot remember the community paying attention to it. Two is that while there were very active Zionists among us, most of the community looked at them in complete puzzlement. Three is that I can remember listening to Father Coughlin's anti-Semitic broadcasts some evenings . . .

LB: Perhaps those three memories explain something about the conformity of the Jews in Iowa.
    What did you study at the University of Chicago?

EG: I had many, many interests. Some have said I have ADD. I studied philosophy and then social work.

LB: So how did you come to be a rabbi?

EG: Philosophy and social work! What better profession to combine the two? I went to the Jewish Theological Seminary – although I might have been better served at the Jewish Institute of Religion . . .

LB: The Reform seminary.

EG: Yes, in Cincinnati. The students at JTS were mostly East Coast; their backgrounds were so different, Jewishly, from mine; their levels of observance were more rigorous. On the other hand, Louis Finkelstein was there, Abraham Joshua Heschel was there, Saul Lieberman, Louis Ginzberg, Mordecai Kaplan . . .

LB: What other influences have affected you as a rabbi?

EG: When I was in seminary, I was in psychoanalysis for three and a half years, with a lay analyst, Vienna-trained, very orthodox. Fifteen dollars an hour! Three to four times a week. I was coping with depression and the inability to express myself. It helped a lot in those areas.

LB: Did you have psychedelic experiences in the 1960s?

EG: Yes, I did, including at Millbrook, which was the mother church of psychedelics, and with such guides as Dick Alpert, who became known as Ram Dass. But my experiences were not so positive and did not leave much of a spiritual residue.

I was more shaped by my experiences in the South during the civil rights struggle. I was jailed in the desegregation campaign in Albany, Georgia, where Dr. King and SCLC were up against a very savvy police chief named Laurie Pritchett, who conducted mass arrests but very carefully avoided mass violence. I got my bail money back twenty-three years later – without interest, unfortunately!

I was also in Birmingham, Alabama, which was under the rule of Sheriff Bull Connor. I helped to organize a JTS rabbinical delegation that flew down. They had a convoy to take us from the airport to the hotel. At certain intersections, we were told to bend down out of view, because there were snipers out, and if they saw an integrated car . . .

LB: Did you have contact with Jewish communities in the South?

EG: Yes, there was another delegation that met us at the airport in Birmingham: from the local Jewish community, representatives who tried to dissuade us from participating and offered to pay all our expenses to return home. I understood the difficulty of their situation – we were going to come and go, while they lived there in that terrifying place – but I couldn't accede to their request.

Birmingham *was* a terrifying place, and in a terrifying time. Connor and his men brutalized people – but as you know, the effect of that was to mobilize the conscience of the whole country.

Finally, this time with Mary also, we were at the Selma march, the second one, at which Dr. King turned us all back from crossing the Pettus Bridge. We were disappointed not to march, but he was right; just around the corner from where we were, the Reverend James Reeb, a Unitarian minister, was clubbed to death.

I saw Dr. King at work more than once. He was extremely impressive.

What I experienced in all three of these episodes was acute fear, certainly, but also the sustaining force of solidarity, enforced by all the activity, the group training: the singing, the walking in silence, the hand-holding, the sense of group, the discipline of nonviolent activism.

LB: Here you are, 87, and this is your first book, Everett. And it doesn't really have a "summing up" essay, which is one reason why I wanted to have this conversation with you. For what would you like to be most remembered?

Not among your intimates, but in terms of your career?

EG: In relation to the tradition of nonviolence, I hope I've made a contribution to the understanding of its place in Judaism. I now feel an urgency to get into print, at last, the many pages of the startling, original pacifist writings, based firmly on Jewish sources, of Rabbi Aaron Samuel Tamaret [1869-1931], which I've translated over the years. I'm also grateful for the opportunities I've had to contribute, within the Tibetan community, to an understanding of the practical tools and the efficacy of nonviolence. It has proved itself in many, many critical situations.

I hope that I have made a contribution in restoring and renewing a sense of the life of the land to Judaism, which was so very much an agricultural faith in its holidays and traditions. I hope that people will continue to adopt and sustain some of my innovations – the Jacob O'Lantern, the Sun Wheel, the planting and reaping for Sukkot, and so on – for their own personal and communal satisfaction and for the renewal and strengthening of Jewish tradition.

At my 85th birthday, my family set up a website called the "Gendler Grapevine," which is meant to endure for five years and give small grants of seed money to carry on some of this work, especially involving environmentalism and social action, at Jewish summer camps, seminaries, synagogues, and other institutions. Hopefully, too, this book will find its way into the hands of individuals with similar sensibilities to mine, and help them enter into a mindset in which the universe has some direction, an overriding purpose. There is no lamb lying down with the lion, and we must live with all the uncertainties, the ambiguities, the challenges – but also with the confidence that *khey ha-olamim,* the Life of the Universe, has us still firmly in hand.

The wager on us humans may have been one of God's less wise decisions: The Divine could lose, we could really destroy what we have been blessed with. But my sense is that there's still a good chance of transformation, there are stirrings among human beings in so many positive directions. If some of my insights, and some of the joys I express in my writing, can help tip that balance, I'll be very, very satisfied.

www.ingramcontent.com/pod-product-compliance
Lightning Source LLC
Chambersburg PA
CBHW071647160426
43195CB00012B/1379